# MARK HAYES

# THE IDEOLOGY OF FASCISM AND THE FAR RIGHT IN BRITAIN

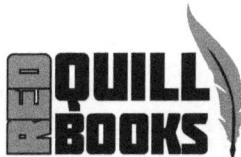

RED QUILL BOOKS

© Red Quill Books Ltd. 2014
Ottawa

www.redquillbooks.com
ISBN: 978-1-926958-31-6

Printed on acid-free paper. The paper used in this book incorporates post-consumer waste and has not been sourced from endangered old growth forests, forests of exceptional conservation value or the Amazon Basin. Red Quill Books subscribes to a one-book-at-a-time manufacturing process that substantially lessens supply chain waste, reduces greenhouse emissions, and conserves valuable natural resources.

**Library and Archives Canada Cataloguing in Publication**

Hayes, Mark, 1960-, author

The ideology of fascism and the far right in Britain / by Mark Hayes.

Includes bibliographical references.
**ISBN 978-1-926958-31-6 (pbk.)**

1. Fascism—Great Britain.
2. Right and left (Political science)—Great Britain.
3. Ideology—Great Britain. I. Title.

DA578.H39 2014 320.53'30941 C2014-902618-8

RQB is a radical publishing house.
Part of the proceeds from the sale of this book will support student scholarships

For Mia, Evie and Millie....

# ACKNOWLEDGEMENTS

Naturally, whilst taking full responsibility for the contents of what follows, I have incurred many debts during the course of writing this particular text. As is customary I would like to take the opportunity to thank a few people. Firstly I would like to mention RQ editor George Rigakos who has been patient, provided sound advice and handled the review process with sensitivity and skill. RQ deserves its reputation as a premier, radical author-friendly publishing company.

My other debts are both personal and political. Research for this book was interrupted for some time by spells in hospital (including intensive care) and I shall always be grateful to the NHS, its staff and the humanitarian principles which underpin its mission. The NHS is a marvellous institution. I should like to thank my family too for their love and support, especially my children Amy, Jim, Lotty and Mick. They all bring me the greatest joy. I also ought to mention Allison Burns, who tells me that she has been "a constant source of inspiration and support". This assertion is actually close enough to the truth to warrant public disclosure.

As for my friends, there are too many to mention individually but it would be true to say that they have all played a part in the writing of this book – some as a result of discussion and debate, others as a consequence of their political dedication. Many of my closest friendships have been forged in the context of serious political conflict and adversity. I regret nothing and I respect them all. My friends have been thoughtful, generous, understanding and, at times, incredibly courageous. They know who they are and they are the reason this book was written in the first place.

In the interests of transparency and in a spirit of openness and honesty I should admit to having been a committed member of Anti-Fascist Action and Red Action. I have seen fascists at very close quarters, especially during the period when they were intent on "controlling the streets" in Britain. It was unpleasant. In many ways it was this political experience that provided the impetus for this project. In effect it has been motivated by the desire to resist. However, actually researching and writing about fascism, and the misery that invariably accompanies it, can be exceedingly depressing. Reading about racism, violence, destruction and death is a debilitating task and not to be recommended for anyone of a fragile cast of mind. Indeed at times it required a considerable, conscious effort to remember that the overwhelming majority of ordinary people are kind, decent and honourable. If ever I began to have serious doubts on this score I invariably reflected on my brother Paul and his wife Jacky in Australia. They have a daughter Zoe who suffers from myotonic muscular dystrophy and autism, a very serious condition which requires constant care and attention. Paul and Jacky, like many thousands of others, climb mountains every day to make the lives of others worth living. Love like this will always be stronger and more resilient than the spiteful prejudice and hatred that is so often spawned, encouraged and legitimized in society today. These are the evil impulses, engendered by inequality and injustice, which fascism seeks to exploit. To the purveyors of such putrescent wickedness I say this - you can do your worst, you will never defeat us.

Finally I would like to dedicate this book, respectfully, to the memory of two men – Fenians both, working class and proud. My paternal grandfather Michael Hayes, through whom I learned the importance of freedom and equality, and volunteer Brendan Hughes ("the Dark") who fought for both. I will not forget.

Beir bua

Mark Hayes, Southampton/Kinawley March 2014

# TABLE OF CONTENTS

# iΠTRpDU CTiPΠ

## EXAMINING FASCISM AND THE
## BRITISH EXPERIENCE

I
t is essential at the outset to be absolutely clear about the precise purpose of this text. It is not designed to be a comprehensive account of fascism in Britain, still less can it claim to be a thorough examination of fascism in more general terms. The rather more modest (but nevertheless vital) objective is to identify the precise nature of fascism as a political project, and locate the British experience within this. This account makes, therefore, no extravagant claims about the depth and scope of its content – it is, rather, designed to be an extended essay in clarification.

It is also important to note that this text makes no lofty claims about the need for "academic  objectivity": the only logical and rational starting point for any work on fascism, given historical experience and the contours of its ideology, is unremitting hostility. Fascism has been responsible for some of the most grotesque cruelty in human history, therefore political neutrality and academic objectivity are deprived of any real meaning since: "fascism is wholly unacceptable, as a method of political mobilization, as a series of ideas, and as a system of rule" (Renton 1999 p.18). Fascism has cast a very long shadow and the heavy subsidiary cost of victory against such a creed must be eternal vigilance. As a consequence this text does not claim to stand above the conflict in a condescending effort to avoid the heat of battle, but adopts an explicitly anti-fascist perspective. This text is underpinned by an unambiguous commitment to *anti*-fascism in theory *and practice* - it is not simply an evaluation of fascism, but a call for resistance. This account therefore reflects the belief that it is a moral and political duty to try to understand the nature and purpose of fascism in order to oppose it. It is crucial that the analysis of such a dangerous credo should not degenerate into an academic game, or provide a pretext for intellectual point-scoring – the reality of dungeons and death camps demands a response that resists the temptation to treat the study of fascism as a simple exercise in scholarly debate *per se.* Of course we can never solve the conundrum of explaining fascism by counting corpses, but it is incumbent upon all who examine the phenomenon to remember that fascism results in barbarism, destruction and death. There is no need for undue digression here, apart from simply reiterating that this text makes no claims to an objectivity which is not felt by the author. The simple intention here is to produce a critical analysis of fascism with reference to theory and practice, analyse the specificity of the British experience, then evaluate the various interpretations of fascism in an attempt to elucidate precisely what fascism really is, and how best to resist it [1].

As we will discover, the far right in Britain has an unquestionably fascist heritage - that is, the parties, groups, and individuals which together constitute the British far right owed their inspiration primarily (if not exclusively) to the fascist movements which emerged on the continent in the 1920s and 1930s. Therefore in order to evaluate the precise nature of this ideology in Britain it is necessary to analyse fascism in its classical formation. The fact is that the "reference" regimes provided a kind of blueprint for a myriad of subsequent imitators and admirers. Moreover, an analysis of classical/historical fascism is also critical because in order to understand and explain fascism as a political/ideological phenomenon it is imperative to look at fascist practice and its relationship to fascist theory. The study of fascism in power is a crucial element in the study of fascism because it is only through practice that the precise nature of fascist ideology is actually revealed (Renton 2001 p.xii) [2]. Obviously this is impossible if we focus entirely on the British fascist example, given its relative political impotence. Fascism as an ideology is revealed in power. As a result an examination of historical fascism (as a source of inspiration for the vast majority of those on the far right in Britain) can serve a key purpose - it can explain what fascism really is, thus throwing the British version of fascism into a much sharper light.

In attempting to get a much clearer picture of the nature of fascism (which necessitates an analysis of both theory *and* practice) the classical fascist regimes in Italy and Germany have been taken as the primary reference area. Although many European countries have experienced fascist movements/regimes, all were/are either mere copies or puppets of the two major movements/regimes, and a detailed consideration of these would not add considerably to what may be learned from an examination of the Italian and German experience. The Italian example provides us with the an opportunity to examine the archetypal fascist movement and regime, whilst German Nazism enables us to assess the most radical and dynamic version of fascism, both of which prompted mimetic reproductions elsewhere (see Kallis 2000a p.99). Indeed "had not the fascists taken over in Italy and Germany there would have been no fascism in Europe worth speaking of" (Schuddekopf 1973 p.72). The two primary historical examples also have the advantage of facilitating the required assessment of fascism in both its "movement" and "system" phases because the true nature of fascism is only ever really fully revealed after the regime stabilises (Poulantzas 1974 p.13 and p.66-67; see Mommsen cited in Laqueur 1982 p.156). As Guerin exclaimed: "to define fascism - how can this be better done than by studying that phenomenon in the countries in which it manifested itself in an altogether characteristic form, those countries where it, so to speak, assumed its classical form - in Italy and Germany?" (Guerin 1973 p.19).

There is another issue here of course, given the distinct qualitative difference between Italian Fascism and German Nazism, and that is the nature and extent of Nazi exceptionalism. As Kershaw correctly points out "it is universally recognized that, within the general typus of fascism, Nazism was itself exceptional by virtue of the dynamic force of its ideology, the radicality of its praxis, the force and extent of its repression, and the scale of its destructive capacity" (Kershaw 1989 p.56-57). In taking both the Fascist and Nazi experience as classical examples, it is important to note that National Socialism will be treated as an intensive or extreme form of fascism, although possessing certain unique features (see Bessel 1998). The validity of using "fascism" as a generic term and viewing National Socialism as a distinctive yet related manifestation of fascism will, it is hoped, become apparent as the analysis develops [3]. The over-riding purpose or ultimate objective is to try to ascertain the true nature of fascism in order to more clearly understand the nature of and prospects for British fascism, and "...it is important to emphasise that it is impossible to understand the meaning and implications of contemporary fascism unless one commands some basic knowledge of those movements that rose to the zenith of their power in the 1930s and 1940s..." (Wilkinson 1981 p.29, see Levy 1999).

It is true, however, that another more specific method-ological difficulty arises as a result of attempting to fulfil the tasks outlined above - the study of fascism has produced a vast quantity of empirical and theoretical literature and obvi-ously, given the scope and purpose of this text, this account cannot possibly be exhaustive. Indeed no scholar or activist could aquaint themselves with all the literature – there are literally thousands of books on the Holocaust alone (Marrus 1993 p.5-6). As a result, whilst acknowledging the fecundity of fascism as a subject worthy of study, an attempt has been made to be selective on sources and to avoid being drawn into an expansive discussion of issues which, though intrinsically interesting, are not entirely relevant to the specific purpose of the text. However the extended reading list consisting of texts utilized in the course of producing this mono-graph might serve as a preliminary guide to more sustained reading and research.

## NOTES

[1]  This account therefore stands in stark contrast to the perspective adopted by, for example, Goodwin (see 2011 p.18, see p.186) who stresses the need for objectivity, and criticizes the fact that "studies of extreme right parties" have been "highly politicized, with anti-fascists and journalists producing a plethora of opinionated, speculative and emotional studies" (Goodwin 2011 p.186). These sentiments follow very closely those of Mudde who suggests that the fact that the study of the far right has been dominated by its opponents has led to accounts that are analytically weak and politically normative (see Mudde 1996). Evidently Goodwin and his neutral, dispassionate academic colleagues are keen to save us from politically motivated displays of emotion. It is worth noting that Goodwin informs us that, for his most recent work, interviews were conducted with 27 BNP activists, and hence he was given "unprecedented" access to the party. He also tells us, like a credulous college student, that his interviewees (for the most part) did not conform to the conventional stereotypes. At least he has the good grace to acknowledge that their complicity might have had something to do with the fact he is a white male (Goodwin 2011 p.187). The possibility that the interviewees might have been tailoring their message for the fascinated academic does not appear to have overly concerned Goodwin.

To take another example, Passmore, despite stressing an "anti-fascist" scholarly approach, argues that we need to distinguish between academic study and moral judgement: "thanks to their professional training, historians, sociologists, and political scientists can justifiably claim to have a special ability to answer these sorts of questions" however, "academics are not the judges of morality" (Passmore 2002 p.152). Of course academic analysts may not be the sole arbiters of morality, but they cannot evade moral responsibility either, and the distinction between right and wrong, good and evil is pretty straightforward in *some* cases. This account has not relied on any interviews with fascists or their fellow-travellers, and the idea that academics can sit on the lofty perch of objectivity is simply condescending nonsense. The very act of apolitical "impartiality" in effect endorses a particular political status quo, and even essentially descriptive analyses often betray a bias by the selection and prioritization of particular facts. As Barrington Moore noted many years ago, there is a tendency to assume that mild-mannered statements in favour of stability are "objective" and that criticism is a form of "rhetoric" (Barrington Moore 1966 p.522). The fact is that truthful analyses, given the way society is configured, are bound to have a critical tone. Indeed, sympathy with the victims of historical processes provides an essential safeguard against being seduced by the dominant mythology (see Barrington-Moore 1966 p.523). In the study of fascism, therefore, a critical approach is perfectly logical, sensible and appropriate given the historical evidence and the suffering of its victims. Fascism was/is an evil creed. Indeed, accusations of coprophilia notwithstanding, Donny Gluckstein's comment that "it is not possible to investigate the contents of a cesspool without looking at excrement" is particularly apt (Gluckstein 1999 p.2).

[2]  Renton therefore argues against the fashionable turn toward "fascism studies" which tends to focus on the realm of political ideas, and in favour of analyses that are more deeply rooted in social and historical reality. Renton correctly maintains that "the only way to generate a consistently anti-fascist approach toward the history of fascism is by relating the ideas of fascism to its actions" (Renton 2001 p.xiii). This issue (and related questions) will re-emerge when the various interpretations of fascism are examined.

[3] Of course some experts on the subject deny the validity of the generic taxonomic approach, arguing that the qualitative differences between Fascism and Nazism are too significant and that each case should be treated *sui generis* (see for example: Allardyce 1979, Pearce 2002, Mack Smith 1985, Burleigh and Wippermann 1991, Sternhell in Copsey 1994 p.102). However, the assumption underpinning this text is that, despite the absence of academic consensus and the existence of fascist heterogeneity, and whilst acknowledging the considerable difficulties created by terminological inexactitude, there *is* an identifiable fascist "minimum" or set of common denominators than can serve as a paradigmatic basis for analysis (see Kallis 2000a). To develop a generic model and treat Nazism as a form of fascism is *not* to deny its uniqueness (Griffin 1995 p.93). For the alternative perspective in its most strident form, for example, see Allardyce (1979), and/or Sternhell (1994, and cited in Griffin 1995 p.305). Thurlow also argues that the differences outweigh the similarities (1980 especially p.9), as does Hildebrand (1985) whilst Bracher (1988) and Renzo De Felice take a similar line (see Paxton 1998). Nolte (1969), Kitchen (1982) and Poulantzas (1974), among many others (Griffin, Eatwell, Payne, Kedward, Mosse, O'Sullivan, Woolf etc) see fascism as an appropriate generic term (see Griffin 1993a).

# 1. THE IDEOLOGICAL COMPONENTS OF FASCISM

Despite the fact that the study of fascism has produced an extraordinary volume of scholarly material and a plethora of definitions and explanations, there remains a conspicuous lack of unanimity on the subject [1]. Indeed in many cases the label "fascist" has degenerated into a term of abuse, thereby obscuring and mystifying the concept, indeed as early as 1928 Togliatti referred to the "error of generalization" being made, with the use of the word to designate every form of reaction [2]. As a slogan or a curse the word loses its force and precision: "the modish use of the general catchword 'fascist' explains little and produces many clichés" (Bracher 1982 p.202; Pearce 2002 p.2-3; Griffiths 2005) [3]. Yet, new versions such as "cyber-fascism" and "designer-fascism" continue to emerge, creating even more confusion and controversy (Griffiths 2005 p.1). This problem has led some analysts to argue that the term should be discarded completely, or restricted for use only by historians [4]. However, the fact that unanimity is absent (indeed unattainable) and that the word is often misused, should not inhibit or preclude an analysis - after all, how much unanimity really exists over such concepts as "socialism", "liberalism" or "democracy", and how often are words such as "Stalinist" or "Trotskyist" used as terms of abuse with little concern for intellectual precision? Certainly fascism is composed of many disparate, chaotic and contradictory elements, derived from many sources and held together in an uneasy synthesis, but they are discernible and can be evaluated (see Mann 2004).

In fact the simplest way to examine fascism is to unpack those components which together constitute its theoretical and practical totality. Whilst acknowledging a great deal of overlap and interpenetration between the respective elements it is nevertheless possible to assess each theme individually as a distinctive feature of the overall fascist experience [5]. Of course this is not to argue that each theme is, in itself, inherently "fascist", but that the combination of facets in a particular configuration can plausibly be designated as a specifically "fascist" synthesis. It is also important to note that the utility of providing (yet another) "model" of fascism is not to deny that in crucial respects fascism was a process (rather than an entity), but it does make it much easier to chart a path through the extraordinary mass of empirical evidence. The construction of such a paradigm constitutes, in essence, an effort to identify meaning and enhance understanding - it is certainly no more than that.

## Zeitgeist: Romantic Anti-Rationalism and Social Darwinism

The first element to be aware of when dealing with classical fascism is that underlying its theory and practice was a basic irrationality, or put more precisely, the relationship between thought and action was not entirely straightforward, which makes conventional ideological analysis rather more problematic. Fascism "does not rest explicitly upon an elaborated philosophical system" and "it has not been given intellectual underpinnings by any system builder, like Marx, or by any major critical intelligence, like Mill, Burke or Tocqueville" (Paxton 2005 p.16). As Paxton colourfully concludes, fascism "was an affair of the gut more than of the brain" (Paxton 2005 p.42). In fact for the fascist, in a sense, action preceded and often precluded rational calculation because "experience" and "deed" were deemed to transcend mundane intellect and purposeless speculation. Fascists would much rather burn books than read them, and this reflected the belief that reasoned debate was to be replaced by an emphasis upon a more sensual experience which was designed to liberate the emotional impulse of the masses. In fact, as Greil (1977-78) has argued, the appeal of fascism lay very much in its "romantic epistemology" as an anti-intellectual theory of knowledge [6].

In many ways fascism began from an assumption about intuitive, pre-theoretical consciousness, which emerged essentially as a consequence of a revolt against modern, post-enlightenment rationalism. Certainly, in the late nineteenth century many of the apparent certainties emerging from the enlightenment were held up to much closer critical scrutiny, and although religion had relinquished its tight grip on western societies, the explanations contained within the new scientific discourse were also being challenged as unsatisfying and inadequate. Scientific "truth" was held to be, in some quarters, just as rigid a cage as conceptions of theological verity. Science, like religion, was being seen by some as futile, and they felt that both should be rejected in deference to the power of human instinct. At the same time democracy, ushered in by the political philosophers who facilitated the French revolution, seemed singularly incapable of solving the successive political, financial and economic crises that enveloped western societies, and even its esrstwhile exponents expressed certain doubts about its long term utility (Griffiths 2005 p.59). Democracy "was seen by many to be ineffective in face of the realities of modern life. Added to this was the impression, in many circles, that democracy was fundamentally corrupt and self-serving" (Griffiths 2005 p.62). Rational discourse and democratic decision-making based on reason were therefore maligned by an emerging scepticism about the practical utility of both.

Consequently, although the fascist movements did attract some intellectuals (such as Ezra Pound, Martin Heidegger, and certain individuals who coalesced around Marinetti's "Futurists"), fascists generally expressed a deep suspicion of conventional notions of cognitive coherence and, more particularly, its political manifestations. For fascism, abstract theoretical systems served simply to prevent positive action. Indeed, the stress on doctrine and theory was considered an integral component of the decadence of bourgeois life (see Neocleous 1997 p.13). Sedentary reflection could only ever produce spectators - faith and intuition were more reliable and should therefore prevail over reason. Writers like Henri Bergson, Henrik de Man and Jules Soury had insisted that the instinctive *elan vital* or life force was more important as a dynamic motive than intellect, and Freud had apparently already established the significance of the irrational, instinctive id, which the conscious mind or ego could barely comprehend, still less control. In fact Giovanni Gentile was probably the only fascist who made a serious attempt to theorise the anti-intellectualism of his adopted movement, with reference to what he termed "actualism", the notion of the unity of theory and practice i.e. thought as pure act [7]. Gentile explained: "'I am convinced that the true doctrine is that which is expressed in action rather than in words or books, in the personality of men and in the attitude they assume in the face of problems, and this is a much more serious solution to problems than abstract dissertations, sermons, and theories'" (cited in McGovern 1946 p.544). However, somewhat paradoxically, the self-styled "philosopher" of Fascism was criticised (and sometimes even ridiculed) for his own excessive rationalism.

What was required, the fascists believed, was a return to sounder and more trustworthy instincts - instincts which had been dulled by years of lifeless contemplation. Vitality was truth. Hitler was especially fond of expressing this view: "'We must distrust the intelligence and the conscience and must place our trust in our instincts. We have to regain a new simplicity...'"(cited in Rauschning 1939 p.222) and "....in political matters feeling often decides more correctly than reason" (Hitler 1974 p.159). People should be offered myths, and men are more likely to be motivated by belief rather than pure logic or rational deduction on the basis of evidence. Indeed Italian Fascism "explicitly rejected rationalism, and praised mythical thinking both as a mental attitude and as a form of political behaviour" (Gentile 1990 p.241). All dilemmas would be resolved by faith and a commitment to act - as Mussolini proudly proclaimed in 1919 "our doctrine is action". Consequently, "in a movement like fascism, based on irrational premises, the role of precisely formulated ideas in guiding political action will tend to be small" (Lyttleton 1973 p.11).

Therefore, when appraising fascism it is inappropriate, indeed fruitless, to search for a coherent or systematic body of ideas - hence the need to pay particularly close attention to political practice when evaluating the fascist phenomenon. As Kitchen points out, fascism was based on "half-baked and cranky ideas... (it) never produced anything like the systematic body of ideas found in Marxism-Leninism" (Kitchen 1982 p.28). Fascist "ideas" could be contradictory and confusing, and the fascists themselves not only acknowledged and accepted their theoretical incoherence, it was positively celebrated as a sign of their vitality. Yet the fact that there were few philosophers or theoreticians among the fascists, and that Hitler's *Mein Kampf* or Mussolini's *Political and Social Doctrine* did not contain a high degree of intellectual rigour, was unimportant given their instinctivist premises because rational ideas carried little weight. As Mussolini explained, "'fascism was not given out to the wet-nurse of a doctrine elaborated beforehand round a table. It was born of the need for action'", "'the century of fascism will see the end of intellectualising and sterile intellectuals...'" (Mussolini cited in Lyttleton 1973 p.45 and cited in Guerin 1973 p.170) [8]. Hitler concurred, "'the right feeling is more important than all understanding'", and "'only the man who acts becomes conscious of the real world'" (cited in Bytwerk 2008 p.25 and Rauschning 1939 p.221). Thus fascism digs a grave for those inclined toward thoughtful appraisal and sober analysis, and would eventually bury inanimate and moribund philosophy - for the fascist it was very much a case of I need not (must not) think, therefore I am.

This general irrationalism and preference for action rather than theory was, however, a reaction not only to what the fascists felt was the excessive rationalism and inquisitive intellectualism of European experience since the enlightenment, but also an explicit rejection of the philosophical materialism which underpinned both liberalism and Marxism (see Passmore 2009 p.15). As Mussolini put it, "'fascism is a reaction against the flabby materalistic positivism of the nineteenth century'" (cited in Lyttleton 1973 p.40, see Mussolini cited in Weber 1964 p.21). In many respects therefore fascist irrationalism and instinctivism reflected a desire to supersede or escape the banality of the bourgeois world, its commercialism, its spiritless and soulless materialism, as well as its modes of thought. In the period that saw the germination of the fascist creed many people were concerned about the consequences of urbanisation, standardisation, and the alienation that had accompanied the dramatic social transformations that followed in the wake of industrialisation. The experience of the Great War (1914-18) was also critical in taking this discontent a stage further, and it could be argued that this seismic conflagration was the catalyst which completely undermined older nineteenth century values and assumptions, precipitating the development of an existential anxiety which permeated all levels of society. As Otto Strasser was to remark of the immediate postwar period, "the past was in ruins, the present shattered, the future without hope" (Strasser 1940a p.26). There ensued, as a consequence, what Fest terms "a fashionable pessimism" which became progressively more fascinated by tragedy, doom and adventure (Fest 1973 p.95). It was pessimistic post-war commentators, like Oswald Spengler, who caught the mood, and his brooding upon the decadent decline of western values helped create the intellectual and cultural context within which fascist notions could gain credence. Fascism emerged out of this dark spirit of cynicism and mistrust, and sought social, moral and political regeneration by exalting the values of courage, contempt for risk and even the celebration of death. Indeed it has been persuasively argued that fascism had a particular fascination for the "heroic", "immortal" dead, as captured in the slogan "Long Live Death!" (see Neocleous 2005).

Perhaps inevitably such values were particularly prominent amongst those demoralised and rebellious war veterans who could not re-adapt to "normal" bourgeois or civilian life (see Stern 1975 chapters 2 and 3, also Guerin 1973 p.56-57). Indeed Griffith refers to the "cult of the ex-serviceman" and (quoting Ernst Junger) the "'communion of the trenches'", which precipitated an attitude that stressed commitment, heroism and sacrifice (Griffith 2005 p.29). This kind of proto-fascist nostalgia and romanticism coaleasced in *The Manifesto of Futurism*, written by Tommaso Marinetti, which expressed a love of "'energy and rashness'", as well as "'courage, audacity and revolt'" (cited in Pollard 1998 p.15). "'The fascist'", wrote Mussolini, "'disdains the comfortable life'", and he confessed that personally he was "'insensible to everything except adventure - mad adventure'" (Mussolini cited in Lyttleton 1973 p.40, see Rossi/Tasca 1938 p.23). Indeed the vibrance and sense of romantic adventure which fascism conveyed (and which so impressed Oswald Mosley and others in Britain) was an extremely important element in its success, and is perhaps best expressed by the Italian Fascist slogan *me ne frego* (which, loosely translated, means "I don't give a damn"). Italian Fascists, such as Guiseppe Bottai, spoke of spiritual renewal and the need for a new fascist man in a new age (see Mosse 1979 p.10). As Linz explains, "'fascism had a strong romantic component - an appeal to emotion and sentiment, to the love of adventure and heroism, the belief in action rather than words, the exaltation of violence and even death'" (Linz 1982 p.54).

It is hardly surprising, therefore, that critics like Antonio Gramsci actually likened the fascists to the "'monkey people'" in Kipling's *Jungle Book*, hurling mud and insults and spoiling for a fight (Gramsci cited in Forgacs 1986 p.39); whilst the historian A.J.P. Taylor described Mussolini as a frustrated, over-aged "'rocker'" with his love of the violent gesture and his black shirts (Taylor cited in Kedward 1971 p.201). Somewhat facetious though these critical comments may have been, they do touch on an important component of fascism, derived from its instinctive irrationalism as a "style of life", an "attitude" and a "great adventure". However, "in gloryfying the untamed instincts fascism repudiated not merely reason and tolerance, but even the more humane emotions" (Smith 1979 p.54). Here the ideas of syndicalist Georges Sorel, who saw violence as a cleansing, cathartic process, are also significant because violence was written into the very deoxyribonucleic acid of fascist practice. Whilst Gentile referred approvingly to Fascist party members who saw the Browning pistol as their inseparable lover (see Bosworth 2002 p.163), Mussolini, apparently infatuated by danger, fought numerous individual duels. The Nazis too enthusiastically embraced a culture of violence, and took it to the streets as a political tactic (see Rosenhaft 1983). So the rejection of reason did not stop at ritualistic book-burning - the *squadre d'azione* and the *sturm abteilung* were also born of such a repudiation. The fascist gangs and the tactics of intimidation, the cudgel and the castor oil, were also the practical, organisational manifestation of their irrationalist, instinctivist premise. Fascist violence was designed to destroy the opposition, promote solidarity and project an image of strength and vitality. "For fascists 'creative violence' is contrasted with the insipid cowardice of liberal intellectualism: violence is not just a means to an end, but an *intrinsic value* in itself" (Woodley 2010 p.105). An emotional, aesthetic and tactical commitment to violence was therefore an important component of fascism.

Closely connected to irrationalism and instinctivism, and underpinning much of fascist experience in Italy and Germany, was the fascist belief in and adherence to an unrestrained social Darwinism which emphasised the notion of "natural selection". Social Darwinist theory stemmed directly from a distorted version of the iconoclastic work of Charles Darwin, whose book on the *Origin of Species* (1859) exploded conventional Christian ideas on the genesis and nature of man. In some quarters Darwin's extraordinary research precipitated a more general re-evaluation of man's position and status in the world, his ontological purpose and, more specifically, man's proximity to the animal kingdom. Fascism therefore developed in an age when there emerged a belief that man was in fact subject to the very same "aristocratic" principles of nature that governed the animal world. This instrumental version of Darwinism suggested that certain scientific "natural laws" could not be abrogated, ignored or transcended - man could comprehend the laws but never escape them. Nature's inviolable principle of "natural selection" and "survival of the fittest", which led inexorably to the domination or destruction of the weak, was held up to be the natural thrust of existence, and this "truth" was linked to those innate and long suppressed instincts within man (see Guerin 1973 p.176). As Sternhell explains, "as the notion of social Darwinism gained widespread acceptance it stripped the human personality of its sacramental dignity. (It) made no distinction between the physical life and the social life, and conceived of the human condition in terms of an unceasing struggle..." (Sternhell 1982 p.335). Man, according to Mussolini, was driven by a "'divine bestiality'" (cited in Bosworth 2002 p.121), and Hitler concurred, arguing that "'struggle is the father of all things...It is not by the principles of humanity that man lives or is able to preserve himself above the animal world, but solely by means of the most brutal struggle...it is always the stronger who triumphs. Is not that the most reasonable order of things? If it were otherwise, nothing good would ever have existed'" (cited in Rees 2005 p.34).

So the fascists enthusiastically embraced Darwinist conceptions, indeed Mason argues that the Darwinist idea of struggle and competition was "the basic axiom of Nazi thought and practice. It was the only ideological axiom that consistently informed all political practice" (Mason 1993 p.6). From this perspective mankind was simply another animal engaged in a permanent struggle for survival. This bleak and unyielding exhortation to compete and subdue had profound implications in terms of its impact on notions of morality and social purpose. For instance, the extension of the "aristocratic principle of nature" to the sphere of human relations led to a qualitative difference in the nature of violence - brutality was justified, not as in the service of a laudable idea, or even perpetrated in the name of God, but merely as an end in itself to ensure one's survival on the planet (see Trevor Roper's Introduction to Hitler 1973 p.xxxvii). Thus a particularly crude and instrumental version of Darwinism was also very much part of the *zeitgeist,* which fascism was able to exploit for its own particular political purposes.

It might also be noted that this social Darwinism was powerfully reinforced by the philosophical musing of certain prominent individual theorists like Friedrich Nietszche, with his explicit emphasis on transcendent purpose, "will to power" and the inevitable pre-eminence of the powerful over the weak. According to popular interpretations of Nietszche's complex ideas, the pathetic Judeo-Christian values of humanity and compassion, and their palid political offshoots, democracy and socialism, placed intolerable constraints on individual creativity, corrupted mankind and created a slave mentality. The only escape was to recognize that man was engaged in a struggle for survival, and that the fate of mankind should be governed by the "highest types", the *"Herren-Rasse"* (see Griffiths 2005 p.13). A "'Superman'" called by destiny would overcome the pity ethic, rescue society from decadence and decline, transcend facile notions of humanism and restore a genuinely spiritual community (Eatwell 1996 p.8). The Nietzs-chean perspective therefore emphasized the need for a new spiritual and aesthetic form of politics. Meanwhile sociologists like Vilfredo Pareto and Robert Michels were insisting on the inevitability of elites in society and the "iron law of oligarchy". Such notions, which were inevitably distorted, accentuated and embellished, pervaded fascist ideas, and clearly informed the actions of both fascist regimes. Indeed the fascists eagerly embraced such ideas as a pseudo-scientific justification of the ultimate sovereignty of the strong – "might" really was "right". Mussolini believed that blood alone could turn the wheels of history, a process designed to induce defererence to superior force. Meanwhile Hitler punctuated *Mein Kampf* with numerous references to the eternally valid truths rooted in nature and, despising pity, he persistently proclaimed the right and duty of the strong to dominate the weak (see Hitler 1974 p.223, and especially chapter 8 book II). Fascists came to assimilate such ideas, and "scientific" elitist and social Darwinist assumptions were reflected in practically all spheres of fascist activity, especially with regard to economic and foreign policy (this will become evident as the other "themes" of fascism are elaborated and considered).

## Nationalism and Xenophobia

Nationalism, as one of the key concepts of the twentieth century, was absolutely crucial to fascism, indeed fascism itself can be described as an "idiosyncratic and extreme variant of hyper-nationalism" (Kallis 2000a p.96) [9]. In both Italy and Germany the fascists recast and radicalized pre-existing nationalist themes, impulses and imagery. For the fascists, the nation was the object of all their efforts, and since it embodied the essential *elan* of the group it was the single most important organic entity, to which everything had to be sacrificed. Indeed Mosse argues persuasively that notions of nationalism gave the fascist credo a degree of coherence, unifying the many disparate elements of its ideology (Mosse 1979 p.20). Nationality was, in effect, a common bond uniting the community of people, reinforcing and consolidating its sense of collective identity and transcending any internal differences that existed. Differences in wealth and status, for example, were considered superficial and yielded in deference to the higher, unifying significance of nationality and patriotic purpose. Hence, nationalism provided a way of integrating lower income groups by offering them the chance of participation in a powerful national community, and indeed this allegiance produced a communitarian consciousness that offered some tangible compensation for the lack of material resources (see Stackelberg 1999 p.20-21). Significantly, in representing and articulating an often grossly inflated patriotic sentiment the fascists claimed to stand above class politics and beyond sectional interest, and it was certainly this component of its ideological synthesis which enabled it to annex, with little difficulty, much of the bourgeois world. It is also important to note that this emphasis on nationalism even resonated amongst many workers, especially after the Communist International had effectively capitulated to nationalistic forces prior to 1914 (Sewell 1988 p.11). While the bourgeoisie was always more favourably disposed toward a more vehement nationalism, the collapse of what Rosa Luxemburg referred to as the "stinking corpse" of the Second International provided ample scope to create a new, more broadly based, mass nationalism. As Passmore remarks, "nationalism would incorporate workers into the nation and regenerate the bourgeoisie, forcing it to abandon 'feminine humanitarianism' and degenerate liberalism" (Passmore 2009 p.22).

So powerful was this patriotism that, in essence, a new spiritual divinity was expressed via nationhood and the nation became an ersatz God. Hitler, for instance, always tirelessly professed his devotion to the "Fatherland". In rejecting the more conventional notions of civic patriotism, Hitler's nationalism was far more mystical and reverential, constructed upon conceptions of ethnicity rather than citizenship (see later). Although there was some initial doubt about Mussolini's position (given his early flirtation with socialist republicanism), by 1923 all ambiguity was eliminated when he consummated his ideological relationship with nationalism by absorbing the Italian Nationalist Party. As Gentile explained at the time, for the Italian Fascist "'politics revolves entirely round the concept of the nation state'" (cited in Lyttleton 1973 p.306), and Mussolini confirmed this position, "'our myth is the greatness of the Nation! And to this myth, to this grandeur, that we wish to translate into a complete reality, we subordinate all the rest'" (cited in Kallis 2009 p.99). It is clear therefore that the nationalism of the fascists extended well beyond the normal affinity a people might feel toward its homeland. The usual nationalist aspirations of autonomy, identity and security were, under fascism, surpassed in spectacular fashion. The fascist nation-state was much more than an administrative unit covering a given territory, it was an idealized instrument reflecting the power of a mystical, unified entity, underpinned by the unswerving loyalty of the people.

Both Italy and Germany achieved nationhood late in comparison with other European countries, and both were unified as a result of power politics, pursued primarily by Bismarck and Cavour. The fact that each country, possessing significant economic and political potential, had arrived late on the scene during the nineteenth century, when other European nations such as Britain and France had long since secured status and empire, also created resentment and produced a sense of unfulfilled expectation. This resentment, most powerfully felt in Germany, resulted in the Great War. Defeated, but militarily intact, Germany's treatment at Versailles merely fuelled the flames of national bitterness. In Italy meanwhile, despite having entered the war on the "winning" side, there existed a strong feeling of wasted sacrifice, and of having missed out on the spoils of victory. Territorial claims were ignored and massive debts incurred, therefore the idea of a "mutilated victory" in Italy meant that, far from being the realization of a patriotic apotheosis, war had accentuated feelings of national discontent and betrayal (see Corner 2002). Consequently fascism was, to some considerable extent, constructed upon these festering national resentments. Once established, the fascist regimes were determined to attain and secure the "rightful" positions of the two emerging European nations, and not only were they committed to establishing and sustaining their status in the international context, they were perfectly willing to countenance the deployment of military force to ensure that their objectives were achieved. Territorial expansionism may not have been a trait deployed exclusively by fascist states, and may indeed have been fused with pre-existing patriotic attitudes (derived in part from experiences in war), but it was nevertheless seen by those regimes as a "natural" and "historic" necessity, derived from underlying assumptions about superiority and civilisation (Kallis 2000 p. 28).

Thus, having assimilated mythical notions of national salvation, re-birth and renewal, in practice the nationalism purveyed by the fascists was necessarily aggressive and militarist. The German fascists, of course, built upon a tradition of Prussian militarism that was unrivalled in the early twentieth century, and which had survived the ignominy of 1918. The *Freikorps*, the Pan-German League, the Navy League and various other *Volkisch* militaristic formations still gloried in the semi-mystical heritage bequeathed them by Germany's military past. Indeed the army, especially for Hitler, was a crucial component of German life, and his experiences in the Second Bavarian Infantry Regiment evidently reinforced his admiration for an organisation which, he felt, embodied the national virtues of responsibility, order and courage. "What the German people owes the army", Hitler wrote, "can be briefly summed up in one word: everything" (Hitler 1974 p.254, see Maser 1970). Indeed the aggressive militarism of fascism was quite clearly reflected in the military-style formations of the movements themselves, which drew heavily from ex-servicemen. In Italy, for instance, the *arditi* were attracted by the "*trincerismo*" (trench-mindedness) of the Fascist movement. As Renton says, "the experience of war shaped a generation. The former soldiers returned brutal and angry. They had learned to kill and were impatient for change. Many ached for a return to the discipline of the front" (Renton 2001 p.1).

More importantly, as well as exploiting and emphasising the importance of the military as an organisation, the fascists saw war itself as natural and, indeed, inevitable. A nation, they believed, could only really discover its true value in conflict and adversity,  indeed perpetual peace was unattainable, undesirable and detrimental to the development of a healthy nation. In fact war was seen "as an opportunity for changing the rules of politics. War will restore a proper hierarchy of political ends, in which the power of the sacralised nation must take the highest place and relegate all partial political interests to a lower plane of significance" (Lyttleton 1998 p.18). Prophetically, the proto-Fascist D'Annunzio spoke openly of the "'ghastly stench of peace'" and glorified acts of war in a manner designed to appeal to ex-military desperadoes (cited in Knox 2000 p.37). Whilst Mussolini himself said, "'war alone brings up to their highest tension all human energies and puts the stamp of nobility upon the peoples who have the courage to meet it'", and he maintained that it was "'better to live one day like a lion than a hundred years like a sheep ... a minute on the battlefield is worth a lifetime of peace ... My objective is simple; I want to make Italy great, respected and feared'" (Mussolini cited in Lyttleton 1973 p.47 and cited in Halperin 1964 p.47, see Mussolini 1939, 1976) [10]. Thus, Mussolini "never tired of repeating that Italy must become a society permanently mobilized for war, that Italians must become more ruthless and militant" (Whittam 1995 p.102). As Bosworth says, "Fascist rhetoric was unrestrained in extolling the virtues of war and killing, each being inscribed as the essence of Fascist manhood" (Bosworth 2005 p.3). Similarly, Hitler spoke frequently of the innate, instrumental morality of conquest: "every healthy, vigorous people sees nothing sinful in territorial acquisition, but something quite in keeping with nature" (Hitler 1961a p.15). Indeed Hitler's attitude to war can be clearly gleaned from his observation that "'the victor will not be asked afterwards whether he told the truth or not. When starting and waging a war it is not right that matters, but victory. Close your hearts to pity. Act brutally. Eighty million people must obtain what is their right. Their existence must be made secure. The stronger man is right'" (cited in Kershaw 2009 p.498). Clearly, for the fascist "war shapes man's spiritual character and is the defining characteristic of nature. The state of war is thus the universal norm; this means that there is no real distinction between politics and war" (Neocleous 1997 p.18). This was certainly true of the two fascist regimes in question, both of which embraced a military ethos and glorified war.

Adolf Hitler obviously had hopes of continental hegemony for his new Nazi Germany. Derived, most probably, from Professor Haushofer of Munich University (who taught Rudolph Hess), and elaborated more fully during his detention at Landsberg, Hitler's plan envisaged alliances with Britain and Italy in the West and an Empire in the East at the expense, primarily, of Poland and Russia. The unambiguous aim was to secure *lebensraum*, (living space) for the German people (see Hitler 1974 p.587, also 1961). The Germans, according to Hitler, could only sustain themselves by expanding their territory, so in this sense it was not a choice between "guns or butter" but the prioritization of the former in order to attain the latter (see Tooze 2007). As prominent Nazi Walter Darre explained "'we will settle this space, according to the law that a superior people always has the right to conquer and to own the land of an inferior people'" (cited in Tooze 2007 p.198). Moreover, Hitler stated emphatically in *Mein Kampf* that "Germany will either be a world power or there will be no Germany" (Hitler 1974 p.597). Mazower maintains that "Hitler's reading of how the British ruled India showed that what counted for him at bottom was force. A ruling power, according to him, should not even pretend that what it was doing was in anyone's interest but its own" (Mazower 2009 p.587). Indeed, for the Nazis war and *Wiederwehrhaftmachung* (military preparedness) were very much integral to the process of social reconstruction, a transformation which was, therefore, premised upon the domination of other nations (Geyer 1987, see p.61 and p.66). In fact Hitler, speaking to senior military officers in February 1939, even suggested that Germany was destined for mastery of the entire world (see Knox 2000 p.104) and Rauschning confirms, in his (otherwise dubious) recollections, that the dictator undoubtedly had global aspirations, especially in South America (see Rauschning 1939 p.72, see Kershaw 1985 p.108). Evidently, "given Hitler's reluctance to tolerate limits to his power, it is most unlikely that his foreign policy would have remained purely continental" (Williamson 1998 p.52).

Meanwhile Mussolini and the Italian Fascists, for their part, desired colonial expansion as the natural task and rightful reward for an aspiring young "proletarian" nation. As Mussolini put it "'imperialism is the eternal and immutable law of life'" (cited in McGovern 1946 p.540). Italians, Mussolini claimed, were entitled to a greater share of the earth, even if it meant confrontation with the British Empire (Knox 2000 p.69). Demographic reality and national (Roman) pride dictated that the geo-political privilege of the strategic *spazio vitale* around the Mediterranean would be claimed as an entitlement for Italy and established by force if necessary. As Mussolini self-confidently and emphatically expressed it, "'we have a right to empire'" (cited in Hayes 1973 p.53). For both Mussolini and Hitler therefore, as for most fascists, war, conflict and conquest were very much part of the essence of life itself, inevitable and necessary. As Kallis says, "the notions of *spazio vitale* and *lebensraum* became figurative and composite expressions both of a general propensity for expansion – as an open-ended, permanent state of affairs – and of concrete aspirations, reinforced by historical, geopolitical and ideological factors specific to each country and regime...but timing and planning were greatly determined by external opportunities and limitations" (Kallis 2000 p.196). Each fascist regime therefore exploited, in a pragmatic and flexible fashion, the various geo-political and foreign policy opportunities as they arose.

So the fascist movements, and the regimes they created, were virulently nationalistic and militaristic, with an innate imperialist impulse. Their ideology was based on the belief that war was a morally purifying activity and that conflict was an inevitable and positive facet of life - and that the spoils belonged rightfully to the victor. The military values, embodied in graphic terms by historical and mythological reference to the Romans and the Teutons, dominated fascist praxis and legitimized violence and war. It is, therefore, hardly surprising that tentative moves toward the formulation of some kind of fascist International (for example at Montreux in 1934) were effectively stillborn. Despite Mussolini's grandiloquent claims about fostering a "new civilization" and references to the century of "universal" fascism, multilateral initiatives were undermined by the inherent national parochialism of the respective movements (see Knox 2000 p.63). As Woolf says, "for movements born of exacerbated nationalistic feeling and nurtured on the exaltation of war and the bloody oppression of the weak, fascist internationalism was a contradiction in terms" (Woolf 1981 p.17, see p.15-17).

Of course in practical terms this undisguised xenophobic desire for national self-aggrandizement eventually resulted in a world-wide conflagration. Fascist Italy revealed its intentions as early as 1923 with the bombardment of Corfu, and Mussolini discovered that the invasion of Abyssinia in 1935, whilst posing only relatively minor logistical and military problems, could enhance national prestige and distract public attention from rather more pressing domestic difficulties (Schmidt 1973 p.137, see Rodogno 2009). The Italian Fascist nation would be constructed via conflict and territorial expansion, and "ideologically driven wars waged by Italian Fascism were murderous and resulted in hundreds of thousands of victims" (Rodogno 2009 p.257). The Italian Empire was proclaimed in 1936 amidst much euphoria, and intervention in Spain in support of Franco reinforced a sense of national and ideological purpose. However from that point onwards (and especially after the signing of the Anti-Comintern Pact in 1937, and "Pact of Steel" in 1939) Italy became increasingly subordinated to her stronger northern neighbour - henceforth Italian Fascism was dragged along in the wake of Nazism (see Chabod 1974 p.81).

The Germans, having withdrawn from the League of Nations, remilitarized the Rhineland, occupied Austria (*anchluss*) and annexed Czechoslovakia via a combination of bullying, blackmail and international complicity. After those who had sought to appease the dictator had learned harsh lessons at Munich in 1938, the invasion of Poland in September 1939 precipitated the Second World War. The complete contempt for international agreements and the stunning diplomatic *volte face* via the Nazi-Soviet Pact indicated with the utmost clarity the Nazi regime's voracious expansionism and Hitler's intention to pursue his particular foreign policy objectives by force, in complete disregard of conventional diplomatic procedure and international protocols. Dominance in Europe via pre-emptive war was therefore Hitler's primary objective, and the establishment of a New Order on the continent was a prelude to the activation of global geo-political aspirations (see Mazower 2009 p.2-3). When Mussolini (although unprepared) joined Hitler on 10 June 1940 at the height of German success, Hitler's armies having swept through Holland, Belgium and France, it seemed that fascism had fulfilled its own prophecies about the predominance of the strong over the weak. General Erich von Manstein's brilliant, calculated wager in the Ardennes  had apparently paid off with spectacular results, and Field Marshall Keitel solemnly proclaimed Hitler to be *Groesster Feldheer Aller Zeiten* – the greatest military leader of all time. Undoubtedly hubris reinvigorated the Nazi regime's ideological resolve in the subsequent *blitzkrieg* against Russia which was, according to Tooze, "the last great land-grab in the long and bloody history of European colonialism" (Tooze 2007 p.462). "Operation Barbarossa", launched in June 1941 against the Slav *untermenschen*, initiated "the most destructive and barbaric war in the history of mankind" (Kershaw 2009 p.621). This attack, the largest invasion in military history, represented another extraordinary gamble by Hitler. Initially, as German tanks swept eastward into the vastness of Russia, it seemed as though Hitler's instincts were to be spectacularly vindicated. Indeed, in July 1941 the Chief of the German Army General Staff Franz Halder wrote in his diary that the war in the east had been won (see Rees 2005 p.147), and by the end of 1942 Germany occupied approximately one third of Europe's landmass, governing nearly half of its inhabitants: "the swastika flew over the Channel Islands in the west and over Mount Elbrus in the Caucasus, from northern Norway to the Sahara" (Mazower 2009 p.223).

Of course fascism's "plutocratic" enemies in the west were more stubborn, and the invasion of the Soviet Union proved to be a fatal mistake. General Jodl had predicted that the Russian colossus would prove to be a nothing more than a "'pigs bladder'" (cited in Rees 2005 p.158), although it soon became clear, in the winter snows outside Moscow and Leningrad, that the reach of the German High Command had exceeded its grasp. They would be made to regret their arrogance. After the decisive battle at Stalingrad, where the German 6th Army was decisively defeated by the Red Army in January 1943, and the invasion of Normandy in 1944, the fascist dictators eventually capitulated to a gigantic pincer movement coordinated by the Allies. Mussolini was eventually captured whilst trying to escape and shot by partisans on the Swiss border, his corpse hung upside-down on a meat-hook along with his mistress Claretta Petacci in the *Piazzale Loreto,* Milan. Whilst Hitler committed suicide with a Walther 7.65mm pistol in his bunker in Berlin as the Soviets entered Potsdamer Platz, the Nazi leader evidently unable to bear the ignominy of defeat at the hands of the "Asiatic hordes". Thus, in a sense, fascism's rampant nationalism, militarism and imperialism followed a predictable course through armed aggression, territorial acquisition, conflict and war. The only difficulty for them proved to be that the "decadent" Western democracies, and the "inferior" Slav peoples destined to be conquered to the East, proved too strong and determined in practice to play the role allotted to them in fascist ideology.

## Authoritarian State and Disciplined Society

Closely linked to the concept of nationalism, as interpreted by the fascist, was the belief in the necessity of a strong, centralized, authoritarian state and a hierarchically ordered, disciplined society (see Poulantzas 1974 Part 7). Whilst Hitler proclaimed ominously that, "you do not alter the destinies of nations in kid-gloves" (Hitler 1974 p.621), the official political journal of Fascism, founded by Mussolini himself, was entitled *Gerarchia*-hierarchy. Discipline, duty and servitude were deeply woven into the fabric of fascist ideology and experience.

Fascists believed that man was self-evidently a social animal, and individual "freedom" could not exist beyond rule-bound social arrangements. For Italian Fascists "society is the unity of the universal and particular, and constitutes a whole which is greater than its immediate parts" (Gregor 1969 p.218 see p.213). Consequently Gentile criticised those who claimed that "the particular individual man must be recognised as free or as substantially independent of the social aggregation through which he also becomes a member of society ... the conception of the individual as a social atom is a pure fiction ... at the root of 'I' there is a 'We'", hence "the individual ... does not exist; individualism is only a shadow that looms over the field of politics and makes it sterile" (Gentile 1960 p.80-82 and p.169). Fascism was therefore predicated upon the superiority of collective interests over and above individual interests, and it emphasised an organic conception of society. Society was considered a living entity, an integrated formation, the fabric of which had to be protected by the state. The state was seen, in this context, as the embodiment of the will of the nation - the juridical incarnation of the collective will. The state's authority was felt to be derived not from any obscure liberal idea of a (hypothetical) "social contract" between citizen and state, but stemmed from its organic relationship with its citizens via the Fascist party (see later). The individual was seen as unambiguously subservient to the state, and "freedom" meant, in effect, performing one's duty toward, and/or on behalf of, the Fascist state (see Mosse 1979 p.30). The notion of a free or autonomous realm of civil society had no purchase in fascist perceptions beyond the professon of loyalty by the people. The Italian Fascist Alfredo Rocco put the position succinctly: "'individual liberty is only a concession granted by the state to the individual'" (cited in Guerin 1973 p.175).

There was certainly little scope for individual conscience or critical independence, since "according to fascism every citizen's duty is total obedience to the state; the individual should willingly sacrifice everything, including life itself, if it is demanded for the greater glory of the fascist nation" (Wilkinson 1981 p.12). The state's infallible interpretation of the common, national interest and collective will simply made individualism superfluous.

Yet the state was, in an important sense, populist as well as authoritarian in that it was closely identified with the masses and relied, at least in part, on plebiscites for legitimacy (for example, the plebiscite in Italy in March 1929 after the Concordat had been signed with Pius XI; and the German plebiscites of 1933, 1934 and 1938). Fascism was, in Mussolini's words, "'organised, centralized, authoritarian democracy'" (cited in Lyttleton 1973 p.50). This emphasis on the authority of the state, which was popularly endorsed (if not democratic), was born of a deep hostility among fascists towards conventional liberal parliamentary norms. However, in this context it is important to note that the parliamentary systems in Italy and Germany did not possess the tradition and stability of other European countries. In Germany the Weimar Republic was viewed with contempt by many as the politically manufactured product of defeat and, moreover, held responsible for the detested Versailles settlement imposed by the victors. In Italy the weak and corrupt liberal regimes of Giolitti and others did little or nothing to convey the virtues of parliamentary democracy, and as a result the Italian political system could not count on the support of the population at large (Pearce 2002 p.39). So in both countries a significant percentage of the citizens were never actually reconciled to their respective parliamentary "systems" and political conflict was never fully institutionalized. In fact it could be argued that severe economic crises and acute social conflict led to state repression in the pre-fascist era, which in turn paved the way for a much more authoritarian alternative. Certainly the fascists served notice on the political structures and processes of their adversaries with the utmost clarity and consistency. Mussolini proclaimed unambiguously that "'the century of democracy is over ... the ideals of democracy are exploded ... the new generation are not going to let the corpse of democracy block their way to the future'" (cited in Rossi/ Tasca 1938 p.237); whilst Hitler claimed that "the Western democracy of today is the forerunner of Marxism", and "the parliamentary principle of majority rule sins against the basic aristocratic principle of nature" (Hitler 1974 p.72 and p.74) [11]. Parliamentarianism and liberal democratic constitution- alism were viewed by fascists as a cowardly and irresponsible product of bourgeois decadence, if not the precursor to the calamity of communism.

However, both Hitler and Mussolini used the pre-existing political system to achieve power (and indeed in this they were aided by state elites in the army, police force and judiciary). Mussolini saw the parliamentary system as irredeemably effete, and democracy as effeminate – counting rifles was much more important than counting votes. However, despite the scorn and opprobrium heaped upon democratic struc- tures and processes, Mussolini's Fascists also contested elections and paid a certain procedural lip-service to liberal democratic forms. Fascists performed very poorly at first and it was only after Giolitti invited the Fascists to join the National Bloc, prior to elections in May 1921, that the Fascists substantially increased their representation. However the Fascists ultimately displayed contempt for the legitimacy of liberal constitutionalism by conducting the so-called "March on Rome", an act of political choreography by which Musso- lini managed to threaten and bluff his way to a position of power (see Halperin 1964 p.31). King Victor Emmanuel III actually "invited" Mussolini to head the government of Italy and the invitation was "applauded by the vast majority of that segment of the national political world which possessed wealth, status and power" (Bosworth 1998 p.41). The Italian Establishment, in collaborating with Fascists, had effectively subverted democracy and sanctioned a coup d'etat.

Hitler became convinced of the need for "legality" after the fiasco of his Munich putsch on 9 November 1923 which was probably inspired by Mussolini's successful "March on Rome". Hitler, along with disaffected war veteran General Ludendorff, led the local *Deutscher Kampfbund* in an attempt to launch its own fateful *Machtergreifung* (seizure of power). Hitler believed that if he could take control of Munich the civil and military leaders would be forced by public opinion to support him and his ultimate plan to move against the federal authorities. However, the challenge to the authority of Weimar ended abruptly when the local army and police declined to support the provincial uprising and fourteen insurgents were killed. Hitler was sent to Landsberg prison after being convicted of treason (Kershaw 2009 p.129), and although Hitler received a derisory sentence, he was able to use his trial to dramatic effect by publicizing his political perspective. Hitler undoubtedly realised that his movement stood much more chance of achieving its objectives by utilizing the state for his own purposes, rather than attempting to overthrow it directly by armed insurrection. As Hitler remarked "'instead of working to achieve power by an armed coup, we shall have to hold our noses and enter the Reichstag'" (cited in Pearce 2002 p.55). Yet Hitler was perfectly clear about his ultimate goal, "'it is not for seats in Parliament that we fight'", he declared in September 1930, "'but we win seats in Parliament in order that one day we may be able to liberate the German people'" (Hitler cited in Baynes 1969 vol I p.189) [12]. There is no doubt that for the Nazis, "the bullet and the ballot box were complementary tools of power", and the threat of violence was never abandoned, in effect "votes and elections were treated cynically as instruments of formal political legitimation" (Evans 2006 p.44). Of course the Nazis never won a majority of the popular vote, and despite being the largest party its share of the vote was diminishing in the last election (November 1932) before Hitler took power. Hitler used his gambler's instinct to hold out for the Chancellorship and it was, in effect, the political establishment that invited Hitler to assume the reigns of power. In David Schoenbaum's memorable phrase, the "stowaways" suddenly found themselves "in control of an ocean liner" (Schoenbaum 1967 p.47). Those conservative elements in the German state, who were so pleased that Hitler could deliver mass support and a Parliamentary majority that excluded the ideological left, handed authority to Hitler in a cynical backstairs deal.

Hence in both countries the fascists assumed the authority of state via "legitimate" (or at least quasi-legal) processes, whereby conservative elements agreed to share power. In neither case was the democratic mandate overwhelming – conservative elites effectively capitulated to the fascists as a consequence of a tawdry combination of cowardice and self-serving political machination. The Fascist and Nazi adventurers had made themselves too important to ignore, and had been encouraged and indulged by conservatives elements because of their anti-communism (see later), then those very same social elements in both countries, who held the keys to state authority, decided that the possibilities they offered outweighed the disadvantages of allowing the ruffians to exert power (see Paxton 2005 p.99). Of course, ultimately, the fascists would not be absorbed by liberal parliamentary norms, nor would they be constrained by constitutional structures, and despite manufacturing a certain level of "plebiscitary acclamation" (Kershaw 1995 p.203) the fascist regimes were fundamentally anti-democratic. As Paxton explains, "having unleashed their militants in order to make democracy unworkable and discredit the constitutional state, the Nazi and Fascist leaders then posed as the only nonsocialist force that could restore order" (Paxton 2005 p.103-4). The fascists were therefore invited to impose their will on the state.

Thereafter, the authoritarian state was used by the fascists to organise society. Political parties, churches, trade unions, the media, schools, the family and so on were all co-ordinated in the attempt to secure and ensure fascist domination. Yet, beyond this common objective of establishing control of society, there existed a distinct difference in purpose between Italian Fascists and German National Socialists which needs to be acknowledged and explained. The objective of the Italian Fascists was to achieve the "*stato totalitario*", because for the Italian Fascist the state was the sovereign focal point of society since "social life without the state would be impossible" (Gregor 1969 p.153). As Mussolini's famous slogan succinctly put it, "everything inside the state, nothing against the state, nothing outside the state". For Mussolini the state was of critical importance, and everything was to be subordinated to it, even the party, as he said "'for Fascism the state is the absolute before which individuals and groups are only relative...individuals and groups are conceivable only within the state...the state has become the true reality of the individual...for the Fascist everything is in the state, and nothing human or spiritual exists or has value outside of the state'" (cited in Guerin 1973 p.175, see Mussolini 1968 p.38). Moreover, any decisions to be made about individual liberty had to be made by the state, as Mussolini said, "'in such matters the individual cannot be the judge, but the state only'" (cited in McGovern 1946 p.558).

Giovanni Gentile (although only becoming a Fascist in 1923) emerged as the foremost theoretician of the Italian Fascist idea of the state. He perceived the state as an ideal, ethical (even divine) entity, embodying the "purest" form of democracy. As he explained; "'against individualism, the fascist conception is for the state, it is for the individual in so far as he coincides with the state, which is the conscience and universal will of man in his historical context'" (Gentile cited in Lyttleton 1973) [13]. Thus although there was a distinctive denial of diversity, which reflected a conspicuous antagonism toward all forms of political and social pluralism, there also existed an emphasis on the authority of the state as an ethical force, a pedagogue as well as a disciplinarian. This fact accounts for Gentile's odd belief that the new Fascist state was destined to be more "liberal" than the old state, for Gentile "always insisted that fascism was the embodiment of genuine liberalism" (Harris 1966 p.151) [14]. Hence Gentile saw the Fascist state as a Hegelian synthesis which would resolve all social contradictions and realise the true identity of man and society (see Gentile 1960 p.121 and especially chapter VI "The State"). In effect the state *becomes* the will of the individual, and any attempt to separate or counter-pose them are invalid. Thus the political, social, cultural and moral unity of the people, the nation, is realised in the living reality of the state. As a consequence the state, by definition, cannot be coercive, but simply represents liberty on a much higher plane, as Gentile claimed, "'the notion of a state involves law and authority. This authority cannot but present itself initially as a limit to liberty, precisely in order that liberty may be able to express itself in its full concrete infinity'" (cited in Harris 1966 p.123). Gentile concluded that "'the maximum of liberty coincides with the maximum strength of the state'" (cited in McGovern 1946 p.558). Gentile aimed to align Fascism with the neo-Hegelian's doctrine of the ethical state, thereby providing it with a heritage identified with the Risorgimento period. In this way Fascism was designated as the true heir of the Italian liberal tradition. Indeed, Gentile maintained that "'Fascism has restored to the state its sovereign functions by claiming its absolute ethical meaning, against the egotism of classes and categories'" (cited in Mussolini 1968 p.38). Thus we can see in Italian Fascism the kernel of a frustrated liberalism and, as Lyttleton quite rightly points out "we must recognize that there was a powerful strain in Italian Fascism which originated in an exasperated and disillusioned liberalism" (Lyttleton 1973 p.18, see Harris 1966). Thus Italian Fascism saw the state as an ethical *end in itself*, and practiced in effect what Pope Pius XI perceptively referred to as "statolotry".

In its early period of control at the helm Italian Fascism never achieved its ambitious objectives with regard to the role of the state. From 1922 to 1925 (despite altering electoral law in 1923 to ensure increased Fascist representation in the Chamber of Deputies in April 1924) [15] Mussolini seemed perfectly content to head a coalition of sorts, to rule within a parliamentary framework and tolerate the persistence of bourgeois civil liberties. The monarchy, the army, the bureaucracy and the church all played a key role, in the initial stages, in strengthening state power. As Mussolini claimed, he could have immediately transformed the Italian Parliament into a bivouac for his Fascist squads – but in the early period of Fascist rule he simply chose not to (see Morgan 1995 p.69). It was only after the murder of the socialist deputy Matteotti in June 1924 (who had complained of election irregularities), and the emergence of the "Aventine" opposition, that Fascism lurched tangibly toward its self-expressed "totalitarian" objectives. In fact "the Matteotti crisis proved that though Mussolini had no clear plan for dictatorship when he came to power, Fascism could not coexist within even the modified framework of the Liberal parliamentary state" (Pollard 1998 p.53).

Mussolini's speech of 3 January 1925 marked a new departure and what Lyttleton refers to as the "second wave" of Fascism (Lyttleton 1979 p.45). Through the Exceptional Decrees of November 1926 state controls were tightened and civil freedoms eroded. For instance, legal codes were reformed and the death penalty introduced for certain political offences; the civil service was "made Fascist"; the autonomy of local provinces and municipalities was restricted by centrally controlled prefects; freedom of the press and of association were curtailed; and political exiles were deprived of their citizenship (see Halperin 1964 p.43 and Documents). In 1927 the Italian secret police, the *Organizzazione per la Vigilanze e la Repressione dell'Antifascismo* (OVRA), was set up and its vast clandestine, capilliary network of agents and informers had two over-riding functions – repression and deterrence (see Corner 2002a). Although the precise meaning of the acronym is contested, there is no doubt that this mysterious and unpredictable organization was effective in limiting dissent (see Duggan 2013 p.156-57). The operational activity of OVRA was accompanied by the extensive use of Special Tribunals to deal with "political crimes". Meanwhile the detention centres on the isles Lipari, Ponzi and Tremiti were used to incarcerate anyone suspected of subversive activity and Fascist Italy's largest concentration camp, which was situated at Ferramonti di Tarsia in Calabria, housed many thousands of Jews, Greeks, Yugoslavs and "enemies of the state". Torture, beating and physical intimidation was not uncommon, and the impact of such techniques on the perception of the wider public must have been profound (see Corner 2002a). The boundaries delineating "unacceptable" behaviour were therefore expanded dramatically as the regime focused on control, surveillance and regimentation. Suspicion that someone *might* be intending to engage in activity to the detriment of the state was often enough to precipitate a punitive response. Indeed, tens of thousands of "dissenters" were sent to *confino* – placed, in effect, under house arrest and rendered politically inoperative by the regime. The coercive capability of the state was thereby considerably enhanced by the Fascists.

The electoral law of 1928 decreed that only a single list of candidates would be put forward in an election, in effect those endorsed by the Grand Council of Fascism – Italy became a one party state. The state was simultaneously centralized and denuded of its, albeit limited, democratic structures and procedures. The numerous attempts on Mussolini's life and the orchestrated anger that inevitably followed, created the context for tightening the Fascist grip on the state. By 1929 Mussolini was head of no less than eight ministries, he also led the Fascist Party, the Fascist Grand Council, the National Council of Corporations, he was Commandant of the Militia and later the armed forces, and he headed a plethora of committees and commissions. As Morgan noted, "government came to resemble Mussolini in endless dialogue with himself" (Morgan 1995 p.94). Thus, by virtue of the sheer extent of Mussolini's personal authority the Fascists could justifiably claim to have substantially augmented the authoritarian nature of the state (see Schmidt 1973 p.49). In reality, "meaningful parliamentary government had given way to a centralized and unaccountable system of executive rule, vested in Mussolini and the state bureaucracies" (Morgan 1995 p.94). Even the Catholic Church came to terms with the state in February 1929 with the Lateran Pacts which, whilst affording the Church certain rights, nevertheless enabled Mussolini to harness the status and prestige of the Vatican to his regime. "Italy's overwhelmingly Catholic population was now free to support Fascism without reservation" and the established Church had, thereafter, a vested interest in supporting Mussolini (Knox 2000 p.86). Importantly, "the regime met no serious opposition from established institutions or from traditional economic and social interests as it set about demolishing the liberal state. The monarchy, the armed forces, and the industrial and agrarian bourgeoisie accepted the demise of parliamentary government with little evident sign of regret, and seemed more impressed by the advantages that the new regime had brought them by restoring order and discipline in Italian society, and in particular over the workers" (Gentile 2002 p.155). All the currents within Fascism, syndicalist or nationalist, radical or conservative, were supportive of measures to reinforce law and order, and Justice Minister Rocco, when he introduced the Public Safety Law in 1926, explicitly repudiated all doctrines of natural law and individual rights (see Sarti 1990 p.22). Protecting the state and protecting the Fascist government became, for all practical purposes, identical (see Corner 2002a). The Special Tribunal set up to defend the state and adjudicate in appropriate cases, employed judges who were either ex-army, Fascist Militia or able to demonstrate their "national" credentials – that is, in practice, pro-Fascist sympathies. "By 1929 almost all those political figures who continued to argue that it was possible and desirable to be an Italian and yet not a Fascist had been driven into exile or sat disconsolate in Fascist jails" (Bosworth 2005 p.246). In his autobiography Mussolini talked of a sense of seriousness pervading all citizens and all classes in society - disorder, he said, had been "abolished" (Mussolini 1939 p.253). In effect the *fasces*, the bundle of rods and axes carried by a lictor in classical times, symbolized not only collectivism but the public meaning of a regime which had eventually created a vertically ordered society where the power of the state prevailed over all else (see Bosworth 1998 p.37).

However, despite the regime's "totalitarian" pretentions and evident authoritarianism, there was a real sense in which Fascist aspirations remained unfulfilled, although it is important not to succumb to the temptation, induced by Mussolini's theatrical antics, to see the regime as more comic than coercive (see Corner 2002a). The Italian Fascist state was unquestionably coercive, but its power incomplete. Under Fascism, for example, the persistent conflict between Turati, Farinacci and Starace conformed to a Hobbesian pattern as each functionary engaged in mutually hostile machinations designed to procure the favour of Mussolini. Moreover, despite the efforts of people like Rocco and Federzoni, important centres of power continued to exist outside the Fascist state's central control: the Monarchy, the Senate, the Roman Catholic Church, the Army, parts of the civil service, sections of large scale capital and indeed numerous provincial leaders of the National Fascist Party itself (*Ras*) – all retained varying degrees of autonomy. The institutional components of the Fascist regime existed in uneasy equilibrium, depriving the Fascist state of uninhibited authoritarian control. In a very real sense, as De Grand has pointed out, Italian Fascism was a "hyphenated" phenomenon because a "modifier" was always added to it, whether it was Catholic, Nationalist, Monarchist or even Syndicalist (see De Grand 2000). Italy may have been a dictatorship, but the leader of the state was not all-powerful (Pearce 2002 p.66) and the idea of Mussolini as an omnipotent overlord was essentially a fiction perpetuated by the Fascist party (see later). Indeed it was the existence of centres of influence beyond the scope of Fascist control which proved effective in providing the focal points around which the opposition to the Duce could eventually coalesce. As events took shape, concerned sectors of society were able to rally around the Monarchy, Army and Church and make terms with the allies, leaving Mussolini to be crushed between the partisan hammer and German anvil in his ragged republic to the north (see later).

The Nazis, quite unlike the Italian Fascists, saw their state more as a means toward other objectives, rather than as an end in itself (see Caplan 1993, Maser 1970 chapter 9, Hitler 1974 vol I chapter 12, and vol II chapters 2-3). As Hitler explained, "the state is a means to an end. Its end lies in the preservation and advancement of a community of physically and psychically homogenous creatures...it should not be forgotten that the highest aim of human existence is not the preservation of the state, let alone the government, but the preservation of the species" (Hitler 1974 p.357 and p.88; see Noakes 2008). Such was Hitler's view of the state – an instrument with which to maintain and reproduce the racial integrity of the German people or *Volksgemeinschaft* (see later). As Pois says, "the role of the National Socialist movement - embodying the will of the volk - superceded that of the state, which ideally was to be merely its administrative and juridicial appendage" (Pois 1970 p.30, see chapter V p.191; see also Cecil 1972 p.118). In fact Hitler believed that the Germanic race had "created the notion of the state...by compelling the individual to be a part of the whole" (Hitler 1973 p.34). Hence if a task was considered too important to be entrusted to the state, he simply bypassed it, but Hitler's expectation was that the state should simply be a vehicle for the implementation of Nazi ideology (Kershaw 1989 p.64). With his over-riding racial objective in mind Hitler's National Socialists managed to fashion, in a remarkably short period of time, an authoritarian state which made Mussolini's look decidedly moderate (see Kedward 1971).

Hitler maintained that the Nazi state must be based on "tradition", "force" and "popularity" (Hitler 1974 p.471), building upon the assets he felt the Germans had inherited from the old Reich, namely the civil service, the monarchical infrastructure, and especially the army. Moreover, a new state, the Nazis believed, would emerge out of the NSDAP as comprising the best elements of the German nation. "Command and responsibility" was to be the key phrase in creating a state which would embody the very essence of "German" identity. Indeed Bullock noted that "as soon as Hitler began to think and talk about the organisation of the state it is clear that the metaphor which dominated his mind was that of an army. He saw the state as an instrument of power in which the qualities to be valued were discipline, unity and sacrifice" (Bullock 1962 p.403). The individual would therefore be subordinated to the state as a prerequisite for social order. Hitler started from the premise that in the National Socialist state there was no place for individualism or those who valued personal freedom, and the idea that the state was a voluntary or contractual association of independent individuals was anathema to all Nazis (see Mazer 1970 p.127).

In fact the authoritarian conception of the state envisaged by the Nazis was prefigured, to some extent, by events which occured toward the end of the Weimar period when the constitution was routinely abrogated by President von Hindenburg via Article 48, which was only supposed to be invoked in the event of an emergency. Bruning's two years in government had already seen the resort to rule via emergency decrees, a period when authoritarianism became effectively normalized. Evading democratic accountability and ruling without reference to the Reichstag was justified, to a large degree, by the juridicial analysis of Carl Schmitt, who eventually became the Third Reich's chief legal expert. Schmitt, in the pre-Nazi Weimar period, put forward an exalted view of the state as the protector of security and order. Given the political turmoil that characterised the Weimar period many conservatives, who had not come to terms with the loss of the monarchy, were prone to advocate authoritarian solutions, and Schmitt was simply the most articulate of them as "one of twentieth century Germany's ablest political and legal philosophers" (Frye 1966 p.824). Schmitt criticised liberalism and the pluralism of democracy as inherently destructive of stability and order. According to Schmitt the state had to be above politics in order to represent the nation as a whole, and he justified the utilisation of Article 48 of the Weimar Constitution. The state was to have few restrictions upon its jurisdiction because "from his (Schmitt's) perspective the freedom of the individual was secondary to the grandiose task allotted to the state", indeed Schmitt himself wrote, "'no individual can have autonomy within the state'" (cited in Bendersky 1983 p.12). Schmitt's "Concept of the Political", which outlined his "friend-enemy thesis", was his most significant intellectual justification for the authoritarian German state. The philosophy of "decisionism", which was designed to forestall political chaos, meant the "exceptional" state was to have the sole authority to identify and deal with "friend" or "enemy" (see Schmitt 1976 p.26). Schmitt therefore argued, in an explicit juridicial fashion, for "a return to an authoritarian conception of politics and an authoritarian state" (Frye 1966 p.824). Although originally an authoritarian conservative, Schmitt joined the NSDAP in October 1933 to become a significant intellectual apologist for the Nazi dictatorship, and his prefigurative ideas gave important impetus to the Nazis in their desire to erect an authoritarian state structure [16]

Hitler's "*Gleichschaltung*" (co-ordination) of state and society was swift and effective, and the Nazis adopted a strategy of what Nolte called "war in peacetime" to construct their authoritarian edifice (Nolte 1969 p.440). "In practice *Gleichschaltung* meant the elimination from German society of all diversity and dissent" (Stackelberg 1999 p.105). Indeed Shirer, in his famous study, claimed that "Hitler...conquered Germany with the greatest of ease" since there was very little practical political resistance to the process (Shirer 1985 p.204, see especially chapter 7). At an early stage Hitler warned that the desire to establish social order could not be constrained by constitutional structures or legalistic requirements. The Reichstag fire in February 1933 (apparently started by Dutch Communist Marinus van der Lubbe) provided the preliminary pretext to extend the suppression of political opponents, with Hindenburg signing a Decree for the Protection of People and State in February 1933, which suspended all sections of the constitution relating to free speech, free press, free assembly and so on (see Rees 2012 p.111). The Decree also authorized wiretaps, the opening of personal mail, and sanctioned search and indefinite detention without a warrant. In March the

Reichstag met to consider and pass the Enabling Bill which transferred full legislative and executive authority to the new Chancellor. It was, in effect, a coup. Waves of arbitrary arrests followed and the Decree against Malicious Attacks even criminalized hostile remarks made against party leadership and state. Criminal and political offences were thereby conflated, affording enormous discretionary power to a multiplicity of coercive state agencies.

As a consequence of the Enabling Act (Law for Removing the Distress of People and Reich, 23 March 1933, described by Schmitt as the provisional constitution), the Emergency Regulations for the Protection of People and State, and the Law for the Safeguarding of the Unity of Party and State (1 December 1933), the National Socialists secured a stranglehold over state structures. After the death of Hindenburg in August 1934 Hitler effectively combined the posts of President and Chancellor, and "the Fuhrer" became unassailable as supreme leader and head of state, thus acquiring a position far stronger than Mussolini ever enjoyed in Italy. Under the cloak of legality (and without, technically, even abrogating the Weimar constitution) Hitler proceeded to permeate state institutions with the Nazi *Weltanschauung*. As Evans says "the Nazi assault on existing institutions affected the whole of society. Every state government, every state parliament in Germany's federal political system, every town and district and local council was ruthlessly purged; the Reichstag Fire Decree and the Enabling Act were used to dismiss supposed enemies of the state, meaning enemies of the Nazis. Every national voluntary association, and every local club was brought under Nazi control...in short, the whole fabric of associational life was Nazified" (Evans 2006 p.14).

It also soon became clear that the Nazi's were willing to countenance the most extreme violence in order to ensure the stability of the state. The signs were already evident before the Nazis came to power with the attempt to intimidate all serious political opposition. After Hitler acquired control of the state, that intimidation took on an even more sinister dimension, as the power of the government was used to endorse and enhance the terror tactics of the Nazi stormtroopers (see Bessel 1987a). Indeed Goering passed a decree prohibiting the police from prosecuting members of the SA, and then incorporated them as an auxiliary arm of state coercion (Mason 1993 p.75 note No.73). The "auxiliary police", composed of members of the SA, SS and *Stahlhelm*, therefore orchestrated a coordinated campaign against all the opponents of the new regime. This state endorsement of Nazi paramilitarism constituted the cynical deployment of thuggish violence in defence of social order (see Bessel 1987a p.15). However the resulting upsurge in the use of force was far too unruly, unpredictable and uncomfortable for established social elites in the army and aristocracy to accept, and pressure was placed on Hitler to deal with those elements who appeared to be intent on deploying disreputable methods.

The purge of June 1934, which physically eliminated all opposition to Hitler, was crucial in establishing a pattern of authoritarian state order (Stackelberg 1999 p.113). Ernst Rohm's vague talk of a "second revolution" and the general lawlessness of the SA left Hitler with an opportunity to convince the *Reichwehr* that he would not tolerate insubordination from below (see Kershaw 2009 p.315). Rohm's execution, along with other SA leaders and Gregor Strasser, removed the threat of further radicalism, and the opportunity was taken to settle old scores with the likes of ex-Chancellor von Schleicher who was murdered, like many others, in cold blood. Hitler used the blood-letting as a chance to establish his credentials as a ruthless leader, and the pitiless purge was described as a "clean-up of dangerous and degenerate elements" (Evans 2006 p.37). The army, via General Blomberg, expressed its sincere gratitude and President Hindenburg sent a telegram congratulating Hitler on his "'gallant intervention'", while the rubber-stamp Reichstag applauded Hitler's retrospective self-justification (see Stackelberg 1999 p.116).

Importantly, this act of blatant pre-meditated murder by Hitler's henchmen was justified in judicial terms by the aforementioned expert on public law Carl Schmitt, who argued that since legal power actually rested with the leader of the state his actions could not, by definition, be unlawful. As Schmitt said with regard to the so-called "Night of the Long Knives", "'the *Fuhrer* preserves the right, when in the moment of danger, to use his supreme authority to be the highest judge...the *Fuhrer's* action was part of his natural jurisdiction, not proceeding through legal forms but in itself of supreme justice'" (cited in Corni 2009 p.287). Rational legality had been finally subjugated to the requirements of arbitrary executive power. Hitler, in Carl Schmitt's terms, decided the "friend-enemy" distinction and his power was effectively unrestricted. As Schmitt himself confirmed: "'the strength of the National Socialist State lies in the fact that it is from top to bottom and in every atom of its existence ruled and permeated with the concept of leadership'" (cited in Griffin 1995 p.138-39). With this justification of terror Schmitt not only consummated his marriage to a murderous authoritarian dictatorship but paved the way for the Fuhrer to take unilateral decisions, such as the "Night and Fog" Order of 7 December 1941 whereby opponents of the regime could be interned without even the semblance of a trial or even the notification of families. Hitler's personal will was henceforth accorded supreme executive authority possessing the force of law within the regime - state power became, in essence, *Fuhrer*-power. As Dr. Hans Frank, Commissioner of Justice and Reich Law Leader explained "'the Fuhrer is supreme judge of the nation...there is no position in the area of constitutional law in the Third Reich independent of this elemental will of the Fuhrer'" (cited in Welch 1998 p.45).

In practice, the speeches of Adolph Hitler became the basis for interpreting legal sources. Certainly the law, as interpreted by legal experts like Ernst Rudolf Huber, offered little protection to individuals because the Fuhrer's authority in articulating the common interest of the *volk* was exclusive, comprehensive and unconstrained. Interestingly, "the regime found no difficulty in finding lawyers to serve on the

Special Courts. They were mostly men of upper-middle-class backgrounds, conservative nationalists...Few had qualms about Nazi jurisprudence. Most lawyers detested the Weimar Republic, were anti-democratic and pro-Nazi" (Kitchen 1995 p.184). Consequently, in practice, National Socialist jurisprudence was an irrational Carroll-like "wonderland" where truth was subordinated to falsehood, and fact merged with fiction - Hitler, of course, as the custodian of the national will and purveyor of summary and capricious state justice, acted as "Queen of Hearts" (see Stern 1975 p.119; see Kitchen 1995). The judiciary lost all semblance of autonomy and, quite simply, Adolf Hitler *was* the law, as Hans Frank concisely confirmed, "'the Constitutional law of the Third Reich is the legal formulation of the historic intentions of the Fuhrer'", "'our Constitution is the will of the Fuhrer'" (cited in Caplan 1993 p.106 and Bullock 1962 p.403, see Evans 2006 p.73).

Hitler and the Nazis proceeded to neutralize all opposition. Independent political parties were effectively abolished or made redundant, the Communists and Social Democrats were proscribed whilst the "Law Against the Formation of New Parties" simply formalized the reality of single party rule as the conservative and liberal parties dissolved themselves. What Goebbels referred to as the "'ape's theatre'" of parliamentary party politics came to an abrupt end and a one-party Nazi state was declared on 14 July 1933. The Nazis abolished the *Reichsrat* in February 1934 and effectively turned the *Reichstag* into a rubber stamp for the ratification of executive action. Moreover, the state had been centralized via the law for the Reorganisation of the Reich of January 1934 whereby, with the Nazi Gauleiters as Hitler's loyal regional chieftains, all semblance of representative self-government was effectively eliminated. Subsequent plebiscites were strictly controlled to ensure appropriate results, for example the dictatorship itself was endorsed in August 1934 by 89% of votes cast amidst murder, destruction and the violent intimidation of political opponents. Meanwhile independent trade unions were dissolved and their assets seized. Hitler had more or less secured the subordination of the army via reform of the High Command while the personal oath by the *Reichswehr* to the Fuhrer, in the eyes of most military officers, not only secured their acquiescence but deprived any resistance to the regime of any moral validity (see Knox 2000 p.91). The *Geheime Staatspolizei* secret state police (Gestapo) soon acquired a fearsome reputation for surveillance and coercion, enforcing the law (Hitler's will) with brutal effect against "enemies of the state" (Evans 2006 p.117). Although recent research suggests that, given resource constraints and structural inadequacies, the idea of the Gestapo as "omniscient, omnipotent and omnipresent" was to some extent a convenient myth to justfy popular acquiescence, there is little doubt that the consequences of resistance, or even non-compliance, could be swift and brutal (see Mallman and Paul 1995). As Evans says "vague and wide-ranging laws and decrees gave the police almost limitless powers of arrest and detention, virtually at will, while the courts did not lag far behind in applying the policies of repression and control" (Evans 2006 p.80). The Gestapo and SS (*Schutzstaffel*), having been given free reign to intimidate and coerce, were merged in 1936 under Himmler. Meanwhile the means of communication were effectively monopolized under Goebbels as independent or critical media outlets were either coerced into compliance or physically co-opted.

Certainly Nazi rule became increasingly personalised, especially after 1937. As Rees says, Hitler "had destroyed the normal apparatus of the state which would have served as a check on his absolute power" (Rees 2005 p.328). There were no meaningful Cabinet meetings to apply some manner of collective restraint, no national assembly to act as an institutional check, indeed no clear constitutional framework to delineate precise limits on Hitler's freedom of action. Consequently Hitler felt able to interfere in a vast range of areas and he issued dictats and instructions on a variety of issues - from the strength of beer in Bavaria, to the utility of fishing permits, from the level of garage rents, to the type of food given to visiting functionaries, from the production of artificial honey to the number of violins in the Vienna symphony orchestra (see Laqueur 1996 p.31). Certainly no-one could deviate from the guidelines he set. As SS officer Rudolf Hoess pointed out, "'orders, issued in the name of the *Fuhrer* were sacred. They brooked no consideration, no argument, no interpretation. They were carried out ruthlessly and regardless of conse-quences'" (cited in ABSM 1995 p.68). All of this led Bullock to claim, with some justification, that "if ever a man exercised absolute power it was Adolf Hitler" (Bullock 1962 p.381).

However, having said this we must be careful not to suggest that the Nazi state structure was totally monolithic or that Hitler was omnipotent. The Nazi state structure was not as uniform or efficient as conventional wisdom might suggest. In fact Noakes and Pridham argue that, "perhaps the most outstanding characteristic of the political system of the Third Reich was its lack of formal structure" (Noakes and Pridham 1974 p.248). Kershaw has also observed that the regime was characterized by a degree of polycentrism, noting that Hitler became "at one and the same time the absolutely indispensible fulcrum of the entire regime, and yet largely detached from any formal machinery of government. The result, inevitably, was a high level of governmental and administrative disorder" (Kershaw 2009 p.323). Indeed Noakes, whilst acknowledging a common functional impetus, nevertheless suggests that numerous state, party and hybrid power-holders were locked in a mutual struggle for ascendancy which precipitated an administrative chaos that "resembled a war zone" (Noakes 2008 p.88). This fact has led Geyer to argue that governing in the Third Reich consisted, essentially, of attempting to manage a competitive interaction between institutions which were engaged in a vicious and chaotic struggle for power and resources – indeed, he maintains that "there was no coherent system of government" (Geyer 1987 p.60). So in some senses Nazi rule was not only personal, arbitrary and authoritarian, but haphazard. Indeed Hildebrand, following Fest, talks of an "authoritarian anarchy" which was the consequence of bureaucratic inertia, overlapping jurisdictions and competing fiefdoms, for example between the Labour Front, Four Year Plan Office and Ministry of Interior (Hildebrand 1985 p.62, Fest 1973). Interestingly, "it has been estimated that there were 42 separate agencies with executive power to implement policy within the central government machine of Nazi Germany" (McDonough 1999 p.31), therefore "there was nothing neat about the administration of the Third Reich, and the idea that it was a smoothly functioning, completely centralized state has long since been abandoned by historians" (Evans 2006 p.49). Indeed General Keitel, who was undoubtedly in a position to know, characterized the system as a "'war of all against all'" (cited in Mason 1996 p.72). The incontrovertible evidence of polymorphous confusion and cynical self-interest, with Hitler in some cases actually fostering and exploiting competition among his subordinates, was a key characteristic of the state. However, Hitler acted as "supreme arbiter", and "all important drafts of proposals by heads of departments and party leaders required his personal approval; there was never any collective responsibility within the government" (Mason 1996 p.59). Hitler, in arrogating to himself the largely mythical status of omniscient overlord, nevertheless stood above a chaotic, labyrinthine state bureaucracy, as the sole source of political legitimacy (see Noakes 2008).

Perhaps the key insight into the way the Nazi state actually worked has been provided by Kershaw who made reference to a phrase used by Werner Willikens (Secretary of State in the Ministry of Food) in a speech in February 1934, which asserted that it was the duty of everyone to "'work towards the Fuhrer along the lines he would wish'" (cited in Kershaw 1993). Caplan captured the same point with reference to Hans Frank's exortation to German bureaucrats that they should "'act in such a way that if the Fuhrer knew of your action, he would approve the action'" (cited in Caplan 1993 p.196). Nazi state functionaries, and indeed the German people, were therefore encouraged to use their own initiative in interpreting precisely what Hitler wanted, and they continued to do so until the policy was either corrected or retrospectively legitimised. As Rees says, deploying Kershaw's perspective, "the system could not have functioned without Hitler or without those subordinates who initiated what they believed were desired policies" (Rees 2005 p.54). Functionairies therefore proceeded on the basis that they were doing Hitler's bidding or acting in conformity with the ideas and policies he espoused. So, for instance, the Reich Chancellery, the Chancellery of the Fuhrer, the office of the Presidential Chancellery, and the office of the Deputy Fuhrer (Martin Bormann) might compete over respective jurisdictions, but all looked to please the Fuhrer as the ultimate source of authority. Consequently, despite a degree of administrative anarchy the locus of power at the very top was not necessarily diminished by such confusion, and indeed may even have been enhanced by it. As far as the amorphous state bureaucracy itself was concerned, the consequence was corruption, adulteration, deficiency, fragmentation and excess, detatched from any meaningful mechanism of democratic control (see Caplan 1993 p.108).

In fact some analysts argue that the irrational organizational confusion of the state was a critical dynamic for the murderous radicalism of the Nazi regime (see Mommsen 1982, 2001). Ultimately this is a difficult proposition to prove conclusively, although there was a certain "shapelessness" to Nazi rule because the "leadership principle" cascaded down through the social and political pyramid (see Paxton 2005 p.127). In any event, whether because of, or despite, the polymorphous nature of the state and the confusing competition between agencies and organizations, the Nazi regime possessed a radically coercive capability. Certainly, gauged by most modern standards, the National Socialist state was an extraordinarily formidable authoritarian edifice (see Kitchen 1995). Indeed, "everything that happened in the Third Reich took place in this pervasive atmosphere of fear and terror" (Evans 2006 p.118) and, as Robert Ley remarked, "'the only person still leading a private life in Germany today is someone who sleeps'" (cited in Gluckstein 1999 p.148). In fact the all-encompassing authoritarian ambition of Nazism was conveyed quite clearly by Heydrich's extraordinary plan for the "'total and permanent police supervision of everyone'" (cited in Stone 1992 p.164).

There were similarities therefore in classical fascist experience in terms of authoritarian structures, coercive practice and the competing forces beneath the over-arching structure of the state, and even if the "total terror" model is simplistic, neither regime is conceivable without the aggressive application of state authority. As Alexander De Grand has correctly pointed out, what made the fascist system unique was "the vertical authoritarian context within which institutions developed and the almost Hobbesian struggle between leaders who were forced to compete for the favour of the supreme leader without any fixed rules to regulate the competition" (De Grand 1995 p.34). However, the Nazi state form, although similar to the Italian model in its essential authoritarianism, was qualitatively different for two reasons. Firstly because of the level of the authoritarianism - the extent of the terror was far greater in Nazi Germany, for instance more than 40,000 people were condemned to death via the courts in the Third Reich, whilst Mussolini's Italy did not re-introduce the death penalty until 1931 and there were 88 executions during the Fascist dictatorship (Kitchen 1995 p.176). Secondly, because of the respective purpose(s) of each state - the Nazis attempted to utilize it as an instrument in the pursuit of their racial fantasies (see later), whilst the Italian Fascists revered it as an end in itself, in the quest for a new kind of Hegelian freedom. In both cases, however, the methods of repression were brought to a "high degree of perfection" (Guerin 1973 p.276).

The social consequences of this authoritarian repression were entirely predictable, and the social preferences of both regimes squared with those conservative values that already prevailed, indeed "the traditionalism of the fascist movement coincided with existing society's most basic moral values" (Mosse 1999 p.20). Both societies were severely disciplined under their respective fascist regimes and the state produced a sterile culture of conformity, especially in Germany. As Herbert correctly points out "the ideological foundation of National Socialist social policy was the conviction that a large part of social deviance, or phenomena that suggested social maladjustment had biological causes. This biologisation of the social – a core concern of racist thought was based on the concept of the *Volk* as an autonomous, overarching suprain-dividual biological and cultural entity" (Herbert 1996 p.27, see later). For example welfare policy under the Nazis was used in deference to much broader social (racial) objectives, rather than simply to provide a minimum standard of living or social safety net. Thus "People's Welfare" and "Winter Aid", in effectively extorting charitable contributions from the general population, provided some material assistance to Germans in need, but the ultimate objective was didactic in terms of establishing popular acquiescence to the regime and securing absolute obedience as a pre-requisite for entitle-ment. The conscience and generosity of the *volk*, mobilized via voluntary activism and state bureaucracy, was reserved for genuinely "valuable" Aryan national comrades only whilst so-called "ballast existences", such as beggars and alcoholics, were routinely rounded up and effectively imprisoned in workhouses. "Welfare ceased to be a general entitlement to state compensation for the misfortunes of life, but rather became state marshalling of privately funded assistance for the prospective contribution the family 'cell' would make to the 'national community'" (Burleigh 2001 p.226).

Meanwhile in Italy, to take a pertinent example, the *Opera nazionale per la maternita ed infanzia* (the National Agency for Maternity and Infancy, ONMI) expanded welfare programmes to facilitate the achievement of  the Fascist regime's broader demographic objectives, such as the rapid expansion of the population. Women were encouraged to have more children, bachelors were taxed in order to subsi-dize families, and various medical and athletic programmes were introduced because demographic degeneration was deemed to lead to a whole host of social ailments, including alcoholism, tuberculosis and even premature death (see Gillette 202 p.41). By the 1930s spending on welfare in Italy had increased from 1.5 billion to 6.7 billion lire (Duggan 2013 p.239). Welfare, based on the motivating criteria of national strength and solidarity rather than social justice, was also used as leverage to induce conformity. Discretionary control over the allocation of public housing was, for instance, often a political decision – in effect the Fascist state rewarded collaboration and reinforced its control (Corner 2002a). Such welfare assistance, although partial and politically determined, was nevertheless used as a mechanism of propaganda and social discipline, although it is interesting to note that many of the schemes (e.g. pensions) benefited the *impiegati* (white collar, clerical employees) disproportionately (see Corner 2002a). At the same time the *Istituto Nazionale di Cultura Fascista* (INCF), created in 1925, sought to educate the masses about their ancient Roman heritage and point the way toward a specifically Fascist future by inculcating particular social values such as duty, responsibility and obedience (see Gillette 2002 p.54-55). In this way the state was used vigorously to endorse various Fascist social preconceptions and preferences.

Cultural life under fascism was also guided into specifically prescribed and officially sanctioned channels. In art, literature, music and architecture the regimes stifled originality and the so-called "decadent" forms were derided and marginalised. Fascism did not invent anything new in this regard, but simply annexed long held traditions and pandered to some popular tastes, thereby symbolizing a standard designed to secure the unity of the community or nation. "There was no room for avant-garde trends and constantly changing fashions whose aesthetic value was uncertain. Instead art had to be heroic or tragic, to preach devotion to the soil, the family, and, above all, the native land. It stood not for bloodless (and rootless) objectivism but, rather, the 'healthy instincts' of the people, such as patriotism" (Laqueur 1996 p.60). As Mosse says "the frequent contention that fascist culture diverged from the mainstream of European culture cannot be upheld; on the contrary, it absorbed most of what had the greatest mass appeal in the past" (Mosse 1999 p.29). Hence fascist cultural tastes were relatively mundane and mainstream. Moreover, the cultural "establishment", despite some grumbling at the margins, cooperated pragmatically with the appropriate fascist authorities.

In Germany for instance, "authentic art was not determined by the conditions of a particular age or by changes in fashion; it was the timeless expression of the innermost character of a particular people. True art, Nazi pundits intoned, emanates from the soul of the people and expresses its ideals" (Stackelberg 1999 p.133, see Fraenkel 1940). Vulgar peasant tastes were idealized and the innovative complexity of modern art was disparaged as the product of anti-social deviation. Hitler, with characteristic vanity, personally chose the pictures to go on display at every major German art exhibition, where his own pedantic puritanism and "execrable taste" pervaded the various programmes (Fraenkel 1940 p.366-67). At a huge exhibition of German Art held in Munich during 1937, there were 150 portraits on display and fifty were of Hitler himself, while the rest of the collection focused rigidly on landscapes and agricultural life (see Aycoberry 1999 p.77). The ritualistic monologues delivered by Hitler at the Berchtesgaden, recounted to captive audiences of adjutants and secretaries, provided the clearest illustration of the arid intolerance of Hitler's cultural vista, and his narrow-minded, parochial rigidity was reflected in the priorities of the regime itself. Goebbels, as Director of the Reich Chamber of Culture which was set up on 22 September 1933, attempted to combat degenerate artistic "Bolshevism" and he made sure that no writer or artist could publish, perform or exhibit without the imprimatur of the Nazi party. The Nazis banned, for instance, the music of Mendelssohn and Mahler, and forced into exile writers of the stature of Thomas Mann and Bertold Brecht. A similar fate befell artists such as Wassily Kandinsky and Oscar Kokoschka, film directors like Fritz Lang and Otto Preminger, and the architect Walter Gropius. At the same time swing music was derided as a decadent American import, and jazz dismissed as a worthless negroid creation. However the Nazi-imposed, state-led dispensation of culture, reflected most iconically in the monumental architectural creations of Albert Speer and the muscle-bound sculptures of Arno Breker, was completely incapable of compensating for the clear artistic and cultural deficit it had created. Thus although the Chamber of Culture assiduously endeavoured to divert cultural activity (especially art) into "healthy" avenues, there was a "sickening decline in cultural standards" in Germany (Shirer 1985 p.242). State-directed, pro-Nazi cultural activity was designed to serve the national cause and glorify the regime, but in so doing it precipitated, for the most part, sterile drivel.

In Italy the National Institute of Fascist Culture and *Miniculpop* (the Ministry of Popular Culture) performed a similar task by prioritizing the cult of *Romanita* as the bedrock of "civilized" values, thereby prescribing a stultifying conformity via reference to a particularly narrow interpretation of ancient classicism. This imposition of values was, for instance, clearly evident in Italian Fascist architecture where some urban settings were transformed by an austere Fascist version of the classical form, such as the *Foro italico* in Rome, whilst the imposing colonnaded structures of Marcello Piacentini, the Fascist regime's favoured architect, remain a mute testimony to the prevalence of structural neo-classicism under Fascism. Such architectural monuments, by their very presence, had an instrumental symbolic value in contributing to a Fascist mythology of permanence and strength (see Gentile 1990 p.246). The same state-led ideological effort to manage cultural outcomes was also made in film, literature and art, with rather less success (see Bosworth 1998). For example, famous musicians, such as Ottorino Respighi and Pietro Mascagni were courted by the regime but retained a certain critical detachment, while American films and literature were much preferred by the Italian public. Famous painters such as Giorgio Morandi, Felipo De Pisis and Felice Casorati chose to stay and work in Italy, and there was even a lively group of abstract artists who managed to resist the "official" call for a return to conservative verities (see De Grand 2000 p.158). The popular author Alberto Moravia is perhaps emblematic of the inherent ambiguity of much artistic endeavour under Mussolini's regime, in that he published some of his work in Fascist journals but claimed to be opposed to the regime. As Bosworth explains with regard to art, "for every Spartan portrait of a militant *Duce* or of his new legionaires, a later art historian can find countering examples of non-represen-tational art" (Bosworth 1998 p.175). So, despite state-inspired efforts to impose conformity, there remained a measure of autonomy for artists in Fascist Italy, providing that they posed no tangible threat to the existence of the regime.

However, education was very closely monitored by the Fascist state: certain books were banned in Italy after education was re-organised by Gentile's law of 1923, and membership of the Fascist party became obligatory in 1933 for all new teachers in the secondary and tertiary sectors. In October 1931 univer-sity professors were forced to take an oath of allegiance to the regime and only a miniscule minority bravely refused. The effect was to produce a dull regimentation in public and intel-lectual life (see Halperin 1964 p.145). In similar vein the Nazi state launched a systematic campaign against recalcitrant intellectuals, and one of the most enduring images of the Nazi era is that of the public book-burning of "un-German" literature on 10 May 1933, organised by Goebbels. School textbooks and the education curriculum in Germany were comprehensively Nazified, as were universities, which offered little resistance beyond silence or emigration. Hypocrisy and servility characterised both societies, and as critical voices were isolated and persecuted, so those of the sycophant and place-seeker grew louder and more assertive. In Italy the state certainly had to contend with more underlying diversity and had greater difficulty imposing uniformity (see Bosworth 1998), and the idea of a "new" fascist culture should be treated with considerable circumspection, but the emphasis on social control, conformity and order in compliance with a fascist template, was unmistakable in both countries.

Interestingly, the fascist states also sought to enforce other pre-existing social structures and sentiments, in that they attempted to inculcate what might be termed "traditional values". Mosse, for instance, talks of a pervasive "puritanism" under fascism, and conceptions of appropriate social arrangements were undoubtedly coloured by the prevailing hegemony of reactionary conservatism (see Mosse 1979 p.18). Both fascist regimes, for instance, emphasised the critical role of the family and a "traditional" role for women, who were to be (mostly) confined to the domestic and reproductive sphere. Within fascist movements the majority of women "were confined to activities generally considered to be suited to their nature – essentially welfare work" (Passmore 2002 p.130). Indeed, "every fascist movement and regime has viewed women as unfit to occupy the leading positions in the party and in the state. The female role was seen to be almost entirely centred on the home, family and the bearing and upbringing of children..." (Wilkinson 1981 p.26).

The evidence indicates quite clearly that "to the Nazi leadership, the female of the species was, above all, an actual or potential mother" (Stephenson 1996 p.169). As Hitler said, "'our first task ... is to help the development of family ties. The decline of the family would undoubtedly be the end of any superior form of humanity ... it is the smallest but most important unit in the building of the whole state...'" (cited in Poulantzas 1974 p.346). As Goebbels explained, more succinctly, "'the mission of the woman is to be beautiful and bring children into the world'" (cited in Evans 2006 p.332), whilst the male breadwinner, as head of the household, was expected to display appropriate masculine virtues, such as athleticism and pugilism. In Nazi Germany the family was seen as the "natural" or "appropriate" venue for the female where home-making was an obligation: "*kinder, kuche, kirche*" (children, cooking, church) was the Nazi slogan for women. Such was the Nazi state's desire to confine women to the home as child-rearer that restrictions were placed on the employment of married women in public service, whilst in 1933 the Marriage Loan Scheme provided a small grant for couples intending to marry on condition that the wife-to-be gave up her job. Indeed the emphasis on the reproductive function is clearly illustrated by the fact that after 1938 infertility or refusal to have children became grounds for divorce (Stephenson 1996 p.173 and 175). Women held no leadership positions in party or government, except in organizations specifically intended for women, such as the National Socialist Women's Union (*Nationalsozialistische Frauenschaft*) or the League of German Girls (*Bund deutscher Madel*) which prioritized themes of house-keeping, childcare and cookery. For her part, the head of the politically insignificant Nazi Women's movement (*Deutsches Frauenwerk*) and "Reich Mother-in-Chief" Gertrud Scholtz-Klink preferred the less than inspiring slogan "the German Woman is Knitting Again!" (Stone 1992 p.76, see Stephenson 1996). Indeed Hitler, who was always fond of being photographed with blonde maidens, resisted until 1943 calls for the conscription of women, even though Germany experienced periods of acute labour shortage. Naturally abortion and birth control were anathema, legally constrained by the state and actively discouraged as a reflection of the degeneration of "healthier" values and instincts (see Cecil 1972 p.143-44, Halperin 1964 p.48 and Passmore 2002 p.125). Hitler explained that a place had been reserved in the *volk* for "'women who turn their gaze not at the rights offered them by a Jewish intellectualism, but at the duties which nature imposes'" (cited in Schoembaum 1967 p.189). As Schoenbaum clearly recognized, in Nazi Germany "anti-feminism functioned as a kind of secondary racism" (Schoenbaum 1967 p.187 see later).

Meanwhile Mussolini insisted that the female's natural role was to care for a new generation of warriors (see Eatwell 1996 p.64), and Gentile articulated similar sentiments: "man is the family...the family is the perennial moral nursery of humanity" (Gentile 1960 p.172). As Turati put it "'the family is the basic cell of the State, the Nation and the people. It is the only possible safeguard, the only trench defending us against the corrosion coming from the various amoral, immoral and dissolvent forces around'" (cited in Bosworth 2002 p.231). Women had to reproduce in the conventional familial context and, in private conversation, Mussolini was characteristically blunt in his assessment of the choices available for women - it was a case of "'either children or beatings'" (cited in Bosworth 2005 p.264). The idealized notion of the fecund *Donna madre* was the role model for all women in Fascist Italy to aspire to, and those that did not understand or failed to assimilate that particular message were to be instructed appropriately by a male didact. The Rocco Criminal Code of 1932 reinforced bans on contraception and abortion, entrenched the legal and financial power of a husband over his wife and even made adultery a punishable crime for a woman, but not a man (see Pollard 1998 p.80). Such was the attitude of the Fascist regime toward women.

Hence fascism was inherently patriarchal – the political and social emancipation of women, and the modest gains secured during the inter-war period, were considered to be nothing more than a mistake. Indeed Passmore describes fascism as "a quintessentially male ideology...as deeply opposed to feminism as it is to socialism" (Passmore 2002 p.123, see later). It is, however, still important to avoid reductive generalizations, and as Durham has pointed out, the notion of a masculine movement pursuing a misogynist agenda ignores some complex empirical data (Durham 1998, see von Saldern 1995). Some women clearly participated beyond the confines imposed by the regime. Indeed, as Claudia Koonz has pointed out, the equation that links all females to the status of victim is perhaps excessively simplistic, and it must be remembered that some women, such as the aforementioned *Reichsfrauenfuhrerin* Gertrud Scholtz-Klink, participated enthusiastically in the fulcrum of a murderous regime (see Koonz 1987). Nevertheless it is true that, despite some evidence of differentiated experiences, pragmatism and contradictory relationships, in practice most women were subordinated to men in fascist societies, which were structured around the logic of supposedly "natural" and immutable biological categories (see Koonz 1987 p.3-6, Burleigh and Wipperman 1991 p.242).

Unsurprisingly under the fascist state homosexuality was a punishable offence. It was seen as both a sexually "deviant" practice and fundamentally evil due to its deleterious impact on the demographic future of society (Peukert 1987 p.219). In fact the Nazis in Germany saw homosexuality as not only degenerate, but the "'evil lust of the Jewish soul'" (*Volkischer Beobachter* cited in Stumke 1996 p.156) and so sought to criminalize every act of inter-masculine sexual contact. Indeed in 1938 the Reich Supreme Court deemed "optical arousal" as sufficient proof of criminal malevolence and "Himmler's SS was unremitting in seeking out and punishing known and suspected gay men" (Stephenson 2008 p.104). Raids on gay gatherings were commonplace and some homosexual men were even the subject of experimental surgical operations to implant the male hormone testosterone (see Burleigh and Wipperman 1991 p.195). Those condemned to wear the pink triangle often ended up imprisoned in concentration camps where they were destined to receive the harshest treatment, not only by guards, but often by fellow inmates (Burleigh and Wipperman 1991 p.183). Although Nazi practice was characterized by a pathological homophobia, lesbians were seen as deviant rather than "racial saboteurs" and therefore not subjected to formal prosecution, although there is no doubt that heterosexual sexism pervaded more general societal notions of "decency" under fascism.

The objective of social engineering did not stop at efforts to manipulate culture or replicate a particular pattern of familial relations and specific gender roles. The regimes exerted considerable energy in attempting to guide leisure persuits into what were deemed to be appropriate avenues. In Italy the *Opera Nazionale Dopolavoro* (OND) was established on 1 May 1925 and was designed to incorporate the masses into the regime by controlling certain leisure activities. The organization grew from 250,000 in 1926 to four million members by 1939 (Whittam 1995 p. 73) and it provided sport facilities, summer camps, subsidized excursions, cheap travel, inexpensive access to theatres and concerts, whilst performing limited welfare functions for families in need. Although some of these schemes pre-dated Fascism it would be fair to say that for many Italians the OND provided their first glimpse of the Alps or trip to the sea, their first experience of rail travel or regular entertainment – facts which were not inconsiderable in the lives of ordinary people, irrespective of the condescension of the onlooking upper classes. The OND was in fact "the most popular institution of the Fascist period...precisely because it enabled millions of Italians to enjoy its resources without the obligation of any full commitment to Fascist ideals or practice" (Whittam 1995 p.75). Of course in reality the regime did everything in its power to reinforce the connection between its various leisure schemes and Fascist ideology. In Germany under Nazism organized leisure time "afforded an opportunity for increased political supervision and indoctrination" (Mason 1993 p.160). Nazi newsreels and radio broadcasts portrayed happy people enjoying cruise holidays, receiving cheap cinema tickets and attending the "People's Theatre", whilst various sporting and leisure activities were coordinated via the *Kraft durch Freude* (KdF) "Strength through Joy" movement, which by 1939 had an annual turnover of RM25 billion (Mason 1993 p.160, see Herbert 1996 p.28). Set up with the confiscated assets of independent trade unions the KdF scheme included subsidized theatre, concerts, exhibitions, films, dances, hiking, adult education courses and holidays. Via this programme workers listened to symphonies which were conducted in factory grounds, families utilised the newly constructed open-air swimming pools, and people participated in community athletic events, all of which required a significant commitment of resources and a relatively high level of bureaucratic organization and oversight. According to "official" statistical evidence the number of people taking holiday cruises jumped from 2.3 million in 1934 to 10.3 million in 1938

and participation in "leisure activities" leapt from 9.1 million
to 54.6 million in the same period (Mason 1993 p.160). Even if
the statistics are treated with a degree of circumspection, and
whilst taking into account the benefits to the regime in terms
of inducing loyalty and increasing productivity, "there is no
doubt about the popularity of 'Strength through Joy'" (Mason
1993 p.160). Therefore it has to be acknowledged that the
Nazi regime was able to produce powerful, socially unifying
forces capable of binding society together as a unit (see Frei
2001). The idea of a united *Volksgemeinschaft*, based as it was
on regimentation rather than emancipation, was nevertheless
not a complete fiction.

Fascist regimes also exalted the idea of youth and invested
great energy and resources in setting up youth organizations
to establish control and facilitate mobilisation. For instance
under Fascism the *Opera Nazionale Balilla* (ONB) was founded
in April 1926 and offered a combination of leisure pursuits
and political indoctrination under the tutelage of the fanatical Renato Ricci. Young Italians were placed under severe
pressure to join the organisation, and membership eventually
became compulsory in 1937, with members having to swear an
oath to carry out the Duce's wishes without discussion or hesi-
tation (Wanrooij 2002 p.180). "The principal function of the
ONB was to prepare the young for their future roles in society:
boys to be soldiers and girls to be the mothers of warriors"
(Duggan 2013 p.192). Membership of Nazi youth movements
became compulsory in 1936, and from the ages of 10-14 young
boys joined the *Jungvolk* and girls the *Jungmadel* before joining
the Hitler Youth proper, which was organized under the
auspices of Baldur von Schirach. By 1934 1.25 million young
people between the ages 14-18 belonged to the Hitler Youth
or the League of German Maidens (Burleigh and Wipperman
1991 p.202). As Geary says, "to refuse to allow one's children
to join the Hitler Youth or the League of German Maidens
could be dangerous" (Geary 1994 p.40), and these social
organisations were designed to indoctrinate fanatical loyalty
to the Fuhrer and his regime. Children were even encouraged

to report any "unsound" political views expressed by their parents to appropriate Nazi officials (who themselves became a significant source of authority to compete with parent, clergy and teacher). Although there were some forms of youthful sub-cultural resistance, such as the Edelweiss Pirates, which capitalized on the idea of an alternative "life-style", and at times there were undoubtedly pockets of apathetic, apolitical youngsters immune to Nazi exhortation, there is no doubt that the Nazi youth organizations predominated and set the social tone for many young people. In this way young Germans were compelled to conform and submit to state authority and military-style discipline. For many adolescents who were shaped by Hitler Youth, a hierarchical social order was something taken for granted and to which there was no real alternative (see Peukert in Bessel 1987 p.25).

Overall, the idea often conveyed by critical accounts of fascism which stress a totally subservient society laboring under an oppressive authoritarian state are essentially true, but this has to be qualified somewhat because it must be acknowledged that the regimes managed to engender feelings of hope amongst large sections of society after years of desperation and despair. The fascists realized that terror, per se, would never suffice to subdue a society. Shirer's first-hand observations of Germany in the mid-30s are interesting in this context since he talks about a widespread enthusiasm and confidence, at least initially (see Shirer 1985 chapter 8), and Peukert even refers to the fact that some state terror was met with popular approval (Peukert 1987 p. 197). Similarly, while Renzo De Felice's controversial contention that Fascism was based on a consensus in Italy is clearly overdrawn, and the idea of *il fascism bonario* is a gross misrepresentation of reality, there is still nevertheless a sense in which the Fascist state met at least some of the requirements of the Italian people (see Corner 2002a). The fascists had come to power promising to liquidate the past with all its attendant failures and disappointments, and offered a brand new start for society. Many in the population were prepared to believe practically anything given the calamitous years preceding fascism, even if it did prove eventually to be a false dawn. It is interesting to note that even after it became perfectly apparent that the respective regimes were austere and murderous dictatorships constructed upon the subjection of others, many maintained their loyalty and commitment to their state. Of course there were many more, atomized and fragmented by political and cultural oppression, who simply craved normality, and whose "retreat into privacy" effectively crippled efforts at resistance (Peukert 1987 p.79, see Fraenkel 1940). The overall impression in both cases (although in Italy to a lesser degree) is of society strictly controlled by the ideological and coercive instruments of a harsh authoritarian state, although the impulse of the masses to accept, if not embrace, the situation, given the circumstances, is an uncomfortable truth which cannot be easily dismissed. Having said this, in the final analysis fascism repressed its enemies in brutal fashion, and ensured social conformity and discipline with comprehensive and systematic coercion. The reality of some popular endorsement must always therefore be weighed in the context of the underlying and ubiquitous intimidation and subjugation of the "other". Fascists were determined to use the state as a coercive instrument to secure obedience and enforce certain social preferences – this, they hoped, would effectively reverse the tide of moral anarchy, decay and disorder that had, according to fascism, been unleashed by the spurious notions dating back to the French revolution. Liberty was to be abolished in deference to duty, and conformity was demanded by the fascist state at the cost of civil freedom.

## Charismatic Leader and the Mass Party

Another important component of the fascist schema was the place and purpose of the mass party. The National Socialist German Workers' Party (*National-sozialistische Deutsche Arbeiterpartei*, NSDAP) and the National Fascist Party (*Partito Nazionale Fascista* PNF) were indispensible cogs in the fascist machine, designed essentially to function as the mechanism through which fascist ideology could be put into practice. Although this objective was common to both classic examples, key qualitative differences in performance can be identified. Nevertheless, the fascists demanded participation in the political process via their respective parties and in this sense they reflected, and accentuated, the trend toward mass participatory democracy in the early twentieth century. Fascism, as a populist phenomenon, mobilized the population via mass based political parties, with their membership and support derived from people across the entire social spectrum. In Germany membership of the NSDAP peaked at 8 million, whilst the PNF eventually reached 4.7 million members – they were mass parties by any conventional standard of measurement, reaching into every village, town, city and region  (see Laqueur 1996 p.35-36).

The fascist party was designed to act as a repository for the vast discontent that grew in their respective societies after 1918, and they were indeed what might be termed "catch-all" parties in the sense that they were attempting to win broad popular support by making many promises to a variety of different constituencies. The aim of both parties in the "movement" phase was to attract the widest possible support, win elections and achieve power, even if this meant making contradictory claims or pursuing a policy agenda that lacked any kind of programmatic coherence. Although both parties were "anti-system" parties, the fact that they contested elections meant they had to try and attract a broad cross-section of the population. In Germany the Weimar Republic had never really established its legitimacy, given the circumstances of its formation after defeat in war and in the face of implacable opposition from nationalists and communists alike, and in Italy parliamentary government based on limited suffrage and blatant election fixing produced governments dominated by a corrupt and self-serving oligarchy. So in both countries, ostensibly liberal institutions were undermined by severe, systemic weakness. Therefore both fascist movements articulated and channeled hostility toward parliamentary forms that appeared to be completely incapable of resolving the severe social and economic crises that occurred immediately after the First World War. In fact fascists "quickly profited from the inability of the centrists and conservatives to keep control of a mass electorate. Whereas the notable dinosaurs disdained mass politics, fascists showed how to use it" (Paxton 2005 p.78).

In Italy the germ cell of the PNF, formed in November 1921, may be traced back to the *fasci d'azione revoluzionaria* of 1914, but as an organisational entity can really only be dated from 23 March 1919 with the emergence of the *fasci di combat-timento* in Milan, following a meeting of the so-called "Fascists of the first hour" in the Piazza San Sepolcro (Pollard 1998 p.23). The term "Fascism" was derived from *fascio* which in turn was a reference to the Latin word *fasces,* the bundle of rods containing an axe which was a symbol of authority in ancient Rome, and the PNF made a clear effort to identify itself with the power and prestige of imperial Rome. In contrast to the Nazis, the PNF was primarily based in urban metropolitan areas to begin with and it spread outwards to the countryside where local leaders (*Ras*) were afforded, and able to sustain, a high level of operational autonomy. Like medieval barons, they exploited the sympathy of state authorities, such as legal prosecutors and the *Carabinieri,* and used armed squads to dominate their local areas.

The NSDAP emerged out of Anton Drexler's German Workers' Party (DAP), which was formed on 5 January 1919. Hitler, having been selected by the army as an anti-Bolshevik propagandist and "liaison officer", was sent to investigate the embryonic DAP in order to nurture its activities in the hope of creating a patriotic front (Welch 1998 p.11, Fritzsche 2008 p.53). Hitler was evidently so impressed that he joined the party in September as member number 555 (given that Drexler numbered the cards from 501 to make the party appear larger and more popular, this made Hitler number fifty-five, and not member seven as Hitler liked to claim) (see Kershaw 2009 p.76, Stone 1992 p.26). Nevertheless this party, indistinct in the early stages from numerous other nationalist or *volkisch* organizations, was soon to be dominated by Adolf Hitler, who became its leader in August 1921. Hitler thrived in the febrile atmosphere of patriotic radicalism and established his pre-eminence after an internal confrontation with Drexler, which left the latter with only the valedictory title of "Honorary President" (see Welch 1998 p.16). Hitler's conception of a political party was clearly influenced by Georg Von Schoenerer's German National Party, the Catholic Christian Social Party led by rabble-rousing Mayor of Vienna Karl Lueger and, significantly, by the Marxist parties, especially the SPD (see Hitler 1974 p.161, Kershaw 2009 p.32 and Rauschning 1939 p.16). Based primarily in rural Bavaria in the early years the party gradually spread north into the more industrialized zones of Germany. The party organization reflected Reichstag district constituencies, and each area was supervised by a Gauleiter, below which were branches staffed by local activists. The party was organized vertically to ensure its subordination to the leader (Williamson 1998 p.6), and Hitler became absolutely central to the party's success during and after the so-called *Kampfzeit* (period of struggle). Indeed so closely was Hitler identified with the party that when Germans went to the polling stations the ballot cards would read "Hitler movement" *(Hitlerbewegung)* rather than NSDAP (Welch 1998 p.23).

Yet the fascist party was much more than an electoral vessel designed to collect the disparate elements of social discontent. They were mass parties that developed a special relationship with the middle classes, the young, and ex-servicemen. Both the Italian and German parties attracted a disproportionate number of middle class sympathisers who saw fascism as a solution to the economic difficulties that had beset them. The NSDAP and PNF were able to accomplish this by offering a so-called "third way" between the threat of communism and unfettered capitalism (see Sparks 1980, Peukert 1987 p.93, and Carrocci 1975). Meanwhile, the younger generation succumbed to the impression that the fascists conveyed of themselves as parties of direct action and of generational

revolt, indeed as Lyttleton says, Fascism achieved "the insti-
tutionalization of a permanent adolescence" (Lyttleton 1998
p.20). In fact twenty-five per cent of PNF members were under
twenty-one, while sixty per cent of SA members were under
twenty-five, and few of the prominent fascist leaders were over
fifty years of age (Mann 2004 p.102, p.148). Moreover, fascist
parties manifested themselves in a form that constituted a fatal
attraction for many military veterans. In Germany "so many
ex-soldiers were involved in the early Nazi party, it is probably
best described as an army propaganda unit" (McDonough
1999 p.11), whilst in Italy "thousands of discontented and
disillusioned ex-combatants, officers and men, were to play
a key role in the development of the Fascist movement, and
in the formation of the paramilitary squads in particular"
(Pollard 1998 p.27).

Nevertheless, it is also true to say that despite the particularly close links the fascists had with certain components
of their respective communities, fascist parties managed to
attract members and voters from *all* sectors of society, even
the industrial working classes and the unemployed. In the
German context this fact has been the subject of sustained
academic debate, and although "workers were far less likely to
be members of the NSDAP or vote for the party than middle
class elements" (Geary 1994 p.25) there is now little doubt that
the Nazis achieved cross class support. The fascists were able
to attract a significant number of unemployed and members
of the working class, particulary into the SA, principally
because this social strata had very little to lose by joining a
fascist party, and stood to gain, at the very least, a regular hot
meal and a uniform. Some may even have developed, through
their party, a sense of identity, belonging and purpose. In
fact some analysts go further and Fischer, for instance, maintains that the working classes represented as many four in ten
party members and voters, with a higher percentage in the
associated ancilliary organizations (Fischer 1995 p.30). Consequently Sewell's contention that the Nazis "completely failed
to win support amongst organized labour" (Sewell 1988 p.67),

although forming a part of conventional wisdom, is somewhat overstated (although any conclusion here is of course contingent upon the precise definition of the term "organized"). Certainly, as Kershaw points out, "the NSDAP was no mere middle class party, as used to be thought. Though not in equal proportions, the Hitler Movement could reasonably claim to have won support from all sections of society" (Kershaw 2009 p.205; see Evans 2006 p.9). This uncomfortable fact is confirmed by Muhlberger, who argues that the re-evaluation of the empirical evidence by psephologists in recent years has resulted in the so-called *Mittelstandspartei* hypothesis being replaced by the *Volkspartei* thesis, and therefore "it was the ability of the Nazis to generate support from all social classes which ultimately gave the Nazi Movement its potency" (Muhlberger 2003 p.79). There is little doubt that "the party offered an antidote to anomie, atomization and deracination, holding out a lamp to the millions cut loose from primary ties of family and intermediary associations to drift unmoored on the seas of a hypertrophied *Gesellschaft*" (Baldwin 1990 p.9-10). Hence, although it is also worth bearing in mind that established social circles were significantly over-represented in both the membership and leadership of the fascist movements, party membership and support cannot be neatly dismissed as the political project of a particular social class (see Mann 2004). In short, fascism "attracted a motley crew of followers from different backgrounds and of all classes, even though the bourgeoisie provided the backbone of the movement and most of the leaders" (Mosse 1999 p.22).

In order to attract and sustain such diverse membership and support the fascists used a wide and novel range of political propaganda techniques, exploiting new technologies. Clearly part of the attraction of fascism lay in the intensity of the message (see Mann 2004 p.364). Many of the political techniques developed by fascism had first been elaborated by Gabrielle  d'Annunzio and his *Arditi* during his Fiume adventure of 1919-20, when he and his irregular army tried to reclaim the Adriatic city for Italy from the newly formed state of Yugoslavia (Pearce 2002 p.40) [17]. The use of uniforms, flags, songs, salutes, parades, marches and other symbolic, quasi-theatrical techniques enabled participants to transcend the tedium of everyday life whilst enabling the party to obscure more divisive social categories. The fascists did not possess a monopoly on the use of ostentatious para-military paraphernalia or flag-waving displays of strength but they were exceptionally skilled exponents, and this helped surround the respective movements with a certain quasi-military mystique. The carefully choreographed ceremonials which took place at Nuremberg, for example, were extraordinary in their magnitude and meticulous preparation (see Stone p.77-78) and after the party secured power, the techniques of Dr. Goebbels as Minister for Popular Enlightenment and Propaganda were crucial in co-ordinating such events. All newspapers and radio stations were controlled by the state in the interests of facilitating support and unity through the party. Both parties utilized state-of-the-art techniques, such as film, broadcasting and air travel, in order to convey their message and sustain support, and this curious mixture of technological modernism and medieval mysticism resulted in what Mommsen has called the "aestheticization of politics" (Mommsen 1982 p.154, see Winkler 1979 p.144).

Central to the success of this political show was the fascist leader, who in stark contrast to the prevarication of their parliamentary contemporaries, spoke confidently of national resurgence and "projected an image of bold determination" (Pearce 2002 p.58). Such an assertive confidence was a rare and valuable commodity in the context of a continental Europe deep in economic crisis and mired in social turmoil. The "leadership-principle" was ruthlessly established and adhered to by both parties, with Hitler and Mussolini standing at the apex of the organisational pyramid (see Corni 2009). As Corni explains, "in both cases, the power of the *Duce* or *Fuhrer* was represented in propaganda as absolute, and decision making was meant to occur vertically and in a hierarchical manner" (Corni 2009 p.286). However, the dictator did not owe his authority to any constitutional process or democratic framework, since the organisational infrastructure was just a matter of expediency, a necessary evil (Hitler 1974 see p.314). As Weber argues, "the leader (did not) hold his position because of any particular intellectual or moral superiority, but by a mystic pre-selection; he is not so much the representative of his people as its medium", his selection "was similar to that of pirate or robber chiefs or that of certain military castes in which a bond of honour and mutual devotion unites the leader to the men he leads... " (Weber 1964 p.81-2). Thus the leader, standing above the party, intuitively understood and articulated the hopes and desires of his followers, and he was the personal embodiment of their will. In fact the leader assumed an almost quasi-religious significance for hordes of deferential party members for whom he was a prophet, a man of destiny sent by providence, instilling awe and acting as the party's key mechanism of integration and mobilization.

In the German case the "charismatic domination" of the *Fuhrer* and the concept of "working towards the leader" were crucial in explaining Nazi success (Kershaw 1991; see Rees 2012, and earlier). The predominance of Hitler in the party can be traced to its inception, but became much more significant after Hitler's incarceration in prison, as he began to take himself more seriously as the potential political saviour of Germany. The example of Mussolini in Italy seems to have inspired Hitler to emulate his political mentor, and Hitler never denied the influence of the Italian Fascist blueprint (see Schieder 2001). As Kershaw says, "the Hitler myth was consciously built up within the movement as a device to integrate the party" (Kershaw 1987 p.43) and the introduction of the compulsory *Heil Hitler* salute among party members was a visible sign of their messianic devotion to their leader. In effect, the personification of National Socialism in Hitler provided the central point of reference for the multiplicity of personalities and auxiliary organizations within the movement, the point where disputes would be resolved and from which other Nazi leaders derived their own authority (Fischer 1995 p.69).

Hence, contrary to Hans Mommsen's claims that Hitler was in practice a "'weak dictator'" engaging in haphazard, inconsistent leadership, "Hitler's power was real, and immense, not a phantasm" (Kershaw 1989 p.55). As Goering eloquently put it "'when a decision has to be taken, none of us count more than the stones on which we are standing. It is the Fuhrer alone who decides'" (cited in Rees 2012 p.157). The basis of Hitler's authority was his direct relationship with the German people via the party and the widespread assumption that he had been called by destiny to lead it.

Although the Hitler myth was neither a static or stable phenomenon, that it facilitated the prominence of the demagogic dictator as the key locus of power in the regime is beyond serious dispute. Indeed deference to Hitler's demonic magnetism was unquestionably a critical component in constraining the centrifugal tendencies of internal party factionalism, and it was central to securing the accommodation between the Nazi party itself and pre-existing conservative social elites. Hitler was portrayed as a leader with whom all sectors of society could identify and "many ordinary Germans were overwhelmed by the scale and intensity of this propaganda" (Evans 2006 p.123). A flavour of the obsequious content that underpinned the cult of personality is provided by the *Volkischer Beobachter* which proclaimed: "'The Fuhrer is the highest synthesis of his race...He embodies the universalism of Goethe, the depth of Kant, the genius of Frederick II, the realism of Bismarck as well as the tumultuous inspiration of Wagner, the perspicacity of Spengler...'" and so on (cited in Eatwell 1996 p.113). Goering even noted that "'we love Adolf Hitler because we believe, deeply and steadfastly, that he was sent by God to save Germany...There is no quality that he does not possess to the highest degree...For us the Fuhrer is simply infallible in all matters political and all other issues concerning the national and social interests of the people'" (cited in Rees 2012 p.130-31). However it should be noted that at least until the fall of Stalingrad, loyalty was not simply a matter of mass manipulation, because Hitler was genuinely popular amongst many Germans as the selfless personification of national unity and strength. Hence the penetration of the "Hitler myth" was exceedingly deep and Hitler became, in essence, the beneficiary of a cult of personality, the consequences of which eventually bordered upon modern political deification (Kershaw 1995). "Unquestionably, the adulation of Hitler by millions of Germans who may otherwise have been only marginally committed to the Nazi ideology, or party, was a crucial element of political integration in the Third Reich" (Kershaw 1987 p.54). Hitler himself was crucial to the stability of the Nazi regime.

Similarly, in Italy the leadership cult formed the "fulcrum" of the regime: "the organisational energies of the regime were permanently mobilised around the exercise of this cult; millions of Italians deified Mussolini" (Melograni 1979 p.75). As Thurlow says, "through the use of mass rallies, choreographed displays, loudspeakers, new forms of lighting and brass bands, Fascism developed a politics of charisma. The emphasis, particularly under Starace's direction, was on the greatness of the *Duce*" (Thurlow 1999 p.30). Mussolini sat at the epicenter of a regime sustained by a cult of personality of extraordinary dimensions. Indeed, "the individual was the state, and the state was Italy, and Italy was fascism, and Mussolini was all of them" (Gregor 1969 p.326). In fact, according to Mack Smith, the personality cult was "the most novel and effective feature of Italian fascism" (Mack Smith 1985 p.142). Although he claimed otherwise (somewhat disingenuously), Mussolini actively encouraged the cult of "*ducismo*", and he was certainly aware of Gustav Le Bon's theories regarding the psychological manipulation of mass sentiments and instincts. Mussolini was also, obviously, in a perfect position to foster such myths given Fascist control of the media and the absence of effective opposition.

The School of Fascist Mysticism, established in 1930 under the auspices of the party, was specifically designed to propagate the myth of the Duce and induce deference amongst an adoring population (Whittam 1995 p.59, see Gentile 1990 p.237). The notion was promulgated that Mussolini could do no wrong, and the most striking slogans were declared about the man who had pioneered Fascist dictatorship, such as *"Mussolini ha sempre ragione"* (Mussolini is always right). However the hero-worship was by no means confined to the masses (who perhaps might be excused on the grounds that the desperate are most anxious to believe), for example one Professor Giglioli wrote at the time that in Mussolini there had been assembled the organising will of ancient Rome, the noble piety of the Christian faith, the wisdom of the great men of the renaissance, and the constructive passion of the Risorgimento (see Melograni 1979 p.83). Indeed, both the craven complicity of the intelligentsia and the pivotal role of the leader in Fascist party politics is perhaps best revealed by Gentile's juvenile eulogy to Mussolini: "'He strides ahead crowned by a halo of myth, as if a man chosen by God, tireless and infallible, the instrument elected by providence to create a new civilization.....'" (Gentile cited in Lyttleton 1973 p.315, see Gentile 1960). As Bosworth confirms, "regime propagandists spread an extreme and in retrospect ludicrous personality cult in which Mussolini was elevated into an all-seeing all-knowing god, a Man who, Italians were assured, radiated a divine light and possessed an omniscient intuition" (Bosworth 2005 p.3). The success of this strategy in influencing ordinary people should certainly not be underestimated. As Duggan's analysis of diaries and memoirs written at the time confirms, for many individuals the talismanic (and apparently blameless) figure of Mussolini was crucial to their emotional and political engagement with the regime (see Duggan 2013).

Nevertheless, having noted the hysterical hero-worship, there is a sense in which Mussolini "survives in memory, everywhere except in Italy, as a joke, a ham actor, rolling his eyes, waving his hands and jutting his chin, bellowing, bullying, boasting, blundering" (Bosworth 2009 p.262). Mussolini is sometimes portrayed as a "sawdust Ceasar", a "dictator minor", and a figure whose sense of   self-importance far outweighed his actual historical significance (see Bosworth 1998 p.58-59). Thus the vanity, crass theatricality and incompetence of Mussolini has somehow afforded him a fool's pardon in some accounts, the savage cruelty of his regime receding behind the cartoon image of the boastful buffoon. Bosworth suggests that such an interpretation owes at least something to Anglo-Saxon prejudice (Bosworth 2002 p.2), but it is also perhaps a reflection of the fact that Mussolini's unremitting quest for complete dominance over Italy was never quite accomplished, and the contrast to Hitler's dictatorship was so stark. Mussolini's efforts in the sphere of coercion, control and mass manipulation look decidedly amateurish when compared to the accomplishments of the Nazis in Germany, and the self-assigned epithet "totalitarian" by Mussolini concealed the erratic inconsistency of a brutal dictatorship led by a cynical imbecile.

The leader was, for fascism, unquestionably both messiah and messenger. As Kershaw explains, "the Leader was the 'central point' or 'preserver' of the 'idea'. This demanded, as Hitler repeatedly reiterated, blind obedience and loyalty from followers. The cult of the Leader was thus built up as the integrating mechanism of the movement" (Kershaw 2009 p.181). The National Socialist reverence for Hitler, and the techniques of political ritual used thereby, probably deserve greater study than they have so far received (see Taylor 1985) since "propaganda, for Hitler, was the highest form of political activity" (Kershaw 2009 p. 96). Of course Hitler himself was an extraordinary orator who could manipulate and exploit the emotion of an audience with great skill, and descriptions of his "power" over his audience are legion (see Carr 1978). It was a skill honed in the beer halls of Munich and developed to perfection by the demagogic agitator in front of the masses at Nuremberg. In his classic study Bullock (1962) refers to the ability of Hitler to release hidden emotions by an appeal to mass instinct, and Albert Speer, at his post-war trial, spoke eloquently (despite the self-serving sub-text) about Hitler's mystical-hypnotic effect. Even Otto

Strasser stated that "Hitler responds to the vibrations of the human heart with the delicacy of a seismograph ... enabling him to act as a loud-speaker proclaiming the most secret desires, the least admissible instincts, the sufferings of a whole nation ... His words go like an arrow to their target, he touches each private wound on the raw, liberating the mass unconscious, expressing its innermost aspirations, telling it what it most wants to hear" (Strasser 1940 p.74 and p.78). In the context of a Nazi meeting, which were masterpieces of theatrical art, Hitler's talent was utilised to maximum effect, articulating fears and hopes via simplistic slogans designed to inspire and mobilise. Hitler was "above all else a consummate actor...the delayed entry into the packed hall, the careful construction of his speeches, the choice of colourful phrases, the gestures, the body-language. Here his natural rhetorical talent was harnessed to well-honed performing skills" (Kershaw 2009 p.174). The extravagant mannerisms, the subtle undulations of diction, the vivid prose, which rose eventually to a climactic crescendo, were all specifically designed to seduce the assembled multitudes. In retrospect it is easy to read the text of the speeches and deride them as a collection of unsubstantiated assertions and boastful trivialities, but there is no doubt that at the time many in the audience were swept away (see Aycoberry 1999 p.68).

Interestingly, in mobilizing support for their leaders the fascists were not averse to deploying religious metaphors. Fascists spoke of Mussolini as the "new Messiah", and references to "divine Caesar", "spiritual father" and "sublime redeemer" perpetuated the illusion of omnipotence (see Ottavio Dinale cited in Pearce 2002 p.67). Even the Pope referred to Mussolini as a "'man of providence'" although he was perhaps less comfortable with the fact that children were told not only to love God, but that the "God of Italy" was *Il Duce* (see Whittam 1995 p.59 Schmidt 1973 p.70) [18]. Moreover, Mussolini consciously and assiduously cultivated an "aura of holiness" (Gentile 1990 p.236), which was eagerly seized upon by his supporters. The journalist Asvero Gravelli encapsulated the mood: "'Homer, the divine in Art; Jesus the Divine in Life; Mussolini the divine in Action'" (cited in Bosworth 2002 p.310). The references to religion were, of course, entirely deliberate and used cynically and unscrupulously by the likes of Augusto Turati and Achille Starace to induce an aura of mysticism and awe. Predappio, where Mussolini was born, became a place of pilgrimage for the Italian people. In Germany too the leader was elevated to the status of the divine, indeed, if anything theological inferences were even stronger in the Nazi context. Hitler was referred to as the "Saviour", whilst those who had died in the failed putsch of November 1923 were described as "apostles". Followers were urged to have "faith" in the "immortality" of the German people who had "risen". The descriptive language was infused with references to "salvation", "martyrdom", "blood", "incarnation" and "resurrection". A prayer, read in kindergartens in the 1930s, is indicative: "'Dear Fuhrer, we love you like our fathers and mothers. Just as we belong to them so we belong to you. Take unto yourself our love and trust, O Fuhrer'" (cited in Rees 2005 p.14). Julius Streicher even explicitly compared Hitler with Jesus only to arrive at the extraordinary conclusion that "'Hitler is far too big a man to be compared with one so petty'" (cited in Rees 2005 p.14). Hitler was, therefore, worshipped as a divinity, but to clarify the analogy Hitler was not, and could never be, the sacrificial Christ who facilitated spiritual redemption, he was if anything the Christ of the millenium, the second coming of the wrathful Messiah destroying his enemies and leading his believers to the promised land and ultimate salvation (see Taylor 1985 p.182, and Guerin 1973 p.67; also Mosse 1979 p.9 and Stern 1975 chapter 10). In fact the Nazi party "ransacked the various religious traditions of the German churches and reproduced their ritual form in political celebrations" (Taylor 1985 p.187; see Evans 2006 p.257-58), and specifically Nazi celebrations (e.g. Hitler's birthday, Party Day) were accompanied by non-Nazi cultural festivals which were cleverly transformed for Nazi purposes (e.g. mothers' day, May Day etc). Hence, "Nazi emblems, signs, words and culture permeated everyday life...Not only were film, radio, newspapers, magazines, sculptures, painting, literature, poetry, architecture, music and high culture increasingly informed by Nazi ideals, or confined within the boundaries they set, but everyday culture as well" (Evans 2006 p.211).

The Nazi/Fascist party world view and *Fuhrer/Duce*-worship, endorsed by techniques of mass suggestion, reinforcing images of obedience, social harmony and common sacrifice, were therefore extremely important in both legitimising and mystifying fascist rule, providing both a focus for loyalty and source of identity in a period of severe crisis and uncertainty. "Before all else", Guerin suggested, "fascism offers its followers mysticism" (Guerin 1973 p.63). Certainly this is true to a large extent, but this should not lead us to undervalue its importance. It is too easy to dismiss or mock, in retrospect, the images of Mussolini speaking upon a white horse or from a gun-turret, or Hitler, whipping the assembled delegates into a frenzy at the Nuremberg *Parteitag*, and forget that they not only demanded, but actually received to a significant extent, unquestioning allegiance. Fascism effectively "exploited the mystical longings of the little man for a saviour", and offered hope to those in society seeking some form of personal or collective transcendence (Schmidt 1973 p.42, and Stern 1975 p.92). As Weber explains, the identity created between the mystical leader and his followers "permitted every sparrow to fly vicariously on eagles' wings and enjoy the eagle's triumphs and magnificence as if they were his own" (Weber 1964 p.35). As a result it would be unwise to underestimate the value of such techniques in attracting and maintaining support, and in creating the general impression of gathering and unstoppable momentum. The fanaticism, the emotive symbolism, the devotion to the leader, and the obvious quasi-religious faith in the cause resonated with many people who saw fascism as a potentially positive development in a period of unparalleled disunity, strife and uncertainty.

Although the fascist party mobilized for elections and facilitated the cult of personality, it is important to note that upon achieving power the role that was expected of each mass party was qualitatively different. As we have seen the NSDAP became the only party in Germany after 14 July 1933 and Hitler, although retaining no formal position within the NSDAP, managed to maintain his position of predominance. This is important because Hitler placed great emphasis on the role of the NSDAP in German society. Hitler believed in the priority of talent and the natural aristocracy of those with superior strength and will, which led him to believe in the inevitable supremacy of party over state (see Hitler 1973). The party, as a vehicle for the Nazi *weltanschauung* promoting and preserving the Aryan race (see later) would, of necessity, assume a high profile in guiding society. In July 1933 Hitler ostentatiously declared that "'the party" had "become the state'" (cited in Williamson 1998 p.24), and via the "Law to Ensure the Unity of Party and State" of December 1933 the party was made a public corporation - it was therefore said to be "'the bearer of the concept of the German state" and "'inseparably linked to the state'" (cited in Williamson 1998 p.24). In 1935 the Nazi party swastika became the official flag of the German state, which reflected the fact that the party's task was to educate, inform, indoctrinate and purify, directing the whole nation toward the desired goal of racial homogeneity and strength. As a result, the multifarious Nazi organisations such as Nazi Teachers Association, Union of German Nazi Lawyers, Hitler Youth, League of German Maidens and so on were expected to perform auxiliary functions for the state (see Noakes and Pridham 1974 p.234). "The Nazis began to honeycomb society with party associations and institutions: at the onset they competed with existing bodies, but by degrees they got the upper hand and either absorbed or displaced them" (Hildebrand 1985 p.6). This led in practice to a degree of overlap and even fusion between state and party bodies, for instance Himmler as Reichsfuhrer of the SS became Chief of German Police in June 1936, and the SS subsequently became an integral part of the state. Although the party itself was wracked with internal rivalries, and was often paralysed by mutual recrimination and mistrust, there is no doubt about its critical role as the superior instrument designed to mobilize the masses in order to fulfil over-riding ideological objectives. As Baynes pointed out, in Nazi Germany "there is no escaping from the fact that the party is the primary element, the state is but secondary'" (Baynes 1969 p.417) [19].

In Fascist Italy "the party was a capilliary organization that operated uniformly throughout Italy and involved all Italians in an experiment in political socialization that had no precedent in Italian history" (Gentile 2002 p.164), although in practice the situation was more complicated, and quite different from the German experience. For a start Mussolini had greater difficulty controlling the National Fascist Party (PNF), and certainly the chain of command from the Duce down through the Party Secretary, the Grand Council, National Council, Provisional Secretaries and so on to ordinary members, was far from unequivocal. Moreover, from the beginning Mussolini was forced, to some extent, to delegate authority to powerful Fascist subordinates like Dino Grande, Italo Balbo, Guiseppe Bottai and Achille Starace, and his relationship with the Fascist *Raz* was always fractious (Bosworth 2009 p.267, see Bosworth 2005 p.150). Tension between the Duce and radicals like Michele Bianchi was commonplace, especially before 1926 (see Lyttleton 1979 p.47-48) and the fact that Mussolini attempted to formalize Fascist control in statutes laid down in October 1926, the *leggi fascistissme*, made little practical difference. As a result of this and, more importantly, as a consequence of the Italian Fascist conception of the state (see earlier), Mussolini was not prepared to see the party play a pre-eminent role, much less usurp the functions of the state. As Melograni says, "Mussolini made little use of the party for purposes of government. Instead he used the state..." (Melograni 1979 p.73, see Lyttleton 1979 p.45).

As a result it would be accurate to say that in Italy, despite the fact that a dual structure emerged, with party and state

paralleling and often duplicating one another, the latter ultimately predominated. The PNF and the militia (MVSN) were
kept very much in the background by Mussolini, who used
them more as a threat when expedient, if a particular state
institution proved intransigent or if he wanted to influence
public opinion or the king. The fact that the party was always
subordinated to the state was also reflected in the fact that,
for example, Chief of Police Bochinni had far more genuine
power than Party Secretary Starace. Despite the introduction
of some explicitly pro-party measures (for instance the holding
of public posts was made dependent upon party membership),
the PNF remained in the shadow of the state form (Whittam
1995 p.53). In the end the PNF became a de-politicised, poorly
organised, structurally schlerotic shell, which consistently
struggled to come to terms with the systemic corruption and
slow pace of Italian public life, indeed within a relatively short
time frame it had transformed itself into a vehicle for time-
serving careerists, a bloated bureaucratic leviathan devoid of
any genuine political purpose. In effect, the PNF penetrated
Italian life far less than might be supposed and remained,
essentially, satisfied with pretentious images and ostentatious
propaganda (see Forgacs 1986). As Pollard confirms, "as the
party became depoliticized and bureaucratized, its functions
inside the Fascist state were reduced...the party performed
a largely decorative and propagandistic role in Fascist Italy
– mobilizing its members in endless parades and demonstrations of support for the policies of the Duce" (Pollard 1998
p.63). The contrast here with the radicalizing penetration of
the Nazi party in Germany could hardly be clearer.

## Corporatism and Autarky:
## the " Third Way"

It has been claimed, with some justification, that fascist
socio-economic programmes were so full of ambiguities and
contradictions that they cannot possibly withstand serious
analysis (see Wilkinson 1981 p.14). Nevertheless there were

some preferences and aspects of policy which reflected a common economic perspective. For example, the idea of "corporatism" (or "corporativism") and autarky were emphasised by both regimes (especially by Italian Fascists) and these were seen as an integral part of their overall plan for socio-economic development in the context of a so-called "third way" (see Mussolini 1975 p.28 and p.48). On this basis alone it is therefore necessary to devote some attention to the nature and purpose of these particular policies.

Economic corporatism emerged as a possible solution to the grave social and economic difficulties that had beset both Italy and Germany after 1918. In Germany the scale of the economic crisis after the war was enormous. The brief period of stability and prosperity after the great inflation of 1923 gave way to a deep depression and massive levels of unemployment by 1930 (Sewell 1988 p.57). In Italy similar difficulties, such as inflation and food and raw material shortages, led to the strikes and factory occupations of the *biennio rosso* between 1918-20. In both countries, therefore, severe social problems resulted from acute economic instability, and the notion of corporatism might be seen as an attempt to address directly these difficulties by solving, permanently, the primary social problem, namely the apparently inevitable contradiction between labour and capital. The expectation was that corporatism, as well as providing a mechanism with which to regulate the economy, would reduce industrial strife and mobilise productive potential in the interests of the nation.

Certainly in Italy the notion of class collaboration was absolutely crucial in providing the impetus for so-called corporatist solutions. As Mussolini put it, both capital and labour would have equal rights and duties and become "'brothers in the fascist family'" (cited in Scmidt 1973 p.75, see Mack Smith 1985 p.75). Corporatism was thus viewed as a "third way" between a capitalism which was self-evidently prone to cyclical crisis, and a communism which was considered wholly impracticable and undesirable. In effect corporatism would institutionalise the ideal of class co-operation, as Carocci confirmed, "one of the fundamental principles of fascism was the collaboration between capital and labour" (Carocci 1975 p.42). In fact it might even be argued that "Italian fascism's chief claim to political creativity lay in the construction between 1925-1939 of the Corporate State, a system purporting to be revolutionary yet socially unifying, to guarantee economic progress and social justice by bringing employers, managers and workers together within a legally constituted framework" (Blinkhorn 1994 p.29).

Mussolini, in his *Political and Social Doctrine of Fascism* maintained that the Corporations lay at the centre of the Italian Fascist regime, and certainly the practice of corporatism was most fully developed in Italy. The concept itself, expounded by the likes of Gino Arias, was partly derived from the initial preference of some Fascists for syndicalist or productivist economic ideas. The notion of "productivism" focused on the creation of wealth rather than its distribution, emphasizing the need for more efficient management of resources and an over-riding conception of national purpose. Similarly, syndicalism originally envisaged an integrated network of self-governing workplace unions or "syndicates" composed of worker-producers. There is also a sense in which corporatism reflected some of the social teachings of the Catholic church about the need for co-operation and the value of labour, indeed Pope Pius thanked Mussolini for implementing the teachings of *Rerum novarum* (Mann 2004 p.126). However corporatism, as it evolved under Mussolini, was suffused with a nationalist credo, focused on the employers (rather than workers) as the key actors, and had the Italian state superimposed upon it. The primary piece of legislation on the subject was passed in February 1934 when twenty-two Corporations were established in sectors of the economy such as textiles, building, metal and engineering, arts, professions and so on (see text of the law in Mussolini 1975 p.107 and p.91, also 1968 p.173 for a comprehensive list of functions). In 1929 the National Council of Corporations was set up to coordinate economic activity, and in 1939 an Assembly of Corporations, in effect, replaced the Chamber of Deputies as the major representative institution of the state (see Morgan 2009 p.157). The idea underpinning these structures was to honour and represent each citizen as a producer in society, to transcend selfish sectional interests and to integrate productive individuals into an organic economic unity for the benefit of the community as a whole. Within each Corporation members of each sphere of economic activity were brought together and representatives from the employers, employees, and the state were supposed to meet and decide policy. If a dispute arose, those assembled were to decide in favour of the "national interest", which meant, more often than not, that the state (government) decided the outcome.

In fact, as Whittam argues, Mussolini never really took the idea of tripartite "corporativism" seriously, although he realized its significance in symbolic and propaganda terms (Whittam 1995 p.62). Indeed Morgan makes the interesting observation that "corporatism, where the Fascist state compelled to be brought together, under a single institutional roof, representatives of all those involved in the productive process of a given sector of the economy, workers, employers, managers, technicians, was conceived of as educative, as much as economic, in function" (Morgan 2009 p.152). Evidently corporatism had a didactic function at a basic level in the sense of setting the parameters of what was economically possible. The aim was to eliminate divisive and counter-productive class conflict via consultation and prepare the nation for the realization of broader economic objectives. However, in practice the overarching corporate framework was cumbersome, top-heavy, unresponsive to ordinary workers, prone to bureaucratic inertia and subject to inter-ministerial disputes over areas of competence and jurisdiction – in effect Fascist corporatism was "a superstructure without any capillary substructure, a centre without a periphery to manage and coordinate" (Morgan 2009 p.157). Moreover, when faced with the prospect of a confrontation, "Mussolini refused to allow the corporative institutions to determine policy" (De Grand 2000 p.80).

In practice Mussolini, in collaboration with party leaders and, crucially, after consulting with prominent business leaders, made most of the key strategic economic decisions. Moreover, the severity of the economic crisis in the 1930s actually ended any lingering hopes that ordinary workers might receive some residual benefits from the corporatist framework. In effect Italian Corporatism, despite the grandiose syndicalist rhetoric of Bottai and others about "social responsibility", meant little more than a pragmatic way of securing the subordination of labour in the interests of employers and the state – it was in effect an elaborate façade designed to obscure the reality of endemic corruption and continued exploitation. While "the corporative institutions busily spun their wheels and went nowhere", it confirmed the fact that Fascism "did not create its own unique economic system but rather grafted further statist and bureaucratic tissue on the existing body of Italian capitalism" (De Grand 2000 p.166 and p.167). Essentially corporatism was an elaborate "illusion" (De Grand 2000 p.79) and the idea of a "corporate state" performed the function of a "myth", a noble lie, designed to mask the underlying reality of bourgeois power and class conflict.

However, it might nevertheless be noted at this point that this more "collectivist" attitude toward the economy, which was reflected in the rhetoric of corporatism, also led to several state-inspired attempts to ameliorate the worst excesses of the economic depression. The so-called "battle of  grain" and the "battle of production"; the programme of land reclama-tion (1928-33); the creation of the *Instituto Mobiliare Italiano* (IMI) in 1931 to subsidize banks in supplying credit; and the setting up of the *Instituto di Ricostruzion Industriali* (IRI) in 1933, as a state holding company – all of these initiatives led to an increase in government intervention in the economy via higher levels of public expenditure. Industries in crisis as a consequence of the economic downturn could thereby be re-organised, re-financed and returned to the private sector while "strategic day-to-day handling of these publically owned industries was in the hands of  big businessmen and private enterprise managers, whose own interests straddled the public and private sectors" (Morgan 2009 p.162). That business interests predominated in this arrangement was a fact personified by the IRI President Alberto Beneduce, who was a multiple corporate director *and* state functionary. The overall objective was to facilitate cartelization, maximize production and thereby sustain the capitalist economy (see later). It is in this, limited sense, that "the state drove the economy, not the economy the state" (Morgan 2009 p.153).

Taken together these state-led measures were designed to resolve the systemic crisis of capitalism and facilitate some form of social justice in Italy. Indeed as early as 1933 Mussolini made the extraordinary claim that this combination of corporatism and state direction meant that the capitalist mode of production had been transcended. Under corporatism, he maintained, private property had lost its private character and had become "social" (see Schmidt 1973 p.156 and Mussolini 1975 p.18). As we shall discover in more detail later, such claims are little short of absurd. Suffice to say at this juncture that corporatism simply masked the domination of the employers, who were always strong enough to ignore workers and avoid being dictated to by the state. As Morgan says, "the regime's syndical and corporate machinery was the means and channel by which wage and salary cuts were imposed on the workforce" (Morgan 2009 p.154). Moreover, "in its concrete workings, the corporative system did not limit the power of the capitalists, whereas it sanctioned the destruction of the power of the trade unions" (Lombardini 1968 p.161) [20]. If there was class collaboration it was "like the collaboration of horse and rider" (Schmidt 1973 p.79). Corporatism in Italy was a useful propaganda weapon but it did not even achieve the limited objective of class co-operation, let alone the eradication of capitalism as an economic system. As Halperin concludes on the subject, "the corporative institutions had little authority and no autonomy, they neither originated nor formulated economic policy...the disparity between pretense and practice could scarcely have been greater" (Halperin

1964 p.57-8). Corporatism was therefore an "unrealised idea" in Italy and became part of Italian Fascism's "'revolutionary' myth" (see Mack Smith 1985 p.137, Morgan 2009 p.156).

Hitler and the Nazis adopted similar macro-economic methods in order to stimulate the German economy although they proceeded, predictably, on a much larger scale and with more spectacular results. This has led some analysts to comment positively on the consequences of Nazi economic policy, for instance Kedward claims that "Hitler promised to solve economic problems and he was successful" (Kedward 1971 p.119). However, it would be fair to say that this "success" owed more to contra-cyclical demand-management, state investment and fiscal policy, rather than any grand corporatist economic plan. There is a sense in which Nazi economic policy has been relatively under-researched and Tooze (2007) makes the interesting observation that the study of Nazi economic history has not progressed at the same rate as, for example, the analysis of racial policy. However, we can nevertheless still discern the broad contours of an identifiably Nazi approach to economic matters, indeed Tooze himself has done much to re-frame and re-position the economic narrative, questioning popular assumptions about the strength of the German economy under Nazism (Tooze 2007). In fact Tooze, in his compelling study, argues very persuasively that it was the underpinning economic rationale, specifically the effort to keep up with emerging economic power-house of the USA which, from a Nazi perspective, not only posed an existential threat to Germany but actually provoked Hitler's regime to engage in some of its more desperate foreign policy gambles. Economics can therefore offer much in the way of an explanation for the actual trajectory of Nazism in Germany (see later).

Certainly corporatism, as a mode of economic and social organization, was the focus of considerable aspirational attention in the early years of Nazism. For instance Rosenberg, a key Nazi ideologue and one of the architects of the Nazi regime, declared in June 1933 that "'the corporative organisation which is begun in Germany will represent real socialism, twentieth century socialism'" (cited in Guerin 1973 p.203), and great faith was placed in the proposed Corporatist Constitution. However, the contradictory nature of this concept can be gauged from the fact that while Rosenberg spoke of its "socialist" content, Hans Reupke, who was funded by the *Reichsverband der Deutschen Industrie* (National Association of German Industry) to research corporatism in Italy, concluded that the system was the "'pioneer of the capitalist system'" (cited in Schieder 2001 p.44). Indeed, even some of its exponents, such as Robert Ley referred to the notion of corporate organisation as a confusing "'chaos of ideas'" (cited in Mason 1993 p.90). Nevertheless, despite its inherent ambivalence, the notion of corporatism and the *Reichstande* appeared frequently in Nazi literature and was well publicised inside the Nazi movement before 1933 (Barkai 1990 p.116). In the German context, according to Barkai, corporatist methods "designated the modeling of economic and social organization on pre-industrial society, namely, in corporate professional bodies of workers and employers that would take care of conflicting interests in industrial relations, competition, prices and the market in a more or less autonomous manner" (Barkai 1990 p.116). However corporatism, given its vagueness, could be used to envision an economic arrangement suitable to seduce any special interests although, in much the same way as in Italy, the practicalities were actually designed to ensure working class subordination (Mason 1993 p.89, see later).

In practice, the National Economic Chamber, The Reich Corporation of German Industry and the German Labour Front, set up by the Law for the Organisation of National Labour on 20 January 1934, attempted to achieve the familiar corporatist objective of uniting capital and labour in the "national interest". The Law on Trustees of Labour of May 1933 had established twelve state officials from the Reich Ministry of Labour, whose task it was, in corporatist fashion, to monitor and regulate wages and conditions of work, and to maintain cordial relations between workers and bosses.

Although these arrangements were shrouded in the language of feudal reciprocity this simply obscured the predominance of the employers (Evans 2006 p.460). The Ministry of Economics, meanwhile, was ultimately responsible for, and in theory coordinated, economic activity via regional Chambers of Economics. However, Max Frauendorfer, head of the party Bureau for Corporate Structure, had very little real decision-making authority, and tentative moves toward genuine corporatist decision-making in agriculture were not extended to other areas (Barkai 1990 p.135-36, see p.138). In reality it could be argued that when the Reich Estate of Germany Industry was formed in the summer of 1933 "any pretence of corporative organization was abandoned" (De Grand 1995 p.44). Direct administrative intervention and collaborative self-management in the sphere of economics was thereby kept to a minimum, despite the imposing corporatist façade. As Mason says, when it became clear that the various corporatist-style structures offered few practical solutions to the contradiction between labour and capital it became a simple question of power, with the odds stacked firmly in favour of the industrial elites (see Mason 1993 p.94). At the same time Hitler, persistently preoccupied with foreign policy schemes and racial fantasies, was perfectly prepared to let the corporatist structures wither on the vine.

Nevertheless, although corporatism was moribund, state intervention in a broader sense (to guarantee investment, impose exchange controls etc), and public expenditure (on public works, railways, motorways etc), were used to some considerable effect to rejuvenate the German economy. Indeed, according to Barkai, "the state's supreme authority in economic matters was a cornerstone of the Nazi's economic principles" (Barkai 1990 p.137). As we shall see later, this is an exaggeration, although in important respects the state did retain overall strategic control of the economy. German economists were well aware of the ideas of John Maynard Keynes (indeed were fond of quoting him), and many Nazis saw them as practical, "active" remedies which conformed to a Germanic, authoritarian, organic state tradition that was sceptical about the virtues of unrestrained free enterprise capitalism. Hence a reconstituted Keynesianism worked with the grain of German preconceptions about the role of the state, indeed Keynes' notions not only found fertile soil in Germany they also, incidentally, seemed to confirm the view that even the lackluster liberal democracies were beginning to accept the idea that the state should impose some kind of strategic, regulatory framework (Barkai 1990 p.66; see Mazower 2009 p.124). Although it has been argued in some quarters that the Nazi's, in encouraging state (rather than private) demand, impeded the multiplier effect thereby distorting the Keynesian prescription (see Buchheim 2001, Tooze 2008), there is no doubt that Nazi ideas were derived from the basic Keynesian principle of deficit financing. In this sense Hitler was able to exploit a nascent economic consensus about a more pro-active economic role for the state, and pursued it on a massive scale.

By using basic Keynesian contra-cyclical deficit-financing and fiscal reflationary techniques, accompanied by a compulsory Reich Labour scheme (June 1935) and conscription (March 1935), the National Socialists were able to effectively eliminate unemployment from a level of six million in 1932. The Nazis used the *Reichsbank* (rather than conventional loans) as "an ingenious novelty" (Stone 1992 p.75), and public works schemes were created and used to stimulate the economy, the most iconic of which being the building of the *autobahn* (although that idea actually preceded Hitler) (see Barkai 1990 p.167). The Nazis promised work for the German people and the techniques produced the desired outcome, indeed "Hitler's boast that he would solve the unemployment problem within four years of taking office seemed to have been triumphantly justified" (Evans 2006 p.333). Moreover, the economic recovery was so swift that the actual state deficits were reduced quite quickly by economic expansion and the return of prosperity (Stone 1992 p.75). Although wage levels were extremely low, and despite the fact that labour was often coerced to work, in poor conditions, and even though the expansion was constructed primarily upon the armaments industry and preparation for war, it appeared to be an impressive economic achievement, especially given the pessimism that pervaded the democratic countries about the apparently insoluble nature of economic problems such as unemployment. As Griffiths has correctly pointed out, "the economic recovery was a major factor in the growing popularity of Hitler. The solving of the unemployment problem not only brought the Nazis great support among the workers; it also played a large part in the favourable impression made by the new regime in many circles abroad" (Griffiths 2005 p.73; see Barkai 1990 p.106).

However it is important to note that although the scope and depth of dirigist state intervention was a relatively new phenomenon, there was very little central planning as such (Barkai 1990 p.5). In fact the initial priorities were re-armament, repudiating foreign debts, and saving German agriculture, rather than developing and executing any grand plan for state-led economic recovery (see Tooze 2007 p.25). As Tooze says, "the 'Keynesian' issues of work creation and unemployment were never as prominent in the agenda of Hitler's government as is commonly supposed...Hitler's economic miracle was in fact a highly ambiguous experience" (Tooze 2007 p.32 and p.33). Actually, in many ways Nazi fiscal policy was "pragmatic, cautious and surprisingly orthodox", indeed dominated by the economic preconceptions and prejudices of the depression era (James 1993 p.120, see p.132). Moreover, the Nazi regime was fortunate to benefit from an upturn in the global economic cycle after 1933 and the cancellation of reparations payments (which had in fact been negotiated by the Bruning administration at Lausanne in 1932). Actually the Papen, Schleicher and Bruning governments had all prepared similar plans which conformed broadly to Keynesian principles, but they had been unable to execute them due to their dependence on foreign finance (Barkai 1990 p.161, see James 1993 p.115). Clearly much of Nazi policy in this sphere had been prefigured by politicians in the Weimar republic, but of course the strife-torn, tattered Republic could not match the confidence, euphoria and sense of purpose generated by the lurid propaganda of a Nazi party in full control of the mass media in a modern industrialised state. The reality is that Nazi economic policy was less effective than many have supposed (Tooze 2007) and is better viewed as an, albeit important, adjunct to Hitler's broader ideological objectives regarding re-armament and foreign policy. Nazi policies should certainly not be seen as reflecting a serious commitment to secure and sustain any deeply held socio-corporatist principles.

Related to the concept of the corporatist state, and state intervention in the economy, was the desire of both fascist movements to achieve national self-sufficiency/autarky (see Guerin 1973 p.233). The idea of a nation state as a self-contained economic unit has an important historical lineage (see Hayes 1973 p.104), and in the German case goes back at least as far as Fichte's ideas on the *Closed Commercial State* (1800). With the onset of the worldwide economic depression after 1929 there was a distinct trend toward protectionism anyhow, but in Italy and Germany such notions had a special significance. Autarky as a goal was visible in Nazi policy from an early stage because of Germany's over-reliance on imports, and was given impetus in Italy by League of Nations sanctions after 1935. Autarky, in practical terms, meant a concerted attempt to produce internally everything that the domestic economy required (Evans 2006 p.345, Fischer 1995 p.51). This involved constructing a programme of indigenous product substitution, along with the imposition of tariffs on imports and exchange controls. According to autarkic prescriptions trade was to be based more on a bi-lateral barter system constructed on notions of reciprocity and mutual benefit, rather than relying on the free play of market forces across international frontiers.

Hitler spoke quite frequently of his desire to insulate the national economy from the vicissitudes of the free market between nations and cautioned against the consequences of international commercial interdependence, indeed he looked forward to the time when Germany would only import tea and coffee (see Hitler 1973 p.72-3). For the Nazis international trade precipitated economic dependence which eroded national autonomy. As a consequence the Reich Food Estate set up in September 1933, which was incidentally intended to function as a Corporation, aimed at autarky in foodstuffs. There followed some limited successes in terms of self-sufficiency in commodities like bread, potatoes, sugar and meat, although the expense to the consumer, in the form of higher prices, was considerable (Evans 2006 p.346-349). At Nuremberg in November 1936 Hitler announced a plan to make Germany self-sufficient in raw materials, and therefore immune to the tactic of economic blockade (which had been deployed against Germany in the Great War). Experimentation on new technology was stepped up in order to substitute those commodities which were imported on a large scale such as rubber and textile fibres, and factories were constructed, for example, to manufacture synthetic gasoline from coal. Product development in this context obviously required a degree of state direction since the short-term profit levels could not attract the requisite private investment and therefore the state itself set the autarkic objectives. Overall, however, the policy of "autarky" in Germany amounted to little more than a generalized effort to renege on "unfair" foreign debts and restrict imports, which underpinned a strategy of selective economic disengagement directed primarily against Britain, France and the United States (Tooze 2007 p.86).

The story in Italy has a similar plot line. In Italy the First World War had revealed the extent of Italy's dependence upon foreign coal, cotton, oil and wheat and the Fascist government set about re-configuring the economy. Mussolini officially used the term "autarky" on 23 March 1936 to define the regime's long-term goal of economic self-sufficiency. Consequently the Italian Fascists introduced a programme of intensive agricultural production to improve domestic output, along with the imposition of import-tariff controls, whilst hydroelectric power was encouraged as an alternative to coal and oil. The state also entered into joint ventures with industrial giants to explore the development of synthetic fuel and rubber (see De Grand 2000 p.107). However autarky, somewhat erratically pursued by the Italian administration, certainly did not alter Italy's financial and technological weakness relative to its more powerful northern neighbours (Bosworth 2005). Indeed the contradictions inherent in the official Italian commitment to autarky are highlighted by the fact that, throughout the period, the most remunerative industry remained tourism (Bosworth 1998 p.151). Although the practical economic virtue of autarky as a policy was debatable, given that Italy was poor and depended to a considerable degree upon imported coal and oil, the propaganda benefits were clearly evident in terms of promoting the idea of national economic independence and self-sustainability (see Halperin 1964 p.62). As Knox says, "Italy's massive dependence on imported energy and strategic raw materials made genuine autarky impractical, but furnished yet another argument for expansion" (Knox 2000 p.98). Similarly, in Germany full scale self-sufficiency was only achieved in cereals, so neither regime was successful in escaping its dependence on imports (Barkai 1990 p.156). Of course if the Nazis could not produce the raw materials required, then they would also have to "acquire" them elsewhere hence, for instance, Hitler's envious glances toward the Ukrainian oil fields. In fact, given their lack of colonies and their limited supply of raw materials, the economic imperative of autarky, as pursued by Italy and Germany, merely provided further impetus to the territorial expansionism inherent in the nationalist-militarist-imperialist component of its ideology. Indeed, "autarky was literally unrealizable for both Fascist Italy and Nazi Germany within their current territorial confines, and, hence, its attainment became a self-fulfilling or self-sustaining myth and prophecy. Autarky, for the fascist regimes, was both means and end, a reason for and a product of wars of expansion" (Morgan 2009 p.154).

In actual fact despite the apparent "successes" of Hitler's economic policy and the corporatist aspirations of Mussolini, neither fascist regime could be said to have really elaborated a "third way" between capitalism and communism. In essence the so-called "Corporate State" in Italy achieved remarkably little and performed no serious function, except to confirm the rigid subordination of labour to capital. In Germany there was no fundamental change in the structure of the economy, and even when employers accepted the idea of corporations it was only after the concept had been emptied of all genuinely collaborative content. The capitalists demanded economic control and continued to dominate economic policy, which precluded any kind of industrial harmony based on some kind of mutual consultative status or negotiated partnership under the auspices of the state. As far as autarky was concerned: "Mussolini's autarkic policies kept the overall rate of Italian economic growth at almost the same level for two decades and made sense only as a device for maintaining the economy and the masses in the barrack-room state of unity which Hitler in a more successful way, imposed upon Germany" (O'Sullivan 1983 p170).

The abject failure of the so-called "third way" may be best seen, however, when analysing the anti-communism, "socialism" and "anti-capitalism" of fascism. It will become apparent that whilst anti-communism was as important and consistent reactive ingredient of fascism, its self-professed socialism and anti-capitalism was merely a demagogic device, which served simply to mystify the reality of socio-economic relationships. Indeed, not only was there no serious attempt to move in the direction of socialism or transform the capitalist mode of production, it might be justifiably argued that fascism was, in effect, the "life-belt" of capitalism (see Sternhell 1982 p.374).

## Anti-Communism, Pseudo-Socialism and Rhetorical Anti-Capitalism

Both types of fascism, Italian and German, were fanatically anti-communist in theory and practice, although the Nazis in particular did profess adherence to certain "socialist" beliefs. After 1918 Italy and Germany were both character-ized by the existence of serious social conflict between labour and capital, indeed both nations, prior to the ascendancy of fascism, contained assertive labour movements with a signifi-cant revolutionary contingent. In Germany the existence of a strong Communist Party combined with episodes such as the aborted *Raterupublik* in Munich and the Spartakist uprising in 1919, illustrated the belligerency of the organised working class (Sewell 1988 p.30); whilst in Italy the socialist threat manifested itself most vividly with the *Biennio Rosso* and the occupation of the factories between 1919-20. Although it is factually incorrect to suggest that fascism forestalled the forthcoming socialist revolution (see Zetkin's perceptive contributions in Beetham 1983) because the socialist threat at the time was undoubtedly exaggerated, it is nevertheless fair to say that, following hard on the heels of the Bolshevik revolution in 1917, working class activism produced an anxious and frightened bourgeoisie. Fascists were well equipped to exploit such fears and "it is true that fascism was more successful in those societies in which the bourgeoisie had been deeply scared by revolutionary attempts, however unsuccessful, and where the labour movement held on to a maximalist revolutionary rhetoric even when it was unable to mobilize for revolution" (Linz 1982 p.43). As a result "its supporters put forward fascism as the antithesis of commu-nism, and many supported it as the only real alternative to red revolution" (Pearce 2002 p.38). There was, therefore, a ready-made reactionary constituency, primed and receptive to an anti-communist movement with an unambiguously anti-communist message. In fact antipathy toward Marxism constituted a negative essence in the ideology of the two classic fascist movements, indeed "violent anti-communism lay at the core of all fascisms" (Markwick 2009 p.344).

The Nazi hatred of Marxism is well documented and beyond dispute (see Wachsmann 2008 p.123). Hitler detested Marxism as an integral part of a Jewish plot (see later), but the whole Nazi movement was based on a vehement and vitriolic anti-communism. Communism, the Nazis believed, divided society and subverted the natural hierarchy of men and nations. In effect the NSDAP set out to win the masses back from Marxism, to exterminate Bolshevism, and to save good Germans from the Communist menace [21]. As Fest rightly pointed out, Nazism derived a considerable part of its emotional appeal and political cohesion from a defensive attitude toward the Marxist threat, as Hitler said, his party's aim was the "'annihilation and extermination of the Marxist world view'" (cited in Fest 1973 p.92; see Nolte cited in Pearce 2002 p.31). Indeed Hitler asserted in 1924 that "'we shall make Marxism understand that National Socialism is the future master of the streets and that it will one day be master of the State'" (cited in Aycoberry 1999 p.18). It is in this context that Bullock identified a very important distinction: "...while Hitler's attitude toward liberalism was one of contempt, towards Marxism he showed implacable hostility. The difference is significant. Liberalism he no longer regarded as a serious threat, its values had lost their attraction in an age of mass politics...Marxism however, whether revisionist or revolutionary, was a rival weltanshuung able to exert a powerful attractive force..." (Bullock 1962 p.405). It is interesting to note that Goebbels' provocative slogan in "red" Berlin was "Adolf Hitler devours Karl Marx". The speech Hitler gave to the *Hamburger Nationalklub* on 28 February 1926 outlined clearly his view that the bourgeoisie was completely incapable of destroying Marxism, which he identified as the primary task of the NSDAP. As Kershaw explains: "national revival through terroristic anti-Marxism built on the cynical manipulation and indoctrination of the masses: that was the sum total of Hitler's message to the upper-crust of the Hamburg bourgeoisie" (Kershaw 2009 p.179). Indeed "even in private, dictating the speeches to his secretary, when it came to passages on Bolshevism Hitler, red faced and eyes blazing, would work himself into a frenzy, bellowing at full volume his thunderous denunciations" (Kershaw 2009 p.381). Adolf Hitler's consistently held, fanatical detestation of communism is also clearly indicated by the fact that it lasted until the bitter end of his life - in his very last political testament Hitler claimed that he had been misunderstood by the west and that his one overriding objective was to save Europe from the evils of Bolshevism (Hitler 1961b p.34).

However, the self-proclaimed "'socialism" of the German fascists has caused some considerable confusion, partly because of the deliberately ambiguous nature of Hitler's rhetoric and, indeed, the pliable nature of Nazi ideology. Hitler and the Nazis always claimed to be "socialist" in some respect, and Hitler made great play of having been a manual labourer in Vienna (a claim for which, given the paucity of sources, there is no reliable empirical evidence) (see Hamann 2001 p.24). Nevertheless Hitler continued to claim adherence to certain socialist ideals whilst reiterating his credentials as a man of the people. For instance, in an article in the Sunday Express on 28 September 1930 (cited in Baynes 1969 p.92-3), Hitler claimed that whilst not being Marxist he was a "true socialist", and many of his speeches acclaimed the virtue and value of German workers.

In fact the early Twenty-Five Point NSDAP party programme did indeed refer to the need for such policies as the abolition of interest payments on borrowed money, the confiscation of war profits and even, in some circumstances, the elimination of unearned income (points 10-14 and 17). "Though phrased vaguely enough to admit a variety of interpretations, a number of provisions had a distinctly anti-capitalist tenor designed to attract workers in the revolutionary climate...For Hitler the program was designed to attract various discontented social groups and at the same time exercise a broad emotional appeal" (Stackelberg 1999 p.86). Socialist-sounding anti-capitalist rhetoric was extremely important in sustaining the electoral viability of the Nazi party in the industrial areas of Germany where support from workers had to be secured.

Obviously the German fascists could not ignore the condition of the masses if they sought power by electoral means so they were effectively forced to engage in a tactical bid to out-radicalise their political opponents by making reference to certain "socialist" themes such as the value of labour and the importance of workers. Certainly the rhetoric of *Gemeinnutz geht vor Eigennutz* ("common good before the good of the individual") was extremely seductive, with underlying resonances of collectivist socialism. It also seems that several commentators have accepted at face value the idea that the Nazis were actually socialists in some significant respect: Weber for instance, states that they "certainly did not lack concern for the worker" (Weber 1964 p.53), whilst Hildebrand finds it impossible to overlook the fact that Nazi policy tended toward equality and the elimination of class differences (Hildebrand 1985 p.8, see Woolf 1981 p.100 who makes essentially the same point). Similarly Hayes talks of "a considerable socialist content" in Nazism whilst stressing Hitler's empathy for the poor given his own destitution for a time in Vienna [22], after all, exclaims Hayes, they were the National "Socialist" German "Workers" Party (Hayes 1973 p.63 and p.66). Clearly great care needs to be taken here, because if we take "socialism" to mean the pursuit of egalitarianism (by whatever means), or even social justice, such conclusions are completely misguided, if not deliberately mischievous. As Cecil has rightly said "there was nothing egalitarian about Nazism at any level" (Cecil 1972 p.64). The Nazis might have appropriated some of the rhetoric, tactics and iconography of socialism, but the vast majority of Nazis, and especially Hitler, were not socialists in any meaningful sense at all and we can prove this beyond any reasonable doubt.

Take as evidence Hitler's discussions with Otto Strasser on the subject (22 May 1930): "'with what right do the workers demand a share in the possessions of the capitalist, not to speak of a share in control?'", the capitalists "'have worked their way to the top through their capacity, and on the basis of this selection...they have a right to lead...Do you think that I should be so mad as to destroy business life?....the only thing which the present system lacks is the ultimate responsibility to the nation'" (cited in Baynes 1969 p.111-12) . And again to Strasser, "'the great mass of working men want only bread and circuses, they have no understanding for ideals of any sort'" (Hitler cited in Baynes 1969 p.988). As Hitler explained to Rauschning, "'my socialism is not class war but order'" (cited in Rauschning 1939 p.178). Disparity of income mattered little to Hitler, still less ownership and control of industry, since in an authentic Aryan state all would feel a collective sense of purpose irrespective of class or status (see later). As Hitler said, "'why need we trouble to socialize banks and factories? We socialize human beings'", moreover "'whoever is prepared to make the national cause his own to such an extent that he knows no higher ideal than the welfare of his nation; whoever has understood ... that nothing in the wide world surpasses in his eyes this Germany, people and land - that man is a socialist'" (Hitler cited in Rauschning 1939 p.92, and cited in Shirer 1985 p.85). Indeed Hitler declared, without a hint of irony, that the "'highest socialist organization" was in fact "the German army'" (cited in Gluckstein 1999 p.29). Again, in a speech on 1 July 1933, Hitler outlined his unique, indeed perverse, conception of socialism: "'socialism is nothing else than the natural ordering of people according to its inborn capacities'" (cited in Shirer 1985 p.85, and in Baynes 1969 p.483). Such an idea may have some intrinsic merit, and even a sophisticated ancient philosopher like Plato might have approved, but then he was not reknown for his socialism either. Social inequality was "natural" for Hitler, part of nature's "law", which was only logical given his social Darwinist premise. What was required, according to Hitler, was leadership, authority and responsi-bility, not equality - indeed according to Rauschning the very mention of the word "equality" "seemed to lash him into a fury" (Rauschning 1939 p.76). "Despite their anti-bourgeois rhetoric, superficially so similar to that of the left, the Nazis did not want to re-distribute income or change the social and economic structure in any way that might inhibit full and efficient production" (Stackelberg 1999 p.124). The Nazis might have detested the other profiteering "plutocracies" of the west, but they were not about to risk the productive potential of their preferred economic model in order to pursue some vague "socialistic" plan.

Nazi "socialism" consisted of nothing more than the advocacy of an ordered, regimented and hierarchical society, with a degree of meritocratic mobility and a measure of economic state paternalism, which was dictated more by the requirements of war preparedness than any genuine social commitment. Hitler was though "cunningly vague" in his use of terminology (Taylor 1985 p.129), and the quasi-religious idealization of the German "peasant" and "worker" certainly might have created the impression of a regime sympathetic to the lower orders, but this was simply an illusion. As Nicholls quite rightly points out, "the workers themselves might have been flattered by the Nazi claims that only they and not the ageing bourgeoisie were capable of asserting Germany's position in the world; they might have had their social ambitions stimulated by Geobbels' insistence that the term 'proletariat' was a degrading Jewish invention, and that in National Socialist Germany they would receive the recognition due to them...but status promotion of this kind did not imply a major economic re-organization for the benefit of the working class" (Nicholls 1981 p.67). The duplicity and deceit, which was deeply woven into Nazi ideology, is clearly discernible in Goebbels' Nazi newspaper *Der Angriff* ("The Attack") which had as its motto the suitably radical sounding "For the Oppressed! Against the Exploiters!". Close scrutiny of its actual content reveals an emphasis on crude anti-semitism and the projection of the Fuhrer-myth – references to socialism are conspicuous by their absence (see Welch 1998 p.29). In short "the Nazis used propagandistic appeals, not economic policies, to combat the class system" (Stackelberg 1999 p.124).

However, an important caveat must be inserted here. There was a section of the NSDAP, centred around the Strasser brothers, which did take their professed commitment to radical social policies rather more seriously. As Bullock says "the Strasser brothers did not share Hitler's cynical disregard for any programme except as a means to power" (Bullock 1962 p.136). These Nazi radicals advocated a kind of nationalistic state feudalism, with a de-centralised corporatist and autarkic economy (see Strasser 1940a p.92). Otto Strasser's idea was to fuse the best elements of "left" and "right" into what was often referred to as "volkish socialism", and the *Kampfverlag* publishing house in Berlin was used to purvey Strasser's odd concoction of mystical nationalism and social radicalism. The Strasser brothers envisaged a vertically integrated and culturally distinct society, underpinned by a mystical volkish nationalism. "Strasserism" vehemently rejected the twin internationalist evils of communism and finance capitalism, but persistently argued for the economic emancipation of the workers. This has led to some analysts to refer to these ideas as "a form of leftist 'universal' fascism" (Griffin 1995 p.114). Nevertheless, it is important to note that this vision of "socialism", just like the more mainstream version of Nazism, did not imply equality, and Gregor Strasser maintained that the great discovery that he and his brother had made was that "'true socialism is identical with true nationalism'" (Gregor Strasser cited in Strasser 1940b Appendix p.250). Socialism, they argued, had been "'Hebraically falsified'" and Germany needed to re-acquire the "'Teutonic notion'" of the tribe (cited in Strasser 1940a p.250). This "socialist" perspective was therefore explicitly elitist, with an emphasis on the creation of a new nobility of chivalrous "Knights" (see Griffin 1995 p.114-115). Oblique references were also frequently made to the need for de-urbanisation and a "revolution of the soul", which was apparently the prerequisite for the freedom of the German people. This may indeed constitute a more radical perspective, but it is hardly socialist. Certainly for the Strassers the "idea" was crucial, which bore at least some resemblance both to Hitler's rhetorical preferences and perhaps to Italian syndicalist conceptions of a "third way," but for Hitler conceptual arguments could not possibly override or impede loyalty to the party leader, who was the only person qualified to make and interpret policy. Although the ideological tension between the Strasserite radicals and Hitler was resolved in favour of the latter, the "radical" vision of the former should not be misconstrued as somehow socialist.

It would therefore be unwise and inaccurate to describe this radical Strasserism as somehow constituting a "Nazi left" (see Renton 1999 p.38). According to Guerin, "economic liberalism had hurled them (the Strasserites) defenceless into the capitalist jungle. Merciless competition ruined them and sent them into the working class, and so they sought to bar the march of progress and return to a stage before capitalism" (Guerin 1973 p.88). Similarly Hildebrand has referred to the "social romanticism" of the Strassers, which sought to replace both unethical capitalism and divisive socialism, whilst Taylor says that Strasserism "represented par excellence the notion of a petit bourgeois 'middle way' which claimed to bring together the 'healthy' qualities of both bourgeoisie and proletariat" (Taylor 1985 p.89-90). Strasserite ideas were therefore characterised by fundamental internal contradictions, and they were shrouded in ambiguity – for example, despite their ostentatious professions of commitment to social harmony they not only remained fiercely nationalistic, they also refused to relinquish explicitly racist notions about the nature of Jewry (see Noakes and Pridham 1974 p.71). Although it is true that Strasser accused Hitler of being bewitched by Prussian militarism and of planning a sell-out to conservative forces, and Hitler considered Otto Strasser an "'intellectual white Jew, totally incapable of organization, a Marxist of the purest ilk'" (cited in Kershaw 2009 p.201), the plain fact is that neither was socialist in the slightest respect.

In practice this ideological cleavage resulted in a number of party crises and internal disputes. The Strassers were based in Berlin, and found the industrial north more receptive to their ideas, and naturally this alarmed the Nazi leadership in Munich (especially since Hitler courted wealthy backers for his movement). Disputes surrounded, for instance, the issue of whether certain strikes should be endorsed, or whether the German royal houses should be expropriated. The Nazi conference at Bamberg on 14 February 1926 was designed to resolve the festering ideological dispute but merely resulted in the papering over of clear differences of opinion (it also resulted in the defection of Goebbels to the Hitler camp). On 4 July 1930 Otto Strasser left the NSDAP to form the Revolutionary National Socialists, later known as the Black Front. Gregor Strasser chose to stay with Hitler and "having eliminated rivals from within the movement and reshaped its organizational structure in his own image Hitler imposed his unimpeachable authority over the movement" (Welch 1998 p.22). Henceforth Nazism would be precisely what Hitler wanted, and it certainly excluded socialism, although the idealistic social programme associated with the Strassers remained important to certain sections of the SA (brown-shirts) (see Noakes and Pridham 1974 p.201) [23]. As Kershaw put it, after the internal party crisis had resulted in the ultimate ascendancy of Hitler, "Leader and Idea were one and the same" and there would be no more talk of social revolution (Kershaw 2009 p.201). In short "'Hitler got rid of social revolutionaries like Otto Strasser who wanted to challenge property relationships, however slightly" (Mosse 1979a p.7). In June 1934, on the so-called "Night of he Long Knives", a bloody fate awaited Hitler's more radical political opponents in the Nazi movement, as he took the opportunity to eliminate enemies in the SA who were threatening to embarrass him and de-stabilise the regime.

We can also illustrate quite clearly that *anti*-socialism was a feature of the Nazi regime in practice – the evidence is incontrovertible. As early as July 1933 Hitler made it perfectly clear that he was not prepared to lead a social revolution against the army and existing elites, "'the full spate of revolution must be guided into the secure bed of evolution...'" he declared (cited in Taylor 1985 p.161) and Hitler's National "Socialists" were an unmitigated disaster not only for the Communists, whom he outlawed, interned, intimidated, tortured and murdered, but for the organised labour and socialist movement (Evans 2006 p.455). "The total destruction of organized labour was followed by the elimination, through systematic acts of terror, of all underground resistance groups that sought to spread social democratic or communist ideas. In terms of its remorseless efficiency and brutality, the suppression surpassed anything the labour movement had encountered up to that point" (Mason 1993 p.24).

As a consequence, trade unions were brutally disbanded in May 1933 and their assets sequestrated, whilst many union officials were beaten, tortured or murdered. The "Law on the Ordering of National Labour" resulted in the application of the "*fuhrerprinzip*" to all aspects of employment and workers became mere "followers" (*gefolgschaft*) of their own particular factory leader, the *Betriebsfuhrer*. Trustees of Labour, appointed and answerable to the state, ensured that industrial "harmony" prevailed, which in effect meant that they dictated remuneration policy whereby wages were frozen at depression levels, longer hours were introduced and strikes forbidden. As Rabinbach says, the law "established the absolute hegemony of management within the industrial enterprise" (Rabinbach 1979 p.190). Significantly, "most statistical investigations are agreed that the economic situation of the mass of working class wage-earners did not markedly improve between 1933 and 1939...workers were having to put in longer hours just to maintain their existing, very modest standard of living" and income inequality increased as top earners improved their relative position (Evans 2006 p.477-78, see later). Indeed a modest increase in wages for ordinary workers could only be secured for some by a significant increase in the number of working hours – by 1936 the average German industrial worker was working 47.8 hours per week, nearly eight hours a week more than their British counterpart (McDonough 1999 p.37). The fact is that the share of workers' wages as a percentage of gross national income declined from 57% to approximately 52% between 1932-39 "indicating a redistribution of wealth *away* from the working class...the relationship between capital and labour remained fundamentally unaltered between 1933 and 1945: firms stayed in private hands, bosses remained bosses and workers remained workers" (Geary 1994 p.48 and p.50). Moreover, workers were routinely threatened with the Gestapo for "under-performance", whilst welfare and benefit payments were cut (Evans 2006 p.482 and p.491). Meanwhile in the countryside, despite a policy of protectionism, the continuation of subsistence wages and payment in kind, accompanied by increased rents, effectively reduced the rural peasant to the status of bonded serf. Any benefits that were to be derived from state intervention by the Reich Food Estate (RNS) to sustain prices were accrued by larger estates rather than independent farm workers (see Tooze 2008 p.176). In addition, of course, conditions for the 1.5 million foreign workers and 1.3 million prisoners of war, who contributed massively to the German economy, were immeasurably worse (see Mason 1993 p.265). Indeed, any marginal benefits for the German worker occurred much later on, as a consequence of the fact that foreign labour was mercilessly exploited by the regime (see Herbert 1996 p.31-32).

Agencies such as the Bureau of the Beauty of Labour (*Schonheit der Arbeit*), founded on 27 November 1933, which set itself the lofty task of transforming the nature of work by eliminating the compulsion of capitalist wage slavery, were merely part of an elaborate propaganda exercise. Although some commentators have over-stressed the power of symbolism with regard to the regime's focus on manual workers as cultural icons via the "honour of labour", such techniques simply camouflaged continued exploitation (see Ludtke 1995). In short, providing factories with better sanitation, bigger windows, better ventilation and a canteen did not impact significantly on the extraction of surplus value. Giving work a "higher ethical meaning" entailed, in most cases, a simple programme of factory beautification which, in essence, represented a fairly transparent attempt to increase production whilst ameliorating industrial unrest (see Rabinbach 1979 p.189). (It is perhaps worth remembering in this context that the Nazis were masters of such cynical psychological manipulation – bands playing to greet arrivals to the death camps, and blooming flowers in window boxes of the crematoria, set amidst meticulously manicured lawns, are but the most obvious examples. See later).

Along with this emphasis on the aesthetics of production, the regimented leisure programmes of *Kraft durch Freude* "Strength through Joy" sought to achieve similar objectives via state intervention (as we have already noted). The first May Day of National Socialist rule (1 May 1933) not only marked the creation of the German Labour Front (DAF) but presaged the official slogan "Honour Work and Respect the Worker", and the Nazis contented themselves with empty words and facile sloganizing. As Herbert explains, "many of the socio-political offerings of the Nazis were little more than proof of a purposeless activism, which had no actual impact on the situation of the working class" (Herbert 1996 p.28). In the Beauty of Labour scheme the utopian promise of an industrial society where class was abolished was given an administrative form, but its ultimate aim was to defuse any potential industrial relations conflict and "'integrate the German worker, deprived of political and economic representation, into the 'façade' socialism of the Labour Front'" (Rabinbach cited in Gregor 2000 p.221-222). Even the Nazi workplace structure *National Socialistische Betriebszellen Organisation* (NSBO) was so mistrusted by the party leadership that after January 1934 it was re-organised and subordinated to the German Labour Front (*Deutsche Arbeitsfront*) under the leadership of Robert Ley (see Mason 1993). The primary objective of the Front was to control and  placate workers and defuse any potential industrial unrest. Although in some respects the Front always remained suspect because of its mass base, it was thoroughly infiltrated by secret police and eventually dominated by the employers, who also controlled the Reich Economic Council.

The reality of the workplace under the Nazis was more clearly reflected in the fact that deaths from industrial accidents rose by 33% (McDonough 1999 p.52), whilst the experience of workers at *Volkswagon* factories after they were converted to armament production is still more instructive. Workers for VW encountered systematic surveillance conducted by the Gestapo, and the SS *Werkschutz* patrolled factory corridors with guns and dogs, administering severe punishments for the slightest infraction of company rules (see Gluckstein 1999 p.195 and Siegfried 1996). Many workers were beaten, confined to factory cells or taken to concentration camps such as Labour Camp 21 at Hallendorf where deaths were so frequent that the company "incorporated the deaths of these prisoners into their business calculations" (Siegfried 1996 p.43). Given the intimidation and terror deployed in the everyday lives of workers there was, in effect, a straight line leading from the factory to the factory-as-concentration-camp (Mason 1993 p.274). The space for non-suicidal collective resistance by labour was thereby dramatically diminished in practice as the regime imposed its draconian restrictions on the work force.

In essence, despite the rhetoric of equal status, Nazi concern for the poorest classes in society was negligible and their limited paternal initiatives were defensive in terms of heading off the possibility of revolt and/or purely functional in the sense of winning elections or attempting to secure general acquiescence for their over-riding foreign policy/racial objectives (see later). Despite the rhetorical assertion of equality it was explicitly denied in practice and there was no substantive material redistribution of resources (see Tooze 2008 p.174). However exploitation – the mainspring of class conflict – intensified (see Mason 1996). Thus Robert Ley's grandiose claim that Germany was "'the first country in Europe to overcome the class struggle'" (cited in Evans

2006 p.498) can be legitimately dismissed as vacuous hyperbole because "rich and poor remained in the Third Reich, as much as they ever had" (Evans 2006 p.500). In essence, "the Third Reich remained very much a class society to the end" (Mason 1993 p.369).

In Italy too there existed some ambiguity about the *anti*-socialism of Fascism. This stemmed to some extent, however, from the fact that Mussolini, prior to becoming leader of the Fascists, was a prominent, radical socialist (Renton 2001 p.2) [24]. Mussolini came from a working class background, became editor of the socialist newspaper *Avanti!* and as a young left wing radical he was even admired by Lenin and Trotsky. Indeed Mussolini only broke with his erstwhile comrades over the issue of entry into the Great War which, after all, had precipitated a split in socialist ranks across Europe. Ideological confusion was also sustained due to the fact that the original *fasci di combattimento* began with an impressive populist republican programme, which included proposals for a new constitution, universal suffrage (i.e. giving females the vote), decentralization of executive power, confiscation of war profits, a progressive tax on capital, workers councils, a minimum wage, eight-hour working day, seizure of Church property and the abolition of the monarchy (see Griffiths 2005 p.33). However, as Blinkhorn rightly says, "what eventually proved most significant about this programme was its negligible impact" (Blinkhorn 1994 p.19). At the same time, however, Mussolini actually contradicted these radical programmatic elements with speeches declaring war on socialism and advocating imperialism, so it is best perhaps to view the manifesto as reflecting the "heat and excitement of the moment" (Tasca/Rossi 1938 p.33) [25]. As Morgan suggests, "argument about whether this programme was tendentially to the left or right perhaps misses the point. The amalgamation of radical and nationalist ideas was determined by the perceived outlook and expectations of the constituencies it was meant to attract: left interventionists and ex-servicemen" (Morgan 1995 p.13).

Nevertheless despite Mussolini's early flirtation with socialism (and Marxism), he parted company with the labour and socialist movement amidst mutual acrimony, and he was soon to deride its egalitarian internationalism. In fact, after his very public separation from the socialist movement, any influence Mussolini might have had over workers vanished almost overnight (De Grand 2000 p.18). It might be noted that at the official birth of Fascism, in the meeting room of the Milan Industrial and Commercial Alliance overlooking the Piazza San Sepolcro on 23 March 1919, those assembled there resolved to "'declare war against socialism'" (cited in Paxton 2005 p.5). As Mussolini said, in response to a question about Fascism's manifesto: "'our program is to smash the skulls of the Socialists'" (cited in Laqueur 1996 p.50). Moreover, Mussolini became editor of *Il Popolo d'Italia* (People of Italy), which had been partly financed by business interests such as wealthy entrepreneur Cesare Goldman and the Ansaldo ship-building company, along with contributions from the British and French secret services. Mussolini's publication emphasized the irrelevance of past ideological positions, particularly socialism. As Bosworth says, "although he occasionally remembered that he had grown up a socialist, Mussolini, with his cutting phrases and slashing debating style, was digging an abyss between himself and his erstwhile party" (Bosworth 2005 p.53). Mussolini was soon describing himself as a Fascist and although at this point the precise contours of his new ideology were yet to be formulated, any residual sympathy Mussolini might have had for his socialist comrades had completely evaporated. The hostility was mutual.

In any case, after a disappointing defeat in the elections of 1919, Mussolini's finely tuned political antenna led him to realise that there was little purchase in social radicalism for the Fascists. Thereafter the Italian Fascists began to focus on the evils of Bolshevik Leninism, as Mussolini said "'the socialist party is a Russian army encamped in Italy. Against this foreign army, Fascists have launched a guerilla war, and they will conduct it with exceptional seriousness'" (cited in

Bosworth 2002 p.152). Indeed "Mussolini was at his most verbally consistent in his hostility to socialism" and he was "set on a political course which was, above everything else, anti-socialist" (Bosworth 2002 p.133 and p.138). Mussolini was, however, an opportunist and he sought to plagiarise, mimic and re-mould radical sounding ideas, whilst prioritizing the defeat of socialist agitation. Mussolini detected and developed the latent political potential for a self-proclaimed reactionary movement, for as Mussolini exclaimed "'to be a reactionary is a sign of nobility...the title pleases us'" (cited in Bosworth 2002 p.139). Indeed as Fascism began to evolve, "it did so by presenting itself to the leaders of the Confindustria business federation and the Banca Commerciale as a non-political army of professional strike breakers" (Renton 2001 p.3). As Blink-horn says, "increasingly, moral and financial support, if not always actual membership, was coming from rich *agrari* and, to a lesser extent, industrialists eager to see fascism crush or irreversibly weaken trade unionism and socialism" (Blinkhorn 1994 p.21). Fascism's potential to appeal to the "respectable" classes as a reactionary ant-socialist force increased quickly and dramatically.

One of the first acts by the *fascio di combattimento* was the sacking of the offices of socialist newspaper *Avanti!* on 15 April 1919, which was "sweet revenge" for Mussolini against the former comrades who had expelled him from the Socialist Party (Whittam 1995 p.17). Very soon Fascist gangs began beating socialists, intimidating workers, smashing trade union premises and protecting "blackleg" labour. In effect the squads created a "climate of terror", especially in rural Italy (Morgan 1995 p.51, see De Grand 2000). Better armed and organised than the left (and enjoying the passive acquiescence, if not outright support, of the local police and judiciary) the Fascists "waged war" against labour organisa-tions (see Schmidt 1973 p.43 and Mussolini 1939 p.75). As Markwick says, "colluding with the coercive arms of the state – the police and the army – *squadrismo* acted as an extra-legal arm of the state unleashed against Socialist Party and union organizations" (Markwick 2009 p.343). It is also worth mentioning that Mussolini realized that only by cynically abandoning its commitment to republicanism could his movement avoid confrontation with the royalist officer corps, and thereby secure its path to power. By the autumn of 1922, as a consequence of Mussolini's unscrupulous pragmatism, the initial, apparently "radical" programme of the Fascists had been drastically revised. In fact Mussolini could afford to dispense with social radicals because their places were being filled by an influx of middle class recruits, who could see the socialist threat receding. "In return for money, arms and transport for his expanding movement, in the knowledge that state authorities would be inclined to help rather than hinder his activities, Mussolini was more than prepared to unleash the *squadristi* against the common enemies of both fascism and capitalism" (Whittam 1995 p.30).

Thus although Mussolini was prone to speak in eulogistic terms about the "power and glory of labour", there existed in Fascism no commitment at all to egalitarian objectives. As Mussolini himself confirmed, "Fascism affirms the irredemable, fruitful and beneficent inequality of men" (cited in Lyttleton 1973 p.49, see Mussolini 1975 p.40). There is no question that for Mussolini, "Darwin weighed more heavily on his mind than Marx had ever done" (Bosworth 2002 p.121) and therefore Mussolini spoke of the need to transcend class divisions not eliminate them. As Mussolini said in November 1921 to the Third Fascist Congress, "'the class struggle is a fairy-tale. Mankind cannot be divided. Instead of being separate the proletariat and the bourgeoisie are integral parts of a single whole...'" (cited in Halperin 1964 p.102). *Il Duce* was perfectly prepared to shed the blood of his former comrades in order to prove it. Therefore, "its programme might seem to have many colours, but the battle which Fascism waged was fundamentally directed to winning the class war against the socialists" (Bosworth 2002 p.153, see Marwick 2009 p.342) and the Fascists were intent on keeping the promises they made about destroying socialism.

When in power Fascism quite simply served as an instrument for the regimentation, rather than the emancipation, of labour. The Charter of Labour (*Carta del Lavoro*) of 27 April 1927, which was hailed by the regime as the greatest social document in history and the highest form of industrial self-management, simply ratified a few minimal workers' rights (some of which had actually pre-dated the war) such as free Sundays, extra pay for night-work and so on (see Mack Smith 1985 p.138, Halperin 1964 Document No.14 p.129). On the other hand independent trades unions were "made Fascist", strikes were made illegal, the eight-hour day was ended, and factory committees abolished. The statutory prohibition of lock-outs by employers was emblematic of a number of superficial palliatives offered to workers (how likely is a lock-out if strikes are outlawed?). Real wages for workers fell, for example Renton records a reduction in pay between 1927-32 of 50% (Renton 1999 p.32, see Pearse 2002 p.70-71). Although economic figures were systematically distorted by the Fascist regime it is nevertheless clear that living standards declined for most industrial workers, whilst in the countryside there existed a state of exploitative, semi-feudal serfdom. The promised re-distribution of the land did not materialise, and impoverished peasants were forbidden to move to the cities to look for (better-paid) work (see Mack Smith 1985 p.142). Fascism, despite the rhetoric of ruralisation, impinged only slightly on parochial peasant lives that were defined by the persistence of disease, endemic poverty, and the enduring power of landlords. Organisations such as *Dopolavoro*, the leisure institute, set up on 1 May 1925 provided some social activities, such as sports and subsidized holidays for workers, but was far more valuable to the Fascists as a means of disseminating pro-government propaganda (as noted earlier).

Although Mussolini continually protested that his government did more for the worker than any other, as Mack Smith says "he reiterated this so frequently as to suggest that he knew it was a debatable point" (Mack Smith 1985 p.183). Thus, "Mussolini and the Fascists had made the reactionaries their main allies and the Reds their main rivals. But in making this alliance Mussolini wittingly, and many other Fascists unwittingly, had brought about the counter-revolution desired by the big landowners and businessmen, along with the monarchy, the military and some of the higher civil servants…(and)…the church also preferred Mussolini" (Tannenbaum 1972 p.54). In the scheme of priorities outlined by the Fascist regime the plight of ordinary people hardly registered, and the response to genuine hardship barely moved beyond the regurgitation of turgid platitudes.

It has however been argued that Mussolini's so-called Salo Republic captured more successfully the radical essence of Italian Fascism. Although the regime was born out of adversity in 1943, after the *Duce* had been rescued from *Gran Sasso* by German commandos and installed in the northern territory, some observers have viewed the episode as an attempt to recapture certain socialist ideals which had never really been abandoned (see the Salo Manifesto of November 1943 in Gregor 1969 Appendix B p.387, Schnapp 2000 p.198). For example Thurlow has argued without qualification that Salo "represented Mussolini's return to his revolutionary socialist policy which he advocated prior to 1915", and Gregor refers to an "emphatic socialist content" in the newly constituted Fascist Republican programme, whilst Griffiths says it was a return to Fascism's "radical roots" and "guiding principles" (Thurlow 1980 p.20 and Gregor 1969 p.286; Griffiths 2005 p.38 and p.141, see p.143). Similarly Eatwell concurs, claiming that Salo revealed "a clear ideological desire to return to radical roots" (Eatwell 1996b p.316). Hence the Salo republic has been portrayed by some as a period of socialist redemption, a radical renaissance reflecting the ineliminable essence of Italian Fascism.

In fact the apparent syndicalist social-radicalism of Mussolini's tattered republic was severely compromised by a number of factors: a firm commitment to private property; a virulent anti-semitism (Jews were rounded-up and dispatched to their fate in the east); German over-lordship (Mussolini was referred to dismissively in some quarters as "the *Gauleiter*"); and the extensive use of violence by officially sanctioned death-squads (see Mack Smith 1985 chapter 17, De Grand 2000 chapter 9). The regime was also clearly corrupt and incompetent and "lurched along the edge not so much of social revolution as of anarchy" (Bosworth 2002 p.23). Mussolini might well have wanted revenge against the bourgeoisie and monarchy that had betrayed him, but to refer to the policies pursued in this temporary and artificial little quasi-statelet as somehow "socialist" is highly implausible. Indeed Mussolini's social radicalism was probably motivated by the necessity of appealing to the industrial workers of the North where the regime was based, rather than a real attempt to redeem himself and fulfill long-suppressed socialist ideals. As Blinkhorn says, "if in theory the Social Republic embodied a return to social 'leftism', in reality it demonstrated nothing more than fascism's utter subjection to Nazi Germany" (Blinkhorn 1994 p.52). Del Boca and Giovana are undoubtedly closer to the truth when they argue that, "he (Mussolini) knew that it was mere propaganda, a verbal subterfuge, an expedient to make a struggle for survival seem more noble" (Del Boca and Giovana 1970 p.75). Thus, as Schmidt noted (as early as 1939), it was characteristic of Italian Fascism in practice to reject socialism: Fascism embodied "a virulent and selfish hatred of proletarian socialism, a determination to punish the workers and reduce them to their old and 'proper' status of docile servants" (Schmidt 1973 p.42) [26].

Consequently fascists in Italy and Germany, despite some rhetorical ambiguity and the existence of certain vague collectivist notions, did not believe in, nor did they seek in any meaningful or substantive sense, socialism or radical social change. As Renton says, "fascism won popularity through its revolutionary promises, but fascism in power acted in a reactionary way. Indeed the results of fascism have never been in any meaningful sense revolutionary" (Renton 1999 p.106) [27]. The fascist leadership in effect betrayed those petit-bourgeois elements on the fringes of the movements who had urged a more radical course, and fascism in practice was a force of social reaction, not emancipation, as both the leaders were well aware [28]. Indeed, as Barrington Moore quite correctly pointed out, "the fascist outlook stressed not only the inevitability of hierarchy, discipline and obedience, but also posited that they were values in their own right. Romantic conceptions of comradeship qualify this outlook but slightly; it is comradeship in submission" (Barrington Moore 1966 p.447). Both National Socialism and National Fascism "served the destruction of the labour movement and of democracy... it did not provide a systematic critique of existing society nor a guide to radical reform of the social structure" (Kitchen 1982 p.28). Thus "only a fool would have been deceived by these trappings of socialism...Fascism and Nazism are implacably opposed to socialism and communism and always have been" (Wilkinson 1981 p.17 and p.18, see Trotsky 1971, and Poulantzas 1974 p.166-7 and p.290).

Obviously the anti-communism and anti-socialism of the fascists is intimately connected to their relationship with capital, and here again we discover a certain theoretical ambivalence and rhetorical ambiguity, which is not reflected in practice. Fascism was supposed to transform and transcend capitalism in theory - in practice it did absolutely nothing of the kind. Fascist economics was, in effect, an inconsistent mixture of pragmatism and doctrine, synthesized in a system of managed capitalism (see Woodley 2010 p.141). In fact it was in the sphere of economic policy that fascists conceded most to the forces of capitalist conservatism, and in time Italian and German business circles adapted well to their respective regimes - they certainly had far more success in securing overall objectives than the fascist "radicals" (see Paxton 2005 p.145-46).

However, there can be little doubt that the radical sounding anti-capitalist rhetoric of the fascists did attract significant support in the 1920s and 1930s, especially from the middle classes who had been proletarianized by severe capitalist economic crises but who nevertheless could not bring themselves to endorse the socialism of organised labour. In Germany the likes of the Strasser brothers, and especially Gottfried Feder, persistently attacked the capitalist system, particularly that section of it which they deemed parasitical, in effect that class of finance capitalists who, unlike the productive industrial entrepreneurs, merely used interest rates as a means to accumulate unearned wealth. Indeed there is certainly some evidence to suggest that the vehemence of the anti-capitalist rhetoric in some quarters alarmed elements of the property owning classes (see Winkler 1979 p.147). Paragraph 17 of the original Nazi programme, for instance, made reference to the possible expropriation of private property for community purposes, which caused some considerable consternation amongst the bourgeoisie, to such an extent that Hitler felt compelled to assuage the party's wealthy benefactors. As Hilberg explains, the provision "was authoritatively interpreted by Hitler to mean that only Jewish property was involved" (Hilberg 1985 Volume One p.32, see later). Hitler's intervention on this issue belied the fact that his actual knowledge of economics was meager, indeed "Hitler's own understanding of economic technicalities was not more than could be gleaned from a cursory reading of the business sections of the right-wing press" (Stone 1992 p.58). Yet, as Weber explains with reference to the persistence of anti--capitalist verbiage, "the electorate had seemed to like these ideas but big business did not ... such concepts were therefore soon abandoned" (Weber 1964 p.83-4). Despite the bombastic discourse (and the disproportionately small section of the movement which took it seriously) Hitler and the NSDAP had absolutely no intention at all of breaking the laws of capitalist accumulation or of superceding private ownership of the means of production.

Of course Hitler's reluctance to take seriously the anti-capitalist elements in his own party is connected to the fact that the Nazis relied to some extent on the commercial backing of certain capitalist elements prior to the assumption of power in 1933. For example in the early formative days of the movement in southern Germany Dietrich Eckart opened doors to the local bourgeoisie, and the wealthy Bechstein family, along with the Bavarian Confederation of Industry, provided much needed financial support (see Kershaw 2009 p.95) [29]. As early as 1922 Hitler had been invited to speak at the prestigious National Club, whilst the *Herrenklub*, the Merchants' Guild, and the League of Bavarian Industrialists followed soon after (Gluckstein 1999 p.32). In the early years significant contacts were also made with Bavarian industrialist Dr. Emil Gansser and the so-called "Baltic Baron" Max Erwin Scheubner-Richter. Indeed Jeremy Noakes has noted the success of the Nazis in securing social approval and political legitimacy via their progressive integration into the circles of "high society" (see Noakes 1996). The German nobility and female members of the upper middle class appear to have been particularly susceptible to the brash charms of the Nazi leader and his radical rhetoric of national renewal. Members of the aristocracy, like Duke Eduard of Saxe-Coburg and Prince August-Wilhelm of Prussia, along with a string of lesser nobles, joined the Nazi party, whilst Frau Erna Hanfstangl, a member of the famous art publishing family, sheltered Hitler after the abortive putsch in 1923. Meanwhile Frau Bechstein, heir to the prestigious piano manufacturing franchise, not only loaned the Nazi party jewellery for collateral, she gave Hitler advice on social etiquette! Bourgeois elites in Germany therefore became increasingly attracted by the flattering blandishments of the vulgar bohemian demagogue. After 1926, as Hitler established ascendancy over the Strasserites, the likes of Thyssen, Kirdorf, Bruckmann, Von Stauss, Grauert, Poensgen, Brandi, Tengelmann, Springorum, Vogler, Hugenberg, Von Borsig and other prominent members of the business community began to patronize Hitler's political ambitions (see Gluckstein 1999 p.54). Thyssen, who openly admitted to giving Hitler over one million marks, was instrumental in winning over sections of the bourgeoisie to the Nazi cause, as he admitted: "'I did in fact bring about the connections between Hitler and the entire body of Rhenish-Westphalian industrialists...in consequence of this a number of large contributions flowed from the resources of heavy industry to the treasuries of the National Socialist Party'" (cited in Sewell 1988 p.64; see Gluckstein 1999 p.54). The ultimate aim of such industrial elites was, of course, to secure popular support for pro-business policies and bind Hitler more closely to the conservative establishment, whilst Hitler, for his part, capitalized on the pessimistic view that *"so kann es nicht weitergehen"* (things can't go on like this) which pervaded the upper echelons of German society. The attitude of Paul Reusch, leader of *Ruhrlade*, a secret organization consisting of 12 top industrialists, is indicative: "'after a productive two hour talk with Hitler yesterday...I find myself in complete sympathy with the National Socialists, though they are a bit tactless'" (cited in Gluckstein 1999 p.56).

In fact Hitler did his utmost to allay any capitalist fears, and he never missed an opportunity to impress upon the business community how he would guarantee private property and business activity. Hitler emphasized repeatedly how much he admired the "captains" of industry (see Nichols 1981 p.78). Indeed Hitler was totally committed to private ownership of property and free enterprise, and he confirmed unambiguously to party colleagues that, "I absolutely insist on protecting private property", adding that he believed the drive for profit and capital accumulation were perfectly "natural" (Hitler 1973 p.363). As Hitler allegedly commented to Rauschning, any attempt to abolish private economic interests was as ridiculous as attempting to abolish sexual intercourse by decree (see Rauschning 1939 p.187) [30]. Hitler therefore offered himself as a personal guarantor of private enterprise and big business profitability. If there was any "anti-bourgeois" reference at all in Hitler's rhetoric it was not a question of criticizing that class as "exploiters" but simply as a "worn-out" group that lacked the courage, commitment, vitality and dynamism to defend their own (and German) interests (see Mosse 1999 p.26). The bourgeoisie, according to Hitler, was incapable of winning over the masses for its political project of defending their business interests, and in order to do that it required a "'fundamentally new world view'" (Hitler cited in Bytwerk 2008 p.20).

As a consequence Hitler tried anxiously to legitimize his movement in the eyes of Germany's business elites. His speech on 27 January 1932 to assembled industrialists at Dusseldorf is a classic of its kind (cited in Baynes 1969 p.777, see also Bullock 1962 p.196): he stressed the importance of business life in society; the value of personality and creative individuality (and thus the impracticality of equality and bourgeois democracy); he pointed out that competition and struggle had always been, and would continue to be, the motor of history; he maintained that private property was one of nature's "laws" and therefore should not, and could not, be eliminated; and concluded that the National Socialists waged war on Marxism. Not surprisingly the response from the audience was positive and large contributions followed (Bullock 1962 p.199). The same points were made immediately after Hitler's acquisition of power when, on 20 February 1933, those businessmen who assembled at Goering's ostentatious villa were informed that the principles of commerce and leadership would be respected. No questions were taken at the meeting, but it was made clear (by Goering after Hitler had left) that appropriate financial contributions were expected (Tooze 2007 p.99-100). Over the next three weeks donations were received from seventeen different business organizations, the largest coming from IG Farben, Deutsche Bank and the mining industry (ranging from 200,000-400,000 Reichsmarks). The impact on Nazi finances was significant, as Tooze says "the meeting of 20 February and its aftermath are the most notorious instances of the willingness of German big business to assist Hitler in establishing his dictatorial regime. The evidence cannot be dodged" (Tooze 2007 p.101). Hitler promised to put an end to democracy, and for that business was prepared to provide a considerable downpayment, and as a consequence it can be justifiably asserted that Krupp and the other industrialists were "willing partners" in the destruction of political pluralism in Germany (see Tooze 2007 p.101).

Some analysts have been (or remain) unconvinced on this point. For example, historian Henry A. Turner (1985) has sought to qualify Hitler's favourable predisposition toward capital by stressing that big business only played a marginal role in the NSDAP's actual rise to power – party funds were generated internally through rank-and-file members, or came from smaller firms of limited means, rather than from external, wealthy big-business benefactors. As Turner says, "the Nazis themselves, not Germany's capitalists, provided the decisive financing for Hitler's rise to power" (Turner 1985 p.347). Turner argues that the historical evidence (gleaned through company archives) confirms that the captains of industry, despite some grave reservations about the Weimar Republic and democratic government, merely dabbled in politics, were disconcerted by Hitler's plebian, anti-semitic proclivities, and were seriously alarmed by his party's ambivalent rhetoric and idiosyncratic policy preferences regarding economic matters. In short Turner maintains that big business has been wrongly blamed for somehow creating the Nazi menace. Indeed it may be true that, as Turner, Hayes and others have pointed out (see Turner 1985, Hayes 1987), most capitalists like I.G. Farben's Carl Duisberg, or Chairman of the *Vereinigung der Deutschen Arbeitgeberverbande* Ernst von Borsig, preferred to "invest" in Hugenberg's Nationalist Party (DNVP). It may also be a fact that many capitalists hedged their political bets, or perhaps provided funds at a level far too insignificant to meet the Nazi's resource requirements. Certainly, for every magnate who so spectacularly succumbed to the ideological lure of Nazism before they achieved power there were doubtless many others who were, especially in the years before the political breakthough in 1933, more cautious or circumspect. For every Emil Kirdorf or Fritz Thyssen there was a Paul Reusch or Jakob Wilhelm Reichert, both of whom expressed clear reservations about the Nazis.

However, we must not lose sight of the crucial fact that the money that was actually raised for Hitler's movement through business contacts (for example in the important early days in Bavaria) and, more crucially, Hitler's ideological perspective regarding the role of capital, meant that the Nazis were hardly likely in practical terms to do anything to precipitate a break with their actual (or potential) benefactors once they achieved power. The barons of industry may indeed have been diversifying their political insurance in the period before 1933, but this does not invalidate the argument that capitalist backing was critical to the Nazis, irrespective of whether the money provided in the preliminary phase secured them that power in the first place. Whilst Turner failed to find any convincing evidence that big business brought Hitler to power, he essentially ignores the question of who supported him afterwards and, crucially, who benefitted subsequently, where the evidence is far less contentious (we shall have cause to take issue with Turner again). The plain fact is that the actual assumption of full executive governmental authority was enough to dispel any lingering reservations in the business community. The leaders of big business thereafter went from "sleeping partners" to active accomplices in support of the Nazi regime (see Barkai 1990).

Given that Nazi ideology was not antagonistic to capitalist priorities and did not seek or require a re-evaluation of economic organization, Hitler's government in practice clearly reflected this political predisposition. When Hitler was "invited" into office by President Hindenburg it was "to establish a stable right-wing authoritarian dictatorship, upholding the aims of the army, the agrarian Junkers and big business" (McDonough 1999 p.17). It is always worth remembering that the highest percentage of the vote recorded by the Nazis before 1933 was 37.4% in July 1932. In November 1932 the Nazis lost 2 million votes in the Reichstag elections, their share of the vote falling from 37% to 33%, so electorally the Nazis, despite being the largest party in the Reichstag, never won an overall majority of the vote. Indeed the Nazis were actually losing ground electorally when the reactionary conservative elites sought a compromise with Hitler (Peukert 1987 p.27). Hitler was effectively offered power by the German establishment, which included not only members of the military and agrarian elites, but key elements in big business. Under the Weimar system employers had been obliged to recognize unions, adhere to legally binding wage agreements and defer to state arbitration during industrial disputes, hence "the net result was that most of industry wanted to get rid of the Weimar system" (Geary 1994 p.32). Hjalmar Schacht, former head of the *Reichsbank*, was one of a number of financiers and industrialists who, fearful of the increasing electoral threat of the Communists, signed a petition to President Hindenburg asking him to appoint Hitler as Chancellor – in essence the likes of Krupp, Thyssen, Bosch, and Siemens lobbied Hindenburg and Papen on Hitler's behalf (Stone 1992 p.54). Hence it was a cabal of reactionary politicians, backed by certain sectors of the business community, which accommodated the Nazis after the high tide of Nazi electoral success had begun to subside (Rees 2005 p.42). It is therefore fair to conclude that Hitler did not storm the ramparts of the pre-existing regime, the drawbridge was actually lowered by those German elites in industry, the bureaucracy and the army, who wielded power and opted for Hitler because they thought he could be used to serve their interests. This close collaboration was set to continue.

In practical terms therefore it was Franz von Papen, with his myopic political manoeuvring, who facilitated the acquisition of power for Hitler in January 1933. As Hans Mommsen explains: "the complex and opaque processes which led to the formation of Hitler's cabinet give the appearance of a palace coup, but they occurred within a broader social context. They were made possible through the vigorously forced elimination of democratic parliamentarianism by the majority of the bourgeois parties and their related asscociations" (cited in Gregor 2000 p.98). After the consolidation of power via the key election of March 1933 the business community began to pour money into the NSDAP (see Noakes and Pridham 1974 p.21 and Taylor 1985 p.122-3). Hitler's first act as German Chancellor was to call another election in order to break up the coalition, and big business donated 3 million marks to the campaign (McDonough 1999 p.24). Clearly, for some sections of the German bourgeoisie it really was of little consequence who ruled politically as long as economic "stability" was ensured - to quote one industrialist, "'business is not in the least bit concerned whether it is ruled by a tin helmet or a top hat'" (cited in Kitchen 1995 p.42).

Upon achieving power, and having eliminated or marginalized the minority of anti-capitalists, the true nature of Hitler's relationship with large-scale capital became apparent, and it is evident that "on sum, relations between the traditional elites and the Nazi regime were close and largely amicable" (Burleigh and Wipperman 1991 p.271). Hitler aimed to free German firms to manage their own affairs and his regime willingly capitulated to the requirements of large-scale industrial capitalism. Nazi *anti*-socialism secured for its wealthy backers a compliant and demoralised workforce. Naturally, as a consequence of the Nazi's pro-business policy orientation many capitalists did extremely well under the Third Reich. That the prevailing industrial and commercial economic structure was not about to be seriously challenged is illustrated by the fact that the Economic Advisory Council was almost exclusively drawn from the upper echelons of banking and heavy industry. The fate of the radical Nazi Gottfried Feder, who had urged the abolition of interest slavery, is particularly instructive since he was forced to work under Dr. Kurt Schmitt, an insurance magnate who had spent his life lending money and collecting interest. Indeed, when President of the Reichsbank Hjalmar Schacht took over the Ministry of Economics, Feder was unceremoniously dismissed (Shirer 1985 p.261, see Taylor 1985 p.160).

Krupp became *"Fuhrer"* of the Association of German Industrialists (*Reichstand der Deutsches Industrie*) whilst the likes of Carl Krauch of I.G. Farben oscillated between the boardroom and government agencies. Private firms were encouraged to organize into producer cartels by the Law for the Organic Construction of the German Economy (27 February 1934) and access to credit was expanded by the creation of the *Metal-lurgischen-Forschungs GmbH (Mefo)* bond scheme set up by the government and used by industry and banking as a source of collateral to secure investment. In effect this shadowy financial technique had been underwritten by the likes of Krupp, Siemens and Deutsche Industrie Werke, who were certain to benefit, and the captains of industry presided over a period of unprecedented expansion for German capital. Further monopolisation of industry was facilitated by the Stocks and Shares Law of 1937 and the regime bestowed upon the large landowners tax exemptions, subsidies for land development, and a moratorium on all debts (see Guerin 1973 p.265). In 1933 40% of German production was under monopoly control but by 1937 monopolies controlled over 70% of all production (McDonough 1999 p.35). "The combination of rising domestic  demand, an end to foreign compensation, rising prices and relatively static wages created a context in which it was hard not to make healthy profits. Indeed, by 1934 the bonuses being paid to the boards of some firms were so spectacular that they were causing acute embarrassment to Hitler's government" (Tooze 2007 p.108).

Of course this favourable policy predisposition created an economic context which resulted in colossal profits for large private companies and a financial bonanza for entrepreneurs, with profits increasing 433% in the first three years of Nazi rule (see Gluckstein 1999 p.155). Profits from all industrial and commercial enterprises in fact rose a massive 126% (from 6.6 billion to 15 billion marks) between 1933 and 1938 (Poulantzas 1974 p.191-2, see Mandel's Introduction to Trotsky 1971). The profits of IG Farben, to take a specific example, rose from 74m Reichsmarks in 1933 to 240m in 1939 (Renton 1999 p.39). Similar financial profiles existed for AEG, Krupp, Daimler Benz, BMW, Allianz and even Coca-Cola (which was suitably disassociated from its American roots). Foreign companies also benefitted from the Nazi economic boom for businesses, including BP, Dunlop, ITT, Standard Oil, General Motors and also Ford which has been noted for its "extremely pro-Nazi management" in Cologne (Tooze 2007 p.133). Moreover, managers of major industrial companies saw their salaried income increase by 50% between 1933-1939, much higher than any other group in German society (McDonough 1999 p.35). Even after the appointment of Goering to oversee the introduction of the Four Year Plan in 1936 it signified not so much a move toward more extensive economic intervention and planning, but rather denoted a change in the emphasis and tempo of policy in deference toward particular capitalist groups such as the large chemical and electrical conglomerates. Hence any state involvement in the economy was often in accordance with the requirements of the most prominent private companies, and even state-run enterprises imitated the methods, and reflected the priorities, of the private sector. For example state owned plants like the Hermann Goering Steelworks were organized along classical capitalist lines and raised capital by selling shares in the free market (see Williamson 1998 p.36). Even when Goering himself assumed control of the Four Year Plan after 1938 (via his functionary Walter Funk), after which industry became geared more explicitly toward the *Wehrwirtschaft* (war economy) and the fulfillment of Nazi war aims, private industry still flourished. Goering was apt to address industrialists in apocalyptic tones about the consequences of failure, but that he relied upon them for the success of his Nazi vision of military conquest cannot be denied, as he commented "'if we win, then business will be sufficiently compensated'" (Goering cited in Tooze 2007 p.224). Certain businesses, like IG Farben, bought into the Nazi vision in a massive way, a commitment which was symbolised in the appointment of Carl Krauch as head of research and development in the raw materials office of the Four Year Plan. Krauch lobbied hard to ensure that the leadership of all chemical programmes lay in the hands of private industry, not the military, which afforded IG Farben "an absolutely unique place in the Third Reich" (Tooze 2007 p.230, see p.227-28).

Economics in Nazi Germany might have become increasingly subjected to inconsistent political interference, but private ownership was still the norm, and the profit motive remained the ultimate entrepreneurial catalyst for industrial production. As Tooze points out "it suited German business leaders only too well to assist Fritz Todt in mixing the ugly cocktail of Nazi leadership doctrine (*Fuehrertum*) and the self-serving rhetoric of entrepreneurial dynamism (*Unternehmertum*) that was soon to become the guiding ideology of the German war economy" (Tooze 2007 p.352-53). Clearly, Hitler's notion of a *Wehrwirtschaft* military-economy suited the over-riding priorities of those who owned and/or controlled the means of production, although Evans is correct to have identified some increasing unease within the business community concerning the constraints imposed on free trade by the focus on war production (Evans 2006 p.351). Only in the area of agricultural production could it be argued that the fundamental "laws" of the free market were genuinely regulated and constrained via price and production control, in deference to the requirements of the *Reichsnaehrstand* (RNS) and the Reich Ministry of Food and Agriculture (see Tooze 2007 Chapter 6). Nevertheless, the initial alliance formed between Nazi ideologues and established economic elites in industry circles, which was sustained with considerable dexterity by Albert Speer's *Zentral Planung* during the war, remained essentially intact until the very end of the conflict (see Tooze 2007 Chapter 17). Capitalism was certainly being directed, primarily for military purposes, but private industry was still in the driving seat in terms of the organization of production. Significantly, the new economic supremo Speer, in stressing the "self-responsibility" and "private initiative" of industry in Germany's life-or-death struggle with the planned economic leviathan of Stalin's Russia, was clearly identifying a contest between two competing economic systems – a contest which the Nazi's only lost due to the extraordinary effort of the Red Army and the Soviet Union (see Tooze 2007 p.588-59).

As Mandel has maintained, "whether Krupp or Thyssen looked upon this or that point of Hitler's rule with enthusiasm, reservation, or antipathy is not essential...what is essential is private property and the possibility of accumulating capital and realising surplus value. In this respect the statistics speak unambiguously..." (Mandel in Trotsky 1971 p.13 and p.16). Even if we do not accept Mandel's subsequent claim that all interests were brutally subordinated to the requirements of the big companies, it is quite clear that capitalists did extremely well under Nazi rule. The idea that the German economy under Nazism was somehow meticulously "planned" or that the free market system was somehow "destroyed" is clearly erroneous because it was not until 1943 (well into the war) that production of consumer goods was curtailed, so in a sense it might be argued that the British war-economy was "planned" earlier and to a greater degree (Hildebrand 1985 p.64; see Pearse 2002 p.73). As Evans argues, "despite this increase in state intervention, as Nazi economic spokesmen repeatedly insisted, Germany was to remain a free market economy, in which the state provided leadership and set the primary goals" (Evans 2006 p.351). Clearly Overy's contention that Nazi Germany was a "command economy" and that Hitler, as "an enemy of free market economics", rejected economic liberalism, is seriously overdrawn (Overy 1994 p.17 and p.1). Even Avram Barkai, an analyst evidently anxious to acknowledge the credentials of "Nazi economics" as "unique" and "distinctive", accepted that the Nazi economy was "capitalistic, though controlled and guided from above" (Barkai 1990 p.vii and p.248). Consequently it would be reasonable to conclude that "although the scope of state intervention increased markedly there was no major structural change in the German economy under the new regime" (Stackelberg 1999 p.120).

It soon became clear that the only practical anti-capitalist measures taken by the regime would be those carried out in line with Hitler's racial policy of economic Aryanization, directed primarily against the Jews. In fact, giant concerns like Mannesmann, Krupp, Thysen, Flick and IG Farben, and leading banks "were the major beneficiaries, while a variety of business consortia, corrupt party functionaries, and untold numbers of small commercial enterprises grabbed what they could" (Kershaw 2009 p.451; Evans p.378). As businesses were progressively "Ayranised" via government dictat, prominent German firms were particularly keen to participate in the plunder, and the major banks like Deutsche and Dresdner competed fiercely for the spoils (see Tooze 2007 p.276). As Barkai confirms, "as a rule militant Nazis, middle class businessmen and 'respectable' well-groomed industrial tycoons had no moral inhibitions against taking advantage of the desolate position in which Jewish proprietors found themselves" (Barkai 1996 p.39). By 1937 "virtually every large company in Germany was joining in the division of the spoils" (Evans 2006 p.396) and private enterprises benefitted dramatically from the material dispossession of the Jewish community.

Even the SS, the institutional essence of Nazism, could count on the patronage of particular enterprises, eager to formalize their contact with Himmler, a paragon of the regime. Indeed, Himmler raised money by distributing "honorary ranks and titles" to entrepreneurs desperate to exploit Nazi networks, and the money flowed in from businesses, bankers and industrialists. For example the banker Kurt von Schroder set up a special account to channel funds into the hands of the Reichsfuhrer SS (Gluckstein 1999 p.156) whilst the so-called "Friends of the Reich Leader SS" included men like the IG Farben Director Heinrich Butefisch, and representatives from companies like Siemens-Schuckert, the Deutsche Bank, Rheinmetall-Borsig and the Hamburg-America Shipping Line (see Evans 2006 p.51). Actually the SS, its members befittingly attired by Hugo Boss, developed its very own economic empire under the auspices of its Business Administration Main Office (*Wirtschaftverwaltungshauptamt, WVHA*). This enterprise involved around 150 firms engaged in a range of spheres such as mining, foodstuffs, textiles and armaments, which were all combined together and organized via a single trust – the *Deutsche Wirtschaftsbetriebe GmbH* (see Allen 2002). "With the exception of a small number of engineers, these enterprises were manned by forced labor and inmates of concentration camps" (Barkai 1990 p.240) a fact which caused little concern to the capitalists involved. Admittedly the SS zealots themselves were motivated more by a "productivist" racial ideology than the profit motive per se, but they were nevertheless "slave-labor moguls" (Allen 2002 p.5). Indeed the ideologues in the SS, whose "successful" management methodology was constructed on the technocratic imposition of terror, were eager to export their aggressive tactics to private industry, and many enterprises enthusiastically emulated their model (Allen 2002 p.225). It certainly would not have been unusual to see factories filled with semi-starving workers since food was rationed as an "incentive" to work, whilst some facilities were actually littered with corpses as recalcitrant workers were left hanging from the rafters as a warning to others (see Tooze 2007 p.623). "So long as the SS supervisors carried out regular inspections, weeded out those workers whose productivity had fallen below acceptable levels and replaced them with fresh inmates, the employer had little to complain about…clearly ways were found to reconcile the murderous ideological impulses of the regime with a rational system of exploitation that was functional from the point of view of the individual employer, if not the war economy as a whole" (Tooze 2007 p.533 and p.536).

German expansion across Europe was also accompanied by a clamouring of private industry eager to make the most of new opportunities. As Mason points out, "German industrialists certainly took advantage of the victories of the Wehrmacht to eliminate or take over foreign competitors and to extend the interests of their firms into France and Eastern Europe; they sometimes took the initiative in submitting takeover plans to the government" (Mason 1996 p.70). Indeed "many industrialists colluded with the racially-motivated imperialist goals of the Nazis' war effort since arms production meant vast state-guaranteed profits, while the regime's military expansionism promised a considerably enhanced sphere of economic activity and influence" (Herbert 1996 p.47-48). For instance, Krupps procured Dutch shipyards, Belgian metalworks, and French machine-tool factories in the west, Yugoslav chromium deposits and Greek nickel mines in the south. Meanwhile, foreign labour was exploited mercilessly, especially *Ostarbeiter* (Eastern workers), as indicated by Goering's comment that, "'the place of the German skilled workmen is in the armaments industry. Shovelling dirt and quarrying stones are not their job – that's what the Russian is for...the Russians can arrange their own food (cats, horses etc)'" (cited in Herbert 1995 p.222-23). Even if the dynamic, driving force behind this outcome was racial rather than economic (see later), the coercive deployment of slave labour benefitted business and sustained the profits of capitalist companies such as Krupps, Flick, A.E.G., Siemens, Porsche and others. In the east industry could be developed using a slave labour which was a welcome by-product of imperialist expansion and anti-semitism. One company, the German Excavation and Quarrying Company Limited, established brickworks in the immediate vicinity of concentration camps specifically to exploit slave labour which was, in effect, supplied by the Gestapo. The story was the same elsewhere: whether it was in the coal mines near Jawiszowice or Furstengrube, the copper mines near Bor, or the Portland Cement factory in Goleszow; whether it was in the Bata Shoe factory near Chelmek, or the Heinkel aircraft factory near Budzyn; whether in the Skarzysko-Kamienna ammunition factory, or the synthetic rubber, oil and petrol plants at Blechhammer, Monowitz and Schwarzheide - the reality was always the deadly exploitation of human beings for the benefit of big private companies and bosses. Meanwhile "entrepreneurs" like Fritz Scultz and Walter Toebbens had specifically set up industrial installations in the Warsaw ghetto because they knew that slavery was good for business. Here Oscar Schindler was the iconic exception that simply proved the rule. Moreover, by 1944 there were more than seven million foreign, mostly Slavic workers in Germany who were mercilessly exploited as cheap commodities to be worked unremittingly until they were completely exhausted or expired (Mazower 2009 p.294).

Entrepreneurs were therefore ruthlessly cold blooded, indeed barbaric, in their utilisation of basic business principles and commercial calculations, as applied to a subservient work-force which meant absolutely nothing to them beyond profit margins and a balance sheet. Siemens and AEG-Telefunken for example, deployed prison labour from the camps in, among other places, Bobrek, Ravensbruck, Neustadt, Ebensee and Jungbuch. Ravensbruek provided female workers to Siemens, Mauthausen had a productive relationship with Steyr Daimler Puch, Sachsenhausen serviced Daimler-Benz and Dachau was "in business" with BMW (see Tooze 2007 p.532). In many ways the paradigm for state-business collaboration in this regard was the construction of the Buna Works of IG Farben in Auschwitz. The industrial colossus IG Farben was "a bureaucratic empire and a major factor in the destructive machine" (Hilberg 1985 Volume Three p.922). This industrial camp was designed to produce synthetic rubber, and was a facility which increased company profits from 363 million to 822 million marks between 1939-43 (Gluckstein 1999 p.168). Approximately 25,000 forced labourers died at the plant and it was an "open secret" among IG Farben management that inmates who were no longer "fit to work" were killed by poison gas (Frei 2005 p.159). German firms, such as water-supply specialists Wodak, and civil engineers Kluge, profited from the construction of Auschwitz, as did many other companies as the camp was enlarged and its operations expanded (Frei 2005 p.153). The SS even sold some of its labour force to private enterprises (see ABSM 1995 p.36-37 note No.26), for example a number of prisoners from the camp were "sold" to Bayer, a subsidiary of IG Farben, as guinea-pigs for the testing of new drugs (see Rees 2005a p.232). Eventually there were 28 sub-camps at Auschwitz operating close to private industrial facilities throughout Upper Silesia, and it is estimated that they generated around 30 million marks of pure profit for the Nazi regime (Rees 2005a p.222). As Gregor says, "the policy of genocide did not stand in conflict with that of economic exploitation, but rather complemented and reinforced it" (Gregor 2005 p.5).

It is also interesting to note that the unrestrained impulse of creative free enterprise unleashed by the Nazi regime led private firms to seek out other avenues in order to make profits. For example Shirer actually noted lively competition amongst entrepreneurs in the death and disposal business: the Saurer works in Austria supplied the trucks used as gas-vans in the east, whilst German companies IG Farben, Tesch & Stabenow and J.A. Topf & Sons of Efurt supplied Zyklon B and provided the gas ovens used for mass extermination. Meanwhile, gold teeth were extracted from corpses, melted down into ingots and deposited in banks, whilst human hair from victims was used in thread and in the manufacture of mattresses and rope - among the clients who paid 50 pfennings a kilo were the Bremer Wollkammerei wool factory and the Alex Zink felt factory at Roth (Steinbacher 2005 p.103, see ABSM 1995). Human ash was used for building roads and insulating buildings, and the SS sold human bone-meal to a fertilizer company in Strzemieszyce (Steinbacher 2005 p.103) whilst Jewish tombstones were sold to grateful stonemasons (Gilbert 1987 p.289). Indeed one enterprising firm from Danzig even invented and constructed an electric tank for making soap out of human fat! (see Shirer 1985 p.971).

Even H.A. Turner, who has expended some considerable intellectual energy in an effort to exonerate big business from culpability in bringing Hitler to power, says "businessmen experienced little difficulty in adapting to a regime that, even though it gave them no voice in its decisions, held labor in check and, on the whole, respected private property. They took their profits, paid the financial tribute extorted from them by the new rulers, and asked no questions" (Turner 1985 p.338). Turner says that the full story of how big business fared under the regime has yet to be told and that analysis of the role of capitalists has been characterized by narrow anti-capitalist political bias and personal condescension (Turner

1985 p.339 and p.350-51). However, Turner's accusation is feeble and disingenuous. There is no doubt that the basic framework of capitalism (production for profit, private property, vast inequality of wealth etc.) remained fundamentally unchanged. Indeed the social power of capital was guaranteed by the Nazis and the traditional social elites were, unquestionably, the primary beneficiaries of fascism (see Guerin 1973 p.284 and Sole-Tura 1968 p.49). As Kershaw points out, "German industry's direct implication in the Nazi plunder, exploitation, destruction and mass murder in the occupied territories continued to the end. Whereas certain groups within the armed forces and the old aristocracy underwent a development from initial reserve to outright antipathy...industrial leaders were notably missing from resistance circles... the divorce between the radical nihilism of the Nazi bloc and the material interests of German industry only became total during the last phase of the war, in the wild lashings of the regime in its death throes" (Kershaw 1985 p.58-9, see Wilkinson 1981 p.52). Practically every major private enterprise was implicated in the Nazi plunder of Europe, and leading industrialists were conspicuously absent from the conspiracies to depose Hitler, even as he stumbled, in paroxysms of rage, toward his nihilistic "Nero Order".

Quite clearly Nazi ideology was "closely tied in with the provision of a free hand for private industry and eulogization of the entrepreneurial spirit" (Kershaw 1985 p.59, see Hildebrand 1985 p.124), and as Shirer concludes, "a sober study of the statistics ... revealed that the much maligned capitalist, not the worker, benefited most from Nazi policies" (Shirer 1985 p.264). As the *Volkischer Beobachter* succinctly explained, the economic policy of the Nazis "'allows capitalism to function as an engine, but it is National Socialism that changes the gears'" (cited in Aycoberry 1999 p.107). This was one of the few truths to be found in that particular publication. Therefore, "the fact that numerous industrialists not only passively co-operated in the 'Aryanization' of the economy, in the confiscation of firms in occupied territory, in the enslavement of many million people from Eastern Europe and in the employment of concentration camp prisoners, but indeed often took the initiative in these actions, constitutes a damning judgement on the economic system whose essential organizing principle (competition) gave rise to such conduct" (Mason 1996 p.71).

In Italy the record is remarkably similar. The rhetoric of corporatist unity and the "third way" which we identified earlier must be considered in the light of capitalist support for the Fascists prior to 1922, and the subsequent success of big business after Mussolini had taken control of government (see Schmidt 1973 chapter VI). From the summer of 1918 onwards Mussolini developed productive contacts with influential entrepreneurs such as the Perone brothers, Mario and Pio (who ran the Ansaldo industrial complex), whilst the wealthy landowners in the Po Valley provided financial support which undoubtedly gave a powerful stimulus to the anti-socialism of the Fascists. As Sarti says, "business wanted a government willing to pursue policies that were bound to be unpopular but necessary to achieve what they claimed was a wiser allocation of economic resources" (Sarti 1971 p.29) and it was precisely this type of administration that Mussolini promised and provided. Even before coming to power Mussolini began to talk of the need for a "Manchestrian state" which would restrict its economic functions and concentrate on re-establishing social order and discipline (Gregor 1969 p.158). Mussolini, in tones clearly designed to attract the support of wealthy elites, criticized state-run industries and asserted his libertarian economic credentials: "'as far as economics is concerned, we are liberals, because we believe that the national economy cannot usefully be entrusted to collective or governmental and bureaucratic organisations'" (Mussolini cited in Bosworth 2002 p.162). As a consequence of Mussolini abandoning his previous equivocation toward private enterprise, a number of key industrialists, such as Benni, Conti, Olivetti, Agnelli and Pirelli, became much more favourably disposed toward Fascism, despite the fact that some elements of the business elite harboured ongoing reservations about the radical rhetoric of a few Fascist syndicalists (see Sarti 1971 p.29). Mussolini therefore offered appropriate assurances to the business community in private meetings held just prior to the March on Rome (see Sarti 1971 p.37-38). In effect "Mussolini's shrewd tactics assured him the acquiescence of the industrial leaders in his bid for power" (Sarti 1971 p.38) and thereafter "the Fascist movement became the long-sought instrument of bourgeois resurgence" (De Grand 2000 p.32).

From 1922 onwards no-one was in any doubt, least of all Mussolini, that Fascism's interests lay in the development of an amicable and mutually beneficial relationship with Italian industrialists and financiers. As with Hitler, what reservations the capitalists had about Fascism were soon dispelled. At Udine on 20 September 1922 Mussolini said, "'we want to strip the state of all its economic functions. Enough of the state which acts as railway owner, postman, insurance company. Enough of the state which functions at the taxpayers expense...with the police, education, the army, with foreign policy, none can say that the state thus restricted is diminished in stature'" (cited in Rossi/Tasca 1938 p.249). Mussolini was determined to balance the state budget, and in 1923 the Duce declared "'I think that the state must renounce its economic functions, and above all those in the field of public utilities, because in this respect the state is incompetent...the government will accord full freedom to private enterprise and will abandon all intervention in private economy'" (cited in Schmidt 1973 p.52 and p.115). These statements were made in the same year that the merger with the Nationalists took place, which until that point had been the predominant political vehicle for the representation of capitalist interests. The merger was, as Mussolini himself put it in his autobiography, "an act of political sincerity" (Mussolini 1939 p.197). Indeed the pact between Mussolini and the industrialists was formalised in the *Palazzo Chiji* agreement of December 1923 and the *Palazzo Vidoni* agreement of October 1925, whereby "while labour was to be tightly controlled in Fascist syndicates, the industrialists were to have a free hand within the bounds established by the dictator's directives" (Halperin 1964 p.58). Gino Olivetti was honoured with the title *"Duce"* of Italian industrialists, and Mussolini went out of his way to promote figures from the business world into the Senate. Therefore it would be reasonable to suggest that, with the success of Fascism in Italy, "the real victors were the industrialists who now thirsted for revenge on the workers who had held them to ransom for so long" (Pollard 1998 p.29).

The Fascist government's first measures more than met the requirements of industry and finance: cuts in government spending; privatization of the telephone network; deconstruction of the state monopoly on life assurance; relaxation of price and rent controls; the shelving of an enquiry into excess war profits; reduction of direct taxation levels for the wealthy; abolition of tax on family inheritance, and so on (see Schmidt 1973 p.51; Pollard 1998 p.42). Clearly "the support which Fascism had received from industrial and financial circles was amply rewarded by the policies pursued by De Stafani at the Ministry of Finance" (Pollard 1998 p.48). It was a programme of fiscal rectitude "inspired by a laissez-faire philosophy which, in principle, was totally acceptable to business" (Sarti 1971 p.43). In April 1923 the Ministry of Labour and Welfare, which had been extensively criticized by business interests as an expensive concession to subversive elements, was effectively abolished. The leader of the new Ministry of the National Economy, Mario Orso Corbino, was a liberal economist who had the "complete confidence" of the industrialists (Sarti 1971 p.47). From 1925 onwards trade unions were banned and strikes outlawed, and the employers association, the *Confederazione Generale dell'Industria Italiana (CGII)* otherwise known as *Confindustria,* could count on tangible advantages as the move toward the "totalitarian" state necessitated the further subordination of labour. For example in 1934 the workers' passport was introduced which recorded personal details and indicated whether past conduct had been satisfactory from the "national" viewpoint. Workers were effectively vetted for evidence of inappropriate political behavior, as determined by the Fascist regime.

In fact Articles VI and IX of the Charter of Labour enshrined the rights of the employer and reflected quite explicitly the precise economic priorities of the regime: "'the Corporate State considers private enterprise in the domain of production to be the most efficient method and the most advantageous to the interests of the nation ... the state intervenes in economic production only when private enterprise fails or is insufficient, or when the political interests of the state are involved'" (cited in Wiskemann 1969 p.23, see Mussolini 1975 Articles of Charter VI and IX p.66 and p.67). This orientation was confirmed by one of the major Italian industrialists, Alberto Pirelli, who noted: "'they (the Fascists) know that initiative and private property, that indispensable mainspring of human and civilized progress and of collective well-being, demands as a condition and a consequence that management be granted – as the Fascists indeed grant to it – adequate powers for running each productive organism'" (cited in Tannenbaum 1972 p.92). Consequently, "private property and private enterprise remained largely sacrosanct, although the state did reserve the right to intervene if a crisis arose or if the national interest demanded it" (Whittam 1995 p.60).

Of course, in the context of the global conomic depression after 1929, in Italy and elsewhere, the idea of not utilizing public input would have appeared positively peverse, however it is important to note that any government intervention that took place in the economy was positively welcomed by the capitalists. For example the *Instituto di Ricostruzion Industriali* (IRI) was popular among businesses as a reliable source of investment at a time when economic difficulties meant higher risks and an increasing reluctance by shareholders and financiers to provide money for investment. Thus the savings of the Italian people were used to provide long-term loans to business, guaranteed by the state. The decision to keep the IRI as an autonomous institution well outside the corporatist framework, and to place it under the direction of industrialist Alberto Beneduce, symbolized its favourable orientation toward big business (De Grand 1995 p.44). Even as the balance between private and public institutions seemed to be re-calibrated in favour of the latter, in accordance with the prevailing corporatist requirements, this transformation was acceptable, indeed advantageous, to the "industrial leadership" (see Sarti 1971). For example, the *CGII/Confindustria* was unquestionably the most powerful and politically influencial private organization in Italy,  it was recognized by the government as the sole representative of all industrial employers and it took on the status and prestige of a politically sanctioned public agency. As Sarti argued, "the CGII enjoyed both the administrative autonomy of a private organization and the juridicial authority of a public institution" (Sarti 1971 p.76). The citadel of private industry thus became part of the state, but was not controlled by it – private interests were able to pursue their own particular objectives under the guise of public policy (see Sarti 1971 p.80). In effect large business concerns sought and received state assistance whilst avoiding public regulation.

In Fascist Italy many private firms that were under contract to the government (e.g. in the sphere of armaments) were shielded completely from the harsh winds of economic competition and the Mussolini government presided over a distinct trend toward monopolisation in industry. Cartels (*consorzio*) first appeared in 1929-30 as voluntary associations of producers who were anxious to fix prices in a diminishing market, but the state soon made such arrangements compulsory. In 1932 such "consortiums" were sanctioned and protected by law, and by 1937 there were 279 cartels, particularly prominent and powerful were those in the metal, chemical and food industries (see Tannenbaum 1972 p.93). Despite the dubious economic benefits of such a policy – Italian economic growth in the period was less than almost every other European country and economic policy was, in general terms, "a failure" – cartelization nevertheless facilitated the continued economic and social predominance of big business (Tannenbaum 1972 p.111).

Even where economic choices were made which did not obviously benefit the industrialists, they made strenuous efforts to bend them into a shape they could accommodate. Such was the case, for example, with the policy of "Quota 90" announced in 1926 which revalued the lira at a rate which some businesses found uncomfortable. "After initial expressions of concern, industry readily adjusted to the new situation. In fact the large corporations took advantage of the crisis to eliminate their weaker rivals" (De Grand 2000 p.61). Similarly the economic policy of autarky (see earlier) certainly posed challenges for commercial interests because the desire to protect the domestic market had to be balanced against an unavoidable dependence on imported raw materials such as coal, oil and metal ores. However, there were few advocates in elite business circles for a dogmatic adherence to international free trade, so in effect the government could count on commercial support for protectionism, especially in the agricultural sector. The policy of autarky also provided further impetus toward the cartelization of productive units, which was often enthusiastically embraced because that policy afforded more financial leverage to larger companies. Certainly autarky was politically motivated, rather than a purely commercial policy preference, and as such it was laden with emotional, nationalistic overtones, but the industrial and agrarian leadership was prepared to conform, or at least conceal their deeper reservations, in deference to Mussolini's conception of the national interest.

It is also important to acknowledge that key industrialists were also generally supportive of the regime's expansionist impulses, which were seen as an opportunity to extend government contracts and increase profits. Indeed, "regardless of what the industrial leaders thought of Mussolini's foreign policy, industrial firms and cartels were eager to seize all opportunities for economic expansion abroad" (Sarti 1971 p.125). For example the CGII organized cartels to develop Ethiopian natural resources soon after the fall of Addis Ababa in May 1936. Within a short time around 800 firms, organized within seventeen cartels, were profiteering from Italy's newest imperial acquisition (see Sarti 1971 p.125). Similarly, Italian intervention in the Spanish civil war was welcomed by the commercial elites as a necessary measure in order to protect Italian investments. Even the traditional anxieties amongst Italian business leaders about commercial competition from Germany were suspended when the prospect of victory in the war seemed to offer massive opportunities for profitable expansion. The fact that this was a dreadful miscalculation does not obviate the fact that the Italian bourgeoisie would have fallen over themselves to exploit fascist military success.

Consequently the capitalists, as far as economic policy was concerned, had little to fear and much to gain from Italian Fascism. "Fascism had endorsed the view that what was good for Fiat, the banks and even international capital was good for Italy" (Bosworth 2002 p.179). As Griffiths argues, "Fascism, in power, became 'respectable'...and the State became the defender of the capitalism on which its prosperity depended" (Griffiths 2005 p.36-37), therefore "the class which benefitted most from fascist rule was the layer of big industrialists" (Renton 1999 p.33). In practice, although the bourgeoisie was never strong enough to dominate Fascism, "they had been sufficiently influencial to protect their business interests", so in effect "the absence of an economic dimension to the Fascist revolution meant Fascist acceptance of traditional economics" (Sarti 1971 p.132 and p.51). Although there were limits to their power under Fascism, bourgeois elites managed to mitigate the impact of public (political) intervention, whilst maintaining control of the production process, keeping most of it in private hands – overall, in fact, they conceded very little and gained much. The partnership of big business with Fascism was a mutually profitable venture.

In summary, it is clear that both the fascist movements did offer, in theory, what may be termed a collectivist solution to certain economic difficulties, that is corporatism and a degree of paternalistic state intervention. However, this approach was directed primarily against socialist/communist alternatives (see Guerin 1973 chapter VIII) and fascist collectivism was certainly not the same as socialism. While all socialists are,

by definition, collectivists, not all collectivists are socialists –
and certainly not the fascists in Italy and Germany. Crucially,
this collectivist approach by the fascists was not, and was not
intended to be, antagonistic toward capitalism as a mode of
production based on private ownership and control of the
means of production in pursuit of profit. "For fascists, the
dysfunctional capitalism of the inter-war period did not need
fundamental re-ordering: its ills could be cured simply by
applying sufficient political will" (Paxton 2005 p.10). The fact
that there was a measure of state intervention in the economic
sphere, or that one section of capital suffered disproportionately (for instance small-scale concerns), does not indicate a
serious or significant departure from capitalist economics, as
some have suggested. Moreover, state intervention was used,
by and large, primarily as a means of creating extra opportunities for a business community which feared socialism and was
recovering from a period of acute economic crisis. In any event,
on the whole fascists preferred non-interference by the state
in economic processes (see Hayes 1973) [31]. As Poulantzas
asserted, "state control of the economy by fascism has always
been a myth, and even with the war economy it never went
beyond regulation in favour of big capital. Fascism never jeop-
ardised 'traditional' big capital, whose interests it constantly
guaranteed" (Poulantzas 1974 p.258). It is also important to
note that the captains of industry and finance, the capitalist
elite, were also deeply implicated in the most heinous crimes
committed by the fascist states. Thus we may conclude that
"only the naive could have believed that fascism is an actual
economic revolution outmoding capitalism", and "in no case
has a fascist regime attempted to suppress capitalism" (Guerin
1973 p.208 and Wilkinson 1981 p.23). In short, the pseudo-
socialism and phoney anti-capitalism of fascist theory proved
to be, in reality, simple demagogic devices designed to secure
the broadest possible spectrum of electoral support. In Fascist
Italy and Nazi Germany private industry was, more or less,
actively encouraged or left well alone to pursue its self-allotted
task of accumulating vast wealth.

## Varieties of Racism

The last "theme" of fascism which requires attention is racism, which was primarily a National Socialist trait, and it is this facet which, to some extent, sets it apart from more conventional fascisms. As Gordon argues "theorists of generic fascism are dealt a serious (although not fatal) blow whenever they acknowledge the deep fracture – at the level of race – between the first and, in many ways, model fascist regime, and its most violent and cataclysmically consequential epigone" (Gordon 2009 p.297). However, as Gordon implies, the fact that certain divergences exist, which need to be acknowledged and accounted for, does not invalidate the use of the generic term because, in a real sense, the "eliminationist drive" (Kallis 2009) was inherent in the core of fascist ideology and reflected clearly in fascist practice – the differences discernible in each case were a matter of degree rather than kind.

Most analysts agree that racism and anti-semitism are an integral component of National Socialism, and it is reasonable to assert that many aspects of the Nazi experience are inexplicable unless one refers to this feature of its ideology [32]. Racism pervaded practically every aspect of National Socialism and sits at the very epicenter of its political perspective. As Hitler said, "if I try to gauge my work, I must consider first of all, that I've contributed, in a world that had forgotten the notion, to the triumph of the idea of the primacy of race" (Hitler 1973 p.82). Indeed, "in Germany racial ideologies enjoyed the widest currency and the greatest political salience: the Third Reich became the first state in world history whose dogma and practice was racism" (Burleigh and Wipperman 1991 p.23). By contrast, racism in Italy was of a qualitatively different type and, as we shall see, the socio-biological determinism which drove the Nazis was, to a large extent, derivative in the Italian context. It is important to be precise here, since racism was still an important component part of Fascist experience in Italy, but the narrative is different in very important aspects. In effect fascism meant marginalisation, expulsion and, eventually, elimination of the "other" – indeed "it has become impossible to talk about fascism without referring to the millions of people who were ruthlessly persecuted, displaced, and brutally murdered in the fascist 'new order'" (Kallis 2009 p.5-6).

Before examining in greater detail the nature of respective types of racism, it is necessary to acknowledge that both forms of fascist racism were rooted in crude anthropological assumptions, many of which were actually common currency in Europe at the end of the nineteenth century. Indeed it would not be an over-statement to claim that the idea of race saturated social, political and scientific thought during this period as a kind of conventional wisdom, and notions of ethno-exclusive nationalism and Empire, which prevailed across Europe, certainly contained explicit (or implicit) ideas about racial superiority and inferiority (see Neocleous 1997 p.26). European colonialism had confirmed, in the minds of many, the irredeemable superiority of the white race, embedding notions of superiority and subordination. Such attitudes justified the domination and denigration of "inferior" peoples as perfectly "natural" in the name of "civilization". In fact this "race discourse", which emerged across Europe in the decades preceding 1914, was common currency amongst members of the intellectual, political and scientific elites in every European nation (see Kallis 2009 p.83). Concepts of race therefore permeated the perceptions of those who wielded political power across the continent.

Moreover, anti-semitism as a particular component of fascist racism, was constructed upon a very long history of antipathy toward the Jews, much of which was Christian in inspiration. The Jews were often demonized as "Christ-killers" (Gilbert 1987 p.19). Indeed, following the failure of the Jewish uprising against the Romans in AD 69-70 and the subsequent scattering of the Diaspora, the Jews "became targeted for persecution throughout Christian Europe" (Neville 1999 p.4). According to Raul Hilberg, ever since the fourth century anti-Jewish policies fell into three categories – conversion, expulsion and annihilation, and even the most cursory glance at the work of Martin Luther (to take one pertinent example) reveals the depth of hatred toward the Jew as a plague and a pestilence on the Christian community (Hilberg 1985 Vol One p.8, see p.15-16). Therefore, as Hannah Arendt and others have rightly pointed out, racists could draw on a much broader and deeper (especially eastern) European tradition of anti-semitism because the denigration of Judaism had not only existed for centuries, it had a "respectable" lineage based in large part on the Christian antipathy toward the Jew (see Arendt 1962, and Pois 1970 p.14; see Neville 1999 p.4, Cohn-Sherbok 1999). Throughout Christian Europe "centuries of theological damnation, legal persecution and popular prejudice had generated an almost automatic anti-Jewish feeling" which "survived the advent of modernity, the demise of the social influence of the church, and the secularization of identities precisely because it had always operated on a deeper, popular level of prejudice without much understanding of, or attention to, its theological origins" (Kallis 2009 p.36). Therefore, "Jew hatred, with its two-thousand-year-old history, could arise both as a spontaneous outburst of popular instincts, and as a deliberately fanned instrument of scapegoat politics" (Gilbert 1987 p.20). Violent pogroms against the Jews have punctuated European history, especially in the east (see Barkai 1996a) and anti-semitism might even be described as "humanity's longest hatred" (Cohn-Sherbok 1999 p.7).

In this sense "elimination" was always a possibility contained within the concept of anti-semitism, although generating that potential depended upon a complex synergy of agency and structure, some of which was nation-specific (Kallis 2009 p.11). For example the diachronic, pan-European antipathy toward Jewry was accentuated in the German context by Lutheran Protestantism during the Reformation and by a succession of *volkish* organizations along with philosophers like Gottlieb Fichte (1762-1814) who stressed the Jews as essentially alien and corrosive to a specifically German sense of collective ethnic identity (see Neville 1999). In

German history there was never any shortage of philosophers and politicians who, frustrated at the absence of a genuine national German entity, emphasised the particular quality of the Germanic race and the value of its Aryan-Nordic heritage. Thus the ideas of of Herder, Jahn and Schopenhauer, which stressed the superiority of Germanic peoples in terms of cultural value, were reflected in the various "*volkish*" groups and societies (such as the Thule Bund) which emerged to stress the uniqueness of the *volksgemeinschaft* (community of racial people). The composer Wagner, for instance, saw Germans as descended from pre-Christian nature-Gods, called by destiny toward unity and superiority. In the language of *blut and boden* ("blood and soil"), the "*volk*" assumed a special, almost spiritual significance: "at a mundane level it means 'the people' but on a more abstract plane it connotes a system of absolute values, an immutable metaphysical ideal of peoplehood" (Wilford 1986 p.219, see Taylor 1985 p.8). Indeed the notion of the "*volk*" is a peculiarly Germanic concept embodying the idea of a racial entity united by and embodying a transcendental essence of nature, blood and culture. Hence the notion of *volksgemeinschaft* signified a living organism from which Germans could derive the true meaning and essence of their existence (Barkai 1996 p.85).

Moreover, "to be authentically German involved commitment to idealism and rejection of "Jewish" materialism" (Stackelberg 1999 p.48), so the idea of the "German" stood in stark contrast to stereotypical conceptions of "Jewishness" as essentially selfish, immoral and manipulative. As a consequence of this contradistinction a fragile German national consciousness was solidified and strengthened by reference to a mythologized *volksfeind* "other". By the nineteenth century the idea of "Jewishness" was becoming an increasingly racialized concept, based on the apparently scientific "truths" of socio-biology - henceforth the Jew could no longer evade attention via conversion and assimilation which had, historically, provided the usual route toward respectability and/or anonymity.

It is also extremely important to understand that National Socialist racism was based essentially upon this pseudo-scientific biological-determinist interpretation of the world. These ideas, articulated by the likes of Count Arthur de Gobineau, H.S. Chamberlain and Ernst Haeckel, along with a host of scientifically illiterate pundits like Willibald Hentschel, suggested that the history and development of mankind could be explained simply by reference to human biology and race [33]. Drawing upon a distorted Darwinism they saw history as a perpetual struggle between the various races for supremacy and, moreover, stressed how important it was that the Aryan-Germanic race (as the inheritors of Graeco-Roman civilization) should emerge victorious. More specifically Aryans were presumed to be engaged in an eternal conflict, not only with the Semite, but the Negroid and Mongoloid races (Griffiths 2005 p.16-17). Thus, according to this perspective, the natural hierarchy of races, with Aryans at the apex, could be maintained only at the expense of eternal vigilance against racial enemies.

In many ways the most systematic exposition of Nazi-style racism, which built upon the ideas of German *volk*, came from Alfred Rosenberg who was, according to Cecil, "a would be intellectual in a group of instinctive and self-proclaimed anti-intellectuals" (Cecil 1972 p.5). Rosenberg became editor of the *Volkischer Beobachter*, and after 1929 headed the Combat League for German Culture. Although essentially a synthe-sizer of ideas, Rosenberg seems to have actually believed the toxic notions he expounded in his major work *The Myth of the Twentieth Century* (1930) (see Pois 1970 p.11). As Rosen-berg exclaimed "'the belief in the worth of Blood is the basic presupposition in the National Socialist philosophy of life'" (Rosenberg cited in McGovern 1946 p.638) and Heinrich Himmler was still more explicit, explaining to a gathering of Nazi *Gauleiters* that "'I believe that our blood, the Nordic blood, is actually the best blood on this earth...There is no other. We are superior to everything and everyone. Once we are liberated from inhibitions and restraints, there is no one who can surpass us in quality and strength'" (Himmler cited in Rees 2012 p.294).

However, if we are to genuinely understand the nature and essence of authentic Nazi racism we need look no further than the ideas of Adolf Hitler himself, who elaborated his racial ideas most fully in *Mein Kampf*. Although the text is dull, repetitive and verbose, it is nevertheless evident that Hitler believed that he had discerned the fundamental "laws" of human existence. *Mein Kampf* was to become the National Socialist Gospel, indeed the text became "something upon which doubt could not be cast without serious consequences" (Maser 1970 p.106). Mankind, Hitler explained, was divided into a natural hierarchy of races and the highest "culture-forming" race was the Aryan race. With its unique capacity for creativity and social cohesion the Aryans, Hitler believed, were the origin of all that was positive in the world, indeed they alone had the capability of developing beyond the "herd instinct" of other races and subordinating the individual to the kin group - this is what he termed Aryan "idealism" (Hitler 1974 p.271). Racial groups were further sub-divided into "culture bearers" and "culture destroyers" with whom the Aryan was engaged in a constant struggle for survival and supremacy. According to Hitler this battle for ascendancy explained, totally, the historical development of mankind, as he concluded: "all occurrences in world history are the expression of the races' instinct of self-preservation" (Hitler 1974 p.269). Force and strength, as experienced and expressed via race, were the key determining factors in all cases.

For Adolf Hitler, the crucial "law" which the Aryans needed to observe in order to maintain its predominance, was to maintain the purity of the racial bloodline. The mixing of Aryan blood with the lower races would devalue the quality of the race and impair its capacity to survive - civilizations had fallen, Hitler maintained, because of miscegenation and the concomitant decline in the quality of the blood-line. Of course this was self-evident, Hitler argued, if one observed nature, where cross-breeding between species was always punished and therefore rarely occurred (see Hitler 1974 p.259). In actual fact Hitler more or less attributed all of Germany's difficulties, including failures in war and in peacetime, to a mixing of the blood and a sickening of normal, healthy, racial instincts. As Hitler said, "'blood that has once been poisoned cannot be changed...the inner discord of the German people is the result only of mixed blood'" (cited in Bytwerk 2008 p.24-25). As a result, Hitler's primary objective was to sustain and purify the Germanic race: "What we must fight for is to safeguard the existence and reproduction of our race and our people, the sustenance of our children and the purity of our blood, the freedom and independence of the Fatherland, so that the people may mature for the fulfillment of the mission allotted it by the creator of the universe...every thought and every idea, every doctrine and all knowledge must serve this purpose...everything must be examined from this point of view and used or rejected according to its utility" (Hitler 1974 p.195).

As Rosenberg had also made clear, true freedom could only be derived from the fellowship of race (see Pois 1970 p.99). A Germanic state of the Germanic nation was required and society should be organised to fulfill over-riding racial objectives, whilst a programme of selected breeding was required to promote and develop those pockets of the Aryan race which remained pure. The social consequences of such an approach were not lost on Nazi ideologues, as Hitler explained, "it is a half measure to let incurably sick people steadily contaminate the remaining healthy ones...the demand that defective people be prevented from propagating equally defective offspring is a demand of the clearest reason..." (Hitler 1974 p.232). In addition, Hitler argued, living-space (*lebensraum*) was required for this Aryan master race, which could be found to the east, an area destined for colonization by the Germans. In Hitler's vision Aryan soldier-peasants would control the eastern territory, ensuring the subservience of the local, uneducated, disease-ridden Slav population, who were to be treated as "redskins" (see Hitler 1974 book II chapter

1 "Eastern Orientation or Eastern Policy?"). This process of colonization required that "inferior" races be used in much the same way as man had always used beasts like horses and cattle, to lighten the burden of his labour because, as Hitler remarked, "all who are not of good race in this world are chaff" (Hitler 1974 p.269). In fact there is some evidence that Hitler set his sights well beyond this: "'the Nordic race has a right to rule the world and we must take this right as the guiding star of our foreign policy...'" (Hitler cited in Baynes 1969 p.989, see Strasser 1940 p.118-19), therefore "'...our task is to organise on a large scale the whole world so that each country produces what it can best produce while the white race, the Nordic race, undertakes the organisation of this gigantic plan...National Socialism as a whole would be worth nothing if it were restricted merely to Germany and did not seal the supremacy of the superior race over the entire world for at least one thousand to two thousand years'" (Hitler in conversation with Otto Strasser, 22 May 1930, cited in Baynes 1969 p.774-75). A New Order would be created in Europe with global aspirations, the centre of which would be a racially homogeneous *Germania*.

However, according to Hitler's racial theory there was one major obstacle to the success of the Aryan race in the pursuit of its rightful position as a Spartan elite dominating and exploiting the inferior Helot races - the Jew. "In whatever direction one follows Hitler's train of thought, sooner or later one encounters the Satanic figure of the Jew. The Jew is made the universal scapegoat" (Bullock 1962 p.407, see also Maser 1970 p.152). Hitler began his political career on 10 September 1919 with a speech on the nature of the Jewish threat; and he ended it in his last "political testament" of 29 April 1945 with a vitriolic attack on Jewry and its accomplices [34]. Hitler maintained his pathological hatred of the Jews right until the very end, claiming that "it is one of the achievements of National Socialism that it was the first to face the Jewish problem in a realistic manner...I have opened the eyes of the whole world to the Jewish peril" and the world would be "eternally grateful" (Hitler 1961a p.50, p.52 and p.57).

Hitler's fanatical detestation of the Jews probably began in his youth as he assimilated the language of hatred, disseminated via the cheap, virulently anti-semitic leaflet-literature of early twentieth century Viennese politics. Hitler was unquestionably influenced by the populist anti-semitism of his political contemporaries in Austria such as leader of the *Alldeutsche* Georg von Schoenerer and Mayor Karl Lueger. Both denounced the degenerate influence of the Jews in vitriolic terms, referring to them as parasites and insects (see Hamann 2001). Although some argue that Hitler's attitude to the Jews was more ambivalent in this period than conventional scholarship acknowledges, there was, in Vienna at the time, a bitter resentment against immigrants, particularly Slavs and Jews, indeed "the political style and visionary schemes which were symptomatic of right wing agitation in late imperial Vienna left a lasting imprint on Hitler's understanding of society and state" (Hamann 2001 p.23). Hitler also drew on more obscure and sinister sources, for example he had read, and been impressed by, the forged *Protocols of the Learned Elders of Zion*, which he seized upon as documentary "evidence" of Jewish perfidy (see Landau 1998 p.52, Maser 1970 p.164). Hitler was also captivated by the work of the renegade occultist monk Adolf Josef Lanz, alias Georg Lanz von Leibenfels who, via the racist periodical *Ostara,* purveyed esoteric ariosophist visions of blonde haired, blue-eyed Aryan heroes eliminating the Jews and dominating all impure races via an Order of New Templars (see Goodrick-Clarke 1992 Chapter 15 p.192, Kershaw 2009 p.28) [35]. Hitler was also, of course, familiar with the work of Rosenberg who saw Jewish influence as the root of all evil, and his experience of defeat in the Great War, which he blamed on anti-German Jewish elements, appears to have solidified his anti-semitic world view (see Hamann 2001) [36]. Indeed the so-called *Dolchstosslegende,* which evolved in some nationalist circles after 1918, construed the Jews as culpable not only for defeat in war, but for the detested

Versailles treaty and the weak Weimar Republic constructed in its wake. Hitler not only subscribed to this myth, he helped perpetuate it in popular consciousness.

Yet although the Jews were considered racially inferior, according to Nazi ideology they were an extremely cunning adversary. Hitler believed that the Jews were the perpetrators of an enormous conspiracy, which could explain their political power, social prominence and economic success (see Hitler 1974 p.258-300). The Nazis saw the Jews as combining finance capitalism and Marxist Bolshevism in a devastatingly devious plot to subvert the re-emergence of a racially rejuvenated German nation (a threat which proved particularly convincing to the German petit-bourgeoisie threatened by both). This odd collaboration between Soviet Judea and Wall Street (the "Red and Gold International" as Rosenberg termed it) was seen as part of an overall plan to destroy the Aryan race by polluting the purity of its blood. Moreover, this racial defilement was believed to be simply a staging post on the road to a Jewish-led world government. In the midst of this incredible conspiracy-theory even Christianity became entangled, and the organized Christian churches were viewed by Hitler as little more than an instrument of the Jew. As Hitler put it, "Christianity is the invention of sick brains...it is merely wholehearted Bolshevism under a tinsel of metaphysics", the Christian faith, like Marxism, was "a child of Judaism" (Hitler 1973 p.144 and p.146, see Hitler 1961 p.93). As Bullock explains, "in Hitler's eyes Christianity was a religion fit only for slaves; he detested its ethics in particular. Its teaching, he declared, was a rebellion against the natural law of selection by struggle and the survival of the fittest" (Bullock 1962 p.389). In this way Christianity's "pity ethics" were dismissed as a Jewish invention dating back to Saul of Tarsus, and Hitler looked forward (privately at least) to its eventual demise and the emergence of a religion based on pre-Christian Nordic paganism, the swastika, and the purity of German blood [37].

Naturally, given the all-pervasive nature of the Jewish threat, the apocalyptic struggle against them could not exclude any measures, and all options would be seriously considered if they were deemed necessary for ultimate victory. In any case, at bottom, the Jew was "vermin", a "poison", a "virus", a "vampire", a "parasite", and a "racial tuberculosis" bereft of all human characteristics - Germany had to be disinfected or it would itself be asphyxiated by the Jew (Hitler 1961a p.51). As Hitler stated, unequivocally, "'nature is cruel therefore we too may be cruel. If I can send the flower of the German nation into the hell of war without the smallest pity for the spilling of precious German blood then surely I have the right to remove millions of an inferior race that breeds like vermin'" (cited in Rauschning 1939 p.140, see also Hitler 1973 p.79 and p.235). As Kershaw says, "behind all evil that had befallen or was threatening Germany stood the figure of the Jew. In speech after speech he lashed the Jews in the most vicious and barbaric language imaginable" (Kershaw 2009 p.91). Indeed Hitler's perspective actually posited the need for genocidal "extermination" (see Kershaw 2009 p.149). For instance, in *Mein Kampf* Hitler maintained the view that during the First World War it would have been advantageous for Germany to have used poisoned gas against the "Hebrew corrupters" and destroyers of the nation (see Rees 2005a p.38), and on 30 January 1939, as war clouds gathered ominously over Europe, Hitler predicted the fate of the Jewish people in an infamously prophetic speech to the Reichstag: "'if international Jewish finance inside and outside Europe succeeds in involving the nations in another war, the result will not be the bolshevization of the earth and the victory of Judaism but the annihilation of the Jewish race in Europe'" (cited in Carr 1987 p.74-75).

Thus Hiltler's anti-semitism took hatred of the Jews to another dimension by emphasizing blood rather than culture, which effectively destroyed the only escape route for Jews, which was religious conversion – Baptism and assimilation could no longer save them from their fate. As Smith explains, "it (was) of the essence of Hitler's belief that the Jew (was) not simply a Christ-killer or even, as in the older volkish conception, an economic and cultural competitor, rather he (was) a racial disease...the Jew became the incarnation of racial evil, a species of malignant bacillus, the non-race eroding all pure races, the ruin and unseen disease of the Aryan race... the subhuman is not simply outside society, an untouchable, he is a dynamic bacteriological corrupter of mankind. As such he must be annihilated lest he destroy not merely the purified elite, but the whole natural order of castes" (Smith 1979 p.78). Similarly Rosenberg's verdict on the Jews as an invisible, cohesive web of slime fungus or plasmodium and a deadly pathogen meant that they could not be assimilated into the German community under any circumstances - there was no such thing as a "good" or "harmless" Jew (see Bauman 1991 p.68). Although there may be no generally acceptable explanation for Hitler's pathological hatred of Jews, "we can say with absolute certainty that he never seriously doubted the rightness of his Jewish policy" (Maser 1973 p.174) and it was this obsessive anti-semitism which, given historical experience, remains unquestionably the most distinctive feature of National Socialism.

The anti-semitism, so clearly delineated by Hitler and Rosenberg as the key ideologues, was also enthusiastically disseminated via the broader Nazi movement. In fact point No.4 in the original *Dutsche Arbeiterpartei* (DAP) 25 point programme stated that "'only members of the Volk may be citizens of the State. Only those of German blood, whatever their creed, may be members of the nation. Accordingly no Jew may be members of the nation'" (cited in Neville 1999 p.15, see Landau 1998 p.57). Vitriolic articles in the Nazi newspaper *Der Sturmer*, which was launched in 1923, articulated a visceral anti-semitism which was "omnipresent and inescapable" (Evans 2006 p.538). The banner headline of *Der Sturmer* was *Juden sind unser Ungluck* ("The Jews are Our Misfortune") and the malicious content referred to profiteers, warmongering plutocrats, and even speculated about the ritualistic murder of Christian children by Jews. These lurid and insidious diatribes provided the context for the growth of antipathy toward the Jewish community, and offered tacit and explicit encouragement for random acts of violence and inhumanity against the Jewish population (see Friedlander 2009 p.37; Gilbert 1987 p.25). Rabid anti-Semite Julius Streicher even maintained that the Jews were not only a "'bastard race'" but were the "'devil's people'" (cited in Bytwerk 2008 p.88 and p.92). As Barkai says, "every single satanic quality or horrific crime ascribed to Jews on the pages of the *Sturmer* was copied from earlier Judeophobic invective" (Barkai 1996 p.40) while pro-Nazi films such as *Jud Suss* and *The Eternal Jew* portrayed the Jews as vermin rats spreading chaos and disease across the globe (Friedlander 2009 p.188-89). Jews in Nazi literature were depicted in caricature form as medieval remnants with un-natural features, cunningly disguised to evade detection amongst honest and unsuspecting Aryans. The Nazis offered precautionary advice, even to the extent that children's books, such as *The Poisoned Mushroom,* warned young people about the lethal danger posed by the insidious Jew. A seductively simplistic binary formula, good versus evil, *Volksgemeinschaft* versus *Volksfeind,* was deployed to sustain ethnic solidarity and incite racial hatred. One of the Nazi movement's most popular slogans was *"Deutschland erwache, Juda verrecke!",* "Germany awake, death to Judah!" (Gilbert 1987 p.30) and such primitive anti-semitic sloganising would propel a nation toward the abyss of genocide.

Anti-semitism was, therefore, a central component of Nazi practice right from the very beginning. In practical terms the exclusionary ethno-nationalist, racist ideas resulted initially in the general intimidation of the Jewish community – on 1 January 1930 brownshirts in Berlin killed eight Jews, the first Jewish victims of the Nazi era (Gilbert 1987 p.29). The campaign against the Jewish community gathered momentum with the desecration of synagogues and the boycott of Jewish businesses, loosely coordinated by Julius Streicher in April 1933. This process of brutal harassment culminated in the destructive *"Kristalnacht"* pogrom of 9-10 November 1938 which was, ostensibly, revenge for the murder of German diplomat Ernst vom Rath in Paris by the Jewish student Herschel Grynszpant. According to figures collated by the Nazis themselves 800 shops were destroyed, 191 Synagogues set on fire (76 demolished), with damage to property amounting to approximately 25 million marks, while 91 Jews were killed and 20,000 arrested (Welch 1998 p.82). It was the most destructive pogrom in central Europe since the fifteenth century and in retrospect it is clear that *"Kristalnacht"* marked the high-point of Nazi-inspired anti-semitic hooliganism (Neville 1999 p.32, see Gilbert 1987 p.73 who also notes that German Jewry had to bear the cost of the damage to property, and were therefore effectively "fined" for the carnage caused by the Nazis). However, these loosely coordinated "carnivalesque" efforts proved largely inadequate indeed even, to some extent, unpopular and counterproductive, so the Nazi regime, under the auspices of Chief of the Security Police Reinhard Heydrich, resorted to more "rational", legalized anti-semitic racism (see Kallis 2009 p.217, Kershaw 2009 p.464 and Bauman 1991). As Welch says, "the long-term significance of *Kristallnacht* was to convince the Nazi leadership of the limitations of an uncoor-dinated Jewish policy" (Welch 1998 p.82).

The first law to contain the "Aryan paragraph" was the "Law for the Restoration of the Civil Service" of 7 April 1933 (Friedlander 2009 p.11). On 14 July 1933 the "Law Concerning the Revocation of Naturalization and Annulment of German Nationality" made it possible for the government to revoke "undesirable" citizenship naturalizations, and this trend toward formal legal and official discrimination culminated in the so-called "Nuremberg Laws" of September 1935 (see Noakes and Pridham 1974 p.463; Neville 1999 p.26; Evans 2006 p.536). Significantly, the "Reich Citizenship Law" divided the population into ordinary citizens and Reich citizens, the latter being the sole recipients of political and civil rights. "The Law for the Protection of German Blood and German Honour" (September 1935) prohibited marriage and/or sexual inter-course between adults of mixed blood, which was designed to prevent the "desecration of race", an offence later made punishable by death (see Friedlander 2009 Chapter 2 p.32-60). However, "as with any racist legislation, the devil lay in the detail, and in these circumstances reaching a hard-and-fast definition of who was Jewish and who was not was nigh impossible...all solutions the Nazis arrived at in the question of mixed race Germans and mixed marriages were thus in the end entirely arbitrary" (Evans 2006 p.545, see Gordon 2009 p.304). As the body of legislation dealing with race was continuously augmented, the law still failed to yield any definitive conclusions about categorization because the very notion of race was in itself such a slippery and elusive concept, indeed "the question of who should be considered a Jew could never be satisfactorily solved" (Kitchen 1995 p.203, see Burleigh and Wipperman 1991 p.47).

However, the inherent absurdity of fine racial distinctions were but a minor encumbrance for the Nazis. Most Nazi ideologues were simply happy that the issue was being addressed at last, as senior Nazi Hans Frank exclaimed, "'it is a joy finally to be able to deal with the Jewish race. The more that die the better'" (cited in Rees 2005a p.40). The arbitrary and capricious nature of racial categories and the laws constructed upon them was reflected in the fact that Hitler could grant exemptions whenever he pleased. The critical point however was that "the Nuremberg Laws made it clear that the Jews were to be allowed no further part in German life" (Gilbert 1987 p.48) and the momentum of marginalization gathered pace in accordance with the Nazi design. As Hitler had said just prior to the introduction of the Nuremburg laws, the Jews  must be "'removed from all professions, ghettoized, restricted to a particular territory, where they can wander about, in accordance with their character, while the German people looks on, as one looks at animals in the wild'" (cited in Burleigh and Wipperman 1991 p.82).

Following a decree issued in August 1938 the Jews were obliged to use the compulsory first names Sara or Israel and travel documents were subsequently stamped with the red letter "J". In November 1938 another law was passed entitled "Decree on Eliminating the Jew from German Economic Life" (Neville 1999 p.35) which forbade economic activity with Jews and effectively prohibited their gainful employment, and in December the "Decree on the Utilisation of Jewish Assets" ordered the surrender of Jewish capital to the state (Evans 2006 p.596). Jews had to register all assets over 5000RM with the appropriate authorities and they were, in essence, coerced into selling their property at a fraction of the real market value. Such measures led to the "calculated pauperization of the Jewish population" (Burleigh and Wipperman 1991 p.87). In fact the national legislation introduced by central government spawned a huge variety of discriminatory policies at regional and local level regarding, for example, public employment (e.g. medicine and law), voting rights, house ownership, recourse to law, education, taxation, and the Jews were even forbidden to own phones, cameras, radios, bicycles or electrical appliances, drive motorized vehicles, appear in certain public areas/places of entertainment or even keep pets! In fact social ostracism of the dreaded "Jew" became an administrative obsession, with over 2,000 decrees and regulations confirming their status as legally sanctioned outcasts (Stackelberg 1999 p.148). Segregation and demonisation reached its apogee when Jews were forced to wear the yellow Star of David on their clothing, an act introduced in occupied Poland toward the end of 1939 and then in the Reich in August 1941.

Such were (some of) the extraordinary measures taken by the regime in order to systematically isolate, denigrate and expel the Jew (Dawidowicz 1975 p.58). The effect of such measures on the Jewish population was profound, and the specific case of one individual Jewish doctor, Hans Serelman, is indicative - having given a transfusion of his own blood to a non-Jew in order to save their life he was sent to a concentration camp after being convicted of "racial defilement" (Gilbert 1987 p.50). As Friedlander noted, "the symbolic statements the laws expressed and the ideological message they carried were unmistakable" (Friedlander 2009 p.15) and Germany was in effect "turned into a prison for the larger less prosperous section of German Jews" (Nolte 1969 p.479, see Hildebrand 1985 p.6). Meanwhile, as the legal persecution of the Jewish community continued, "the majority of Germans simply chose to look the other way" (Friedlander 2009 p.139, see Gellately 1993). Effective enforcement of the racial measures was not at all dependent upon state coercion, because the Gestapo could rely upon popular acquiescence, if not outright support, as Gellatelly says "it cannot be forgotten that citizens played a crucial role in their own policing and helped make possible the murderous deeds of the regime" (Gellately 1993 p.58).

Yet it was not only the Jew who suffered from legislation designed to sustain and improve the German blood-line. "In steadily widening areas of social policy, health policy, education policy, and demographic policy, a ruling paradigm and guide to action became established, whereby people were divided into those possessing 'value' and those lacking 'value'. 'Value' was to be selected and promoted, and 'nonvalue' was to be segregated and eradicated" (Peukert 1993a p.235). For instance, the "Law Protecting German Blood and German Honour" (14 November 1935) was clarified a few days after its introduction to explain that people of "'alien blood'" included not only Jews but "'gypsies, negroes and their bastards'" (cited in Neville 1999 p.27). Generally speaking the nonconformist ("asocial") Sinti/Roma people were deemed an inferior race which was genetically predisposed toward criminality, and agencies such as the Ministry of Justice and the Reich Health Office applied restrictive racial-hygiene legislation. Himmler's decree of June 1936 for "Combatting the Gypsy Plague" clearly indicates the tone of official discourse and policy (see Kallis 2009 p.196-203). Jehovah's Witnesses and communists suffered too, as did the incurably sick and mentally ill. The "Law for the Prevention of Progeny Suffering from Hereditary Diseases" (July 1933) which took effect from January 1934, facilitated the sterilization of all those deemed "unfit" to procreate. This category was based "on nothing more than social and moral prejudice dressed up as medical reasoning" (Wachsmann 2008 p.134). People suffering from mental disorders, the incurably sick, vagrants, prostitutes and other social outcasts deemed "unworthy of life" by Hereditary Health Courts, were systematically sterilized or liquidated by the programme Euthanasia Action T4 between 1939-41 (see Friedlander 2009 p.16-17 and Kitchen 1995 p.187). The T4 registry, so named because of its address at *Tiergartenstrasse 4*, retrospectively and routinely faked the cause and place of death in order to deceive the victims' families, and as many as 200,000 mentally ill and physically disabled people may have been murdered under its auspices (Stackelberg 1999 p.132). This programme, having reached its initial projected target and having pioneered the use of poison gas, was "suspended" officially in 1941 after protests from families and members of the clergy. The scheme was replaced by "Special Treatment 14f13" whereby operations were moved eastward to help deal with the ongoing "problem" of Jewish "resettlement" (Gluckstein 1999 p.177). By November 1941 most of the participants in the "euthanasia action" had re-deployed their technology and expertise to the east under the operational banner "Organisation Todt" (Kallis 2009 p.174). Experiments in various modes of extermination followed soon thereafter.

Meanwhile phrenology (the technique of reading the character of a person from racial features) and physiognomy (the art of deducing individual character from facial features) were officially encouraged as a way of discerning the irrevocable influence of nature over human temperament, intelligence and talent. Racial profiling was thus considered a subject of the utmost importance, to be studied closely and acted upon. At the same time the *Lebensborn* project, founded in December 1935, set up homes across Europe which offered Aryan women the opportunity to pro-create in secret with SS officers in order to advance the "master race". This programme also facilitated the setting up of institutions which became repositories for "Aryan" children stolen from the Eastern occupied territories. *Lebensborn* was to be the "fountain of life" precipitating a new age of Nordic purity.

Thus the Germanic "New Order" was intrinsically racist and the Nazis did their very best to permeate society with their vitriolic anti-semitism, whilst in the Nazi party itself racial anti-semitism was seen as "a badge of conformity" (Noakes and Pridham 1974 p.467). However, the most potent organisational expression of Nazi racism was the infamous *Schutzstaffel* (Protection Squad, SS), formed originally from Hitler's personal guard. Suffused from the very start by an ethos of loyalty, obedience and discipline, and modelled (at least to some extent) on a paradigm provided by a combination of the Catholic Church's Jesuit Order and the Teutonic Nobility of Medieval Germany, it was to be the nucleus of the new Aryan racial elite upon which the future of Germany depended (see Cecil 1972 p.53, Cohn-Sherbok 1999 p.65, Dawidowicz 1975 p.70). Heinrich Himmler assumed command as *Reichsfuhrer SS* in 1929 determined that, as the "political soldiers" of the new era, they should be the source of racial renewal. The SS was to be the "aristocracy" of the New Order and therefore clearly differentiated from the "mercurial roughnecks" of the SA, and by 1934 it had 200,000 members (Allen 2002 p.22, Stackelberg 1999 p.116). Indeed it was Himmler who "conceived the ambition of turning the SS into the core elite of the new Nazi racial order. In deliberate contrast to the plebian disorder of the brownshirts, Himmler intended his SS to be strictly disciplined, puritanical, racially pure, unquestioningly obedient, incorporating what he regarded as the best elements in the German race" (Evans 2006 p.50). The SS, as the new Order of Teutonic Knights, was destined to be the instrument by which the Nazis would breed a new generation of blonde-haired blue-eyed beasts of prey who would rule the earth.

As a result the SS only recruited from what was deemed to be the very "best" racial stock who could trace their Aryan ancestry back to at least 1750. By the "Betrothal and Marriage Order" of December 1931, inspection of the racial genealogy of prospective spouses prior to marriage was required for SS officers. Interestingly nearly a fifth of the senior ranks of the SS were populated by titled members of the nobility (Evans

2006 p.418) and its expansion was driven by an influx of white collar clerks, managers and lawyers (Allen 2002 p.22). Within the SS, the thoroughly indoctrinated *Totenkopfver-bande* (Death's-Head Units), and *Sicherheitsdienst* (Security Service, SD) were rightly regarded as the most lethally potent elements of this uniquely evil edifice. The ultimate anti-semitic purpose of the organisation was made clear in *Das Schwarze Korps*, the official magazine of the SS, "'no power on earth can stop us, we will take the Jewish question to its total solution'" (cited in Rees 2012 p.193-4). In 1939 Himmler was appointed Reich Commissar for the Strength-ening of German Racial Identity, and Reinhard Heydrich was given responsibility for leading the Reich Security Main Office (RSHA), which incorporated both the Gestapo and the Security Service. These formal postions enabled both men to execute their extraordinary enthusiasm for Nazi racial objectives and they were to become the institutional instruments of racial exclusion, ethnic cleansing and, ulti-mately, genocide.

In line with the desire of the Nazis to expand eastward toward the Urals and secure *lebensraum* and "daily bread" for its race, and in order to destroy Asiatic "Jewish" Bolshe-vism, Germany invaded the Soviet Union on 22 June 1941. Having shrugged off the temporary expediency of the Nazi-Soviet Pact, the decision to invade reflected the ultimate ascendancy of a toxic combination of ideological, racial and geopolitical assumptions, which eventually exploded in the devastating destructiveness of operation "Barbarossa". The invasion constituted a conscious ideological act of the utmost purity and, as Stackelberg says, "for Hitler the attack on the Soviet Union was the fulfillment of the mission of his life" (Stackelberg 1999 p.189). "Barbarossa" was a "mighty Teutonic expedition to establish a vast continental empire" via another *Blitzkreig* (Fest 1973 p.216), but it also precipitated a war of extermination quite unlike anything previously experienced (see Bartov 1996a). It was in fact an ideological-racial war of annihilation which was qualitatively different from the more traditional war of conquest that was occurring simultaneously in the west, which was characterized by conformity with more conventional ethical and legal constraints (see Hildebrand 1985 p.68 and Stern 1975 p.216). The stark contrast between the nature and purpose of Nazi occupation in, for instance, Holland, Denmark or Norway where the Geneva Convention still largely prevailed, and the bestial conquest taking place in the east, could not have been sharper. Indeed it might be argued that the brutal conflict in the east was in many ways a separate "Third World War" (Fest 1973 p.648, see Bartov 1996).

In fact "Hitler stated openly that he wished to see Barbarossa conducted not according to military principles but as a *Vernichtungskrieg* (war of destruction) against an ideology and its adherents" (Forster 1996 p.89, see Streit 1996 p.114). Hence non-combatants, who were clearly no military threat, were massacred in the east by German soldiers (of the *Wehrmacht* and the SS) which presaged a "uniquely savage war" (Barkai 1996a p.138). As Kershaw says, "it was no accident that the war in the east led to genocide. The ideological objective of eradicating 'Jewish-Bolshevism' was central, not peripheral, to what had been deliberately designed as a 'war of annihilation'. It was inseparably bound up with the military campaign. With the murderous onslaught of the *Einsatzgruppen*, backed by the *Wehrmacht* and local collaborators, launched in the first days of the invasion, the genocidal character of the conflict was already established. It would rapidly develop into an all-out genocidal programme the like of which the world had never seen" (Kershaw 2009 p.668, see Gordon 2009 p.311).

As the Nazis sought colonization to the east at the expense of the *Untermenschen* Slavs and *Ostjuden,* the inherent genocidal logic and momentum of their ideology impelled them towards the mass murder of millions of the racially impure and politically unsound. The so-called *Kommissarbefehl* (Commissar Order) of 6 June 1941, by which Communists were to be summarily executed, paved the way for systematic murder. Fittingly Rosenberg became Reich Minister for the

Occupied Eastern Territories in November 1941 and Jews were re-located into ghettos like Lodz and Warsaw, which became in effect "racial dustbins". The latent genocidal dynamic inherent in the policy of ghettoization was clearly evident in the conditions which prevailed in Jewish settlements. For example in the Lodz ghetto 164,000 Jews were crowded in an area of approximately 1.5 square miles in conditions of utter degradation, where individuals barely survived on an allocation of food that amounted to approximately 300 calories per day (see Rees 2005a p.104). A visitor to the Warsaw ghetto, Stanislav Rozycki, described what he saw: "'the majority are nightmare figures, ghosts of former human beings, miserable destitute, pathetic remnants of former humanity...the prominent bones around their eye sockets, the yellow facial colour, the slack pendulous skin, the alarming emaciation and sickliness...on the streets children are crying in vain...every night hundreds of these children die and there is no hope that anybody will put a stop to it'" (cited in Cohn-Sherbok 1999 p.127-28).

Meanwhile, on 31 July 1941 Goering (having already raised the subject in May) commissioned Heydrich to carry out *Endlosung* (the "Final Solution") to the Jewish question. Discussions on the detail of this project took place at a second-tier ministerial level at the Wannsee Conference of 20 January 1942 (Gordon 2009 p.312, Cohn-Sherbok 1999 p.146) which became "the most infamous meeting of modern times" (Roseman 2005 p.131). Gathered at Wannsee were representatives from the Ministries of Justice, Interior, Foreign Office, Reich Chancellery, *Generalgouvernment* and several SS agencies. The clear aim of those assembled was to maximize the efficiency of the killing operation, although the actual minutes of the meeting were deliberately opaque, and euphemisms like "Special Treatment" were utilized in order to obscure the horrific reality of what was intended. Naturally there was no dissent regarding the principle of killing Jews – that was already well-established - but there was some debate about the legal definition of a "Jew" and what to do with "half Jews". In fact in the end Himmler simply ordered territory to be cleared of Jews, yet declined to define specifically what the term "Jew" actually meant, in order to forestall "legalistic meddling" (Kershaw 2009 p.717). There has been some debate as to the actual programmatic significance of the Wannsee conference in historical terms because it was actually more about the SS, Himmler and Heydrich establishing practical control of operations and confirming genocide as official policy - the actual policy was already being implemented, indeed "by the time the *Staatssekretare* (Permanent Secretaries) were sipping their cognacs at Wannsee, mass murder had been underway for six months or more" (Roseman 2005 p.135). Nevertheless, the consequences in terms of the development of Nazi policy were soon evident and "what had hitherto been tentative, fragmentary and spasmodic was to become formal, comprehensive and efficient" (Gilbert 1987 p.283, see Longerich 1999/2000). Wannsee ensured the effective co-ordination of what had, hitherto, been a collection of disparate local initiatives.

It is also worth noting that prior to Wannsee (15 July 1941) Himmler had already received a draft of *Generalplan Ost*, written in part by SS Colonel Professor Konrad Meyer-Hetling. This plan, itself a response to other simililar proposals (see Kallis 2009 p.190-91 and p.195), dealt with the issue of "Germanisation" and the non-Jewish population of the East, and it envisaged the displacement of up to 45 million people, most of whom would be left to persish by starvation. Although there was no precise detail or prescriptive clarity about the ultimate destination of displaced peoples "what cannot have been in doubt is that the process of 'evacuation' would involve mass death on an epic scale" and therefore the plan, agreed by all the relevant agencies of the Nazi state, "should be taken no less seriously than the programme outlined by Heydrich at the Wannsee conference" (Tooze 2007 p.467 and p.468). The Reich's genocidal ambition, in re-drawing ethnic boundaries and setting a timetable for the extinction of entire populations, was absolutely staggering. It was only when the prerequisite for this plan   (i.e. the subordination of Soviet territory) became increasingly problematic, that the Nazi zealots began to turn toward more immediate and dramatic alternatives.

In fact acts of the utmost brutality and barbarism, including mass murder, had already become commonplace in the east shortly after the invasion (see Gilbert 1986 p.218 who notes, for example, the nineteen thousand Jews in Odessa assembled at a square near the port, sprayed with gasoline and burned alive). Indeed genocide had already begun under the auspices of the Reich Security Department against the Polish intelligentsia and Soviet Commissars, using summary execution by firing squad and mobile carbon-monoxide asphyxiation by units of *SS Einsatzkommandos* supported by the *Wehrmacht* (who kept precise statistical records) (Cohn-Sherbok 1999 p.153). In July 1941 Himmler made the fateful decision to include women and children as targets for extermination (Rees 2005a p.79). These so-called "'useless eaters'" would be shot next to open pits, in a process so gruesome that even some of the members of the vastly expanded and specially trained *Einsatzgruppen* would balk at the practicalities. By November 1941 systematic extermination was well underway (Burleigh and Wipperman 1991 p.103). However, it is also significant that evacuation and extermination gathered pace dramatically after the entry of the USA into the war in December 1941, which seemed to confirm, for Hitler, that the conflict was somehow being orchestrated by international Jewry (Rees 2005a p.111). The Nazi vision for the Jews became progressively more apocalyptic and the critical moment appeared to have occured on 12 December when Hitler spoke to assembled *Gauleiters* after which, according to Goebbels, those assembled were left in little doubt that there would be a systematic annihilation of the Jews (see Mazower 2009 p.375-76). Thereafter there followed large-scale and coordinated efforts to organize the transportation of Jews from across the occupied areas to designated camps in the east where they would be slaughtered. The continued efforts to deploy more "efficient" and less emotionally demanding methods of killing had led to experiments in "gassing techniques" which were expanded, and this process soon resulted in the obscenity of mass, mechanised extermination by poison gas at Chelmno, Belzec, Sorbibor, Treblinka and Auschwitz-Birkenau. The "Final Solution" had taken its ultimate, final form.

It has been persuasively argued that "Auschwitz, through its destructive dynamism, was the physical embodiment of the fundamental values of the Nazi state" (Rees 2005a p.8, see Bergen 2008). Mass murder using Zyklon B began at Auschwitz in September 1941 when gas was tested on Soviet POWs and sick inmates, and developed into mechanized murder on an industrial scale. Here, as camp commandant Rudolf Hoess described it, "'vigorous young men and women walked unsuspecting to their death in the gas chambers, under the blossom-laden fruit trees'", where the extermination was carried out "'without pity and in cold blood'" (Hoess cited in ABSM p.75 and p.79). At the height of its efficiency, according to Hoess, Auschwitz was able to gas 10,000 people per day (cited in Burleigh and Wipperman 1991 p.106). Many inmates were deliberately starved, worked to death, or tortured in the infamous Block 11 under the tyranny of the bestial *Untersturm-fuhrer* Max Grabner, whilst others were pressed into service as *Sonderkommandos* to perform the gruesome tasks of burning and burial (see Rees 2005a p.143, ABSM 1995). Other unfortunate inmates were the victims of gruesome "scientific" experiments undertaken by the so-called "angel of death", Josef Mengele. Such sadistic "medical" procedures included injecting "patients" with phenol, petrol or chloroform, and performing grusome "experiments" on twins, such as vivisection or sewing veins together, in order to identify genetic differences and/or test spurious racial hypotheses (Gilbert 1987 p.581 see p.689; Cohn-Sherbok 1999 p.187, see p.192). Other techniques were tested out on inmates to examine the limits of human endurance, and data was gathered on the effects of freezing, burning, high altitude, starvation and drinking sea water. Some were infected with deadly diseases like malaria and typhoid so that symptoms could be studied, whilst Nazi gynecologists tried new and bizzare methods of

sterilization. Unfortunate inmates became, in effect, labora-
tory rats destined to facilitate a macabre scientific curiosity.
Occasionally boiled bones were sent to the Anthropological
Museum in Berlin and elsewhere to enrich anatomical collections, and sometimes the skin of victims was used to make
lampshades, or the ashes of the bodies used to fertilize the
gardens of German officers.

Such were the portents of the "New Order" to be created by
the Nazis in the east. In many respects the absolute barbarity
of it all remains difficult to comprehend, still less convey in
words - the death camps were nothing less than the distilled
essence of an evil ideology, the material manifestation of hell
on earth. As Primo Levi said, "the Nazi camps were the apex,
the culmination of Fascism in Europe, its most monstrous
manifestation" (Levi 2008 p.390) [38]. The eventual figure
given at Nuremberg for those executed was 5,700,000 (see
Noakes and Pridham 1974 p.493; see Renton 2001 p.12) and
as Gilbert says "neither compliance, nor resistance, could stop
the juggernaut of death" (Gilbert 1987 p.452). Millions were
de-humanised and destroyed in a manner which beggars the
imagination – the conscious mind simply recoils at the very
thought of such depravity. Yet it happened.

The clinically efficient, morally detached dynamic which
drove the process of annihilation is clearly indicated by the
testimony of Rudolf Hoess, Commandant of Auschwitz: "'I have
never personally hated the Jews. It is true that I looked on them
as the enemies of our people...You can be sure that it was not
always a pleasure to see those mountains of corpses or smell
the continual burning. But Himmler had ordered it and had
explained the necessity and I really never gave much thought
to whether it was wrong. It just seemed a necessity'" (cited in
Landau p.80-81). Interestingly, although Hoess detested the
"'evil machinations'" of Jewry, he expressed "'disgust'" at the
"'sensationalism'" of *Der Sturmer* "'which played on people's
basest instincts'" (cited in ABSM 1995 p.55). Hoess, a self-
confessed "'fanatical National Socialist'" (cited in ABSM 1995
p.55), who believed in the ultimate rectitude of Nazi racial

policy, evidently felt that he was above the more vulgar forms of prejudice, yet he was the primary instrument of genocidal ethnic cleansing by the Nazi regime. For his part, at his last visit to Theresienstadt, Adolf Eichmann was over-heard to say, "'I shall gladly jump into the pit, knowing that in the same pit are five million enemies of the state'" (cited in Gilbert 1987 p.792), whilst Himmler himself infamously claimed that "'...we had the moral right, we had the duty to our people, to destroy this people which wanted to destroy us...we have exterminated a bacterium'" (cited in Noakes and Pridham 1974 p.492-93; see Kershaw 2009 p.776-77, and Burleigh 2001 p.661). Such was the grotesque "moral" imperative of the Nazi's racial ideology, revealed in all its bleak, icy darkness. So we can see clearly in retrospect, as Raul Hilberg so eloquently explained in his meticulous study, the various levels in the attempted destruction of European Jewry: definition, expropriation, concentration, deportation and annihilation (see Hilberg 1985 Volume One p.53-54).

There has inevitably been sustained debate about the causes of Nazi "genocide", a phrase initially coined by legal scholar and Jewish refugee Raphael Lemkin in 1944 (see Engel 2000 p.2, Browning 1992). This discussion has focused primarily on whether the *Shoah* can be considered *sui generis*, and on the debate between so-called "intentionalists" and "structuralists"/"functionalists" (see Browning 1993, Landau 1998 p.177, Cohn-Sherbok 1999 p.82, Cesarani 1996). The "intentionalists" (such as Lucy Dawidowicz, Karl Hildebrand, Saul Friedlander, Alan Bullock, K.D. Bracher, David Bankier) see a direct, linear, consistent, almost inexorable connection between ideological belief, political intent and practical outcomes. As Dawidowicz claimed, "the nexus between idea and act has seldom been as evident in human history with such manifest consistency" (Dawidowicz 1975 p.3). The Holocaust, according to Davidowicz, was never really in doubt because Hitler willed it. As Bankier argues, despite the occasional tactical compromise and propitious prevarication, the anti-semitic measures implemented by the state were "a faithful translation of Hitler's wishes", indeed "Hitler was not the prisoner of forces, but rather their creator" (Bankier 1988 p.1 and p.17). On the other hand the "functional-ists" or "structuralists" (for instance Martin Broszat, Hans Mommsen, Christopher Browning, Karl Schleunes) tend (to varying degrees) to emphasise the idea of de-centred impro-visation, cumulative radicalization, incremental bureaucratic momentum, pragmatic polycratic reaction to crises, and a more chaotic, "twisted path" to genocide (Schleunes 1970, see Engel 2000, Neville 1999, Thurlow 1999, Marrus 1993, Broszat 1981, Mommsen 1982). This perspective, in rejecting premeditated programming, focuses on the internecine power struggles in the organizational jungle of a regime faced with complex logistical challenges, which produced formless, fragmentary and irrational policy outcomes that, in turn, precipitated genocide (see Broszat 1981). In this scenario the semi-autonomous, polycratic nature of state structures and the short-term process of micro-level experimentation and stock-taking are as significant in producing particular policies as any fixed, longer-term and consistently held meta-political purpose. This view sees Hitler less as an omnipotent dictator imposing his will, and more as a prevaricating, indecisive procrastinator – Hitler as Hamlet!

There has also been a related debate about exactly when in 1941 the final order was given regarding the Jewish ques-tion, and whether the order(s) for extermination reflected the "euphoria of victory", or the "frustrated rage" at mili-tary setbacks (see Browning 1992, 1993 p.222 and 1996 p.137, who claims the former). Marrus, for instance, focuses on the "momentus" decision to halt Jewish emigration and block all exits toward the end of 1941 (Marrus 1993 p.27-28), whilst others consider the plans to re-locate the Jews to Madagascar or Siberia as evidence that the drift toward genocide was extemporal, although given the likely practi-calities it should be noted that the Nazi policies of forced emigration and extermination were never mutually exclusive (see Williamson 1998 p.75, also Carr 1987). Of course there is no definitive, documentary proof to confirm any specific position or to resolve conclusively the debate regarding the "Final Solution", since "no written order for a comprehensive killing programme, from Hitler or anyone else, has been found" (Engel 2000 p.54; see Neville p.39). There was no definitive blueprint and the actual decision was, as Hilberg explains, accompanied by "irresolution" and "cryptic intimations" (Hilberg 1993 p.16). Although this fissure in the historiography has been eagerly seized upon by the likes of David Irving, with his malevolent revisionist agenda, Christopher Browning is undoubtedly correct to have highlighted the fact that this was not how the *Fuhrer* operated anyhow – the line of responsibility to Hitler was clear even if the written record does not reflect that (see Cesarani 1996 p.7). As Hilberg says, written laws and decrees gave way to oral directives as the sources of authority became "more and more ethereal" (Hilberg 1985 Volume Three p.996).

In fact Steinbacher is probably correct when he argues that the plan for systematic murder of the European Jews was not the result of a single 'order', but the product of a lengthy decision making process, which found concrete form in autumn 1941, and was put in motion step by step, before being systematically undertaken in the early summer of 1942 (Steinbacher 2005). Genocide was not so much directed from above as the result of a gradually radicalized policy, intensified to an extreme that probably came into being spasmodically, in a process of "'cumulative radicalisation'" (Steinbacher 2005 p.82). The lack of central direction therefore facilitated private initiative, which forced the pace of radicalization in accordance with the over-riding objective set by the Fuhrer and his eliminationist ideology (see Kershaw 1989 p.65). An extraordinary number of agencies (in the civil service, the military, the party and business) were drawn into the process of liquidation (see Hilberg 1993 p.20) and consequently there is a real sense in which the Final Solution was derived from regional initiatives and local autonomy, as functionaries "worked towards" the Fuhrer (Kershaw 2009 Chapter 12). In effect the assault on the Jews gathered pace incrementally, in an "ascending spiral" of murderous violence (see Paxton 2005 p.158). In fact the recent scholarly trend is to see the genocide as the product of local Nazi subordinates, a policy outcome arrived at in a fragmented, improvised and chaotic manner, rather than a clearly defined and singular plan imposed centrally by the regime. As Hilberg says "the process of destruction unfolded into a definite pattern. It did not, however, proceed from a basic plan" (Hilberg 1985 Volume One p.53). In this sense it could therefore be argued that "the ad hoc nature of the Nazi state encouraged a cumulative radicalization of policy" (Renton 2001 p.13), and "the annihilation policy was radicalized within the context of the expanding war" (Longrich 1999/2000 p.7). However it is important to reiterate that identifying the institutional dynamic underpinning Nazi barbarism should not in any way deny the moral culpability of Hitler, who instigated and approved all major policies, it is only to insist that a single individual cannot carry the entire burden of explanation (Mason 1996 p.220, see Browning 1993).

Although there may have been no single "grand design" or definitive date for a specific decision, all racial policies were adopted and implemented within the framework of the genocidal logic inherent in Nazi ideology. The neglect of the ideological dimension, as the "intentionalists" are anxious to point out, is a categorical error. Indeed, fundamentally irresolvable discussions about timescales, structures and processes need not detain or distract us unduly, precisely *because* there is no escaping the ideological dynamic, despite the strenuous efforts of some revisionists to evade it. It is ideology that holds the key to understanding the Holocaust, and which reveals the true location of responsibility. To overstress the functional context of circumstances, systems and bureaucratic procedures sometimes provides a distorting prism which dims the clarity of the object under scrutiny. In this sense discussions about the precise "moment" when genocide began, or how the process developed, or exactly when a decision was made to use industrial gassing methods, or which official gave the actual order, actually tend to obscure rather than elucidate. Hence while Wannsee might, quite legitimately, pre-occupy the historian, those seeking an actual explanation for the *Endlosung* should fix their eyes elsewhere. The key to explanation and responsibility lies in the very idea of racial utopia and the lethal intent which resided in the ideology, however vague or unformulated. We can illustrate this point with reference to a particularly pertinent example.

In his work on Rosenberg, Cecil points out that "it is a striking fact that Rosenberg who is, of all the Nazi leaders, most closely associated with anti-semitism, should have made so little effort, when he had the chance, to pursue his speciality in any systematic way - it is as if the author of a manual on surgery, on finally entering the operating theatre, found that he could not stand the sight of blood" (Cecil 1972 p.115). Moreover Cecil seems to imply that, given his reticence, Rosenberg was somehow more humane than many of his contemporaries in his dealings in the east. This may or may not be the case, but it is surely not the point. To develop Cecil's analogy, the most important point was that the "manual on surgery" was written and, crucially, that it was acted upon, albeit by others. The parameters of what was necessary or acceptable were unquestionably set by those at the top of the Nazi hierarchy. Similarly David Irving's argument that Hitler never gave the order for genocide, or indeed was even perhaps unaware of the perpetration of mass murder (given the absence of written notification as documentary evidence) does not exonerate Hitler at all. Certainly Hitler never did any actual killing (nor did Himmler for that matter) but he had the panoramic view and the power - and what he did was far more important – he advocated it, demanded it and justified it.

The Nazi ideology, which Hitler and Rosenberg formulated and represented, and which eventually permeated the regime, contained the very seeds of genocide, with its ideas on the master-race, sub-humans, anti-semitism, and genetic determinism. The logic of extermination was (is) inherent in the very ideas of Nazism, which were clear long before the legal discrimination, the "territorial solutions" and the gas ovens. The haunting images of the horrendous death camps at Auschwitz, Belsen, Treblinka and elsewhere, manned by the "elite" *Totenkofverbande* units of the SS and inhabited by innocent men, women and children, are a graphic reminder of the true essence and reality of National Socialist racism. Genocide was always a possible, if not inevitable, outcome of a consistently held racial, biological-determinist ideology with access to power - the dystopian project which led from the identification of racial enemy to harassment and legal repression, proceeded logically to the Final Solution. In a very real sense those who assimilated, elaborated and disseminated Nazi-racist ideas were every bit as responsible for the deaths of the nameless millions as those who actually herded the victims into cattle trucks or manned the ovens. It is as well to remember that most participants in the genocide did not even shoot a rifle, still less kill a child, but the ideology enabled party bureaucrats and businesses to destroy people "by sitting at their desks" (Hilberg 1985 Volume Three p.1024). Turning such a merciless ideology into practice was, in many ways, a mundane task even if the outcomes were invariably wretched (see Bauman 1991). As Barkai says "Auschwitz was latent in the anti-semitic obsessions of Hitler and his Party from the beginning, in the way in which the embryo is in the egg or fruit within a bud" (Barkai 1996a p.89).

Hence Nazi ideology and the notion of socio-biological racism was (is), quite simply, lethal. As Raul Hilberg pointed out "when in the early days of 1933 the first civil servant wrote the first definition of 'non-Aryan' into a civil service ordinance, the fate of European Jewry was sealed" (Hilberg 1985 Volume Three p.1044). There was an inexorable, sequential logic at work here, from abstract theoretical disquisition to death camp. To this extent Dawidowicz is surely correct, the so-called "Final Solution" "was not just another anti-semitic undertaking, but a metahistorical programme devised with an eschatological perspective. It was part of a salvational ideology that envisaged the attainment of Heaven by bringing Hell on earth" (Dawidowicz 1975 p.xiv). The road to genocide and annihilation may indeed have been "twisted", but Nazi ideology had furnished the map and compass, and the destination was very clearly marked for all to see. Yet by the time Hitler began to contemplate taking his own life to spare himself the ignominy of defeat, perhaps even shortly after Stalingrad, he must have realised that his race had failed in its historic task as he saw it. Germany's Aryan heroes were not worthy of Hitler's faith, and his "scorched earth" policy, pursued in retreat, revealed his contempt for those who had failed him. Now we can turn to examine the experience of racism in Fascist Italy.

In Italy racism of the specifically bio-genetic Nazi type was not integral to Fascist ideology and consequently did not produce the same results [39]. This has led to the perception that Italy was a "safe haven" for Jews, a myth which in many ways obscures a much more uncomfortable truth (Nidam-Orvieto 2005 p.158, see Zimmerman 2005). In practice under Fascism there was not only a centralised imposition of cultural uniformity underpinned by a clear notion of "Roman" supremacism, the deployment of crude racial categories precipitated a hateful prejudice toward "inferior" peoples. However, despite Mussolini's persistent exhortations about a "New" Rome and the blatantly supremacist nature of the Fascist invasion of Abyssinia, the motivation behind Italian racism was not racial in precisely the same socio-biological and genetic sense deployed by Nazis, although it can nevertheless still be described as unambiguously "racist" (Renton 1999 p.33).

Although the Italian Fascists purveyed a different type of racism, the emphasis on race existed right from the beginning. As Mussolini said, as early as 1921, "'fascism must concern itself with the racial problem; fascists must concern themselves with the health of the race by which history is made'" (cited in Gillette 202 p.4). Mussolini referred to the magnificent linguistic and cultural attributes of the Italian people and their characteristics of audacity and adventure, and he stressed the greatness of Italian history and culture as a consequence. That pseudo-biological racism of the National Socialist variety was not central to Mussolini or his movement at this stage is illustrated by the fact that Mussolini ridiculed such biological determinism as "unscientific'" and "'ridiculous'" (cited in Whittam 1995 p.95). In fact Mussolini made a series of unflattering remarks about the Nazi obsession with race as, essentially, a "meaningless fixation" (see Kallis 2009 p.223). Indeed as late as 1932, after ten years in power, Mussolini was quoted as saying that "'there are no pure races left; not even the Jews have kept their blood unmingled'" and he stated that the notion of "race" was "'a feeling not a reality... national pride has no need for the delirium of race'" (Mussolini cited in McGovern 1946 p.543). For obvious reasons, given the hybridity of Italian peoples, Mussolini could not comfortably endorse the idea of specifically Aryan superiority and he therefore derided the Nordic obsessions which prevailed north of the Alps (see Wilkinson 1981 p.11, and Mack Smith 1985 p.252).

The ambiguity inherent in Italian Fascist engagement with race has led to some differences of emphasis amongst academics, with some attempting to play down the significance of race. Thurlow goes some way toward endorsing this perspective, arguing that, "for Mussolini race was occasionally used as a synonym for nation, and in so far as other European peoples were concerned, no pejorative ascriptions of inferiority were implied by the use of such a term in his philosophy" (Thurlow 1980a p.12). Mussolini's ideas, according to Thurlow, were derived from the Austrian sociologist Glumpowicz and the anthropologist Sir Arthur Keith who emphasised racial formation as a dynamic historical process, not a static biological concept. The nation was seen as the "race cradle", and as long as out-groups were not too numerous and/or divergent (e.g. Africans) race-mixing was not discouraged. However, this perspective perhaps over-states the case somewhat because there is a sense in which explicit racism was evident in Italian Fascism, at least sporadically, long before 1938 (see Gordon 2009, Schnapp 2000 p.172). Mussolini, despite refusing to endorse socio-biology, still saw the white race as the leader of civilization, and feared the social consequences of miscegenation (see Gillette 2002). Mussolini's racism may have been "vague and vascillating" (Gillette 2002 p.44) in the early period but no-one could seriously deny that it existed and had practical implications.

Fascist racism can be seen, for example, in Italian imperial policy in Africa which sometimes even incorporated pseudo-biological notions of racial superiority (see Gordon 2009 p.302-03). Fascist "pacification" of Eritrea and Somaliland not only entailed the most murderous war crimes by Italian military forces, it implicitly condoned the main premise of biological racism – white supremacy. Similarly, during the Abyssinian conflict the local people were effectively treated as sub-human remnants. The first bomb dropped on Addis Ababa destroyed a hospital, Italian planes sprayed mustard gas over ancient villages, and General Rudolfo Graziani's men happily posed for photographs carrying the severed heads of those tribesmen who had the temerity to resist. As Bosworth points out "after the conquest of Addis Ababa in May 1936, Mussolini cheerfully ordered the liquidation of the Ethiopian intelligentsia", indeed he "adopted fire and sword tactics and sought to extirpate the remains of an Ethiopian national history, preserved in the holy city of Aksum" (Bosworth 1998 p.4). As Mussolini himself proclaimed, in his triumphal declaration from the balcony at the Palazzo Venezia in Rome in 1936, "'the Italian people has created the empire with its blood'" (cited in Paxton 2005 p.165), and he was clear that sustaining an empire would be impossible without the appropriate "race consciousness" (see De Grand 2000 p.115). Miscegenation laws were thereafter rigorously applied to the Italian East African colonial territories, forbidding congugal relations between Italians and natives (except prostitutes), and provision was made for residential segregation. Indeed it was even "enacted that Italians should not be seen by the natives performing menial tasks" and those who did so were described as "moral half-castes" (Robertson 1988 p.51). Moreover, as Mussolini himself explained, "'absolute terror'" was the best approach to governing barbarians in Africa (cited in Bosworth 2005 p.299). Similarly the Slovenes in the border territories of north-eastern Italy, near the newly created state of Yugoslavia, were subjected to sustained and murderous ethnic cleansing, and brutal Italianisation was enforced against Slavs in contested territories. Racism was therefore inherent in Italian Fascist conceptions of nationalism and colonialism, and "for Mussolini the necessity of stressing the domination of the Italians over the Africans was the catalyst for the development of a formal doctrine of racial superiority" (Neocleous 1997 p.34).

In Italy although the notion of race was vague and contradictory, and essentially based on an anthropological and "spiritual" reference to a shared Latin history, tradition, language and culture rather than a shared genetic inheritance, the dynamic was unmistakably "racist" and its consequences malignant. Indeed Pollard refers to a form of "cultural genocide" in the Italian context, which stressed the notion of *Romanita* and the need for the forcible assimilation of "barbaric" ethnic minorities into the culturally superior Italian tradition, with its emphasis on order, discipline and law (see Pollard 1998 p.125). Consequently, the Italian imposition of colonial apartheid and the defence of *la razza* should not be ignored or under-emphasised: "Mussolini was more violent, expansionist and racist than his current historical reputation allows" (Paxton 2009 p.550). As Rodogno argues, "racism, which was certainly not imposed by Nazi Germany in the late 1930s, was the most radical part of the fascist project to transform Italians into a warrior race and was also supposed to play an important role in the organization of fascist 'living space' (*sazio vitale*)" (Rodogno 2009 p.240). So although it is important to remember that the specific emphasis was cultural rather than genetic, and in that sense Fascist notions echoed more closely traditional Western European colonialist assumptions, the rebellious native communities resisting Italian domination in Africa were butchered and gassed all the same.

Yet the Fascist regime went on to publish the Manifesto of Race in 1938 which clearly copied Nazi notions about race, indeed the document not only asserted that a purely biological conception of race was correct, but stated that the "'the population of Italy today is of Aryan origin, and its civilization is Aryan'" and "'this ancient purity of blood is the greatest symbol of the Italian nation's nobility. The time has come for Italians to openly declare themselves racist'" (cited in Schnapp 2000 p.173 and p.174). A new racial paradigm was adopted, based on blood. Moreover, the Manifesto stated unambiguously that "'Jews do not belong to the Italian race'" (cited in Schnapp 2000 p.174). Thus from 1938 onward the Fascist regime appeared to adopt a position on race that was ideologically adjacent, if not identical, to Nazism – indeed the words expressed in the Manifesto might have been penned by Himmler himself. Evidently the adoption by Mussolini after November 1938 of an explicit anti-semitism and certain other Nazi racial ideas can be seen, at least partially, in terms of his increasingly sycophantic attitude toward the Nazis (it is even more shameful when one considers that Hitler never made his alliance contingent upon the adoption of such ideas or measures by Mussolini, indeed the Nazis were somewhat surprised by their adoption). In actual fact there is little doubt that the practical legislative aspect of Italian racism and anti-semitism was, in part, the by-product of Mussolini's personal infatuation with National Socialist Germany, coupled with a desire to re-claim the international limelight (see Kallis 2009 p.224-25). In Italy socio-biological racism was deployed at a time when radical Nazism was in the ascendancy, whilst Italian Fascism appeared to be losing some momentum, therefore this derivative form of racism was used quite cynically by the regime in an attempt to reinvigorate an ageing political creed (Mosse 1979a p.31). Therefore, constructed upon Mussolini's instruction in the Ministry of Popular Culture, the Manifesto endorsed a "biological-determinist" view of race and asserted that the Italians were of Aryan stock.

Although "Mussolini decided to synthesize the Nordic Aryan myth with Romanita in his new racial model" it soon became clear that "this development was quite extraordinary, and seemed shocking to many fascists" since, almost over-night, the Italian people were transfigured from mere Latin supremacists into paragons of the Aryan race (Gillette 202 p.55 and p.56). The evidence appears to suggest that Mussolini hoped that the adoption of a new racial agenda, and demonizing the Jewish "other", would somehow precipitate a new Fascist man *Uomo Fascista* (Gillette 2002 p.4). This new type of Italian warrior would lead to a new unified, disciplined, martial solidarity which would, Mussolini hoped, replace the weak, anarchic, superficial, carnivaleasque country he had inherited (see Gillette 2002 p.53). The "Manifesto of Fascist Racism" introduced in 1938 was therefore a fairly transparent and cynically opportunistic attempt to ape National Socialist legislation, and focused specifically on alienating a small community of around 50,000 Italian Jews. However Italian Jews were not only well integrated into an Italian society with no discernible anti-semitic tradition, they had been generally supportive of the Fascist political project, some even held high office in the regime (see Zuccotti 1987 p.24-25). Nevertheless the Manifesto asserted unequivocally that the Jews could not be assimilated, it highlighted the perils of miscegenation, and it explicitly excluded "Orientals" and "Africans" from the notion of the Nordic Italian. The Manifesto was an extraordinary document, which referred to an omnipresent racial consciousness and the creation of world civilization, but apart from solidifying the Axis with Nazism, the content made little sense otherwise given the Italian context (Morgan 1995 p.160-61). As Gregor says, "the doctrinal attempts to provide a rationale for anti-semitic legislation were almost uniformly inept", and the derivative nature of Mussolini's new emphasis on race was reflected in the fact that Mussolini even wanted his

Italian soldiers to copy the German goose step! (Gregor 1969 p.277 see Appendix A p.383; see Gordon p.306).

Ostensibly an extension of demographic policy, a number of anti-Semitic laws were nevertheless promulgated by the regime thereafter: decrees forbidding Jews from settling on Italian land or owning large businesses; forbidding them to teach in state schools; forbidding them to marry Italians; Jews were also excluded from the military, expelled from the PNF, state or municipal posts, banking, insurance and other professions (see Gordon 2009 p.307, Zuccotti 1987 and Zimmerman 2005). Jews were defined as those people with two Jewish parents, although possible exceptions were made in the case of those decorated in war or for services to Fascism. Subsequent decrees which, for example, meant Jews could not own radios, hold conferences, join sports clubs, list names in telephone directories, or attend certain holiday resorts "constituted pure and simple harassment...the zeal with which these measures were executed varied from place to place, but the suffering was widespread and acute" (Zuccotti1987 p.39-40). As Sarfatti states, "from 1938 to 1943 Fascist Italy was determined to eliminate all Jews, whether Italian or foreign, from Italian soil and from Italian society" (Sarfatti 2005 p.75) and these measures taken collectively had "a profound impact on the life of Jews" in Italy, inflicting "much pain, distress and suffering on the Jewish community" (Nidam-Orvieto 2005 p.160 and p.175, see Levi 2005). This hostility toward the Jew was later taken to another level in the Salo Republic, which was in effect a German puppet state where the Third Reich's plenipotentiary Rudolf Rahn looked menacingly over Mussolini's shoulder. In effect "the Italian government of the RSI put the full weight of its apparatus in the service of the anti-Jewish persecution" (Picciotto 2005 p.215). In a deadly division of labour, the Italian authorities in northern Italy searched for, arrested and interned the Jews, whilst the German overlords organized deportation, and both parties were well aware that extermination was the end result. The fact that only around

6,000 or so suffered death as a consequence of this policy does not diminish in any way its barbarism.

However, it is also worth highlighting the fact that there was actually a degree of ambivalence in Italian anti-semitism for as Bosworth says, "just as the arguments launched by the *Duce* and others were fretted with hypocrisy and confusion, so the practice of Italian Anti-Semitism and other forms of racism was never tempered into steely consistency...the lenience in racial practice in Italian territories and the skepticism in most Italian minds about racial theory indicated that modern racism was an accretion to Fascism and not its epicentre" (Bosworth 2002 p.342 and p.393). Mussolini, Bosworth argues, never possessed the level of racist rigour required to make him a good SS recruit (Bosworth 2002 p.11). Despite the fact that a minority of Fascists, like Roberto Farinacci, Telisio Interlandi, Giovanni Preziosi and Paolo Orano enthusiastically embraced anti-Semitic laws, many Fascists and, more crucially, most of Italian society, rejected them as a sign of slavish subservience to the Third Reich. Italian racism had existed since its inception, as one of the underlying assumptions and manifestations of Fascist ideology, but the explicitly socio-biological version, as it evolved after 1938, was more alien and incongruous, chiming oddly with past Fascist experience - it was a "poor, half-hearted imitation of National Socialism" (Wiskemann 1969 p.70, see Thurlow 1980 and 1980a).

Overall it is quite evident that racism lay at the very core of fascism. Even if we acknowledge the extent to which racial categorization had permeated European intellectual and cultural life in the period before the ascendancy of fascism, and even if we accept that the emphasis on inherent ethnic superiority and/or eugenics (implicit or otherwise) was used to justify colonial hegemony around the world, fascism produced something unique. In fascism as a political movement the element of eliminationist racism was raised to a matter of explicit ideological principle, and the practical consequences were unparalleled in terms of the impact on humanity. Fascism's heterophobia, in exploiting pre-existing prejudice, gave people a licence not only to hate but, by subverting conventional moral, social, legal and cultural codes of behaviour, afforded an open-ended licence to kill with impunity in the most performative and sadistic manner (see Kallis 2009).

Thus the major "themes" of fascist theory and practice have been outlined: its underlying irrationalism and social Darwinism; its xenophobic nationalism, militarism and imperialism; its state authoritarianism; the importance placed upon social discipline; the crucial role of the mass party and dictatorial leader; its uncompromising anti-communism; its collectivist/corporatist approach to economics which, although ambiguous in theory, in practice was antagonistic toward socialism and labour, and sympathetic toward capital; and finally its racism, which was absolutely central to National Socialism but of a qualitatively different type in Fascist Italy. Having described (albeit briefly) the predominant facets of the fascist totality we can now, in the light of what has been deduced, assess the nature of British fascism and thereafter evaluate with much greater clarity the validity of the various theoretical interpretations of fascism.

## NOTES

1]   Indeed one analyst begins his account by explaining that fascism is just one of those "isms", and given that disagreement was inevitable, declined to attempt a definition (see Hayes 1973). Meanwhile Laqueur argues that the search for theories and definitions "matters less than is widely thought" (Laqueur 1996 p.223). See also Blinkhorn (1990), Mosse (1979), and Mandel's introduction to Trotsky's *The Struggle Against Fascism in Germany* (1971).

2]   See Togliatti's work in Beetham (ed) (1983) *Marxists in Face of Fascism*. See also Weissman's (1969) introduction to Trotsky's *Fascism, what it is and how to fight it*. Rees (1984 p.22) uses the term to describe Sinn Fein/IRA, apparently on the basis of one quote! This clearly demonstrates the extent of the problem and the dangers inherent in the ill-considered misapplication of ideological labels.

3]    For the actual historical derivation of the word "fascism" see O'Sullivan (1983 p.207), see also Wilkinson (1981 p.l).

4]    For example see Seton Watson in Mosse (1979 p.371), and Bosworth (2002 p.426-27).

5]    This approach is frequently adopted, although the elements used may vary considerably between accounts. See for instance Hayes (1973), or Kedward (1971).

6]    See Greil (1977-78 and 1977-78a). For an alternative view see the work of Gregor (1977-78 and 1979) who argues that the idea that (Italian) Fascism was anti-intellectual is simply "folk-wisdom" and that Fascism's intellectual credentials are as compelling as any. Many contemporary analysts also give weight to the significance of fascist ideas (see the work of Eatwell, Griffin and others). Of course it is perfectly possible to emphasise the instinctivist dimension in fascism whilst also accepting that fascism is a system of ideas. That is, the focus on the irrational does not detract from or diminish entirely its ideological status.

7]    See Gentile (e.g. in Lyttleton 1973) who wrote the *Doctrine of Fascism: Fundamental Ideas*. Gentile expounded the idea that sentiment was prior to thought and the basis of it, but which was confirmed by reason. See Gentile *Genesis and Structure of Society* which was published post-humously. Gentile was assassinated in April 1944 but never lost faith in the Fascism he endorsed and advocated. See Harris (1966) *The Social Philosophy of Giovanni Gentile* for a sympathetic account (Harris refers to his own work as a rescue operation or an "essay in salvage" p.viii). Harris argues that Gentile's philosophy might be saved if divorced from Fascist practice - hardly a Gentilian approach. Meanwhile Gregor refers to the "genius" of Gentile and argues that his work compares favourably with Lenin or Marx (see Gregor 1979 p.5 and p.14). This is commensurate with Gregor's general view that "(Italian) Fascism as an ideology was a far more complex and systematic intellectual product than many of its antagonists (and many of its protagonists as well) have been prepared to admit" (Gregor 1979 p.26, see p.61 and especially p.205).

8]   In a rare moment of reflexive candour the *Duce* confessed that the only mistakes he ever made were when he had obeyed reason rather than his own more trustworthy instincts   (Bosworth 2002 p.26). See Mussolini's auto-biography (1939 p.34) where his disdain for books is clearly evident.

9]   Smith (1979 chapter 3), however, tends to disagree with this assertion. Interestingly Neocleous argues that the "logic" of nationalism is *necessarily* xenophopic and thus "always remains an invitation to anti-Semitism and racism" (Neocleous 1997 p.32). There is an important element of truth in this observation. However, although racism was undoubtedly a critical component of fascism, and was intimately connected to the idea of nationalism in the European context, the notion that *all* nationalisms point in that direction is difficult to sustain. It is hard to square this perspective, for instance, with the history of anti-colonialism and national liberation movements.

10]  With regard to the obsession with all things military, Mussolini reveals in his autobiography that he was an excellent soldier, and that in 1917 he had twenty-seven operations in one month, nearly all without an aneas-thetic! The autobiography is a predictably dreadful book - indeed it is difficult to make it past the obsequious introduction by Washburn Child – but it provides an interesting insight into the dictator's state of mind, and indeed the masculine vanity that dominated the Fascist movement at the time (Mussolini 1939).

11]  See also Mussolini (1939) chapter IV on "worn out" democracy.

12]  Goebbels was particularly clear on this point, claiming categorically that the Nazis were going to "'cripple the Weimar mentality with its own crutches ...no-one should imagine that Parliamentarianism will tame us...we come as enemies'" (cited in Maser 1973 p.253).

13]  See the first section of the *Political and Social Doctrine of Fascism*, which although attributed to Mussolini, was actually written by Gentile - see Lyttleton (1973 p.41).

14]  See, for example, the letter written by Gentile to Mussolini which claimed that all true liberals must follow Fascism, see Harris (1966 p.167-8).

15]  This extraordinary rule change meant that whichever party received 25% of the vote was entitled to two-thirds of the seats.

16]  Bendersky (1983 p.208) argues that Schmitt never converted to Nazism, even though he joined the party, accepted anti-semitism, and referred to the Nuremberg Laws as the "constitution of freedom". In fact Schmitt's career is a sorry tale of intellectual vanity and complicity with evil. The nature of Schmitt's conservatism and his contribution to Nazi success is particularly pertinent given the comments made in the conclusion to this text.

17]  In the Italian case such techniques might even be traced back to Garibaldi's National Unity Movement/Red Shirts, although given that movement's more progressive agenda this is a more controversial contention.

18]  Mosse (1979 p.26) refers to childrens' books where Mussolini is described as, "as strong as a hurricane" and (even less plausibly) as "beautiful as the sun"! Mussolini's musical biographer, De Renzis, could not ignore the fact that Il Duce was not actually a virtuoso violinist, but claimed "'he is something greater and better – a musician in his very heart and soul'" (cited in Bosworth 1998 p.156).

19]  For an alternative perspective see Poulantzas (1974) who suggests that once transformed the state dominated the party. This is a difficult position to sustain given the pre-eminent role of the party in the progressive radicalization of the regime right up to 1945.

20]   Predictably Gregor (1969 p.303) offers a different inter-
        pretation which portrays Fascist Corporatism much
        more positively as a threat to privilege. The empirical
        evidence to justify such a conclusion is meagre.

21]   References by Hitler to the threat of Marxism and the
        need to eradicate it are legion, but see for example *Mein
        Kampf* (1974 p.142) and the speech given to the Reich-
        stag 17 May 1933 cited in Baynes (1969 p.117).

22]   For the most part Hitler was actually far from destitute,
        see the footnote by Watt in his introduction to *Mein
        Kampf* (1974 p.19). This of course did not stop Hitler
        making the most of the myth of his poverty, as he says
        in his own unmistakable style "'he who has not himself
        been gripped in the clutches of this strangulating viper
        will never come to know its poisoned fangs'" (cited in
        Fest 1973 p.203).

23]   Otto Strasser went on to develop his ideas with regard to
        nationalism, corporatism, autarky, and "entail" (private
        property owned at the discretion of the community). He
        also offered detailed proposals for a federated Europe,
        and argued the need for a new elite vanguard to articu-
        late the revolutionary sentiments of the masses. See
        Strasser *Germany Tomorrow* (1940a).

24]   Gregor, among others, argues that such radical ideas
        remained with Mussolini, (1969 see p.307, p.318)
        although this argument is far from convincing. See
        also, for example, Settenbrini (1979 p.91) who actually
        suggests parallels between Fascism and Leninism.

25]   See Halperin (1964 p.29). Interestingly Poulantzas (1974
        p.131-2 and p.222) argues that the Italian rural Fascist "left"
        was more radical than the Strasser faction in Germany.

26]   Once again see Gregor (e.g. 1979 p.21) for an alternative
        view which stresses (Italian) Fascism's commitment to the
        "humanism of labour", "presumptive equality" and so on.

27]   Thus we can conclude that Gregor's thesis, which explains
        Italian Fascism as a heretical socialist movement, forced
        by circumstances to ally with Conservatives but being

social revolutionary in intent and antagonistic toward capitalism, is a straightforward misinterpretation of historical reality (see Gregor 1969 especially p.376).

28] Those still in need of additional evidence to confirm the fact that the fascist leaders were vociferous anti-socialists might also consult Hitler's speech to the Reichstag 1937 cited in Baynes (1969 p.214-15), and to the Nuremberg Parteitag of 1934 (also cited in Baynes 1969 p.329); also Mussolini's article in *Gerarchia* dated 25 February 1922 entitled "Which way is the world going?" (cited in Lyttleton 1973 p.64) where he actually talks explicitly of Fascism as a "reaction of the right".

29] See Taylor (1985 chapter 4 especially p.116) for specific organizational contacts.

30] See also Hitler's speech to the Reich's Governors on 6 July 1933 for confirmation of his determination to leave the economy well alone (cited in Noakes and Pridham 1974 p.204-05).

31] This observation is reinforced by comparative reference to Britain where there was a relatively high level of state intervention in the economy between 1939 and 1945. Few analysts would seriously suggest that capitalism was terminated or somehow transcended during that period.

32] Weber (1964 p.69) is one of the few to contest this with the implausible assertion that racism and anti-semitism were "not a necessary part" of National Socialism. Others argue that racism makes it so distinctive that it should not be considered as a variant of fascism (see Sternhell in Renton 1999 p.23). It might be noted here, as we embark on the analysis of Nazi racism, that there has also been some acrimonious debate over how far the voices of the victims of fascism have subjectively distorted the reality of National Socialism. The so-called *Historikerstreit* controversy set the likes of Saul Friedlander against Martin Broszat, with the latter arguing for a more rational and dispassionate evaluation of Nazism. On the other hand Orna Kenan, in the Foreword to Friedlander's abridged text, argues against the "smugness of scholarly detachment" (Friedlander 2009 p.xi). That the words of Primo Levi should weigh no less heavily than those of AJ Gregor or Roger Griffin would seem to be, not only eminently reasonable, but actually imperative for a genuine understanding of the Nazi phenomenon.

33] See Pois (1970 p.23) and Burleigh and Wipperman (1991). H.S.Chamberlain, who actually became a German citizen and married Wagner's daughter, even earned a mention in *Mein Kampf* (1974 p.245).

34] His initial speech was provided at the request of his superior officer in the army Captain Karl Meyer; the political testament was written in the bunker just prior to his suicide. See Hitler (1961b) and the work of Maser (1970, 1973 and 1973a).

35] According to some sources they actually met in 1909, and Goodrick-Clarke claims that Lanz von Liebenfels wrote in 1932 that "'Hitler is one of our pupils'" (cited in Goodrick-Clarke 1992 p.192). See introduction by Watt to *Mein Kampf* (1974 p.xxxvii); see also Smith (1979 p.74), Burleigh and Wipperman (1991 p.35) and Maser (1970 p.167).

36] Hitler was, however, ambivalent toward Rosenberg personally because he wanted his own position secure as chief ideologue, see Cecil (1972 p.73) and Pois (1970 chapter IV "The Enemy"). Pois in fact provides a devastating critique of Rosenberg's use of half-truths and distortions to malign the Jewish faith and people – "he simply did not know what he was talking about" (1970 p.25). Rosenbaum highlights the extraordinary claim that Hitler's primal hatred of Jews might even have superceded that of Nazi Neanderthal Julius Streicher, whose thuggish, hateful vitriol even appalled some of his own colleagues (see Rosenbaum 1998 p.190).

37] There are numerous references to this, especially in "Table Talk" (1973), see also Rauschning (1939 p.57-8). Cecil (1972 p.85) refers to Rosenberg's "religion of the blood", while Pois (1970 p.100) analyses Rosenberg's idea of Nordic religion and his distinction between positive and negative Christianity ("honour and love"). It seems that Rosenberg actually believed that Jesus was not Jewish, and that Saul of Tarsus perverted Christian teachings. At Nuremberg in 1937 Rosenberg assured his audience that the German people were not born in sin but in nobility (see also Cecil 1972 p.92). For a more sceptical view see Steigmann-Gall (2005) who doubts that Hitler shared Himmler's interest in projecting Nazism as a neo-pagan religion and points out that Hitler preferred to claim Christ as the "greatest Aryan leader" (see Steigmann-Gall 2005 p.96). The irony of Adolf Hitler attempting to rescue Christ from his Jewish heritage was doubtless a bizarre case of the Fuhrer making the best of being dealt a bad hand.

38] To get some kind of insight into the nature of the suffering see, for example, the statement of Friedrich Grabe on the mass liquidation of 5,000 Jews in the Ukraine on 5 October 1942, the depraved work of Dr. Sigmund Rascher at Dachau or Prof August Hirt, chief of the Anatomical Institute at Strasbourg (who, among other things, made a study of severed heads sent from the eastern front). See also the testimony at Nuremberg of Auschwitz Commandant Rudolph Hoess - see Shirer (1985 p.956, p.979), Fest (1973 p.682), Gilbert (1987) and Cohn-Sherbok (1999). In this context it is worth noting the work of Charles Reznikoff who has constructed powerful verse (originally published in 1975) based upon the factual testimony contained within the publication of the Nuremberg and Eichmann trial transcripts. The result is a powerful artistic record of extraordinary cruelty:

> *"The SS man shook the baby from her arms,*
> *and shot her twice,*
> *and then held the baby in his hands.*
> *The mother, bleeding but still alive, crawled up to his feet.*
> *The SS man laughed*
> *and tore the baby apart as one would a rag.*

*Just then a stray dog passed*
*and the SS man stooped to pat it*
*and took a lump of sugar out of his pocket*
*and gave it to the dog"*
(Reznikoff 2010 p.20-21)

39] In fact, as Zimmerman (2005) has pointed out, the subject of Italian Jewry under Fascist  rule has been under-researched in English language Holocaust historiography. However, although overall Italian racism was qualitatively different from Nazism, the suggestion by Kallis that Italian Fascism "displayed a strikingly whimsical relation to elimination" is over-drawn and a little insensitive (Kallis 2009 p.10).

# 2. BRITISH FASCISM

This section of the text aims to outline the historical development of fascism in Britain. The purpose of this historical perspective is, broadly speaking, to accomplish two tasks: firstly to map the trajectory of far right wing politics and ideology in Britain and thereby to confirm that the contemporary British far right is a specifically fascist phenomenon, with a clear and unambiguous fascist heritage; secondly to assess the relative failure of the far right to make any significant electoral impact on British politics, and to highlight how, nevertheless, the threat of fascism in Britain is still far from negligible. It might also be pointed out that an analysis of fascist poltics and ideology in Britain is actually inseparable from a study of its organisational form and the prominent personalities that have punctuated the historical narrative. Incidentally, the use of the phrase "far right" in this context is deliberately deployed as opposed to the term "radical right" or "populist right" because the former stands in complete opposition to contemporary constitutional arrangements, whilst the latter may only oppose some of the principles and practices thereof. Hopefully the reasons for adopting this particular epithet will become more evident as the analysis develops.

## The Origin and Development of British Fascism

In Britain the far right in the modern era emerged as a response to, and within the context of, developing social and economic problems in the late Victorian and Edwardian era (Webber 1986). As Pugh points out, "alarmed by the pace of social change and the rise of the labour movement, and frustrated by its own impotence, sections of the Edwardian right began to display a serious disillusionment with conventional politics" (Pugh 2005 p.16). However, the birth of the far right, in an organisational sense, is conventionally dated at 1902 when the British Brothers League was formed. Particularly strong in the East End of London the League's primary objective was to curtail immigration in the area, most of which was from Eastern Europe. However, the organisation did not survive the Great War, although that cataclysmic conflict and the Bolshevik revolution were to provide significant impetus to similar groups on the far right, therefore "British fascism's first impetus lay in an ultra-conservative response to the social consequences of the First World War and the rise of Bolshevism" (Baker 1996 p.17). There is also a sense in which the emergence of the far right in this period reflected an anxiety about the relative decline in Britain's global position, as both Germany and the United States increased their share of the world's manufacturing production. Those industries which had sustained Britain's commercial success, such as coal, iron, steel, and textiles, were on a long trajectory of relative economic decline. By 1913 Britain was no longer the dominant player in the international economy, and the Boer War had already highlighted Britain's diminishing military capabilities (Thurlow 1998 p.8). The Empire, it seemed, was in crisis and resistance to it was growing – the Easter Rising in Dublin in 1916 provided stark evidence of this on the doorstep. Therefore elements on the far right in Britain began to seek new political answers. This sense of anxiety on the "right" of the political spectrum about Britain's international pre-eminence and economic prosperity was only partially arrested by victory in 1918, as connections were made to the apparently degenerative effects of mass democracy. Hierarchy and deference were being replaced by a post-war culture of political agitation which reflected a discernible and increasingly audible desire for social reform, as Thurlow says, "the failure of the politicians to create a society which adequately compensated for the horror and trauma of the war produced a mood of frustrated anger which tinted the utopian cravings of many attracted to fascism" (Thurlow 1998 p.15).

One of the more important groupings on the far right in this period was the Britons Society which not only aimed to protect the birthright of British people, its membership was restricted to people who could prove that their parents and grandparents were of "British blood" (Pugh 2005 p.28). Set up just after the war in 1919 the Britons Society led, in turn, to the formation of the influencial Britons Publishing Company in 1922 which was designed to disseminate radical right wing literature (see Baker 1996 p.18). Preoccupied by imperial decline and socio-economic decay, the aim of the Britons Society was to eliminate "alien" influences in British political and economic life (Linehan 2000 p.50). Its founder and President was Henry Hamilton Beamish, who was largely responsible for the articulation of a crude anti-semitic conspiracy theory which, he claimed, "explained" social dete- rioration and the demise of Empire. According to this theory the Jews, by utilising their influence in the press and financial circles, planned for ultimate world domination. The *Protocols of the Learned Elders of Zion* (an infamous Tsarist forgery) was cited as empirical "evidence" of the existence of this conspiracy (see Thurlow 1976a p.27). Beamish even spoke at Nazi meet- ings in Germany and the genocidal nature of his ideas can be gauged by his belief that a Jew-ridden Bolshevik Russia should be immediately invaded, after which, he suggested, half the population should be exterminated and the other half placed in a zoo! (see Thurlow 1998 p.49). Undoubtedly it was the "Jewish question" that preoccupied the Britons, to the virtual exclusion of all other considerations (Linehan 2000 p.51). Although the Britons organization could not be construed as a movement or a party, because it did not seek political power (it actually urged its supporters to vote Conservative), by printing and distributing literature by anti- semitic conspiracy theorists like Nesta Webster and Father Denis Fahey, with their apocalyptic visions and crude racism, its ideological influence on future generations of right wing groups and theorists should not be underestimated.

The inter-war period in Britain was also marked by the growth of numerous embryonic fascist movements, emerging in the wake of Mussolini's take-over in Italy. As Pugh says "the impression that Mussolini had rejuvenated the 'Italian race' and restored national pride and unity made a heady appeal to those who felt disillusioned and alienated from the post-war democracy in Britain" (Pugh 2009 p.493). One such organization, and the first to openly claim the "fascist" title, was the British Fascisti (BF) set up in May 1923 by Miss Rotha Lintorn-Orman. Described by Thurlow as "a spirited young middle-class woman" (Thurlow 1998 p.33) she admired Mussolini and expressed a keen desire to supersede the ideological constraints of conventional Conservatism. The organization, which changed its name in 1924 to the more British-sounding British "Fascists", was financed via Lintorn-Orman's inherited wealth and became preoccupied with treacherous left wing revolutionaries intent on destroying Throne and Empire. Despite containing some working class elements in its membership, most active participants came from the reactionary middle and upper classes. Indeed the BF's General Council and Executive Council were disproportionately staffed by politically disgruntled members of the aristocracy and military, such as BF Presidents Lord Garvagh and Brigadier-General Robert B.D. Blakeney, and Vice-President Rear Admiral A.E. Armstrong. Therefore "the sociological composition of the membership, to a remarkable degree, reflected the reactionary character of the BF's political mission" (Linehan 2000 p.154 see Chapter 6). Structurally hierarchical and divided into sections, the organisation's divisional or district commanders supervised local units, which eventually adopted the blue shirt as an official "uniform" in 1927.

Oddly, at times the BF claimed to be non-political, which in reality meant that at election time they provided practical support for the Conservative party (the BF's "blue shirts" even stewarded some Conservative meetings). Indeed, according to Baker, the BF "was little more than another disaffected middle-class defence league, made up largely of Conservatives obsessed with the dangers of civil strife and Bolshevism, and seeking to maintain public order and guarantee essential services through a network of paramilitary units if Red Revolution should come to the Home Counties" (Baker 1996 p.19; see Griffiths 2005 p.44 and Cross 1961 p.62). As Griffiths confirms, the BF was "basically a Conservative movement, obsessed with the dangers of civil emergency" (Griffiths 2005 p.43). The BF's ideology focused on patriotism and pledged loyalty to traditional institutions like the Monarchy, but it was also "tinged with a heavy moralism" (Linehan 2000 p.64) which opposed sexual promiscuity and vice.  However, the BF did borrow some political ideas from Fascist Italy, such as corporatism, and argued in favour of outlawing strike action by trade unions (Stevenson 1990 p.269). The BF also vociferously supported free enterprise capitalism and even suggested that the best remedy for unemployment was to reduce personal taxation to enable the better-off classes to employ more servants! The BF also urged the purification of the British race by, among other things, imposing a special tax upon aliens. It would nevertheless be true to say that the primary motivation of the British Fascists was fear of, and antagonism toward, "socialism", which was a label covering a multitude of political and social sins. As Cross explained, "the British Fascisti stood simply on the basis of defending King and Parliament against the forces of communism, socialism, anarchism, free love, atheism, and trade unions, which the members tended to lump into a mysterious single entity" (Cross 1961 p.58, see Skidelsky 1981a p.257). Although the BF was a small grouping with few resources and a confused and incoherent policy programme, the fact that it was the first overt and self-consciously fascist organisation is of some significance.

A more important contribution, certainly in terms of ideology if not organisational or electoral impact, was made by Arnold Leese and his Imperial Fascist League. Founded in November 1928 Leese became Director General of the IFL in 1930 and it undoubtedly constituted a more authentic manifestation of the fascist experience. Indeed, according to Baker, "the IFL represented the nearest approximation to a fascist organization in 1920s Britain, being virulently anti-Semitic and fervently pro-Nazi in character" (Baker 1996 p.21). Leese, an ex-colonial vet, had been a member of the BF and was deeply influenced by the work of the Britons Society. In fact Leese had stood for the Stamford Fascists in Lincolnshire who managed to win three local authority elections (two in 1924, one in 1927), the only occasion on which candidates with the explicit "fascist" label have won a British election. However, "Leese's view was that the chief function of the IFL was a training organization for an elite of anti-semitic propagandists, not as a political party in its own right" (Thurlow 1998 p.48). Members wore black shirts and the organisation's emblem was a swastika superimposed upon a union jack, while the IFL's magazine *The Fascist* received donations from German Nazis (Dorril 2006 p.203). The IFL was organized hierarchically into three divisions: the Lictors' Association, the Fascist Legions and the Activist Confederations, although these rather grandiose titles obscured the fact that IFL membership only averaged a meagre 150 and the organization was constantly short of funds (Thurlow 1998 p.41, Linehan 2000 p.73).

Leese, "one of the period's most fanatical, uncompromising and idiosyncratic of fascists" (Linehan 2000 p.71) became the primary ideologue for his miniscule band, and saw racial nationalism as the only sound basis for political endeavour. The IFL's ideology, despite containing vague echoes of Mussolini's corporatist experiment and premised upon an unremitting hostility toward liberal Parliamentarianism, was centred on an unyielding biological determinist belief in a Jewish conspiracy and the need for racial purity. Indeed "it is no exaggeration to say that the 'racial' perspective came to dominate the whole of Arnold Leese's outlook on life, underpinning all his views on politics, society and the world" (Woodbridge 2012 p.44). Utilising a crude and dogmatic pseudo-scientific social Darwinism, Leese obsessively attributed all cultural and historical development to the possession of certain racial characteristics whilst the Aryan-Nordic race was viewed as inherently superior to all others. "Aryans were defined as a unique racial aristocracy, history's principal culture-bearers, who alone, of all the variety of racial types, possessed the appropriate personal and mental qualities to ensure the preservation of higher culture and the forward-thrust of civilization" (Linehan 2000 p.184).

As a consequence of this perspective various eugenic measures were advocated to protect the white race from contamination. The Jews, because of their desire to bastardise the Nordic race, were demonized and detested, and anti-semitism was unquestionably the most distinctive feature of the IFL's ideological position. As Leese himself exclaimed, "'that international finance and Bolshevism are Jewish and allied with one another, both working hard against this country, is a fact hardly worth mentioning'" (cited in Thurlow 1976 p.29). According to Leese the pernicious Jew could be blamed for, among other things, cultural degradation, decadence in art, degenerate democracy, class war, communist subversion, parasitic finance, the corruption of morals, and crime (Linehan 2000 p.179). Indeed, still more bizarrely, Leese apparently believed that Jews were descended from the devil and actually engaged in the ritual murder of Christian children for their blood at Passover (see Thurlow 1998 p.51). Even Christianity, according to Leese, formed an integral part of the all-encompassing Jewish plot, and he even claimed to have detected a disturbing Jewish influence in the Fascist-authoritarian regimes of Mussolini and Franco. The IFL's publication *The Fascist* was therefore devoted to fanatical attacks upon Jews which were scarcely less scurrilous than those contained within Julius Streicher's *Der Stuermer* in Germany. In the February 1935 issue of his journal Leese argued that one Jewish grandparent was enough to indicate active participation in the conspiracy, and given that racial characteristics were (according to his theory) immutable, the only sure way of forestalling racial decline was to physically eliminate the Jew. As Leese explained, "'it must be admitted that the most certain and permanent way of disposing of the Jews would be to exterminate them by some humane method such as the lethal chamber'" (cited in Cross 1961 p.153). So, some years before Nazi death camps became a grotesque reality, Leese was not only engaging in venomous anti-semitic invective, he was advocating genocide. It would be fair to say, therefore, that the other elements in the IFL's political programme, such as an advocacy of a new governing caste, the elimination of popular democracy, and the introduction of a corporate state, were all a product of, or subordinated to, an apparently pathological preoccupation with race and the evils of Jewry.

In some ways it is easy to view the IFL as the product of personality disorder rather than politics, but as Linehan has pointed out, "although it failed to make an impact on the domestic political scene, or recruit a mass following, it would be a mistake to disregard the IFL's relevance for the British fascist right" (Linehan 2000 p.79). In fact there were actually many other tiny fascist and racist groups on the far right in Britain between the wars, quite apart from the BF and IFL: for example, the British Empire Fascists, the Fascist League, the National Party, the Nordic League, the Link, the National Socialist League, the National Freedom Party, the British People's Party, English Mistery, English Array, White Knights of Britain, and the National Socialist Workers' Movement. Most, in articulating the same esoteric, pathologically racist, Manichean ideas were miniscule in size and politically inconsequential. However, by far the most important organisation in terms of impact and ideology was the British Union of Fascists (BUF) led by Oswald Mosley. In fact, interestingly, both the BF and IFL rejected merger proposals by the BUF - the BF Grand Council by one vote and the IFL because Leese (perhaps unsurprisingly) suspected Jewish influence, referring to Mosley as a "'kosher fascist'" (see Woodbridge 2012 p.43). Nevertheless the BUF was a much more important phenomenon given its relative size, the status accorded

Mosley as a serious political theorist, and the overall influence of Mosley and the BUF on the subsequent development of the far right in the period after 1945.

## Oswald Mosley and the British Union of Fascists

The first point to establish before proceeding is that although the BUF was by far the most significant of the inter-war organizations in Britain, its "success" was strictly relative. As Stevenson says, "British fascism was among the weakest manifestations of fascism in interwar Europe" and the BUF "failed to make a decisive impact upon British politics" (Stevenson 1990 p.264). The BUF never won a parliamentary or local council seat, and apart from a very brief spell after 1934, when patronised by Lord Rothermere and his newspapers the *Daily Mail* and *Sunday Dispatch*, it never really looked like achieving power. Nevertheless, the BUF "represented the mature form of the fascist phenomenon in British society, being the only organisation with any pretention to significance in inter-war Britain" (Thurlow 1987 p.92). Moreover, there is a sense in which although there was no "decisive impact", fascism was in fact more central to the history of the inter-war era in Britain than is conventionally acknowledged (Pugh 2005 p.2-4).

The British Union of Fascists was founded, principally by Oswald Mosley, on 1 October 1932, and Mosley subsequently dominated the movement (Skidelsky 1981). Mosley had emerged from a brief flirtation with the Conservatives and a spell in the Labour Party, and he had left the latter in February 1931 after resigning his post as Chancellor of the Duchy of Lancaster in May 1930 over the issue of unemployment. After the rejection of the so-called "Mosley memorandum" he took his economic ideas into the short-lived New Party. Although the New Party was not itself an explicitly fascist party "it did provide the chrysalis within which British fascism developed, and from which the BUF emerged" (Lewis 1987 p.12). The New Party attempted to provide an alternative to the petty squabbling of party politics and aimed to supercede class deadlock by appealing to the higher national interest, however, in doing so it began to attract patriotic anti-communists to its cause (Worley 2010 p.74). The New Party also sent delegations to Germany "with instructions to examine Nazi methods and techniques", which led the *Daily Worker* to declare it a "fascist" organisation (Worley 2010 p.80, see Dorril 2006 p.167 and p.173). This may have been over-stated at this stage but there is little doubt that the NP was infiltrated by crooks, adventurers and incompetents (Dorril 2006 p.188). However, when all 24 New Party candidates failed in the 1931 election "this convinced Mosley that his solutions to the national situation could not be furthered by parliamentary means" (Griffiths 2005 p.69). The two party system appeared to be impervious to the impact of new parties, and by the end of 1931 the New Party was finished in all but name. Mosley turned toward "pure" fascism (Dorril 2006 p.215).

It was apparently after visiting Italy that Mosley became convinced of the necessity of a parallel British Fascist movement and a dictatorial form of government. As Worley says "Mosley adopted the fascist label after much deliberation and with very definite reference to the Italian and German examples" (Worley 2010 p.82). Mosley argued that fascism could be adapted to British requirements, drawing on British conditions and attributes (see Worley 2010). The BUF was essentially designed to replicate the success of the Fascists in Italy and Mussolini actually became a major source of finance for the movement in the mid-30s (Pugh 2009 p.490, see Thurlow 1998 p.105). The BUF not only ostentatiously rejected the so-called "old gang" that had dominated British politics, it anticipated their failure. Indeed Pugh argues that Mosley "calculated that the National government was no more likely to solve the problem of unemployment than its hapless predecessors; having seen both main parties at close hand he thought them ineffectual, unpatriotic, and intellectually bankrupt. In this situation, commiting himself to the BUF was not such a risk; all over Europe Parliamentary regimes were giving way to authoritarian ones" (Pugh 2009 p.489-90). The emphasis on solving unemployment as a key motivating factor may have been genuine but this should not obscure the fact that Mosley was infatuated with the "new" and apparently dynamic fascist movements on the continent. Mosley spoke about the "worldwide faith" of fascism in 1934 (Mosley 1934 p.20), and his subsequent claim that "we do not borrow ideas from foreign countries and we have no 'models' abroad", was simply self-serving, disingenuous nonsense (Mosley 1938 Foreword). There is no doubt that "Mosley was quite explicitly setting out to lead the British equivalent of the fascist movements in Italy and Germany" (Skidelsky 1981 p.292). We can see this quite clearly if we look at key aspects of the BUF's ideology.

According to Mosley only a new movement, saturated with a romantic sense of its own destiny, could resolve the perennial difficulties encountered by Parliamentary democracy, as he said "'we ask those who join us to march with us in a great and hazardous adventure'" (Mosley cited in Lewis 1987 p61). Mosley launched his movement saying "'I have finished with those who think; henceforth I shall go to those who feel'" (cited in Skidelsky 1981 p.336). Indeed BUF members were actively discouraged from thinking too deeply about the coherence of strategy or the consequences of tactics. Indeed, "faith was deemed more important than rational analysis" and "the only justification for thought was when it served as a prelude to action" (Lewis 1987 p.41). In this sense a pre-rational, emotional instinctivism was actually courted and encouraged as an antidote to the stocious, ineffectual bickering of conventional politics and the innate sterility of intellectualism. Rationalism and an excessive propensity for abstraction not only denied man's inner nature, it created doubt, which corroded and deflected the dynamic power of the will. "Attacks on the 'anaemic intellectualism' of the age were also rampant in the BUF press" and the BUF publication *Blackshirt* highlighted the point in 1934 by deriding the "'soft lily-white hands'" and "'scented bodies'" of "'cultured intellectuals'", adding that there "'seems to be no escape from the monster of perverted thought and insipid affection that saps vitality and good sense and kills the instinctive manful appreciation of life'" (cited in Linehan 2005 p.109-110). The BUF portrayed itself as a party of action and it celebrated the forthcoming triumph of faith and instinct over reason.

Mosley also saw fascism as the key to a new civilisation, a new era, a new spirit, and ultimately a new man. Fascism, said Mosley, was a revolt against the materialism of the modern world, and his own party attempted to reflect this in practice (Dorril 2006 p.219). The BUF possessed a rigidly hierarchical internal structure headed by someone who was felt to be (and who considered himself to be) a charismatic leader (Skidelsky 1981). Mosley dominated the BUF as its "man of destiny". In the BUF there was "a heavy emphasis upon the leadership principle which involved discipline, loyalty and unquestioning faith in the leader" (Lewis 1987 p.39). Under the party's constitution the leader was the ultimate arbiter when it came to policy, organizational structure and internal discipline. The "leadership" principle was thus assiduously applied and Mosley evidently believed that, as Britain's prospective Ceasar, he could synthesise Christian notions of self-sacrifice with the Nietszchian doctrine of virility and strength (see Griffin 1995 p.173). Mosley "seems seriously to have believed that he had been born to be the saviour of the nation", and many of his followers shared his belief (Cross 1961 p.55). As a consequence "a leadership cult was encouraged within the movement and Mosley became the object of eulogistic praise and often obsequious pandering by those around him" (Lewis 1987 p.39). Indeed Mosley's followers often wrote and spoke about their leader in awe-struck terms, conveying a loyalty and adoration which vacillated between deference and hero-worship (see Renton 2001 p.70). Mosley's authority within the BUF was, effectively, absolute.

Mosley's movement also utilised a special style and method as befitted, so the BUF claimed, an entirely new social phenomenon. BUF members wore distinctive uniforms, were drilled in military fashion and many were billeted in the so-called

"Black House" in Battersea Park Road. The BUF was organized into area, regions, branches and groups, and at the local level sub-division sometimes took place into companies, sections and units, although the structure proved to be highly bureaucratic and expensive to run, which was a consequence, at least in part, of ineffectual leadership and poor decision-making at all levels (see Thurlow 1998 p.102-04). Indeed, factional disputes characterized the BUF throughout its existence, with accusations of favourtism and rumours of homosexual activity. Finance was always a major issue for the BUF despite a significant subvention from abroad (mostly from Mussolini, but also from some German sources), and there were accusations of embezzlement, indeed some BUF full-time officials were eventually made redundant due to lack of funds (see Dorril 2006 p.236, p.282 and p.337).

East London was unquestionably the epicenter of BUF activity, with nearly half the membership to be found in Bethnal Green, Stepney, Shoreditch and Hackney (Dorril 2006 p.348) although the BUF could claim organizational representation across Britain - the movement even had branches in Berlin, Cologne, Milan, Rome and Paris (Dorril 2006 p.284). BUF membership may have peaked at around 50,000, although there was a rapid turnover (estimates on membership vary greatly, see Lewis 1987 p.71-2, Linehan 2000 Chapter 6). Evidence suggests that BUF membership was largely petit bourgeois in character, with a solidly bourgeois leadership cadre and the BUF had organizations in eleven major public schools (Lewis 1987 p.74, Pugh 2005 p.139). Unsurprisingly the leading personnel included several figures with a military background, and ex-soldiers were drawn to the BUF in significant numbers (Pugh 2005 p.133). The movement also held a particular popularity for the younger generation, who were evidently attracted by the spirit of what Mosley called a new "faith" (Mosley 1934 p.20). The utilisation of the mass meeting was designed to convey the impression of vitalism, action and unstoppable momentum which did much to enhance the BUF's image as a "new" political force (particularly in the eyes of impressionable young people). With Mosley posturing as the stern and virile aristocratic warrior engaging a captivated audience amidst a plethora of union jacks and provocative fascist symbols, the movement appeared to be designed to either repel or attract (Skidelsky 1981 p.336). Such choreography was important since "the focal point of the rally was the Leader's speech and the atmosphere of the occasion was deliberately charged with excitement and enthusiasm to accentuate the Leader's presence" (Linehan 2012 p.12). There was a mystical, almost semi-religious aspect to these theatrical events and it is important to acknowledge the powerful emotions that such gatherings generated (see Cross 1961 p.70). Indeed this aesthetic dimension was a product of a deliberate effort to tap into and exploit deeply held emotions in order to bring passion into politics.

Clearly "Mosley dominated the movement, was an effective communicator, enjoyed privileged access to the means of propaganda and the legitimating stamp of status" (Coupland 1998 p.256). However, Mosley was not only the undisputed leader of the party, but also the BUF's chief theorist: "in terms of ideology he supplied and controlled the intellectual content of the programme" (Thurlow 1976 p.16). Moreover, according to Thurlow, "the BUF produced the most coherent and developed programme of *any* fascist movement" (Thurlow 1998 p.xi italics added). In fact Thurlow argues that Mosley "possessed one of the best minds in British politics in the twentieth century", whilst Cross maintained that "above all else Mosley was an intellectual" (Thurlow 1981 p.26; Cross 1961 p.71) [1]. Mosley's theoretical contribution was made essentially in three works: *The Greater Britain* (written in 1932 and revised two years later), *Fascism: One Hundred Questions Asked and Answered* (1936), and *Tomorrow We Live* (1938) (see Rees 1979 p.137). Roger Eatwell argues that such works represented "the clearest statements of policy ever to be put forward by a fascist group. Here was fascism with a rational-constructive rather than mythical-populist face" (Eatwell 1996 p.182).

Indeed the apparent cogency of some of these ideas has led Pugh to argue that the BUF's alternative "solutions" were "constructive" and "compelling", and that "by the early 1930s (Mosley) offered a programme at least comparable with anything put forward by the conventional parties in Britain and more considered than the proposals of either Mussolini or Hitler before coming to power" (Pugh 2009 p.491). Thus, according to Cullen, there can be "no doubt" that Mosley "advocated a coherent programme for restructuring the political and economic life of Britain" (Cullen 1993 p.245). On the face of it, therefore, the ideas of the BUF (Mosley) need to be taken seriously as an alternative to the programmes and policies of the conventional parties, which had clearly failed in the context of economic depression, mass unemployment and poverty in the 1930s.

Mosley in fact developed the ideas he had advocated in both the Labour Party and the New Party, and his major preoccupation appeared to be how to regenerate Britain's ailing economy. In doing so Mosley elaborated on themes he had already articulated, and he advanced the fascist notion of a "third way" between capitalism and communism. Indeed Skidelsky suggests that Mosley's "political evolution cannot be fully grasped unless one realises that he believed he had discovered the way out of the 'dog-fight' between labour and capital ... the movement towards fascism arose essentially from Mosley's refusal to choose between left and right in a situation of mounting social crisis" (Skidelsky 1981a p.261; see Nugent and King 1977). As Mosley himself put it, referring to the leaders of capital and labour, "instead of being the general staff of opposing armies, they will be joint directors of national enterprise under the general guidance of corporative government" (Mosley 1934 p.37). Rejecting liberal individualism and socialist collectivism the BUF advocated a corporate state and an authoritarian government in conjunction with an exaggerated patriotism. The "national interest", the BUF proclaimed, should always prevail. Mosley and the BUF claimed to offer a qualitatively superior synthesis of concepts from left and right, amalgamating the right's love of country, with the left's professed preoccupation with the well-being of the people.

The BUF also advocated the expeditious passing of a "General Powers Bill", in effect an Enabling Act, in order to implement various constitutional changes because "the overall structure of parliamentary democratic government was deemed to be too cumbersome to undertake the pressing task of implementing a project of dynamic action" (Linehan 2000 p.90-91, see Mosley 1938). The fascist principle of leadership needed to be assiduously applied in the political sphere and alternative political parties would be abolished. As Mosley put it, the fascist government "must be given the absolute power to act" because "the only effective instrument of revolutionary change is absolute authority" (Mosley 1934 p.28 and p.31). Indeed "Mosley frankly characterized this system as 'Modern Dictatorship', that is, the people would entrust power to a leadership which would carry out their will unimpeded by the traditional paraphernalia of parliamentary procedure and partisan squabbling" (Pugh 2005 p.129). Parliament would be dissolved and re-elected on an occupational basis, after which a new corporatist-style National Chamber of Corporations (to replace the House of Commons) and Assembly of Notables (which would replace the House of Lords) would act only in an advisory capacity. Real power would reside in the leader of a government that would be elected by a separate franchise every five years (see Mosley 1938). If the government lost, then the king would decide a replacement advised by the Fascist Grand Council, which would thereby restore the power of the Royal prerogative. Thus, according to the BUF programme, a centralised Tudor-style state, which had been the basis of British supremacy and which had been subverted by Parliamentary democracy, was to be reinstated. It was a candidly authoritarian scheme in which the individual possessed no autonomous rights, save the right to serve the nation and the duty of sacrifice for the common cause (see Nugent 1977). A meritocratic elite would staff the government, members of which would emerge via a complicated hierarchical framework of indirectly elected local, district and zonal councils. Only one party would be legal, the BUF, acting in the interests of the nation, thereby removing divisive class conflict and social sectionalism. In effect the BUF, via the state, would be the arbiter of what was in the "national interest" and the end result would be, as Mosley's oft-quoted aphorism explained, "all for the state and the state for all".

In the political system proposed by the BUF a new National Council of Corporations would constitute a parallel political structure, representing workers, employers and government, thereby eliminating, in theory, all unnecessary and debilitating industrial strife. The National Corporation was designed to be the pre-eminent organ of the entire corporate framework, providing advice to the leader and strategic control of the economy. Twenty-four individual Corporations, designed to include the entire adult population, would bring employers and workers together in order to regulate industry. Indeed Mosley, with a characteristic rhetorical flourish, claimed that "'the main object of a modern and Fascist movement is to establish the Corporate State. In our belief it is the greatest constructive conception yet devised by the mind of man'" (cited in Lewis 1987 p.33). The BUF's version of Corporatism also aimed to exploit the competitive advantage provided by Empire. With the ready availability of natural resources the Empire would not only provide a market for manufactured goods, it would constitute a unit effectively isolated from the global economic system and therefore immune to the visissitudes of unfettered free enterprise capitalism. Empire autarky was seen as the economic way forward for the BUF, and "according to this autarkic model, the mother country and the dominions would observe reciprocal trade agreements, with the former focusing on manufacturing products and the latter on food output" (Linehan 2000 p.90, see Mosley 1934 p.131). Hence Britain would produce that vast majority of what it required at home with raw materials and foodstuffs from the colonies, and would only buy manufactured goods from those nations committed to buying from Britain (Mosley

1934 p.135). The preservation of Empire, for the BUF, was therefore an economic necessity (see Mosley 1938).

A so-called Council of Empire would preside over Britain's imperial domain, which would reflect not only the obvious superiority of the motherland as the ultimate custodian of civilisation, but also the fact that, according to the BUF, most of the "backward" and "illiterate" colonies were entirely unsuited to coping with the responsibilities of political independence (Mosley 1938). As Mosley himself said, Britain's "'right'" to Empire was constructed on "'the power of original conquest'" and the energetic heroism of the British people (cited in Pugh 2005 p.177, see Mosley 1938). Unsurprisingly Britain was deemed to be eminently suited to leadership of an international community which was characterized by the BUF as innately inferior by virtue of culture and history. The BUF was therefore explicitly and uncompromisingly imperialist in its outlook – the Empire would be maintained regardless of claims favouring the rights of colonial subjects and irrespective of any demands for independence. The Empire, for the BUF, was an organic entity and "it was inconceivable for nations to withdraw from a union of this nature, for such an action would amount to the amputation of part of a living organism" (Lewis 1987 p.182). Britain would therefore pursue its own national self-interest ruthlessly, as interpreted by the BUF, without reference to the League of Nations or international law.

Although Empire would offer some protection from the harsh winds of international competition, as far as the BUF was concerned, capitalism would continue to exist, within certain clearly prescribed technocratic guidelines. However, a distinction was to be made between productive capitalism and international finance capitalism, the latter needing to be subject to much firmer discretionary control by the state (see Mosley 1938). Although Mosley attacked finance capitalism and the vested interest of the City (and Wall Street) his perspective was by no means anti-capitalist in outlook (his rhetorical antagonism towards speculators in the Stock

Exchange did not prevent him from drawing income from stocks and shares in foreign companies) (see Pugh 2005 p.200). In effect the BUF's "anti-capitalist" position was little more than an extravagant tactical ploy to outflank Labour. As Coupland says "capitalism would remain, but tamed, and ultimately subordinated to the national interest as interpreted by the fascist government" (Coupland 1998 p.258). In general Mosley "believed that the private enterprise system could be made to work properly provided the men in charge of government were determined to make it work" (Skidelsky 1981 p.303). As the fascist leader himself put it, "'capitalism is the system by which capital uses the nation for its own purposes. Fascism is the system by which the nation uses capitalism for its own purposes'" (Mosley cited in Rees 1979 p.19). Fascism would not transcend capitalism, it would simply return it to prosperity (see Lewis 1987 p.36). Therefore Lewis is undoubtedly correct to conclude that had the economic prescriptions of the BUF's "corporate state" been realized in practice it "would in all likelihood have amounted to nothing more than a euphemism concealing a reactionary capitalist dictatorship" (Lewis 1987 p.56).

Yet Mosley always claimed that his movement incorporated the best aspects of socialism too. This was not "international socialism", which was considered to be the obsolescent instrument of chaos and class envy, but "national" socialism (see Mosley 1938). Here Mosley's ideas were apparently derived from his experience in war, where the feeling of comradeship and sense of mutual sacrifice prevailed. Mosley's socialism "was the socialism of the trenches" which referred to a sense of vertically integrated comradeship rather than the elimination class barriers (Dorril 2006 p.37). It is important to note that this "socialism", as a kind of cooperative synthesis (rejecting "snob" and "parasite"), certainly did not constitute any commitment to material redistribution or the pursuit of egalitarianism in any meaningful or normative sense, since Mosley expressly repudiated any kind of "equalitarianism" as "stupid" (Mosley 1938). Mosley's "socialism" envisaged a meritocracy and equality of opportunity within a more scientific and efficient form of capitalism, which would obviate the need for material redistribution by precipitating harmonious social relations. The sense of common purpose in deference to the national interest would not only make class conflict redundant it would represent, Mosley argued, a form of "socialist" transcendence. Hence, "for Mosley socialism was the modern expression of the feudal idea of community" (Skidelsky 1981 p.134) that is, in effect, a society that is vertically integrated and unified but emphatically not equal.

Hence the Fascist Union of British Workers simply focused on the peril of foreign workers, while the proposed Corporate State posed no material threat to private property or capitalism, and although the Corporate State "seemed to be revolutionary" it "was merely superimposed upon capitalism" (Dorril 2006 p.218). Attempting to energise and rejuvenate a unified community is not the same as making the social system more just. Indeed the quality of Mosley's "socialism" can be gauged by the fact that independent trade unions and the right to strike were deemed unnecessary. Meanwhile private education was applauded, and the party engaged in an apparently limitless sycophantic reverence toward the British monarchy, criticism of which would be made illegal by a BUF government. This craven defence of elitism and privilege indicates, as much as anything else, the complete absence of egalitarianism in BUF ideology. In fact "it is doubtful whether Mosley ever understood socialism in any realistic or meaningful sense" (Lewis 1987 p.14). Of course the BUF detested communists as "'insane fanatics'" and communism as "'the cancer that causes the death of every civilisation'" (cited in Linehan 2005 p.117).

The BUF also clearly endorsed familiar social patterns and prejudices. For example, the BUF claimed that fascism would encourage religious observance by amalgamating the secular and theological dimensions of civil life. There were even some assurances that atheism would perish under the BUF with Christianity being restored to its rightfully privileged position as the nation's religion (see Lewis 1987 p.51). The BUF pledged to continue financial subsidies for denominational schools, and promised political representation for leading clerics within the reconstituted House of Lords. In BUF literature "high culture", exalted via the individual genius of heroic characters like Shakespeare, Elgar and Wordsworth, was counterposed to contamination by a homogenized, commercialized, mass culture. Aesthetic preferences were entirely traditional and based on the noble beauty of the historic Greco-Roman heritage, and at the same time "modern" deviations were seen as a deification of the deformed and the ugly, neurotically self-indulgent and/or tending to promote the dangerous poison of chaos and anarchy. The corrupting influence of modern art and and music (especially jazz) was derided and dismissed as a product of warped minds and moral degeneracy, and they were identified as cultural artefacts which were distinctly "un-British" in origin. Hence "there would be little room for libertarian challenges to conventional morality in fascist art and culture" (Linehan 2000 p.215). The BUF projection of culture and art was, in effect, a bland and unimaginative adjunct to its political propaganda.

The BUF was also dominated by a sense of masculinity and male superiority. As Mosley argued, "women's questions" were usually handled by "ageing spinsters" because most women usually retire to the sphere where their "true interests lie", that is child-rearing in the home (see Mosley 1938 "women's part"). Women, who constituted approximately 20% of the BUF membership, were urged by the male leadership to focus upon their "special" gifts and qualities by devoting themselves to a life of domesticity (see Mosley 1934 p.54-55). Motherhood and home-making would be "honoured" by the creation of its own Corporation (see Lewis 1987 p.53) and the Women's Section of the party was kept strictly segregated, with its own headquarters in Regent Street. As Mosley himself succinctly put it "'we want men who are men, and women who are women'" (cited in Dorril 2006 p.227) and the men, therefore, dictated policy on issues such as birth control and abortion.

The relatively high level of participation by women in the BUF (at least compared to other parties) should not obscure the patriarchal essence of the organization's outlook. In effect "the virility of young males was to provide the cutting edge of fascism's advance through an effete civilization, degenerate with rampant feminism and unchecked matriarchy" (Lewis 1987 p.42).

Cities meanwhile were maligned as the ultimate repositories of decadence and social decay, which were counterposed, in stark contrast, to the BUF's perception of the countryside, which was lauded as the timeless home of honest toil and noble virtues. Mosley himself displayed "a romantic nostalgia for a rural past" (Dorril 2006 p.250), and considered relentless urbanization, which uprooted the population from the soil, to be the harbinger of doom. As Mosley confirmed, "'any civilization that is to endure requires constant replenishment from the steady, virile stock which is bred in the health, sanity, and natural but arduous labour of the countryside'" (cited in Dorril 2006 p.417). Agriculture was seen as capable of embodying the spirit of national vitality in a way that the artificial and soulless urban environment could never achieve. This romantic nostalgia for rural Britain was evident in the BUF's numerous public pronouncements which identified the party as the (self-appointed) custodian of the pastoral idyl. Hence the BUF was, despite the lofty rhetoric about transcending the drab mediocrity of contemporary life, distinctly traditionalist and reactionary in most of its social preferences and policy proposals.

Together this emphasis on nationalism, dictatorship, corporatism and reactionary romanticism constituted the essence of the constructive thinking of Mosley, Raven-Thomson and others in the BUF. However, there was also a racist component in the ideology of the BUF. The BUF expended some considerable energy, especially after 1934, attacking the Jewish and "alien" menace (Stevenson 1990 p.274), although opinions vary as to the importance of this facet of its ideological outlook. For instance Thurlow argues that anti-semitism was not central to the BUF's belief system and claims that Mosley was never an anti-semite, and did not actually believe in a Jewish conspiracy (see Thurlow 1998 p.126, and 1987 p.106 and p.157). Yet Mosley certainly did share the prevailing prejudices which existed against the Jews, claiming that some Jews were acting against Britain's national interest, and he therefore advocated, at various times, segregation and expulsion. In 1936 the BUF became the British Union of Fascists and National Socialists, and henceforth displayed a marked sympathy for specifically Nazi explanations and remedies. As Rees says, "...the BUF did evolve from its earlier more pragmatic Italian-influenced beginning towards a more National Socialist doctrinaire orientation" (Rees 1979 p.10). Indeed, as Mosley himself said in a speech at the Albert Hall in March 1936 "'the strongest passion that can be aroused is the passion against the corruption of Jewish power...the Jew himself has created anti-Semitism – created it as he has always done, by letting people see him and his methods. Even Hitler was not anti-Semitic before he saw a Jew'" (cited in Lewis 1987 p.89). Mosley advocated deporting Jews if engaged in "un-British conduct", and depriving those that remained of British citizenship, yet he declined to define who qualified as a "Jew", or indeed what constituted "un-British conduct". According to Mosley "'Jews, who have placed the interests of Jewry before those of Britain, must leave Great Britain'" (cited in Coupland 1998 p.263). The BUF clearly portrayed the Jew as an anti-social menace, lurking behind the money-lender, the criminal and the communist, the source and symbol of evil (Mosley 1938 Chapter 6). In *Tomorrow We Live* (1938), in a section prophetically entitled "the Final Solution", Mosley attacked the irredeemably "oriental" Jews as physically, mentally and spiritually alien, and advocated finding territory somewhere abroad to allow the Jews to escape their stateless existence (Mosley 1938). Unsurprisingly, attacks on Jews, the desecration of synagogues and the destruction of Jewish property was tolerated by the BUF, if not actively encouraged (see Dorril 2006 p.396 who refers to the "Mile End Road pogrom").

Therefore "there can be little doubt that between 1935 and 1938 the movement was principally identified in terms of its anti-semitism" (Nugent 1977 p.152).

However, there may be a case for suggesting that Mosley's racism was more cultural than socio-biological and genetic, although both forms of racism were endemic within the ranks of the BUF. Mosley's views were, to some extent, based on his interpretation of Oswald Spengler and how best to respond to his pessimistic prognosis about the inevitable demise of western civilisation into barbarism. From Mosley's perspective only a Ceasar-type saviour could protect and enhance western culture, and so deny Spengler's gloomy prophesy. Thurlow argues that Mosley saw himself as just such a saviour, leading a "mutiny against destiny" on behalf of civilized culture, and in the process of outlining his programme of renewal certain ethnic groups were "stigmatised as culturally different rather than racially inferior" (Thurlow 1987 p.18; see Thurlow 1981 p.24). Meanwhile Pugh describes Mosley's anti-semitic prejudice as "fairly routine", "tactical" and "opportunistic" (Pugh 2009 p.503, 2005 p.219). This interpretation suggests a distinct and qualitative difference of emphasis from the genetic determinism of, for example, Arnold Leese and other Nazis.

It is important to be clear on this contrast, because the notion of race was undoubtedly important to the BUF even if the policy detail lacked programmatic coherence. The BUF consistently emphasised its hostility toward Jews as the root cause of decadent capitalism and fratricidal communism, and both were seen as international movements designed to undermine the British Empire/race. As the *Blackshirt* put it in March 1935 "'unfortunately, Jewry is of such virulent growth that it is useless to sever a few branches or members. The tentacles of the Jewish tenacity spread deep-rooted over all the land of his adoption. They must be totally eradicated'" (cited in Lewis 1987 p.104). Thus, although premeditated attacks on Jews and Jewish property were a consequence of this particular political orientation, it presaged far worse if the BUF had ever managed to achieve power. Evidently some high profile and influencial members of the BUF were far more rabidly anti-semitic than Mosley, and urged a more overtly hostile line, for example both A.K.Chesterton and William Joyce were shamelessly anti-semitic. For example Joyce said in 1937 that the "'real struggle lies not between conservatism and socialism, not between capitalism and communism, but between international Jewish finance and National Socialist patriotism'" (cited in Skidelsky 1981 p.343). Indeed Joyce, along with John Beckett, left the BUF to form the National Socialist League (NSL), with the former achieving infamy by defecting to Germany in 1939 and broadcasting propaganda against the Allied war effort as the infamous "Lord Haw Haw", who was hanged as a traitor after the war.

There can be little doubt therefore that racism, cultural, genetic or otherwise, was an integral component of the BUF's credo in this period (Renton 2001 p.73) even if it was partly motivated by Mosley's desire to convince the Nazis he was worth supporting (Dorril 2006 p.306). In the BUF the muscular, square-jawed apostles of white supremacy set the agenda and their vision was to be vigorously acted upon given the opportunity, as Coupland says, "that the Greater Britain would be 'pure' white required no discussion" (Coupland 1998 p.263, see p.264). Indeed, given such an overt position adopted by the BUF itself, if Mosley did not personally believe in the malignance of alien Jewish influences it might be argued that the fact that he nevertheless used the issue to gain political advantage makes his role in the matter even more reprehensible. However Linehan makes the point that "by promoting the argument that Mosley's anti-semitism was a cynical tactical weapon of political mobilization, it fail(s) to recognize that his anti-Jewish rhetoric had its basis in anti-semitic beliefs that were genuinely held" (Linehan 2000 p.191). Indeed there is some evidence to suggest that Mosley had planned anti-Semitism from the very beginning, but did not raise the "Jewish question" initially for purely pragmatic political reasons, in order to get the BUF up and running (see Dorril 2006 p.402). There is certainly no doubt that anti-Semitism should be seen as an integral part of the BUF and therefore any effort to exonerate Mosley as being anything other than an aggressive anti-Semite is controversial to say the least.

Of course events in Europe were to have profound consequences for the success of the BUF. Mosley was almost inevitably drawn into a defence of the continental fascist regimes, and his peculiar brand of pro-German British patriotism consistently undermined the BUF's increasingly flimsy credibility. For instance, Mosley continually cautioned against entering a conflict in Europe and when Mussolini became concerned about the impact of sanctions by the UN after the invasion of Abyssinia, the BUF responded with its "Mind Britain's Business" campaign. In any event Abyssinia was, according to Mosley, only "'a barbarous Negro state existing in the conditions of the Dark Ages'" (cited in Dorril 2006 p.351). Mussolini got good value for money out of Mosley. Mosley even conceded the legitimacy of aggressive expansion by Germany based on the aspiration of racial unification (Dorril 2006 p.344). Moreover, Mosley's preference for appeasement from strength, which advocated leaving (Eastern) Europe for Germany and concentrating on the Empire for Britain, was not only looking decidedly threadbare by May 1940, it was remarkably congruent with Hitler's own foreign policy objectives. The BUF leader was undoubtedly conflicted, as his sympathetic biographer Skidelsky points out, because "the country he loved was fighting against the system he believed in" (Skidelsky 1981 p.455). Indeed even after war had been declared Mosley and the BUF leadership continued to oppose the war as a Jewish-inspired quarrel.

There is no doubt that, in the 1930s, Mosley posed a significant threat to liberal democracy. The BUF "caused serious disquiet across a broad range of opinion", and "the combined use of mass meetings, uniformed parades and the trappings of continental fascism, all at the command of a charismatic leader, had no antecedents in British politics" (Stevenson 1990 p.273). The fact that the BUF generated more suspicion and opposition than support does not invalidate the observation that, given his contacts in the British Establishment, Mosley constituted a genuine menace. For this reason, of course, the BUF aroused substantial left wing opposition in Britain, which led to the well-documented skirmishes at Olympia (June 1934) and Cable Street (October 1936), although the Public Order Act of December 1936 did much to quell the disturbances, which were becoming a frequent feature in places like the East End of London. Mosley was intent on "controlling the streets" and the so-called Fascist Defence Force (particularly the jackbooted I Squad) gained a well-earned reputation for inflicting violence on its opponents (Dorril 2006 p.222 and p.264). Mosley claimed that, "'I organized the Blackshirts to prevent the organized violence of the reds stopping our free speech'" (cited in Cullen 1993 p.247), conveniently ignoring the fact that were the BUF to achieve power the notion of "free speech" would be effectively rendered redundant. Indeed, the coercive implications of the BUF's programme would only really become apparent once power was achieved, and violence would have become a "necessity" against all those who refused to internalize the utopian fascist blueprint (see Coupland 1998 p.262). Resistance and confrontation was therefore inevitable, and occurred regularly at BUF meetings and marches. Indeed there is some evidence that Mosley deliberately provoked a violent response from the left in order to scare the middle classes into supporting the BUF (Dorril 2006 p.266). Despite this, the culpability of the BUF for the violence that occurred on the streets of Britain in the 1930s has been the subject of some debate amongst historians, some of whom are evidently anxious to exonerate the BUF (see Cullen 1993) [2].

In fact the BUF's emphasis on street-level tactics reflected the fact that Mosley never really committed his movement completely to an electoral strategy. As Mosley stated ominously in 1934, whether the BUF would achieve success through democratic means "or whether it will reach power in a situation far beyond the control of Parliament, no one can tell" (Mosley 1934 p.189). The BUF never stood candidates in a General Election, lost badly in three by-elections, and retained an ambivalence about the utility of conventional political representation. Partly this reluctance to engage electorally was derived from a contempt for old-style parliamentary, democratic politics, but it was also a consequence of the fact that Mosley anticipated his elevation to high office via "invitation" after some kind of national crisis. In this context it is important to note the attitude to Mosley and his movement of those with power in ruling class circles (a point which will be developed in the conclusion to this text). The sympathy of Edward VIII for fascist ideas is a matter of public record, an affection that was reciprocated by pro-monarchist rank-and-file fascist activists (Pugh 2009 p.498, see Griffiths 1980 p.240-41). Indeed Mosley assiduously cultivated links with the aristocracy, elements in the armed forces, and certain Conservative peers and MPs via the "January Club", such as Lord Lymington, Lord Erskine, Major-General Fuller, Admiral Powell, Lady Pearson, Viscountess Downe and Henry Rummond Wolff. Indeed the January Club was set up specifically to cultivate links with the "respectable classes" who were instinctively disposed to dismiss the fascists as vulgar and plebian. Lavish dinners were organized with prominent figures connected to the various groups on the far right, such as the Anglo-German Fellowship, the Link, the Nordic League, English Mystery, English Array and so on, where networking inevitably took place amidst the grinding of political axes. In this context "Mosley, for all his contempt for the British Establishment, had no doubt of his ability to seduce enough of it for his purposes" (Pugh 2009 p.501) and the BUF leader clearly anticipated power delivered by ruling class acclamation rather than via the ballot box (Pugh 2009 p.501-502, see Eatwell 1996 p.183-84).

It is also worth remembering that wealthy patrons, like Lord Rothermere, Lady Houston and Baron Tollemache helped to keep the BUF afloat, and that the police and judiciary often displayed a certain sympathy for the BUF (and bias against its left wing rivals) in upholding and applying the law (see Lewis

1987 chapter 6, Dorril 2006 p.307). Pugh endorses this view, making the interesting observation that the Establishment, Home Office and police were "remarkably tolerant towards the paramilitary organization adopted by fascist groups", and "in some cases at least this reflected a widespread fear that society might require some unofficial force to help restore order in the face of the alleged Soviet-inspired machinations such as the General Strike of 1926" (Pugh 2009 p.493). Indeed it is also worth noting that at one point in 1936, during the abdication crisis, Mosley (who had secret contact with Edward VIII) was organizing for the possibility of being invited to participate in a government without Parliamentary sanction (Dorril 2006 p.403-04). It was widely felt that if the King asked Churchill to form an administration, Mosley would be included and at the time "rumours of dictatorship or governmental overthrow were rife" (Griffiths 1980 p.242, Pugh 2005 p.249). Indeed Special Branch feared a "'public uprising'" spearheaded by the Blackshirts, and ceremonial guards outside Buckingham Palace were said to have been issued with live ammunition (Dorril 2006 p.405-06).

Despite such evidence it is nevertheless true to say that even that section of the Establishment "who sympathized with the reasons behind Mosley's revolt saw no reason to forsake the party system to team up with a cavalier adventurer who was trying to turn a foreign tradition into a British political movement" (Thurlow 1998 p.101). As a consequence the British Union of Fascists and National Socialists never stood a realistic chance of achieving power between the wars: the economic crisis was never severe enough to precipitate a generalized crisis of legitimacy; the ruling class was never in any serious danger and therefore saw no reason to desert Conservatism (indeed many Conservatives saw Mosley as little more than an amoral, opportunistic egomaniac); the Parliamentary system was well able to accommodate and absorb the political discontent generated in the 30s; and the BUF's own tactical errors and lack of resources hindered its development. As Dorril says, "having adopted a position which necessitated waiting for history to take a particular turn, Mosley was left marooned when history did not turn in the required direction" (Dorril 2006 p.368).

The BUF, as the principal manifestation of fascism in the inter-war years in Britain, was unquestionably inspired by, and influenced by, continental fascist movements and ideas. We can see this clearly in terms of the movement's romantic irrationalism, fervent nationalism and emphasis on the need for social discipline, certain cultural values and dictatorship, along with the desire for pro-capitalist, pro-imperialist, corporatist solutions designed to transcend socialist or communist alternatives. Moreover, the emphasis on racist anti-semitism even suggests an inclination toward a specifically Nazi version of fascism. The florid rhetoric about ancient Sparta or "merrie" Tudor England could not conceal the fundamental essence of the BUF as a derivative manifestation of its European (Italian and German) progenitors (although even Hitler and Rosenberg commented on the folly of importing and using foreign ideas and labels) (see Dorril 2006 p.343 and p.374). The earnest efforts of Skidelsky and other commentators to emphasise the importance of indigenous influences, such as Joseph Chamberlain's social imperialism, Karl Pearson's social Darwinism or Edward Carson's UVF (Ulster Volunteer Force), cannot obscure the fundamental reality of the BUF's derivative nature, inspired as it was by foreign fascists (see Skidelsky 1981 p.300). Given this fact it was not at all surprising that Oswald Mosley and other leading fascists were interned under Defence Regulation 18B (1a) for the duration of the war [3]. The BUF, along with most other fascist organizations, was disbanded.

## Post War Re-Alignment

The immediate post-war period presented British fascism with obvious and profound political problems. The watershed of internment ensured that henceforth Mosley would be considered a "political pariah", and he would never accquire widespread public sympathy or get to command a genuine mass movement (Macklin 2007 p.10). Moreover, after 1945 "European fascists and Nazis were faced with the pressing question of how to ensure the survival of an ideology that was stigmatized by past associations and, in the case of Nazi Germany, a history of unrivalled criminality and inhumanity" (Poole 1986 p.53). Naturally the experiences of war convinced most people that fascism, and especially Nazism, were destructive and indeed grossly perverted political creeds. Fascism appeared to be a moribund ideology, and not surprisingly the far right was more divided than ever. Some, however, remained unrepentant and on VE day Arnold Leese published *The Jewish War of Survival*, a robust defence of the Holocaust. Leese was subsequently jailed (in 1947) for helping SS war criminals to escape arrest (see Hill 1988 p.78). However, the level of fascist circumspection in this period is well illustrated by the fact that even the fanatical Leese did not actually describe himself as a fascist after the war. Other fascists resolved to tread even more carefully.

Mosley was released on 20 November 1943 on the grounds of ill-health and immediately attempted to capitalize on a sense of "martyrdom" engendered amongst the internees (Macklin 2007 p.30). However, given the furore surrounding the execution of his former Director of Propaganda William Joyce ("Lord Haw Haw") in 1946, Mosley's decision to re-enter the political fray was widely viewed as "a startling affront to common decency" (Macklin 2007 p.35). In fact Mosley told the *Sunday Pictorial* that he had not altered his ideas "'one inch. I do not retract anything that I have either said or stood for in the past'" (cited in Dorril 2006 p.550). Home Office intelligence reports have confirmed that although Mosley was still revered (even worshipped) by his diminishing band of supporters, he was exceedingly unpopular in Britain after the war, with the general perception being that he was not only a symbol of a detested fascist creed, but a traitor to his country (see Thurlow 1998a). Undeterred the ex-BUF leader started a publishing company after the war called Mosley Publications, through which he sought to re-calibrate his ideas and disseminate a new, updated version of fascist ideology. Mosley, evidently refusing to relinquish his beliefs, agreed to form the Union Movement which was launched on 7 February 1948 in another attempt to unite the far right.

As Beckman explains, the use of the same belligerent tactics by "ex-fascists" was deemed to be inappropriate and ineffectual in the new post-war context, and Mosley adopted a "low profile technique aimed at recruiting a new genera-tion of fascists under another name" (Beckman 1993 p.12). Indeed, the weekly publication produced by the Union move-ment, *Union* even had the audacity to suggest that Mosley had never actually been a fascist – as Beckman remarked, if you are going to tell a lie, tell a big one! (Beckman 1993 p.107). The Union Movement was to give organizational expression to Mosley's new political endeavours and this time success would be accomplished by the permeation of ideas and the dissemination of the new credo, rather than insurrection or more conventional electoral politics (see Thurlow 1998a). UM activists were encouraged to "infiltrate" multifarious clubs, associations and organizations (political, social and leisure) in order to spread the word and embed members in local communities. Of course the idea that a few UM supporters could forge and foster grass roots support for fascism via the odd hiking club, cycling team or business association, was an extraordinary delusion. Nevertheless, although the second world war had destroyed fascism, "for Mosley the reasons for his fascist revolt had been reinforced, not made redundant" (Thurlow 1998a p.244).

The first substantial publications by Mosley after the war were *My Answer* (1946), a spirited re-statement of his political position accompanied by a critique of internment, and *The Alternative* (1947) in which Mosley aimed to synthesise concepts relating to heroic leadership and service, whilst combining syndicalism, individualism and classical philosophy into a creed that would fuse "'action with liberty'" (cited in Eatwell 1996 p.261, see Mosley 1946 and 1947). Although Mosley still articulated the idea of a "third way" between capitalism and communism, full scale corporatism was jettisoned in favour of judicious macro-economic management by the state, whilst outright nationalization was rejected as excessively bureaucratic and inefficient (Mosley 1947, Eatwell 1998b p.1193-94). In reality business interests were to remain unfettered, with the vertical pillars of a diluted corporatist framework subjugating (rather than resolving) class conflicts, whilst workers were to be regimented via reference to hopelessly vapid "charters of labour" (see Macklin 2007 p.82). Unsurprisingly, the overall conclusion reached by Mosley and the UM was that only the "thought-deed" Faustian hero could save civilization from the architects of chaos and impending doom and thereby play midwife to historic destiny (Mosley 1947). Britain still needed a great leader.

To some extent, however, Mosley had implicitly acknowledged that his pre-war ideas were too authoritarian and nationalistic for post-war tastes, and he therefore began to espouse the extraordinary geo-political idea of "Euro-Africa" as a kind of mercantilist super-state. Africa would supply for Europe an almost limitless supply of raw materials and labour, and a market for manufactured goods. This was an idea formulated, perhaps unsurprisingly, in conjunction with South African racists like Oswald Pirow, a former Minister for Defence in the Apartheid regime, and Dr. Anton Zischka, a Nazi expert on lebensraum from the German Colonial Office. The tone of Mosley's new thesis is clearly illustrated by his comments that "'Africa will not be developed at all if the end is to be management by the Ju-Ju men'" and "'if they tell us to get off the whole of Africa, we must say that we have not the slightest intention of doing so, any more than the Americans would be willing to leave their continent to the Redskins'" (cited in Eatwell 1998b p.1195 and Dorril p.629). As Macklin points out, "Mosley's scheme was not only reminiscent of the worst excesses of eighteenth century slavery it was also completely unworkable" (Macklin 2007 p.84).

Europe would, Mosley envisaged, become a united entity as a response to the geo-political threat posed by both

American capitalism and Soviet communism – the "New Europe" would not be bought by Wall Street or conquered by the Kremlin. Bolshevik barbarism was explicitly rejected as an "Oriental creed", a materialist dead-end and an egalitarian sin against nature (see Eatwell 1998b p.1191). All the familiar concerns were earnestly expressed about the deleterious effects of negro-semitic culture on European civilization, whilst immigrant crime rates, black sexual debauchery and the consumption of Kit-E-Kat pet food featured prominently as cause for concern (see Eatwell 1998b p.1195). Indeed the emphasis in UM literature from the early 1950s about black immigrants being criminally inclined, sexually promiscuous carriers of disease betrayed a familiar emphasis on unreconstructed racial stereotypes (Poole 1996 p.63). In the UM literature, the word "alien" was substituted as a code-word for "Jew", and the conflict with radical Zionists in Palestine was used as a pretext to re-articulate the same recognizably anti-semitic hostilities (Beckman 1993 p.12). Via his journal *The European* Mosley espoused the idea of Europe as a "'great breed'" and the culmination of a separate strand of racial development (see Poole 1996 p.70).

Interestingly, despite the emphasis on specifically "cultural" superiority, a socio-biological subtext was clearly evident in Mosley's post-war position since cultural developments were deemed to reflect the hierarchical ordering of the races. As a consequence, in Mosley's plan Africa would have to be divided upon racial lines because, as he was keen to point out, one could not cross horses with cattle (Renton 2001 p.73). Even Skidelsky (1981 p.507) acknowledges that Mosley did make more use of genetic arguments after 1945 as the UM leader urged compulsory repatriation (and indeed apartheid in Britain in the interim period). "Britain for the British" was the familiar refrain from the UM, and rabid anti-semitism was never very far from the surface (Renton 2001 p.74, see Mosley 1947).

According to Poole's assessment the UM leader was "undoubtedly a racist in the biological determinist mould because, for Mosley, race determines an individual's nature"

(Poole 1996 p.72). At the same time Mosley still courted ex-Nazi officers and expressed sympathy for the Waffen SS, indeed one of his "advisers" was Alfred Franke-Gricksch, who had been head of the Personnel Section of Himmler's Reich Security Head Office (see Thurlow 1987 p.238, Dorril 2006 p.561). It might also be argued that Mosley actually antici-pated theme of "Holocaust denial" by casting doubt upon the atrocities committed by the Nazis (see Eatwell 1998b p.1191, Macklin 2007 p.114). "'Pictorial evidence proves nothing at all. We have no impartial evidence'" said Mosley of the death camps - although he condemned outright the hangings at Nuremberg as "'contemptible'" (cited in Dorill 2006 p.567). In fact Mosley, in attempting to expunge Nazism's responsi-bility for the Holocaust, became "a central figure in a veritable cottage industry of revisionism and denial, reflecting the fact that the 'Jewish question' remained at the core of post-war fascist politics" (Macklin 2007 p.140-41) On the face of it Mosley was singing the same old chorus in the same old choir.

There has, however, been some significant disagreement over the precise nature of the Union Movement. For instance Pugh maintains that the UM proposals "did not amount to a full fascist programme" (Pugh 2009 p.505), whilst Thurlow has argued that Mosley's post-war perspective was modified to accommodate a more "'democratic framework'" with a greater emphasis on free speech and personal liberty (cited in Renton 2001 p.74-75, see Thurlow 1998a p.248). Rather confusingly, Thurlow's assessment of this period elsewhere is that "in some ways Mosley's thought became more fascist after 1945" (Thurlow 1998a p.247), while Eatwell asserts that Mosleys's immediate post-war writings constituted "an impor-tant statement of fascist philosophy" (Eatwell 1996 p.261). There was certainly no hint of an apology from Mosley for his political past. To those unable to appreciate fine ideological distinctions it all appeared depressingly familiar. There was therefore a strong element of ideological continuity in the UM, even if tactically it was deemed inappropriate to eulogise the old fascist regimes or engage in military style marches and ostentatious salutes. Mosley and his miniscule band of loyal followers seemed to have learned nothing and forgotten nothing. However, "the UM was the pivotal agency through which inter-war fascism was transmitted *as* fascism across the divide of the Second World War to the post-war period…the UM acted as an ideological conveyor belt, transmitting its own particularly malignant set of political and cultural idioms across the chasm of defeat and despair to a new generation of activists" (Macklin 2007 p.141 and p.142).

During this period, the Union Movement and the fascist right had to contend with organized opposition from the Association of Jewish Ex-Servicemen (AJEX), the '43 Group, a well-organised unit of belligerent anti-fascists who formed "commando-style units" to disrupt UM meetings, and later on from the Yellow Star organisation. As in the 1930s the UM meetings became associated with violence and mayhem (Poole 1986 p.59, see Beckman 1993). Indeed it might be argued that such "anti-fascist activities were a major reason why the movement never managed to make even a moderate advance in establishing themselves as a mass political party. Anti-fascists kept the topic of the UM on the agenda if it ever threatened to establish even a tentative hold on the minds of more than a few extremists" (Poole 1996 p.60). At the time, of course, conventional politics reflected a popular social democratic consensus led by the Labour party, which concentrated on the construction of a post-war welfare state that embodied the prevailing wisdom about the importance of social justice. The attention of people and politicians was focused on the practicalities of implementing the Beveridge Report and the new NHS, rather than the grandiose ideological schemes of political outcasts struggling to re-package themselves and shed their fascist baggage. As a result "by the end of the summer of 1949 the Union Movement had declined to a point where it utterly lacked cohesion and direction, and its membership was reduced to confusion and despondency. Their heady dreams of following their revered 'Leader' on a glorious crusade had gone" (Beckman 1993 p.195). Few people cared.

The UM did badly in the 1949 London Municipal Elections (it stood in eight boroughs, coming bottom in all of them), the group's infinitesimal support was therefore fractured even further and the attempt to unite the far right was clearly a complete failure. Mosley went into a short, self-imposed exile, only to return to British politics when the issue of immigration offered the prospect of publicity and support. There is no doubt that the increase in the number of immigrants into Britain seemed to stimulate hope on the far right that the old tunes would begin to resonate with more clarity amongst the general public. In fact the growth of immigration from the New Commonwealth is crucial in understanding the development of postwar right wing politics. The shortage of labour in the advanced Western European countries from 1945 until the early 1960s was solved by importing workers from other countries, in Britain's case from its colonies or former colonies. In the 1950s the growth of such immigration prompted a response from those on the right of the Conservative Party who urged much stricter immigration controls, although the Conservative leadership felt temporarily obliged (although not without serious consideration) to leave the matter well alone (see Taylor 1982 p.11). Given this apparent lacunae in the Conservative party perspective, those on the far right saw the prospect of a political rebirth. Immigration, it was hoped, was going to be the issue to rescue the fascist right from its marginal status on the fringes of British politics. As Thurlow says "the Union Movement was the first significant organization in Britain to attack the 'coloured invasion'" (Thurlow 1998a p.250). The UM continued to accuse Commonwealth immigrants of being predisposed towards all kinds of anti-social criminality, from dope-peddling to rape, although according to Skidelsky "Mosley's attack on coloured immigration was more principled than his attack on the Jews in the 1930s" (Skidelsky 1981 p.507, see Macklin 2007 p.70). The UM, in the mid-1950s, appeared to have discovered an issue through which it could popularize its broader political programme.

By 1957 there were two sizeable groups, in addition to the UM, on the far right: the National Labour Party (set up in 1957) led by John Bean and John Tyndall, and the White Defence League founded in 1956 which was led by Colin Jordan, a disciple of Arnold Leese. Both of these groups were preoccupied with the Jewish conspiracy and the future of the white race, although Jordan's perspective was more pan-European than that of the parochial nationalists in the NLP. That both were authentic manifestations of the fascist genus is incontrovertible, as Thurlow confirms, "Jordan's *Black and White News* was amongst the most scurrilous publications promoting race hatred" whilst Tyndall demanded, in the pages of *Combat,* the elimination of the Jews as a "'cankerous microbe'" (cited in Thurlow 1998 p.233). However, both Jordan and Bean had been members of an apparently more respectable right wing organisation, the League of Empire Loyalists (LEL), which had been created in 1954 by A.K. Chesterton as a pressure group within the Tory party.

The League of Empire Loyalists organized itself in opposition to the consensual "Butskellite" drift of the Conservative leadership after the war. Chesterton himself had been a leading member of the BUF and despite a rank-and-file membership consisting predominantly of traditional "Diehard Tory" types, the LEL also harboured "a well-financed coterie of anti-semitic cranks", many of whom were disaffected fascists or even Nazi fellow-travellers (Searchlight 1989 p.4; see Baker 1985 p.29). Chesterton wrote prodigiously, especially in his own journal *Candour* (set up in 1953), although his major work was "*The New Unhappy Lords*" written in 1965 (Baker 1985) [4]. Most of Chesterton's material revealed his fanatical obsession with the alleged Jewish plot to undermine the British Empire and white race via communism and/or finance capitalism (see Thurlow 1977 p.21). As Chesterton himself put it in 1960, with characteristic verbosity: "'vileness is not too harsh a word for cowardice when one remembers the jackals gathering for the feast with slime upon their snouts and with the hammer and sickle forming a pattern with the dollar sign upon their rumps'" (cited in Thurlow 1976a p.18). Chesterton's racism was based essentially upon generalized anthropological, pseudo-scientific observations and a vulgar social Darwinist perspective, and his primary preoccupation in the 1950s and early 1960s was that large-scale immigration would lead to miscegenation, thereby diluting the quality of British racial stock. According to Chesterton only a rigidly authoritarian state and hierarchical society in service of the national (racial) interest could possibly reverse the inevitable demise.

However, Chesterton came under increasing pressure from his colleagues in the LEL to abandon the emphasis on pressure group tactics and the puerile political stunts with which the LEL had become associated, such as the high profile disruption of Tory conferences. The internal critics argued that the political showmanship should be terminated, and the LEL leadership should concentrate on the serious task of transforming the organisation into a genuine mass movement. Chesterton resolutely refused, and some of the malcontents left to form their own parties. Nevertheless the LEL was a very significant organization for the far right because in many ways it prefigured future developments. As Thurlow explains, "it was to be the ideas of A.K.Chesterton and the growing realisation by some in this group that extremist and nazi ideas could be given a veneer of respectability through being expressed in more moderate language, which was to be the central importance of the League of Empire Loyalists" (Thurlow 1987 p.250).

The so-called "race riots" in Nottingham and Notting Hill in August and September 1958 undoubtedly increased the expectation of success among those inhabiting the fringes of the far right. Indeed, "if the emergence of "race" as a major political issue can be guaged, it is reasonable to take late 1958 and early 1959 as the starting point" (Taylor 1982 p.12). Those on the fascist right felt that the growing discontent induced by immigration and its attendant social problems might provide the basis for future electoral progress, indeed "Mosley was convinced that immigration offered him the chance of political salvation" (Macklin 2007 p.72). However in the General Election of 1959 Mosley (unquestionably the most electorally viable individual on the far right) won just over 8% of the vote in West Kensington, losing his deposit – this ignominious defeat left Mosley and the UM devastated. Mosley's brand of "nostalgic fascism" had failed abysmally (Macklin 2007 p.76). It had become quite evident that the continued disunity of the far right precluded any chance it might have of effectively exploiting the race issue. As a result primarily of this realisation the National Labour Party, led by Andrew Fountaine (who had, incidentally, fought for Franco in Spain), merged with Jordan's White Defence League to form the British National Party in 1960. Fountaine became President (Mrs. Arnold Leese Vice-President) and "policy was almost entirely concerned with the racial question. A Racial Nationalist Folk State was advocated which would exclude Jews and coloured immigrants" (Nugent 1977a p.167).

Meanwhile the LEL continued its largely ineffectual opposition within the Tory party, and as immigration increased from India, Pakistan and the Caribbean, more right wing extremists came to the conclusion that "there was little mileage left in the League's political strategy: there could be no way forward in making appeals to weak-willed middle class Tories who when it came down to it were quite prepared to sacrifice the Empire" (Copsey 2008 p.8). The Conservative party leadership, however, felt compelled to contemplate tougher immigration controls, and an Act effectively reducing unskilled (i.e. mostly black) immigration became operative in 1962. The right wing outside the Tory party, deprived of their major issue (although of course viewing the Act as too weak) began to splinter once more, a process accentuated by the assiduous attention of resurgent anti-fascist organizations like the '62 Group and Yellow Star. At the same time, interestingly, the UM, in looking toward the continent, joined other neo-fascist movements abroad in attempting to form the National Party of Europe. In fact, despite ostentatious publicity and unrealistic claims about progress and co-operation it was clear that, beyond the establishment of a liaison office, little had really been achieved. The far right was still very much on the defensive.

Also in 1962, some members of the BNP (notably Colin Jordan and John Tyndall), who had formed a para-military nucleus "Spearhead", left and created the National Socialist Movement (NSM), formally launched on 20 April 1962 (the anniversary of Hitler's birthday). Jordan solemnly declared, on behalf of the NSM, that "'the greatest treasure of the British people - the basis of their greatness in the past and the only basis for it in the future - is their Aryan, predominantly Nordic blood; and it is the first duty of the state to improve and protect this blood'" (cited in Nugent and King 1977 p.215). The NSM was populated by orthodox, unambiguous Nazis who openly acknowledged Hitler as their spiritual leader, and activists who looked forward to a World Union of National Socialists forestalling the Zionist conspiracy and imposing world-wide racial apartheid. The group's first rally was accompanied by the slogan "Free Britain from Jewish Control", and Tyndall spoke of the Jew as a "'poisonous maggot'" (cited in Hill 1988 p.80). Tyndall's political preferences were clearly articulated in the pamphlet *The Authoritarian State* (1962) which, after identifying perennial conspiratorial themes and explaining the perfidy of the Jews, advocated the abandonment of democracy (see Copsey 2008 p.12). Meanwhile, Colin Jordan's pamphlet *Britain Reborn* spoke of the need to expand "Aryan culture" and "Nordic blood" (Copsey 2008 p.12). The assumption in the group was that violent attacks on ethnic minorities were an inevitable prelude to an impending conflagration that would propel the NSM forward into national prominence. At one point Jordan and Tyndall even managed to smuggle the infamous American Nazi Lincoln Rockwell into Britain and subsequently, in an act of extraordinary self-delusion, Rockwell was named understudy to Colin Jordan as "World Fuhrer" of the World Union of National Socialists. In later years John Tyndall and others would struggle, unsuccessfully, to evade accusations of being Hitler-worshipping

National Socialists, because photos of them in full Nazi-paramilitary regalia found their way into the public domain, and were frequently utilized in the media. Unsurprisingly (if not somewhat disingenuously) Tyndall would later reflect that his involvement in the NSM was a '"profound mistake"' (cited in Copsey 2008 p.13).

The miniscule NSM was subsequently wracked by a split in 1964 caused by conflict between its two leaders, Colin Jordan and John Tyndall, apparently over the favours of wealthy fascist sympathiser Francois Dior. When Jordan married Dior, the niece of the famous French fashion designer, she wore a black and gold swastika necklace, and toasted the Nazi movement to the strains of *Horst Wessel Lied.* Having both declared themselves to be of pure Aryan descent in a ceremony steeped in Nazi ritual, they both cut their fingers and let their blood drip onto a copy of *Mein Kampf.* Tyndall, having failed to wrest control of the organisation from Jordan, left in the spring of 1964 to form the Greater Britain Movement (GBM), claiming that his new organization would more accurately reflect British interests and avoid Jordan's infatuation with Nazi Germany. Yet the very same fascist ideas were expounded by Tyndall and Martin Webster in their journal *Spearhead.* Indeed, according to the official GBM programme: '"For the protection of British blood, racial laws will be enacted forbidding marriage between Britons and non-Aryans. Medical measures will be taken to prevent procreation on the part of all those who have hereditary defects either racial, mental or physical....we hold it to be the Jewish influence in politics and commerce, in morals and culture that is perhaps more than any other factor responsible for the organised filth and corruption that has infected the body of our society. The removal of the Jews from Britain must be a cardinal aim of the new order"' (cited in Rees 1979 p.126; see Copsey 2008 p.14, Hill 1988 p.82 and p.88). Whilst the mutually antagonistic Nazi sects continued to regurgitate their racial bile, and while the UM was busy with its grand Euro-fascist designs, the rump of the BNP tried to establish and develop contacts with other right-wing groups in the apparently diminishing hope of building and sustaining some electoral support.

Although the Conservative party had hoped the 1962 Act would defuse the immigration issue, by the mid-1960s theme was being re-considered as a legitimate area for political discussion. Indeed it might be argued that the Act gave some credence to ideas that immigrants were taking jobs, housing and services from the indigenous white community. (It is also interesting to note that the Labour Party also changed its stance on immigration control, advocating more restrictive measures, to be ameliorated by accompanying Race Relations legislation). So although the far right entered the General Election of 1966 divided, it was still hopeful that the "immigration issue" might bring them votes. In the context of these raised expectations the results were disastrous. After receiving a derisory 4.6% of the vote in Shoreditch and Finsbury Mosley went into exile abroad, leaving the UM to struggle on alone (although he did not formally relinquish leadership until 1973). Meanwhile Tyndall published *Six Principles of British Nationalism* (1966), a plea for unity on the far right which downplayed the usual National Socialist authoritarian and anti-Semitic themes and called on all nationalists to bury their superficial political differences. Given their obvious electoral impotence, negotiations were intensified to unite the warring factions on the far right before their chance disappeared completely. Out of these negotiations emerged the National Front.

## The National Front: The Years of Hope

The National Front was to be, for the next decade and more in Britain, the central focus for radical right wing and fascist activity outside of the Conservative party. Being by far the largest and hitherto most effective of the extremist organizations in that period, and the major inheritor of the interwar fascist tradition, its ideas and impact on British fascist politics need to be analysed and evaluated in some detail (see Taylor 1982 p.18-49 and p.111-70).

The leaders of the LEL and BNP agreed terms for a merger late in 1966 and their respective memberships were presented with a *fait accompli* in February 1967 - the National Front was born. It was without doubt the most significant event on the far right since wartime internment. After seeing off Andrew Fountaine at the 1968 AGM Chesterton governed the new party with the aid of a Directorate composed of the previous leaders of the LEL and BNP in roughly equal proportions. The NF at its inception claimed 2,500 members, although not all came from the aforementioned organizations, some for example came from the Racial Preservation Society, The Patriotic Party, True Tories and the Anglo-Rhodesian Society (see Hanna 1974 p.49). By October 1967 the Greater Britain Movement had been disbanded and its members advised to join the NF, and for the NF's leadership the lure of more members, funds, and a publication (*Spearhead*) outweighed, it seems, initial misgivings about the more overtly fascist/militarist nature of the GBM.

The National Front from the outset sought to map out a more populist perspective and staunchly denied being a fascist, still less a Nazi organisation. However a brief glance at its original programme (The Articles of Association) of 7 February 1967 reveal perennial fascist themes [5]. For instance, the original NF programme advocated a complete termination of non-white immigration and the repatriation of blacks living in Britain in order to "preserve our British native stock" (point 8). The existing Commonwealth of Nations was to be replaced by a white Commonwealth, including Rhodesia and South Africa, under British tutelage. The need for independence from international communism and global finance was stressed, and Britain was to be returned to spiritual and moral health by a "strong" and "courageous" government. As far as economics was concerned the NF considered it essential to aim at self-sufficiency, especially in agriculture, and private enterprise would be retained, albeit subject to "national" guidelines. Interestingly, in his study of the journal *Spearhead* from 1968-72 Harris identified a distinct emphasis on the existence of a "conspiracy" by Zionists, communists, financial elites and liberals, designed to deceive honest Englishmen and pave the way for a de-nationalised and culturally amorphous world dominated by Jews (Harris 1973 p.16). Content analysis of the journal also reveals that it also contained references to the genetic inequality of races, and was characterized by crude and insulting remarks about ethnic minorities, especially Jews. Harris concluded that *Spearhead* (and the early NF) was dominated by "authoritarianism, ethnocentrism, racism, biological naturalism and anti-intellectualism" (Harris 1973 p.16).

Although, therefore, an effort was made to win support on the basis of a populist anti-immigration stance, the NF's inner ideology revealed themes that suggested an unambiguous affinity with the ideas and policy preferences of inter-war fascism [6]. The National Front was "established to present fascist and racist ideas in an electorally 'respectable' manner, without the more obvious trappings of Nazism" (Billig and Cochrane 1981 p.3, see Eatwell 1996 p.266). Thus, according to Billig, the NF adopted an ideology that functioned at two different and distinct levels - "esoteric" which reflected the views of the inner coterie of the leadership, and "exoteric" which was designed for public consumption (Billig 1978). So at one level the core ideas were conventionally fascist, at another they were populist for presentational and propagandistic purposes. This conceptual distinction is critical when analyzing the NF and, as we shall see, the subsequent configurations of fascist praxis.

It is also important to note that, at this time, the NF was provided with additional momentum by the speeches of Conservative Cabinet Minister Enoch Powell. Powell's so-called "Rivers of Blood" speech (1968) attacked successive governments for allowing immigration, whilst referring in apocalyptic terms to the likely social consequences of not dealing adequately with the issue. Powell stated that "'the West Indian or Indian does not, by being born in England, become an Englishman. In law he becomes a United Kingdom citizen by birth; in fact he is a West Indian or Asian still'" (cited in Trilling 2012 p.38). The white community in Britain was being re-cast as a powerless victim by Powell, at the mercy of "foreign" invaders. All the evidence suggests that National Front membership was given a significant impetus by Powell, in Huddersfield for instance the local NF organiser stated that, "'Powell's speeches gave our membership and morale a tremendous boost. Before Powell spoke we were getting only cranks and perverts. After his speeches we started to attract, in a secret sort of way, the right-wing members of the Tory organizations'" (cited in Taylor 1982 p.21). Indeed "there can be little doubt that the National Front would not have survived if Enoch Powell had not unwittingly given it such a helping hand in its infancy" (Thurlow 1987 p.279). The NF definitely saw a chance to capitalize on support for Powell as the only political party which was actually committed to implementing his ideas in practice, although the 1968 Race Relations Act (which made incitement to racial hatred an offence) meant that the language deployed by the unreconstructed racists had to be modified somewhat.

In the 1969 local elections, 45 NF candidates gained a creditable average of 8% of the total vote. However, when the NF contested nine seats in the General Election of 1970, its candidates only achieved a disappointing 3.7% share of the vote. The avowedly Nazi British Movement, set up by Colin Jordan in 1968 as the successor to the NSM, with its Hitler-worshipping SS action squads, did not do much worse. The major reason for the NF's failure was the inclusion in the Tory manifesto of explicit promises to cut immigration - the Conservative leadership may have disliked Powell's language, but could not ignore his popular appeal. The NF, disappointed at its weak election showing, turned inwards upon its leader, and a coup at the end of 1970 replaced Chesterton (who was forced to resign) with John O'Brien (a former Powellite). The change in personnel at a leadership level did not lead to an immediate improvement in the NF's electoral

performance: 84 candidates in the 1971 local elections averaged 5.2% each, and in 1972 O'Brien resigned complaining
of "'evil men'" in the Directorate (see Hanna 1974 p.49).
O'Brien left to form his own National Independence Party,
and his replacement was John Tyndall, who claimed to have
abandoned his Nazi past.

Yet despite Tyndall's reassurances the NF, beneath its
superficial populist emphasis on anti-immigration issues,
remained committed to the familiar racial nationalist
fascist/Nazi creed (Goodwin 2011 p.25) [7]. Indeed the
function of the NF's ideology was indisputably "to convert
racial populists into fascists" (Thurlow 1998 p.263). The
same negative obsessions dominated, but lay just beneath
the surface. The most pressing political and social problem,
according to Tyndall, remained race, and the same old cast of
heroes and villains were placed firmly centre stage. The NF
continued to refer to itself as a party of Racial Nationalism,
an ideology based on the "fact" of inherent racial inequality
and the existence of non-eliminable racial instincts (see NF
Constitution: Statement of Principles Section 2). The unique
character and achievements of the British nation were attributed fundamentally to the racial composition of the people
therein and "the party consistently sought to mobilize intolerance toward immigration by framing immigrants and
minority groups as a threat to the resources and even survival
of white Britons" (Goodwin 2011 p.25). Under Tyndall, who
persistently proclaimed his debt to Chesterton (who had
died in 1973) the NF remained steadfastly committed to
ending black immigration and forcibly repatriating all non-
whites: "'mass coloured immigration and the tyranny of
forced integration are designed to smash our racial identity'"
Tyndall claimed (cited in Thurlow 1977 p.22). The need for
a homogeneous nation was underpinned not, he argued, by
hatred of other racial types but by love of nation, although
this did not preclude ubiquitous references (principally by
Martin Webster) to "'wogs'", "'coons'", "'sub-humans'" and
the "'nigger problem'" (cited in Thurlow 1978 p.5).

Moreover, Tyndall remained convinced of the existence of a secretive Jewish conspiracy conducted by organizations like the Bilderberg Group and the World Bank to undermine Britain's racial stock. The Rockerfellers and the Rothschilds were still seen as the hidden hands pulling the strings in accordance with their own nefarious objectives. As Tyndall explained, "'no race on earth has done more to undermine the idea of the nation state than the Jews'" (cited in Thurlow 1978 p.3). Meanwhile *Spearhead* maintained that "'we must be as merciless as the deadly creatures who seek to destroy our white race, our nation and our civilization....there will be an unanswerable case when the day for the great clean-up comes, to implement the final solution against these sub-human elements by means of the gas chamber system'", indeed according to Tyndall, Hitler "'showed the way to a proper, fair and final solution to the Jewish question'" (cited in Billig 1978 p.184-5). Although these despicable prejudices were not designed for public consumption, the NF world-view under Tyndall constituted a collection of "ethnocentric and racist beliefs which were heavily impregnated by social Darwinism and cultural pessimism. Life was determined according to the laws of nature and the survival of the fittest" (Thurlow 1978 p.2).

In more specific policy terms the NF reiterated its preference for a white Commonwealth and close ties with South Africa, whilst aid to the Third World would become discretionary and based on the commitment of recipient nations to accept repatriated members of ethnic minority communities. Britain, Tyndall argued, should aspire to its former dominance in the world, and policy statements and speeches continued to be suffused with a fanatical, romantic nationalism. Of course in order to create Tyndall's nationalistic utopia certain measures were urgently required and these included, most importantly, strong leadership and an authoritarian state, since democracy, individual freedom and tolerance were seen as unambiguous symptoms of liberal degeneracy. A widespread purge of the "opposition" (so-called "non-patriots"), was also considered to be a prerequisite for genuine national rejuvenation, and capital punishment would be reintroduced for treason. Tyndall's National Front naturally made a firm commitment to defence of the realm, and national autonomy would necessitate withdrawal from all supra-national bodies, such as the EEC, UN, IMF and NATO. As far as the economy was concerned a "racial nationalist" Britain would require the subordination of economics (capital and labour) to politics, in deference to the "national interest". According to the NF a producers' "distributist" economy was required with a widepread ownership of property in order to guard against the worst excesses of capitalism and forestall the fatal attraction of communism. Small businesses would be encouraged, and credit controlled by the government, whilst foreign ownership of commercial concerns would be forbidden by law. People would be encouraged to live and work in rural communities in order to improve not only the economic but the cultural and spiritual health of the nation. Tyndall's NF also advocated, in a minor reworking of Mosley's BUF policy of Empire autarky, self-sufficiency which would be achieved within the context of a white Commonwealth. Quite clearly the NF's ideological content under Tyndall reveals that the tradition of fascism/ Nazism was being continued, adapted and updated.

In fact Tyndall took over the NF just as it was given an issue which enabled it to emerge from the political fringes. The Conservatives had, as promised, introduced more restrictive legislation on immigration in 1971, but any benefit they might have derived from being seen as "tough" on immigration was lost by the decision, in 1972, to admit Ugandan Asians expelled from their own country. Conflict within the Conservative party came to a head at their Conference when Powell openly attacked Prime Minister Ted Heath's decision. Events could not have worked out better for the NF: "feeling betrayed at the Conservative government's leniency over this issue, the racist constituency flocked to the National Front. Membership of the Front doubled between October 1972 and July 1973 and possibly jumped as high as 17,500" (Copsey 2008 p.18;

see Eatwell 1996a). Marches and demonstrations by the NF received unprecedented press exposure as "the disillusioned right-wing Conservatives flocked to join the NF" (Taylor 1982 p.24). Indeed Walker argued that, "the arrival of the Ugandan Asians in 1972...brought so much new support that the character of the Front began to change. New members, new talents from other parties, established local politicians...all welded into a party which was still dominated by the old neo-Nazi cranks who had been scrabbling in the gutter of racist politics for a generation" (Walker 1978 p.9).

At the same time the ties between the National Front and Conservative fringe groups like the Monday Club and WISE (Welsh, Irish, Scottish, English) began to strengthen (indeed Heath was forced to disband some Monday Club branches because of overt NF infiltration) (see Thurlow 1987 p.283). The NF had further opportunities to mobilize support in 1973 because the re-organisation of local government meant that there would be three local elections (as opposed to one): the GLC Metropolitan and Non-Metropolitan County elections (April), the Metropolitan District elections (May), and the Non-Metropolitan District elections (June). The NF put up 35 candidates in the provinces and six in the GLC elections of April where it averaged 7.7.% and 6.8% of the vote respectively. The NF did not contest the May Metropolitan District Elections, preferring instead to concentrate its resources on a by-election at West Bromwich where Martin Webster (described somewhat euphemistically by Hanna as a "jolly buccaneering character") (Hanna 1974 p.53), stood for the NF. Webster received 16% of the vote, thereby saving his deposit. This respectable result was due not only to a sustained and co-ordinated effort by the NF, but also to the fact that Enoch Powell refused to endorse the Conservative candidate because of his views on immigration and the EEC. The result undoubtedly provided the NF with a momentum which it carried into the Non-Metropolitan District elections of June. The NF improved on its April performance and of 28 candidates only three won less that 10% of the total vote,

15 won between 10-15% and 10 won over 20%. The level of NF support may seem surprising in retrospect, but in the context of widespread disillusionment with the major parties (and with the Liberals being the major beneficiaries) the NF's expectations had to be tempered by a realistic evaluation of the overall political situation.

The NF was soon to have another chance to test its support. The General Election of February 1974 saw the NF field 54 candidates, who won a total of more than 77,000 votes. Although this was more than six times the total vote of 1970 the average vote per candidate suggested a significant decline in the level of support. Despite the difficulties involved in comparing the 1973 local elections with the February 1974 General Election, close analysis reveals that the results "indicated unambiguously that NF support had fallen" (Taylor 1982 p.29). There were several reasons for this decline in support including: the disappearance of the Ugandan Asian "invasion" issue (the effects of which were wildly exaggerated by the media in the first place); the importance of other critical issues (such as trade union "power" and economic "stagflation"); and the decision of Powell to urge his considerable following to vote Labour because of its stance over the EEC. NF members were naturally bitterly disappointed with the February 1974 results, especially those recent ex-Conservative recruits who had hoped to capitalize on their former party's apparent weaknesses. Throughout 1974 therefore tension increased within the NF between the so-called "populist" ex-Conservatives and the "ex" Nazi/fascist leadership - the former viewing the latter as the chief reason for the NF's poor electoral display (Copsey 2008 p.18). In the General Election of October 1974 the NF put up 90 candidates. The party's vote increased to 112.000, but this was again the consequence of fielding extra candidates, since the party's average share of the votes in the seats contested remained obstinately low at 3.1% [8]. After the October election the need for the NF to appear unified no longer existed and the rift widened between the ex-Conservative "populists", who wished to broaden the NF's ideological appeal, and the "old guard" who remained determined to adhere to their narrow racial nationalist faith.

In fact the "populists" in the NF were aided by an internal constitutional change in 1974 which meant that all 20 seats on the Directorate were available, and the candidates would be elected by all of the membership rather than the few that could be persuaded to attend the AGM. In October a number of ex-Conservatives (who formed an odd anti-leadership alliance with a few discontented Strasserites) were able to stage a coup against Tyndall, who was subsequently demoted to Deputy Chairman. Kingsley Read became the new Chairman. Internal wrangles followed throughout 1975 as Tyndall attempted frantically to recapture the party by persistently putting forward constitutional amendments, and he was at one point actually expelled. Tyndall managed to get his expulsion revoked on a technicality after judicial intervention, and eventually resumed control of the NF early in 1976, prompting a number of his opponents, including Read, to leave and form their own party, the National Party. (It was, in effect, a repeat of 1972 when O'Brien left, only the consequences were rather more serious for the NF, with the loss of 2,000 members, around one fifth of its total membership, to the new NP) (Copsey p.18-19). The victorious Tyndall faction attacked the secessionists as "National Bolsheviks", "Strasserites" and "National Syndicalist" heretics (see Verrall cited in Rees 1979 p.14 and Evans 1975). Although the National Party claimed to be less authoritarian and cultist, the difference between the two parties was primarily personal rather than political. The NP's preoccupation with race, immigration, conspiracy and so on betrayed some significant continuity in terms of ideological purpose. The NP went on to win two council seats in Blackburn in May 1976 by putting up relatively well known candidates and capitalizing on some sympathetic local media coverage, although eventually "destabilized by internal ideological contradictions, the National Party collapsed in the late 1970s" (Copsey 2008 p.19).

Although the National Party faded into oblivion, and despite the fact that many at the time might have assumed that a similar fate awaited the NF, it was in fact on the verge of another breakthrough, courtesy of a strikingly familiar sequence of events. In April and May 1976 a few (tens rather than thousands) Malawi Asians with UK passports were allowed to enter the country. The event escaped press attention until West Sussex Council housed some of the arrivals in local hotels, at some expense, and as news of this escaped a scare campaign ensued in the press in early May, just before local elections were due to be held. The NF enjoyed arguably its "finest hour" on 7 May 1976 when the results were declared – the party averaged 8.9% of the vote in seats contested, around one in twelve of those who voted [9]. Although these returns were, in fact, once more the result of differential turnout (i.e. NF voters turning out and supporters of other parties staying at home) they were the cause of much jubilation in the NF camp, despite the fact that the NF could not claim a single elected representative. With Powell rampant again and Labour's Race Relations Bill going through the House of Commons, racial tension increased dramatically. The tabloid press, of course, reported items of "interracial" significance in terms which could only lend credence to Powell's persistent warnings.

Yet the NF was unable to benefit further, electorally, from the renewed prominence of race as an issue in this period, since few local or parliamentary by-elections were held in areas that might have been important. Nevertheless, despite the lack of additional electoral opportunities, 1976 can be seen, in retrospect, as one of the NF's most productive and rewarding periods. Certainly the NF's fortunes marked a stark contrast to other right wing fascist groups at this particular juncture, such as the British Movement, which had been taken over by Michael McLaughlin after Colin Jordan was convicted of shoplifting [10]. The BM scorned electoral politics, and McLaughlin combined an interest in "survivalism" with the familiar Hitler-worship that had characterised Jordan's troubled tenure. The journal *British Patriot* spouted the same obnoxious racial hatred, whilst its paramilitary nucleus "Leaderguard" indulged in sporadic, racially motivated attacks on people and property (Wilkinson 1981 p.77; see Eatwell 1996a p.105). Other semi-clandestine Nazi/fascist groups, such as Column 88, SS Wotan, the League of St. George, and the National Socialist Action Party also inhabited the seedy fascist political underworld of the mid-1970s. Meanwhile the NF, by judiciously concealing the core of its ideology and emphasising the populist, anti-immigration component of its political programme, seemed to be making at least some marginal electoral headway, indeed many in the Labour Party and Trade Union movement began to view the NF as a genuine challenger in the quest to capture working class votes.

The NF made a major effort to sustain its support in the 1977 Metropolitan and County Council elections, fielding 413 candidates. These averaged 4.2% of the total vote, a yield less than half the mean of 1976. However this somewhat disappointing return by the NF was  more than compensated by what was perceived to be a quite stunning performance in London (which had not held elections in 1976). The NF contested all the London seats (except Croydon NE), and its 91 candidates won 120,000 votes - more than twice the total vote won in the whole of England in 1974. Consequently, without any immediate "scare" over immigration, the NF had staved off the challenge from the NP and mounted its own assault on the Liberal party for the status of "third party" in the capital (it secured more votes in 32 of the 88 seats contested by both parties). Martin Webster stated shortly afterwards that the NF vote throughout the GLC area was dramatic evidence that the party had firmly established itself on the national electoral scene, whilst some commentators exclaimed ominously that since the National Front had ceased to be an "electoral joke" the only way of preventing its further expansion was to meet some of its demands (Walker 1978 p.225; Taylor 1982) [11]. There is little doubt that, "the 1977 GLC results were interpreted as marking the emergence of the NF as the party of working class protest against the failure of the Labour party at national and local level to make any significant impact upon urban decay and decline in London, and the associated problems to which these gave rise" (Taylor 1982 p.121). "The popular impression was that the NF was now on course to become Britain's third largest political party" (Copsey 2008 p.19). As confidence within the NF soared, its opponents feared the worst. However, as Steed (1978) suggested shortly afterwards, there was a distinct over-reaction to the NF vote in 1977, which could be simply explained in terms of differential turnout - certainly headlines such as "'Poll points to twenty-five Front M.P.s'" were ill-considered and unwarranted, and many commentators were careless in conflating their own discovery of the NF with evidence of a dramatic increase in its electoral support (Steed 1978) [12].

Nevertheless, in subsequent months there developed a genuine fear (perhaps understandable given the widespread misinterpretation of the election statistics and the concomitant media coverage) that the NF was destined to have a permanent place in British politics. The creation of an NF Youth Movement in July 1977 (YNF), and the continuation of high-profile marches and demonstrations, along with the increasing level of violence and racial tension, seemed to confirm these fears (see Adam 1978; Weightman and Weir 1978 p.186-93). Moreover, with the apparent inability of both major parties to deal with persistent inflation and rising unemployment (inelegantly described as "stagflation" in the popular press), it appeared that the objective socio-economic conditions were becoming more favourable for the NF. The existence of a widespread and growing concern inspired both the setting up of the Anti-Nazi League on 3 November (which had over 200 groups affilliated to it by June 1978) and a new Labour party/TUC campaign against the NF. Even the Executive Council of the National Union of the Conservative Party joined the Joint Committee Against Racialism (a kind of ANL for moderates), against the wishes of party leader Margaret Thatcher. Other more autonomous groups such as Christians

Against Racism and Fascism (set up in January 1978) also joined in the opposition against what was widely perceived as the growing spectre of fascism in Britain. "By the end of 1977 an unprecedented range of groups from almost every section of British society spreading right across the political spectrum had declared an intention to oppose the NF and the racism upon which it fed" (Taylor 1982 p.139).

However the local elections of 4 May 1978 simply confirmed the extent of the over-reaction to the previous year's GLC results: the party won 10% of the poll in only eight wards outside London, and the election confirmed the NF's electoral weakness in the provinces. Only the East End of London provided a minor foothold for the party, an area where racially motivated attacks (including several murders) continued to cause public concern, since it was felt that such incidents could not be entirely divorced from the fact that the NF had a presence in the area. Nevertheless the NF held its overdue 1978 AGM on 20 January 1979 in London, where it announced it was going to field over 300 candidates for the forthcoming General Election. In fact, after a considerable organizational effort, on 3 May 1979 the NF eventually managed to put up 303 candidates [13], although the party did little canvassing, relying instead on publicity provided by high profile meetings which would inevitably attract opposition and end in violence. For example, large NF gatherings in Leicester and Southall ended in complete chaos, although Powell characteristically claimed that these events were but the harbinger of the civil war he had predicted (and for which neither he nor the NF could be blamed).

The results of the 1979 General Election dealt a crushing blow to the NF: it won a total of 191,706 votes and a meagre (even by NF standards) 1.3% of the vote (Copsey 2008 p.20). The only regions where the vote topped 2% were London, West Bromwich, Leicester and Wolverhampton. Such results were little better than those regularly secured by perennial joke candidates. Yet the fall in the NF vote was not simply the result of contesting 217 seats it had not contested before in a

General Election, for the NF's share of the vote declined in seats contested in both 1974 and 1979 - nowhere did the party improve on 1974.

In retrospect the reasons for the NF's electoral debacle are clear. Firstly, May 1979 was a General Election where turnout is higher and where NF support (even if constant) would be measured as a smaller proportion of the total votes cast, therefore it could not hope to emulate its local election percentages. It was also a bad year for smaller parties generally with support for the Liberals and Nationalist parties (Scottish and Welsh) also falling, and of course the simple plurality electoral system always militates against a breakthrough for smaller parties. In addition, the activities of the ANL and other anti-NF groups definitely had a tangible effect on the result by imparting negative images to the general public about a party with an unambiguously Nazi heritage advocating hideous ideas – such groups made it impossible for the NF to evade the stigma of its fascist ideology [14]. Finally, and perhaps most importantly, Margaret Thatcher's robust stance on immigration completely undercut the NF's primary source of support. Thatcher's infamous reference to the British people feeling "swamped" by immigration had apparently confirmed her intention to re-package Powell's political preconceptions about race and nationality. As a consequence many of the discontented Tories, who had effectively loaned their support to the NF, returned to the Conservative fold. Henceforth the NF's leadership, which was always predominantly middle class (see Eatwell 2000 p.178), could not rely on support from its own social class in the Conservative political tradition and would have to look again toward those pockets of the working class who continued to feel threatened by immigration. Martin Webster, in the May/June issue of *Spearhead*, remarked with some justification that the "'Tories'" had deserted the NF and therefore, he argued, the movement would have to fall back on "'the guts of NF support'" – in effect that small minority of alienated, white, working class youth in the inner cities (Webster cited in Billig and Cochrane 1981).

## The National Front: Decline and Disintegration

The NF, in the wake of this devastating electoral defeat, turned inward upon itself once more. Tyndall, since his return in 1976, had consolidated his leadership position by altering the eligibility rules for standing as Chairman and, in accordance with his stated preference for an elective dictatorship, it was made much more difficult to stand for the Chairmanship of the NF. However his position could still be challenged from within the ruling inner circle, and this happened in 1979 after a dispute between Tyndall and Andrew Fountaine over the conduct of National Activities Organiser Martin Webster. Fountaine stood against Tyndall for the Chairmanship of the party in October 1979 and lost. It was a prelude to an internal disintegration from which the NF would never recover. In November 1979 Fountaine, having been expelled from the NF, formed the NF Constitutional Movement and, shortly after, the leaders of the large Leicester branch of the NF broke away to form the British People's Party (that name being changed subsequently to the British Democratic Party). With the National Front apparently collapsing around him, Tyndall made one last effort to reassert his authority and on 19 January 1980 he asked the Directorate to convene an Extraordinary General Meeting of the party to confer upon him the extra powers which he believed were required to redeem the situation (and which had been denied him in 1975 and 1979). The Directorate voted 10-2 (1 abstention) not to call an EGM and Tyndall resigned to form his own faction, the New National Front. The primary objective of the New National Front was to wrest control back from the anti-Tyndall incumbents on the NF Directorate.

So by mid-1980 there were three splinter groups from the original NF: the British Democratic Party, the NF Constitutional Movement and the New National Front. At a Directorate meeting of the old NF on 3 February 1981 Andrew Brons was appointed acting Chairman with Richard Verrall (who had been editor of *Spearhead* since 1976) appointed Acting Deputy, and these positions were endorsed as permanent by internal elections on 1 March (they were the only candidates for each post). All three groups put up candidates in the 1981 local elections, and despite the anticipated stimulus of the Brixton riots just prior to polling day, they all fared extremely badly. The average share of their votes combined was a meagre 2.3%, with the "best" results being secured in the East End of London. The National Front, despite being the largest of the fascist groups, was heading back to the obscure fringes of British politics to compete with the British Movement and the League of St. George for the fickle loyalties of skinheads and football hooligans.

However it is important to note that the internal crises in the NF did not precipitate any fundamental ideological re-evaluation. Under the leadership triumvirate of Andrew Brons, Martin Webster and Richard Verrall the NF's ideology remained obstinately racist and dominated by the same negative obsessions. In some respects an even greater emphasis was placed on the "scientific" justification of the same fascist ideas. For example Richard Verrall, as the party's principal ideologue, argued that the NF's ideas were based on the fundamental "truths" of "sociobiology". In essence sociobiology developed the idea that individual abilities and instincts, and hence social behaviour, were predominantly (if not exclusively) reflections of genetic inheritance (see Barker 1982 p.76-100). In short, this neo-Darwinist "theory" suggested that people were essentially pre-programmed by blood, and therefore evolved into separate "races" and "nations". As a result of those inherited racial qualities culture was created by the Aryans and, as usual, the race-nations were ordered hierarchically, with whites being inherently superior to all other racial categories. The greatest racial instinct, according to the NF sociobiological version of mankind, was to protect one's own kin-group, thus racism and nationalism were fundamentally rooted in the genes. In this way elements from anthropology, biology, genetics and psychology were selectively deployed under the rubric of sociobiology and used (with appropriate quotations from the likes of Professors Eysenck, Jensen, Darlington et al) to bestow a spurious "scientific" respectability upon the NF's dismal creed of Social Nationalism (see Thurlow 1987 p.295). As Richard Verrall concluded in an article entitled "'Science is Championing Our Creed of Social Nationalism'", "'sociobiology has shown us that evolutionary processes have genetically and therefore immutably programmed human nature with instincts of competitiveness, territorial defence, racial prejudice, identification with integral behaviour within one kin group (nation)'" (Verrall cited in Barker 1982 p.100). Although, according to Verrall, racial inequality was "'something so obvious, so self-evident that having to prove it strikes one as mildly absurd'", clearly if credence could be provided by reference to certain "scientific" studies, then so much the better (Verrall cited in Thurlow 1978 p.5; see Thurlow 1981 p.26-7). Phased and orderly repatriation (and apartheid in the meantime) was also still required as the essential solution to nearly all social ills.

Moreover, the NF magazine *New Nation* not only argued that the higher races were locked in deadly struggle for survival and supremacy, it insisted that the primary threat remained that being posed by the "worldwide Zionist conspiracy". The Jews aimed to destroy the higher races by encouraging inter-racial blood-mixing. If any further proof were needed that in the NF there remained a nucleus committed to the dissemination of Nazi ideas, it was provided by the continued adherence to historical revisionism. Revisionists claimed either that the mass extermination of the Jews did not take place, or that genocide was greatly exaggerated by the Allied propaganda specialists in the Psychological Warfare Executive and/or by the Jews themselves in a devious attempt to extort reparations from Germany [15]. The conspiracy theory thus remained a central, apocalyptic component of the Front's ideology (see Billig 1989). Ritualistic references were also made to the need to terminate the evils of usury, the failure and betrayal of the old parties, and the importance of transcending the class war in the national interest. The "new" Britain posited by the NF in the early 1980s was to be fiercely patriotic, meritocratic, disciplined, autonomous, well defended, and thoroughly purged of liberal/communist subversive elements.

Clearly the NF remained an unreconstructed repository for the development and dissemination of Nazi ideology. Indeed Taylor, writing in 1982, contended that (after outlining no less than 13 specific similarities), "the most remarkable feature of the NF ideology is the extent to which it corresponds to the ideas set out in 'Mein Kampf'"" (Taylor 1982 p.77-78) and he concluded that the NF was in a large number of respects "identical to that of the German Nazi party before it achieved power" (Taylor 1982 p.175). The familiar purpose of the NF in this period was once more, indisputably, to turn racial populists into hard line fascists (see Thurlow 1987 p.293). The ultimate practical consequence of such an ideology was predictable, as ex-NF activist and organizer Matthew Collins candidly put it - "not that we openly said there would be death camps for one moment but it was fucking obvious" (Collins 2011 p.160).

The two other offshoots of the NF endorsed similar ideas: the NNF/*Spearhead* magazine was no less crude and bigoted, although Tyndall did express the intention of setting up a more elitist organisation via his Special Tactical Activities Group (STAG); whilst the NF Constitutional Movement's attempt to court respectability resulted in abject failure (see Billig and Cochrane 1981 p.14). In fact it soon began to dawn on Tyndall that he was unlikely to retrieve control of the old NF. "Though it was hard to swallow, the fact that Tyndall could no longer recapture the National Front also meant that his claim to the Front's brand name would now have to be sacrificed. If he was to secure a political future, the only alternative was to constitute an entirely new political party" (Copsey 2008 p.24). As a consequence Tyndall chose to abandon his NNF and re-form the British National Party. In so doing Tyndall was attempting to preserve a distinctly fascist ideological heritage and propound those ideas  in opposition to the various other disparate micro-groups that remained thoroughly marginalized as the isolated outposts of the far right, sparsely populated by political psychopaths and football thugs.

For the time being however the National Front was still the primary focus for far right wing politics (despite its relative demise), and it put up sixty candidates in the 1983 election, averaging a paltry 1.1% of the vote (all lost their deposits). However, at this point the NF was on the verge of another split which would indeed alter quite significantly its ideological perspective. The NF's miniscule election return "further encouraged some of its leading members – especially a small but active and relatively well educated group – to turn towards more radical ideological approaches" (Eatwell 1996a p.108 see Collins 2011 p.38). In 1983 the NF's old guard, dominated by Martin Webster, was systematically and ruthlessly purged in what was a major watershed in British right wing fascist politics. The coup, which led subsequently to the expulsion of Webster in February 1984, was staged by a coterie of elitist "national revolutionaries" or "political soldiers", led principally by Nick Griffin, Patrick Harrington and Derek Holland. Along with other self-styled "Strasserites" that had coalesced around the publications *Nationalism Today* and *The Rising* they sought to take the NF in a new, but ideologically related, direction. Andrew Brons became Chairman, and  under his auspices the distributist ideas of Hilaire Belloc and G.K. Chesterton were highlighted. This emphasis on indigenous antecedents was accompanied by a nostalgia for an idealized notion of medieval society in England where peasants, merchants and craftsmen were organized in guilds (see Husbands 1988). However, despite the nod in the direction of a peculiarly English distributism, the new leadership was committed to "a modern version of the anti-semitism, anti-capitalism, anti-Marxism, and syndicalism pioneered by the Strasser brothers in the 1920s" (Baker 1985 p.25). Indeed Baker argues that the radically reconstituted NF leadership looked to focus upon the twenty-five point Nazi programme largely abandoned by Hitler after he reached power (Baker 1985 p.25).

In fact, rather than a full scale commitment to Strasserism this period represented an attempt to merge more economic radicalism with the traditional core value of racial populism which still seemed to unite all sections of the Front. This perspective, however, was accompanied by a growing scepticism as to the value of electoral politics and a revised tactical preference for infiltrating other organizations, such as ecology groups and trade unions. Such a sudden and significant political reorientation caused considerable internal discussion and dissension in the NF, and in May 1984 another split occurred when the so-called "political soldiers" ousted from the Directorate what they referred to as the "reactionary Tory element". Those expelled included Ian Anderson, Martin Wingfield, and even the leader Andrew Brons, whose self-proclaimed preference for "distributism" seemed to resonate with the new mood, felt compelled to resign. Nick Griffin and the others in the new leadership began to develop the idea of a politically educated paramilitary cadre of "political soldiers" adhering to a much more radical and coherent ideological perspective (see Husbands 1988). The self-proclaimed "national revolutionaries" gained full control of the organization and their ascendancy was confirmed after an acrimonious court battle with erstwhile colleagues. Those expelled ex-members went onto form the NF Support Group, which produced a newspaper *The Flag* and a magazine *Vanguard*. While the Support Group complained of "leftist extremism", Griffin, Harrington and the victorious faction made no attempt to conceal their militant credentials - they aimed to build a "fully radicalised National Revolutionary Movement" (NF Directorate 1986 p.65) [16].

The ideas which motivated the new leadership of the Front were perhaps most explicitly expressed in a booklet written by Derek Holland in 1984 entitled *The Political Soldier.* Holland outlined in some detail the parlous and potentially disastrous condition of Britain and talked in apocalyptic terms about the physical and spiritual rape of a sick and dying "Motherland", with accompanying references to, amongst others,

Oswald Spengler. After criticising the various political and tactical mistakes of the older National Front, Holland went on to map his own route toward political redemption. With the country in an advanced state of decay and disintegration and with socio-economic crises looming, what was required, Holland argued, was a "new" kind of man with strength, vision and faith. Hence Holland referred with approval to the ancient Spartan elite, the Christian Crusader and even the Islamic Revolutionary Guard, with their powerful ideals and contempt for death. Holland's was an unambiguous plea for a new caste of National Warriors, a revolutionary elite to advance the nationalist cause [17]. Whilst imparting their political wisdom, replete with Nietschean images of doom and re-birth, it became clear that central to the new leadership's perspective was the perennial fascist notion of a cathartic re-calibration of human nature through instinctive political activism and violence, and here the emphasis on their fascist ideals was inextricably bound up with "boys-own" images of warrior-heroes and ancient folk legends.

On a more prosaic level the new collective leadership of the National Front appeared to make certain other changes in policy. There seemed to be a discernible effort to replace crude and gratuitous racial bigotry with (what they believed were) the more positive values of racial separatism. Indeed, the Directorate spoke of the need to break out of the moronic racist ghetto to which the NF had been consigned by Tyndall, Webster and others (NF Directorate 1986). However, evidence contained within the paper *NF News* and magazine *Nationalism Today* clearly suggested the continued existence of anti-semitism. In fact Jewish Zionists, along with freemasons, communists and large-scale capitalists still appeared to constitute the chief threat according to the newly constituted "revolutionary" NF. Holland, for example, spoke of the need to protect European heritage, culture and traditions from the barbaric hordes of the superpowers, and the Front still looked toward a folk-state by concentrating its efforts on winning over sections of the discontented white working class.

The leadership also pledged to commit itself to such issues as environmental welfare, and the removal of foreign military bases from British soil. Consequently, although it certainly appeared that a distinct effort was being made to emphasise the social component of their ideology, the familiar fascist themes still resonated amongst the "political soldiers".

Interestingly, the NF at this time also declared in favour of an independent Ulster, and it was this rejection of a long-standing policy of supporting British jurisdiction over Northern Ireland that appears to have been one of the chief policy disputes precipitating the split of 1986 (NF Directorate Report 1986 p.26). Strong evidence began to emerge of links between the new NF leadership and Protestant paramilitary groups in Belfast. As the NF Directorate document argued, in Ulster the state was waging war on a section of the nation therefore "it was essential that the NF be seen to be firmly on the side of the nation in its struggle against the state" (NF Directorate 1986 p.27) even if this meant, in the final analysis, a unilateral declaration of independence. In Ulster, where access to sympathetic Loyalist paramilitary groups with weapons was not difficult to organize, the NF saw more possibilities to create its New Order (Eatwell 1996a p.112). The Ulster connection was also significant because it highlights the difference in tactics pursued by the leadership of the Front in the mid-1980s – the "political soldiers" were becoming increasingly fascinated and fixated by the idea of armed insurrection. It was the beginning of a new, and potentially much more dangerous phase in the development of British fascism.

In effect the Front deliberately eschewed electoral activity and went "underground" in accordance with its new clandestine tactical purpose and commitment to the *Terza Posizione* ("Third Position") i.e. neither capitalist nor communist. The new elitist Front leadership were intent on constructing a cadre of well-trained activists to conduct, in effect, terrorist activities in the pursuit of their ultimate objectives. In line with certain ideas expressed by the likes of Italian mystic-fascist Julius Evola (who wrote *The Aryan Doctrine of Fight and*

*Struggle*) and Romanian leader of the Iron Guard Corneliu Codreanu, the NF attempted to de-centralise its organization. The NF re-emphasised ruralism and sought to assemble a second generation of front-line fighters away from the decadence and corruption of the urban environment. There was also significant evidence of contact between the NF leadership and the Italian fascist terrorists NAR *Nuclei Armati Rivoluzionari* (Armed Revolutionary Nuclei) the organization which had bombed Bologna railway station in 1980 killing eighty-five people. It was widely suspected that Italian fascist Roberto Fiore had connections with NAR and was therefore wanted for questioning (Copsey 2008 p.35, Griffin 2011), and after Fiore had fled to London with the help of the League of St. George he made contact with Nick Griffin and other NF leaders. Fiore not only had an influence on the leadership of the NF, he worked with them for a company called Heritage Tours, so the connections were not only clearly ideological, but practical and personal [18].

Extraordinarily the "political soldiers" also had contact with, and spoke approvingly of, Colonel Gaddafi's regime in Libya. More specifically they highlighted the educative value of Gaddafi's *Green Book,* with its emphasis on direct democracy and de-centralisation (see Trilling 2012 p.47). Griffin and Holland even travelled to Tripoli in search of financial support, returning empty handed. Remarkable eulogies were also disseminated via NF literature in support of the Ayatollah Khomeni and the American black separatist Louis Farrakhan (see Eatwell 1996a p.109). This new focus on separatism and identity was indeed qualitatively different from the crude racial populism of the 1970s, and the NF even condemned "anti-semitism" and made approaches to the *Jewish Chronicle* with a view to opening dialogue with the Jewish community. As Roger Griffin points out, as the new leadership continued its mission of translating the party's neo-Nazism into Third Positionism, it produced "a dialect of neo-fascism that must have been utterly strange to the ears of neo-Mosleyite and neo-Hitlerite party faithful" (Griffin 2011 p.196). Whilst the NF delved even deeper into the ideological abyss by supporting an odd rag-tag collection of causes, "the 'political soldier' faction set about destroying its own credibility of its own accord" (Copsey 2008 p.46). The NF became "a coterie of disputatious political neophytes" (Husbands 1988 p.76).

The NF's belief appeared to be that out of the inevitable crises which Britain would experience, a conflagration which would in part be precipitated by the NF tactics of creating "tension and terror", a new fascist force would emerge. The new nationalist phoenix would arise from the ashes of a decadent liberal society. Obviously if a new world was to be constructed upon the ruins of the old, the sooner that society collapsed the better. Violence today would produce the "new order" tomorrow. As the new Directorate stated unequivocally, shortly after the split: "we will make whatever sacrifice is necessary for the salvation of our Race and Nation" (NF Directorate 1986 p.69). As Eatwell has pointed out, "there seems little doubt that the Political Soldiers were willing to use violence to overthrow the system" (Eatwell 1996a p.112). This strategy, which stressed the primacy of political ideas over loyalty to leadership, a common European heritage, and fascist ruralism, obviously had elements in common with the so-called "Third Position" of Otto Strasser. However, while the likes of Griffin, Holland and Harrington flirted ostentatiously with the "Third Position", the NF's membership declined dramatically with some disillusioned members leaving to form the National Democrats (Copsey 2008 p.46, Eatwell 1998 p.145). The "official" NF was constantly on the verge of self-destruction, and the organization effectively disbanded in 1989, with Griffin's clique re-naming itself the International Third Position. Nick Griffin and the Strasserite fascists appeared to be heading inexorably toward terminal crisis and political oblivion.

The NF's pre-eminence on the far right was destined to be short lived anyway because Tyndall's new political vehicle was designed to disseminate the more familiar racial nationalist vision. Indeed it was this new party which would eventually make the most important contribution to far right wing politics since the 1930s – the British National Party. As the NF turned inward upon itself, pre-occupied by esoteric ideological fantasies about "political soldiers" and a pan-European revolution, the BNP became the natural home for those refusing to relinquish their basic adherence to a more straightforward racial-nationalist agenda. With all of the versions of the NF very poorly led and embarrassingly ineffectual in electoral terms, it was left to the BNP to establish itself as the only viable alternative for those wishing to express their right wing fascist political allegiances - conventional racial nationalists were therefore compelled to gravitate toward the BNP.

## The British National Party: From Fascism to Euro-Nationalism?

The British National Party was formed on 7 April 1982 in London. John Tyndall became Chairman and he "merely picked up from where he had left off two years earlier" (Copsey 2008 p.26). However, in a period where Thatcherism appeared to have corralled the remnants of the right wing populists into an electoral endorsement of a new radical Conservative project, the signs for the new BNP were far from propitious. Thatcher's patriotic nationalism and evident concerns about immigration had effectively closed down the ideological space within which the British fascists could operate.

Yet all the familiar fascist themes and priorities were outlined by the new BNP: national unity, opposition to supranational bodies, economic self-sufficiency within a white Commonwealth, the preservation of racial integrity and the repatriation of non-white minorities (BNP 1982, BNP 1982a). Deference toward Britain's glorious imperial heritage and adherence to Nazi ideas on race were still to be the guiding lodestars of the new organisation. As one party document put it "Britain is in the lower league among the advanced nations of the world, plagued with division...an empire has been thrown away, the only legacy of it remaining being the burgeoning coloured populations of our towns and cities, brought here without the consent of the British people ever being sought... It is against this background that the BNP has been formed" (BNP 1982a). The BNP stated unequivocally that, "we are dedicated to the preservation of the British national character...we aim at the establishment in Britain of a government of national unity, which will put an end to the ruinous warfare of parties and classes" (BNP 1982). Law, social order and defence were to be prioritized, economic nationalism and self sufficiency were designed to transcend both capitalism and socialism, whilst the financial system was to be taken out of "private banking interests" (BNP 1982). Britain, the BNP argued, should disband the multi-racial Commonwealth, withdraw from supra-national bodies, end overseas aid and crush Republican "terrorists" in Northern Ireland.

From its inception "the BNP was dominated by ex-members of the NF who profoundly shaped its ideological and strategic direction. There was little incentive to abandon racial nationalism and set out in a new direction" (Goodwin 2011 p.37). The ideological template was still provided by Nazi Germany's toxic blend of sociobiology, anti-semitism and racial nationalism. According to Tyndall, there was no need for a substantive ideological re-evaluation (Copsey 2008 p.26), and perhaps the most significant difference between the new BNP and the old NF of the 1970s was in terms of internal structure. Tyndall was determined to establish and retain full executive authority over the new organization and ensure that he was less vulnerable to internal challenges to his authority. In this he succeeded, initially, by ensuring that any potential leadership candidate had to have served at least five years full membership of the party. However, his concerns were prescient.

At the General Election of 1983, with Margaret Thatcher artfully exploiting a jingoistic post-Falklands euphoria, the political parties of the far right achieved less than 1% of the popular vote. The BNP itself contested 53 seats and gained a derisory 1.3% of the votes cast, despite producing a five-minute pre-election broadcast (Copsey 1996 p.121). Occasional forays by the fascist parties into the electoral fray were met with resounding defeat, if not outright humiliation, and by the time Thatcher had secured her third consecutive electoral success in 1987 "both the British National Party and the National Front had all but vanished from Britain's electoral landscape" (Copsey 2008 p.29). However, with the NF seemingly pre-occupied with its new strategy (or at least viewing voting as a peripheral consideration), the BNP sought to establish itself as the authentic standard-bearer of the far right by focusing on building the party structure, so even for the BNP at this stage elections became a secondary consideration. As Copsey explains, "for the most part this fitful electoral strategy was the consequence of Tyndall's decision, taken after the 1983 general election, to concentrate the resources of his party on long-term organizational development" (Copsey 2008 p.40). It might also be noted, however, that the electoral inactivity may have been, in part, a function of legal conflicts and the short prison sentences given to Tyndall and editor of *British National-ist* John Morse, for incitement to racial hatred. Although they only served four months of a twelve month sentence the impact upon political progress in mid-1980s was tangible and by focusing on internal matters the party leadership might have been making a virtue out of a necessity.

In truth, given the complete ascendancy of Thatcher's New Right version of authoritarian populism, the prospects for the BNP were far from promising. In this context Tyndall's decision to stand just two candidates in the 1987 general election, especially given the dramatic rise in the electoral deposit (from £150 to £500), made some political and financial sense. The leadership of the BNP maintained that contesting elections and persistently securing low votes undermined party morale and credibility, whilst draining diminishing resources, although Copsey claims that this decision was "met with dismay at the grassroots" (Copsey 2008 p.41). Evidently Tyndall, in eschewing elections, was looking toward the longer term, and he began to cast an envious eye across the channel where John-Marie Le Pen was making the kind of electoral impact in France that the BNP could only dream of. Despite the fact that Tyndall saw no need for fundamental ideological re-orientation, he was clearly becoming aware that the continued association of his party with violence and a thuggish hooligan element was an obvious electoral liability.

Yet in terms of political ideas all the tunes had a distinctly recognizable tone, and they had all been originally composed and orchestrated by fascists on the continent in the 1930s. Fascist Italy and Nazi Germany still provided the ideological inspiration. In Tyndall's *Eleventh Hour,* published in 1988, he still spoke in apocalyptic terms about the evils of liberalism and democracy, the collapse of civilization, and the need for a return to authority (Tyndall 1988). A charismatic leader was required to lead the campaign for national re-birth and a new order.  Still stubbornly borrowing from the template outlined by Arnold Leese, Tyndall reiterated the notion of a pure British "race" as the Anglo-Saxon and Celtic essence of "the nation". The survival instinct was, as ever, under threat from the perfidious Jew and a feeble democratic liberalism which caused healthy racial impulses to atrophy. Thus the notion of Nordic supremacy and genetic racism was still the cornerstone of BNP ideology. Repatriation of ethnic minorities and regeneration of the racial stock remained key policy preferences, and despite occasional perfunctory claims to the contrary anti-Zionism and Holocaust denial remained critically important components of the BNP perspective (a fact betrayed by the nature of the publications recommended by the BNP book service) [19]. In *The Eleventh Hour* Tyndall even pondered the racial re-colonisation of Africa for "living space". The ideological themes animating Tyndall's BNP were thus depressingly redolent of previous manifestations of fascism.

Although by the end of the 1980s the BNP had effectively replaced the NF as the pre-eminent "brand" on the far right "it was still firmly entrenched in the political backwaters, marginalized and apparently stagnating on the very edges of British political life" (Copsey 1996 p.124, Copsey 1994). The ideology remained steadfastly illiberal, authoritarian, ultranationalist, racist and anti-semitic, advocating a collection of policies which exhibited "glaring parallels to historic fascism", indeed with its unreconstructed emphasis on socio-biology, the BNP's racism closely resembled the more radical Nazi version of the creed (see Copsey 1994 p.105 and p.107). British society, according to BNP strategists, still needed to be decontaminated in order to forge a racially conscious and homogenous national community. The repetitive rhetoric about national spirit, economic regeneration and the need for real leadership to eradicate pluralistic decadence still pervaded the literature (see Copsey 1994).

In 1989 a BNP party headquarters was secured in Welling South East London and as Collins says, it was from this HQ that "the BNP masterminded race riots, racial violence, Holocaust denial and played a huge part in contributing to the deaths of four young men from South London" (Collins 2011 p.49). Indeed figures from the Greenwich Action Committee Against Racial Attacks suggested that violence in the area increased by 140 per cent in the immediate aftermath of the arrival of the BNP HQ – in effect the BNP legitimized racial violence (see Kushner 1994 p.39). The circulation of *Spearhead* and *British Nationalist* became more regular and sustainable, spreading the message of race-hate from a base in close proximity to multi-racial Plumstead, while racist attacks in areas like the Isle of Dogs (which accommodated many newly arrived Bengali families) caused not only physical harm but significant psychological distress (see Trilling 2012 p.27).

At this stage, in the late 1980s, the tactical emphasis within the BNP was still placed more on meetings and maximum publicity, rather than standing for election. This had been a traditional ploy for fascist parties who were intent on "controlling the streets" in order to "march and grow" by creating the impression of a movement with unstoppable momentum. With the electoral route apparently blocked by a radical right-wing Conservative government, it might be argued that the BNP was simply being realistic, but the strategy of street confrontation and social insurrection had a discernible fascist heritage derived directly from Mussolini and Hitler. The difficulty in deploying this tactic was that the BNP had stimulated determined anti-fascist resistance, and while some groups were very vocal in their denunciations (such as a re-constructed ANL) others, such as Anti-Fascist Action, were committed to driving the fascists from the streets by force. A bloody, semi-clandestine conflict ensued in working class communities across Britain, precipitating what John Tyndall referred to as a "'state of war'" (see Hayes and Aylward 2000). Whenever the BNP attempted to march or hold meetings it nearly always attracted negative publicity due to the ensuing violence, as fascists were literally beaten off  the streets by anti-fascists (see Trilling 2012 p.21). For the new generation of fascists in the BNP the old fashioned "street tactics" were proving to be both personally dangerous and politically counter-productive, and the anti-fascist campaign led the BNP to form Conbat 18 (1992) as a bodyguard to protect members against an increasingly pro-active and determined anti-fascist movement (see Birchall 2010, Lowles 2001 p.10) [20]. As Collins says "C18 was born out of a terrified hatred of the left" (Collins 2011 p.292) and it was perfectly prepared to try and kick its way into public consciousness via lurid headlines in the media.

However, given that Margaret Thatcher had been forced from office in November 1990, the BNP leadership was perhaps entitled to embrace the new decade in a more optimistic cast of mind. The great icon of New Right Conservatism was betrayed by her own Cabinet and cast into the political wilderness, to be replaced by the distinctly uncharismatic grey eminence, John Major. Given his weak leadership, and the evident re-surfacing of divisions in the Conservative party over the issue of Europe, the BNP could once again begin to hope that an ineffectual Conservatism might precipitate some political and electoral dividends. At the same time in East London BNP activist Eddy Butler began to map out a strategy that would be portentious for the future of the BNP. According to BNP activist Steve Smith, it was "a mixture of traditional methods and new tactics, with the emphasis on community-based politics" (Smith 1997 p.6). The BNP decided to focus on local issues like housing, whilst eschewing the pre-election meetings or rallies which invariably precipitated trouble and a torrent of negative publicity. The local BNP put in the groundwork canvassing on the doorstep in East London and it soon paid political dividends. In September 1993 the BNP won its first ever council seat, in Tower Hamlets, East London which, as we have noted, had a tradition of right wing extremist agitation, and where the BNP was able to capitalize upon endemic poverty and an insular culture of white working class antagonism toward immigration. The BNP candidate Derek Beackon won 34% of the vote in the Millwall ward of Tower Hamlets (Copsey 1996 p.125) and as BNP organizer Smith later suggested, important lessons could be learned from the Millwall experiment: "real progress and growth is created by intelligent and consistent political work... genuine community-based politics is the only way forward...it may be slow, and lacking in glamour but it's the only realistic option and the only one so far to have produced the results" (Smith 1997 p.9).

Despite the fact that Tyndall and others claimed that the Millwall result represented a seismic shift in local political consciousness (the *British Nationalist* referred to the prospect of a nationalist government), it is clear in retrospect that Beackon simply benefitted briefly from the continued existence of that residual tradition of racist intolerance in East London that had never really disappeared (see Copsey 1996). However it is also important to note that, even if we disregard the more risible and preposterous predictions of BNP optimists, the result did reflect some very hard work by BNP activists at the local level (see Trilling 2012 p.20). The campaign was constructed around theme of "rights for whites" and the BNP made a clear effort to establish its legitimacy in the eyes of the local electorate (see Eatwell 1998, Lowles 2001 p.36-37). Rather than simply reflecting a straightforward reactionary racist reflex, it was evident that some ordinary white working class voters were making an electoral protest about poor housing provision, unemployment, inadequate services and so on. In reality this limited local success for the BNP reflected a massive practical policy failure for the conventional parties, particularly the Labour Party, which had always portrayed itself as the "natural" vehicle for working class aspirations. In this sense the BNP was making an ambitious claim to represent the legitimate grievances of dispossessed white voters who had been effectively abandoned by the Labour Party. Evidently BNP claims about supporting local white people weighed more heavily in some quarters than evidence of a fascist heritage or negative associations with crime or violence. The BNP also benefitted from what Eatwell has referred to as "syncretic legitimation" (Eatwell 1998) in that the party gained some credibility from local Liberal Democrat tactics – in effect the Liberals, via coded racial signification, underscored the BNP's political position. Put simply the Liberal Democrats identified themselves as the standard-bearers of a specifically local (i.e. white) constituency, thus creating "legitimate" political space for the BNP. By manipulating white working class concerns about housing policy, the Liberal Democrats in Tower Hamlets were partially responsible for underscoring the BNP's "rights for whites" agenda (see Trilling 2012 p.29). BNP success was therefore undoubtedly connected to conventional party failure at both a national and local level.

Even so, the same phenomenon of differential turnout can still explain the level of local success in this specific instance, since in the subsequent local elections of May 1994 a much higher mobilization of the vote meant that the BNP lost its only council seat (despite increasing its share of the vote). The excessively high expectations created in the wake of Beackon's victory were therefore not realized, and the longer term consequences for Tyndall's leadership were profound. Although at the May 1994 local elections 29 candidates received a creditable 13.17% of the vote (Copsey 2008 p.66), and even though Tyndall retained his deposit in the Dagenham by-election in June 1994, the perception amongst the BNP members was that the party had missed yet another opportunity. More menacingly, the unreconstructed Nazi's coalescing around C18 were increasingly unimpressed by the party's conventional electoral strategy, and established their own political wing in June 1994 – the National Socialist Alliance. Consisting principally of members of assorted football hooligan gangs or "firms", the group sought to portray itself as the leading edge of the racial-nationalist movement in Britain. Although individual connections to Ulster Loyalist organizations appeared to underscore the threat, C18 was less competent than some sensationalist accounts suggested (see Lowles 2001). Indeed despite the macho posturing and paramilitary pretentions, the group was prone to disintegrate when faced with a more robust, determined and well-organised opposition (see Birchall 2011, Collins 2011). Nevertheless, the cumulative effect of successive journalistic revelations about C18's apparent involvement in hooliganism (some of them entirely erroneous, such as the role of C18 in the riot by England fans at Lansdowne Road in Dublin in 1995) was to create a moral panic and further undermine the credibility of the BNP's political strategy. Indeed the fact that C18 were perfectly prepared to countenance extreme violence against their political opponents, and that there had been a concomitant upsurge in the number of attacks on ethnic minorities, even drew comment at the highest level from Prime Minister John Major who, in response to a Parliamentary question, described the organization as "'repellant'" (cited in Cronin 1996 p.2, see Collins 2011 p.289) [21]. The friction between the BNP and its posturing "paramilitary" progeny looked set to precipitate an internal party crisis.

Tyndall was, in effect, forced to deal with the issue because C18 were becoming an embarrassing nuisance, indeed he claimed that C18 was part of a conspiracy by the state to discredit the BNP (despite the apparent absurdity of this claim, the subsequent arrest of prominent C18 activist Charlie Sargent for murder, and his exposure as a Special Branch informant, tends to give some credence to Tyndall's account) (see Ryan 1998). At the same time Tyndall sought to forestall potential criticism from the right of his party by re-asserting his ideological credentials and re-admitting hardliners like Nick Griffin back into the organization. Griffin had been introduced to the BNP in 1992 when he was invited to speak at the Croydon branch and he edited the magazine *The Rune*, the tone of which can be gauged from the fact it published adverts for *Waffen SS* posters, and prints of water-colours painted by Adolf Hitler, along with touching eulogies to assorted fascist heroes of yesteryear. The "rights for whites" campaign, Griffin exclaimed, would be accompanied by a robust physical presence, stating quite explicitly that it was "'more important to control the streets of a city than its council chamber'" (cited in Goodwin 2010 p.175-76). Griffin cautioned against trimming the BNP's policies in pursuit of votes, asserting that "'populism'" would be the "'kiss of death'" for the BNP (cited in Copsey 2007 p.67). Indeed Nick Griffin wrote that the electors of Millwall "'did not back a postmodernist rightist party, but what they perceived to be a strong, disciplined organization with the ability to back up its slogan 'Defend Rights for Whites' with well directed boots and fists'" (cited in Trilling 2012 p.35).

In August 1995 Tyndall committed the BNP to standing 50 candidates at the forthcoming General Election, despite the fact that the party was not prepared for a protracted electoral contest. In fact this may well have been, as Copsey argues, "a last-ditch attempt to enthuse and unify the party" (Copsey 2008 p.69). Yet the BNP was still infused with the old ethos of racial nationalism, which stressed the need to foster the natural instinct of racial preservation amongst the British people. As Ellen Strachan put it in the pages of *Spearhead* "in nature, all is a perpetual life-and-death struggle", "survival is the only morality", and "if the British population was still in possession of well-honed instincts for the preservation of their own kind, there would be unanimous support for the policy of repatriation" (Strachan 1996 p.11). According to the BNP, failure to adopt the policies of racial preservation not only reflected a perverse "racial senility", but would lead inevitably, via the ineluctable laws of nature, to racial "extinction" (Strachan 1996 p.11). As Nick Griffin explained, "this tyranny of the insane on behalf of the inadequate is a sin against Nature which will, if not opposed, reversed and uprooted, end in a disaster which will destroy all we have ever held dear" (Griffin 1996a p.12, see Griffin 1996). Tyndall even suggested that racial survival, given limited space and resources in Britain, might be contingent upon acquiring "fresh pastures" in order to "survive and prosper" (Tyndall 1996 p.7). Indeed, according to Tyndall "we will not meet the challenge of overpopulation by means of our own sterility but will do so by redistribution of our numbers into the spacious, and up to now underpopulated, areas of the world which our race controls...the white nations possess an aggregate of military power which, if properly mobilized, will for the indefinite future be quite sufficient to deter, and where necessary repel, any armed invasion of their territories from the non-white world" (Tyndall 1996 pp.8). What was required above all, Tyndall argued, was a return to national pride and "authority" in politics, as a prelude to "moral regeneration" (see Tyndall 1996a). Tyndall's BNP was, therefore, clearly identifiable as a political party advocating overtly nationalistic, racist and dictatorial solutions – in short it still adhered to the classic themes and precepts of fascist ideology as outlined in Italy and Germany before the war.

Having said this, it is clear that at this stage some key "modernizing" elements in the party were seeking to learn lessons from right wing parties on the continent, such as the French National Front and the Austrian Freedom Party. BNP activist Michael Newland, for example, appeared to be advocating a "Euro-Nationalist" strategy, designed to make the party look much more modern and respectable. Similarly Tony Lecomber, a prominent BNP strategist, pointed out that "all of the successful nationalists in Europe are modern nationalists", and he articulated the belief that the erstwhile strategy of "street machismo" was not only misguided but "stupid" (Lecomber 1997 p.17). Indeed Lecomber was quite explicit about the redundancy of past strategies: "the thirties flavour is, like it or not, long past its sell-by date and is a positive voter turn-off. Most people recognize this – even those who would describe themselves as national socialists" (Lecomber 1997 p.199). According to Lecomber the "non-thinking meat-head/fantasists" had let the party down, and community politics was a better way to secure the over-riding nationalist objective of a "mono-racial nation", although this strategic re-orientation certainly did not imply, as he put it, a "kosher sell-out" (Lecomber 1997 p.19). There was, Lecomber concluded "a new way of doing things, a new politics" (Lecomber 1997 p.19). However, in this revised tactical scenario John Tyndall could only really be seen as an anachronistic political liability. With the gathering momentum of the modernizers clearly in mind Tyndall asked Nick Griffin to become editor of *Spearhead* magazine, and Griffin's apparent emphasis on discipline and physical "defence" (i.e. confrontation), and his continued anti-semitic commitment to denying or downplaying the Holocaust apparently coincided with Tyndall's deeply held suspicion of the new, fashionable populist political trends (see Griffin 1997a, see Eatwell 2004 p.69).

However, perhaps surprisingly, the erstwhile hardline Nazi ideologue Nick Griffin (in collaboration with Tony Lecomber), had also been contemplating more critically the futility of conducting high profile meetings and marches, which inevitably descended into nasty punch-ups with anti-fascist activists. An internal party document was produced for discussion which posited the view that there was "no virtue in fighting drunken Red Fenians" – the boot and the fist, it argued, should be decommissioned [22]. Griffin even began to float the idea of a different strategy in the pages of *Spearhead*: "twenty years ago or so, we could make our point to the public with large-scale marches, big meetings in public halls and similar activities. More recently though, bans by the authorities, police pressure and surveillance, Zionist and police threats against hall and hotel owners, and violence from the state's licensed Far Left boot-boys, have all combined to make such tactics largely ineffective under present conditions. We must therefore look for other ways in which to publicise our message, to attract new recruits, to provide them with a sense of belonging, and to demoralize the opposition. The new methods required may best be described as political guerilla warfare" (Griffin 1996a pp.12).

Nick Griffin still maintained his adherence to all the familiar fascist objectives: annihilating Marxist ideology, which was being used as a tool used by those aiming to to destroy the white race; liquidating the "perverted" purveyors of "political correctness"; opposing the "hatchet-faced harpies and roly-poly lesbians" of the left; unmasking organized Jewry; and exposing the dead-end of multi-cultural liberalism – all in the name of the "scientific fact of inequality" (see Griffin 1996 p.13 and Griffin 1996c p.13). Griffin argued that the "juggernaut" of democracy could not be stopped but the BNP could "look for ways to use the weight of its myths and expectations against it", the masses have been "flattered", he said, into believing they should have a say in the affairs of state so "why should we make our pursuit of power any harder by giving them grounds to think that we disagree with them?...even though the misused word 'democratic' may stick in our throats, in a country whose population have a deeply ingrained belief in their right and ability to govern themselves, *realpolitiks* demand that we play the game by that rule" (Griffin 1997 p.15 and p.16). Hence democracy would be used by the BNP for its own nefarious purposes and Griffin went onto clarify that "nationalists of all people should understand that, while certain principles are immutable for all time, systems of government are temporary things..." (Griffin 1997 p.16). Elections therefore had to be fought with a new tactical discretion, which would facilitate political progress whilst the party was intent on sustaining the essential core of its racial-nationalist ideology. Popularity had to be courted via the electoral system whilst somehow maintaining the purity of the fascist ideal. However, as Trilling points out "this developing split in the BNP did not indicate any great disagreement over party doctrine. Both sides – Tyndall, and the faction that now opposed him – were racial nationalists, who believed that non-white immigration was destroying Britain and had to be reversed. Anti-Semitism and an opposition to 'globalism' circulated freely on both sides, while activists all had well-established track records of involvement in fascist movements. Where they differed, however, was in how their ideas might best be presented to the public" (Trilling 2012 p.71). The BNP, according to Nick Griffin and the modernizers, had to become more professional and pragmatic – more suits and fewer boots!

In 1996, as the ideological tensions were exacerbated, some prominent elements in the BNP harboured hopes of decent electoral performances in the near future. However, in the General Election of May 1997 the BNP received a minis-cule 1.35% of the vote (Copsey 2008 p.72). Although the party declared that the aim of participation in the election was to secure a televised broadcast in the hope of generating some popular interest, the results were deeply disappointing. Even if a surge of enquiries was generated by the greater publicity, few were transformed into new members (Spiller 1999 p.10) and "within four years, the BNP had gone from thinking it was on the verge of a major electoral breakthrough to the point of stagnation" (Copsey 2008 p.73). Tyndall's control was becoming ever more tenuous, and some influencial BNP members were viewing Griffin and his acolytes as a poten-tial "populist" alternative to the older leadership faction. This disgruntled section of the BNP began to articulate its perspective via the *Patriot* magazine, launched in 1997, and edited by a "reformed" Tony Lecomber (having recently been released from prison after being convicted of assaulting a Jewish teacher). The modernizers argued that the public face of the BNP had to change, the harsh edges needed to go and the strategy of the party had to be re-calibrated accordingly to procure a softer, less threatening image. Meanwhile Tyndall continued to articulate his austere authoritarian version of racial natonalism by emphasizing the dangers which lurked in those "hypnotic", "infantile" and "libertarian" deviations which prioritized freedom as a political virtue (see Tyndall 1997). As Tyndall explained "the terrible mess in which our own society in Britain now finds itself is something from which we can only escape by being prepared to accept some degree of authoritarianism...to boss people around and tell them what to do. We are at present a rabble army that is losing a war. Total defeat and annihilation are going to be our fate unless *discipline* is introduced" (Tyndall 1997 p.8 see Holmes 1997). Tyndall's continued assertion of his authoritarian credentials was accompanied by an increasingly desperate call for unity across the nationalist spectrum (see Tyndall 1998). It was the plaintif cry of a tin-pot demagogue in terminal decline.

Evidently the Cambridge-educated ex-political soldier Nick Griffin began to believe that he could offer much more as leader of the BNP, and perhaps even rescue the party from its perpetual electoral disappointments. Although clearly personalities played a key role in internal party machinations, the more interesting aspect to the dynamic underpinning Griffin's challenge to the old leadership clique was that he began to identify himself more explicitly with the new so-called "Euro-Nationalist" modernizers. Of course Griffin may have experienced a Damascus-style conversion to what was, ostensibly, a more moderate ideological perspective, but the decision was probably motivated as much by imme-diate tactical considerations. Goodwin, for instance, suggests that there was more than a hint of careerist calculation and personal ambition in the reorientation of Griffin's strategic perspective (Goodwin 2010 p.176).

The fact is that Griffin was less concerned about altering the product than improving the marketing, as he said in *Spearhead* in October 1997 "it's not enough to have the best product, we have to market it as well. So forget the ideals for a few minutes, and think purely about selling them" (Griffin 1997a p.14). Indeed Griffin expressed the need to learn from marketing professionals in order to develop a "slickly presented nationalism" (Griffin 1997a p.14). This point was reinforced in the same issue by Chris Cronshaw, who emphasized the need for the BNP to adapt to altered circumstances in order to make electoral progress, whilst retaining its ideological integrity: "the racial nationalist principles which underlie our ideology and policies must, of course, remain inviolate, but principle without power is worthless vanity" (Cronshaw 1997 p.16). Clearly the importance of "selling" the ideas to a wider public began to carry more weight in Griffin's view, and this was to be achieved by simplifying the message and, importantly, toning down the more bizarre political preferences. Griffin was doubtless aware that the hard-liners would question his ideological credentials, but it was a move designed to establish himself as the standard-bearer of a "reformed", re-constituted political party. In this context the rehabilitation of veteran activist John Bean has some significance, as he was portrayed as the harbinger of a new, more "modern" and "moderate" political project, devoid of the historical obsession with Nazism, biological racism and anti-semitism (see Macklin 2011, and Bean 1999). In effect Tyndall, and the Nazi tradition he represented, was to be airbrushed out of BNP history in an effort to re-brand the party. As Macklin explains, Bean's *Many Shades of Black* was a cipher for Griffin's campaign to expunge the extremists: "Bean's autobiography was seen to buttress the case for 'modernization' made contemporaneously by Griffin and his cohorts" (Macklin 2011 p.23). Griffin's new populist party narrative, disingenuous though it was, given his own Nazi past and fascist views, began to take a recognizable shape.

Unquestionably the new perspective had some strategic political logic, in the sense of courting "respectability" and positioning the party more appropriately to win over disaffected Conservatives, but it also meant the BNP could evade the attentions of AFA, as well as affording Griffin's faction the opportunity to wrest control of the party itself from the perennial political loser, John Tyndall. In February 1999 as the party's Director of Publicity, Nick Griffin announced his intention to challenge Tyndall in order to change the course of British nationalism (see King 1999). After an acrimonious campaign the results were announced in September 1999, and Griffin emerged victorious with 62% of the vote and a clear mandate, he claimed, for reform. Despite accusations of betrayal and treachery Tyndall was forced to concede the leadership of the party to Nick Griffin, and the unrecon-structed racial nationalist Nazi passed the torch of British fascism, somewhat reluctantly, onto the former Strasserite "modernizer". The party stood on the threshold of what Copsey has called "an intensive course of cosmetic surgery" (Copsey 2008 p.3).

Under Griffin's tenure the BNP immediately made an effort to disassociate itself from the negative epithets attrib-uted to it in the past – the references to fascism, Hitler, Nazism and Holocaust revisionism diminished and then disappeared from the party's public lexicon. However it is important to recognize that these ultimate ideological "truths" were not discarded but were to be saved for what Griffin called the "'hardcore'" of BNP membership (cited in Copsey 2007 p.68). Meanwhile the less objectionable themes of security, freedom, democracy and identity were to be emphasized and purveyed in a more professional manner, in an effort to locate the BNP as the repository of the generally held "common sense" of ordinary British people. The new dispensation was reflected in the fact that the party ostentatiously altered the emphasis of its anti-immigration stance by suggesting that those ethnic minorities who were legally established in Britain would be encouraged (via financial incentives), but not compelled, to leave the country and return to their land of origin (Goodwin 2010 p.178). This was a significant change of tone which left some racial nationalist hardliners in the BNP uneasy about the direction of anti-immigration policy. The BNP under Griffin also attempted to recalibrate its critique of multi-culturalism by avoiding any reference to genetics and superiority, and focusing on the need to preserve the cultural identity of indig-enous ("aboriginal") British peoples. "Racism", in the new BNP perspective, was inverted and white Britons were now portrayed as the victims because they were being discriminated against in their own country. It was no longer a question of "racism" or hatred of other people, but of ensuring that British culture, traditions and values were respected and protected. The usual Nazi-style claims about racial supremacy were replaced by an emphasis on preserving a distinct and endangered ethnic identity. The vision was less apocalyptic and the policy emphasis eschewed crude biological categorisation, which meant that the image of the party became much more reasoned and constructive. The party even established an Ethnic Liaison Committee, although the membership was restricted to "whites only" (Goodwin 2010 p.178). Hence the process of "modernization" in the BNP can be dated from 1999 and the ascendancy of a leader who had apparently discovered the necessity of downplaying or de-emphasizing the more obvious ideological manifestations of fascism in an effort to portray a more respectable community-based, populist image.

The BNP contested the European elections in 1999 on a Euro-sceptic ticket, but found its room for manoeuvre severely constrained by the UK Independence Party and, indeed, the Euro-sceptic wing of the Conservatives. The BNP received around 1% of the vote and whispers about the need for an electoral pact with UKIP became more audible. However, undeterred by such a paltry electoral return, Griffin set about trying to professionalize the BNP's political operation. Part of this included designing a strategy to deal with a traditionally hostile media and prioritizing *Identity* (rather than *Spearhead*) as the magazine of the BNP, which was launched in January 2000 and was edited by John Bean. The title of the BNP's newspaper also changed from *British Nationalist* to *The Voice of Freedom*. The new strategic approach also included an emphasis on the internet as an information network that could bypass the usual mechanisms of conventional communication such as meetings and demonstrations. As Griffin himself pointed out, the "virtual HQ" provided the party with all the benefits of a centralized office without being the physical focus around which opposition could coalesce (see

Spiller 1999 p.12). This was considered particularly important given the fact that the party had been forced to close down its old HQ in Welling, South East London, after anti-fascist protests turned into a riot in 1993. The unambiguous aim was to tackle the issue of legitimacy head-on by making the party more approachable and acceptable to the general public. However, this objective was initially made more problematic after evidence came to light of the BNP associations of racist loner David Copeland who bombed London in April 1999, and subsequent accusations by Martin Webster that he had been involved in a homosexual affair with Griffin whilst he was at Cambridge. The effort to secure public respectability got off to a slow start, but Griffin was determined to persevere.

Michael Newland stood for the BNP in the London Mayoral elections of 2000, and five million Londoners received a copy of the party's manifesto. Newland received over 5% of the vote, and the BNP list for the Greater London Assembly received 2.87% of the votes cast, thereby saving the party's deposit. Meanwhile outside London in the sixteen local council wards targeted by the BNP the share of the vote increased from 6.8% to 10.8%. In some ways during this period political space was being opened up for the BNP by a number of favourable issues, such as the existence of "asylum seekers" (as portrayed in the popular press), and high levels of immigration from EU countries. It might also be noted that to some extent the over-reaction of the mainstream political parties to these "issues", who competed with each other to reassure voters of their hard-line credentials, made it much easier for BNP arguments to gain traction. The BNP focused on the threat to British security from asylum seekers, the impact of immigration on crime rates and social service provision, and ultimately the prospect of social unrest as a consequence of both. However, after the 9/11 attacks on the USA, predictably the party shifted, in populist fashion, toward an explicitly anti-Islamic line which stressed not only the incompatibility between the fundamentalist Islamic credo and the notion of "Britishness" (as conceived by the BNP), but between Islam and Western civilization itself. The security agenda began to dominate BNP discourse, and Griffin evidently felt that focusing on Islamic fundamentalism and what he termed the Muslim "'colonization of Britain'", provided an opportunity to exploit a critical issue, indeed he claimed that "'over the next 25 years that is going to be the core issue at the heart of European politics'" (cited in Goodwin 2011 p.69).

It also became clear that Nick Griffin was keen to avoid any kind of factionalism within the BNP and was therefore not inclined to alter the "leadership principle" so assiduously constructed by his predecessor. The National Chairman was to be the final arbiter on all decisions, and there was definitely no question of internal structural pluralism or genuine democratic accountability. Despite this, Griffin still had to deal with a damaging internal party feud which precipitated the suspension of Michael Newland and the expulsion of Deputy Chair Sharron Edwards. Accusations were made about Griffin's role in misappropriating party funds for personal use and the BNP leader's credibility was undoubtedly damaged - there were even rumours of a leadership challenge. According to Trilling, Griffin had alienated his modernizing allies, and he was now "facing growing dissent from the party hard core" (Trilling 2012 p.99). In fact some of the discontented BNP members, centred mostly around the West Midlands, did de-camp to form their own "Freedom Party" in December 2000, although the new party was not able to attract more than a few dozen defectors. With the ultra-Tory populists unable to capitalize on the internal disarray in the BNP Griffin attempted to re-stabilize his party.

In the context of irritating and corrosive internal discontent and, therefore, relatively low expectations, the electoral performance of the party in 2001 came as something of a surprise to the BNP leadership. Indeed it might be argued that 2001 was a watershed in terms of political recognition, because "the party's success at the 2001 general election proved to be unparalleled in the history of right wing extremism in Britain" (Copsey 2008 p.122). Nick Griffin received 16.4% of the vote in Oldham and the BNP, by retaining seven electoral deposits, had apparently discovered some fertile electoral territory. In parts of the North West, where socially deprived residential areas were divided on racial lines, and where an anxious and dispossessed white working class sought to apportion blame for the absence of jobs and public services, some voters turned to the BNP. Inter-communal friction in these areas occasionally precipitated serious social disorder and the BNP cynically exploited those tensions by portraying itself as the only party willing to stand up for the indigenous local community. The BNP clearly benefitted from unscrupulous scaremongering in the local and national press about immigration and the threat of radical Islam but also, to some extent, from a more general disenchantment with the conventional Parliamentary parties at Westminster. The mainstream political parties were seen as distant, if not completely disinterested in such parochial concerns. In fact the BNP took votes mostly from disaffected Labour voters in working class areas and, through assiduous local campaigning and canvassing, came dangerously close to crossing the credibility threshold. Labour Party politicians and strategists were forced to take the BNP more seriously as a genuine rival for working class votes. As Copsey explained "this time round Britain's far right had comparatively more respectability, credibility and professionalism" (Copsey 2008 p.141-42). The accusations by those antagonistic to the BNP, that the party was brimming with skinhead football hooligans and Hitler-worshiping lunatics, were becoming much harder to sustain, and BNP party membership and revenue expanded exponentially (Copsey 2008 p.144). In 2001 Griffin emerged, blinking, from the dark shadows of political obscurity into the well-lit glare of media attention. The BNP, having taken its inspiration from the European national-populist parties, seemed to be on the verge of emulating their electoral success.

The election of three BNP councillors in the Lancashire town of Burnley on May 2 2002 marked another notable electoral breakthrough in local politics. In the May 2003 local elections the BNP fielded 219 candidates and won 17.3% of the vote and 13 council seats. This was an extraordinary success given the fact that the only other two fascist organizations with national pretentions, the BUF and NF, never came close to  matching this performance. Burnley in Lancashire, with eight council seats, became the epicentre of what appeared to be a seismic shift in local electoral support – a national break-through was discussed as a plausible possibility in forthcoming elections. Meanwhile the new right wing populist dynamic within the BNP was reinforced by internal party social events like the "Red, White and Blue" festival, which was evidently modeled on the French FN *Nouvelle Droite* celebration "*Bleu, Blanc, Rouge*" (Goodwin 2007 p.247). At such festivals "cheerful activities such as a football tournaments and stalls offering candy-floss and face-painting would be mixed with racist literature, recordings of anti-Semitic speeches and a rally, at which Griffin and other senior figures would preach racial purity" (Trilling 2012 p.97). Moreover, the implementation of membership training schemes and the teaching of public performance techniques to activists, in order to increase professionalism and make the party more accesible, modern and efficient, seemed to be paying significant electoral divi-dends. The new, positive and proactive political dispensaton, heralded by the arrival of Griffin, seemed to indicate that the BNP had considerable momentum and was on the threshold of a serious electoral breakthrough.

In 2004, anticipating a further significant staging post on route toward national electoral credibility, the BNP made a huge effort. However, the local election performance in May did not meet the exalted expectations of Griffin and the lead-ership (see Renton 2005), although this did little to forestall more optimistic talk within the BNP about a future electoral breakthrough. Significantly, in 2004, the party also received a visit from Jean-Marie Le Pen who carried the imprimatur of Europe's foremost radical right-wing populist party. Le Pen's presence would, it was hoped, stimulate support in the Euro-pean elections, which were identified as a priority for the BNP. Although Griffin chose to stand in the North-West of England

Euro-constituency, an area of growing electoral support, the efforts to capitalize on the BNP's Euro-sceptic rhetoric were undermined somewhat by the fact that UKIP was attempting to mine exactly the same electoral seam. Although Griffin received 134,958 votes, an increased turnout deprived him of success. Even so, overall the BNP won 4.9% of the vote (800,000 votes), rising from just over 100,000 (1.1%) in 1999 (Goodwin 2007 p.241). The BNP had undoubtedly broadened its electoral base, but any satisfaction in the party was tempered by the fact that UKIP won 16% of the vote, indicating very clearly that the BNP was losing out to a party with a similar perspective on the EU and immigration. Despite the fact that the BNP's total vote had increased dramatically, it was clear that UKIP blocked the path to more substantial political progress.

Meanwhile Tyndall, who stubbornly refused to accept his exile and political oblivion in silence, intensified his criticism of the modernizers via the pages of *Spearhead*. Griffin was, in effect, compelled to deal with the recalcitrant Tyndall by expelling him in from the party in 2004, at the second attempt. After Tyndall had been unceremoniously dispatched, the way was open for the BNP to articulate its vision with more consistency and clarity - according to Griffin the BNP could move forward unsullied by old-fashioned traditionalist references to state authoritarianism and undemocratic centralization because the unrepentant Nazi had been symbolically ejected. The focus would continue to be on the modernist themes of freedom, security, democracy and identity (see Trilling 2012 p.73) as part of what Griffin referred to as the new ideological project of "'popular nationalism'" (cited in Copsey 2007 p.61).

The 2005 General Election manifesto *Rebuilding British Democracy* (BNP 2005) emphasized individual liberty, the dispersal of power, and the need for a Bill of Rights. Griffin referred to the document as constituting a "'major ideological revamp'" (cited in Trilling 2012 p.130). The critique of multi-culturalism eschewed explicit references to Zionist conspiracies, but emphasized the exploitative internationalism of neo-liberalism, as the BNP portrayed itself as the legitimate defender of indigenous British people threatened by the impersonal forces of global economics. This defence would require, the BNP asserted, an end to immigration and a scheme of voluntary (not compulsory) repatriation. The tone of BNP literature regarding efforts to deal with the issue of immigration was softening still further, but the British people were still seen as the victims in a cultural war waged by quasi-Marxists who, whilst holding no allegiance to Britain, insisted on the equality of all ethnic identities. Thus the spurious creed of multiculturalism, foisted on the British public by the impersonal forces of international capitalism, was eliminating the indigenous cultural identity of white people in the UK. The BNP was arrogating for itself the role of the most ardent and robust defender of British ethno-cultural integrity, in the context of what they identified as a remorseless drive towards multicultural homogenization. There were also, however, some distinctly odd elements to the newly constructed, populist BNP programme, such as the Citizens' Initiative Referenda, the creation of an English parliament and the proposal for an armed militia of ex-soldiers. Inspiration was also sought from indigenous sources such as G.K. Chesterton and Hilaire Belloc, rather than the usual pantheon of Nazi heroes, and Griffin warned of the electoral dangers inherent in any lingering obsession with Hitler (see Eatwell 2004 p.77). On the face of it the BNP programme appeared to deviate quite dramatically from themes and priorities of the traditional fascist perspective, as reflected in the key examples of Italy and Germany.

In this way Griffin sought to move the party, or more accurately the public perception of the party, beyond an association with the out-dated foreign creed of fascism. As Ford and Goodwin have pointed out "under Griffin, the party now downplays the crude anti-black racism and conspiratorial anti-Semitism that characterised its predecessors in favour of 'differentialist racism' based on ethno-pluralist doctrine" (Ford and Goodwin 2010 p.5). In the BNP the discourse of "difference" and "separation" had prevailed over the language of "superiority" and "compulsory repatriation", which prompted John Tyndall to launch, just before he died in July 2005, a withering broadside against the new Euro-style nationalism and the fashionable turn in radical right wing politics. Racial nationalism, Tyndall opined, was being modernized out of existence. Predictably Griffin rejected the claims of populist opportunism which were made by his hard-line critics, and backed the new manifesto as a realistic attempt to recalibrate nationalism for the twenty-first century. Griffin appeared to be completely vindicated when in the General Election of 2005 the BNP produced a record performance, with the party securing nearly 200,000 votes in 119 constituencies (Ford 2010 p.145).

It is also worth noting that during this period the dramatic interjection of Islamic jihad on the streets of London raised still further the high expectations inside the party, indeed strategist Tony Lecomber claimed that the "terrorist" attack launched on 7 July 2005 in London was "'good news for the BNP'" (cited in Collins 2006 p.8). In the immediate aftermath of the bomb attack Nick Griffin claimed that the 2006 local elections would be a referendum on Islam and the desire by radical Muslims to construct a theocratic Sharia state in Britain. This was evidently an issue which the BNP felt it could successfully exploit, and Griffin grasped further opportunities in 2006 for improving his party's electoral fortunes by focusing even more explicitly on what he referred to as the "evil" religion which spawned Islamic fundamentalism. The BNP leader, his eyes firmly affixed on exploiting the public's understandable anxiety over violent religious fanaticism, not only launched a predictably vitriolic attack on Islam, but also emphasized the importance of Christian values. It was a transparently cynical attempt to profit from a moral panic induced, to a large extent, by the tabloid media. The fear of "terrorism" might have been real enough, but the popular press played into the hands of those on the far right who sought to manipulate the issue for their own selfish political purposes. Indeed Griffin surmised that the so-called "clash of civilizations" between Islam and the West would be "'the threat that can bring us to power'" (cited in Copsey 2007 p.77).

The BNP contested over 360 council seats in May 2006 and secured a further 33 election victories, bringing total representation to 53 local government councillors. Barking and Dagenham elected 12 BNP councillors, becoming the main opposition party in that particular London borough which was becoming infamous as the focul point of a resurgent, right wing radicalism (Lowles 2006 p.4). It was an extraordinary result and, significantly, of those 33 seats, 28 were previously held by Labour. Indeed Searchlight activist Nick Lowles described the election result as "alarming", and claimed that the "respectable" BNP was heading for the mainstream - without decisive action by the alternative parties, he added, the BNP could become a "permanent fixture on the British political landscape" (Lowles 2006 p.4). In 2007 the local elections yielded 300,000 votes for 754 candidates, and while the BNP's overall share of the vote remained relatively small at approximately 1-2%, the geographical concentrations of the BNP vote "enabled the far-right to establish unprecedented levels of representation in local government" (Wilks-Heeg 2009 p.377). The BNP party newspaper *Voice of Freedom* was euphoric at the foothold the party had apparently established in British local democracy, and it reiterated the party's mainstream political credentials. In 2008 Richard Barnbrook became the first ever BNP member of the London Assembly, after nearly 70,000 Londoners voted for him as first choice for London Mayor. This "startling" result by Barnbrook and the BNP captured the attention of the media and appeared to reflect "the renewed vigour of the extreme right in Britain" (Ford 2010 p.145). The BNP still had a very long way to go to reach the summit of political power, but it had apparently established a secure base camp in the foothills, and the destination could be seen clearly in the distance.

Research, conducted as a consequence of the BNP's raised profile, suggested that the party held a particular attraction for poorly educated, middle-aged working class males and people who felt particularly "threatened" by what they perceived as excessive levels of immigration: "our findings suggest that the BNP has succeeded in establishing itself as a credible alternative for working class voters angry about immigration, threatened by Muslims and hostile to the political establishment" (Ford and Goodwin 2010 p.21). The BNP had apparently been able to deflect the obvious charges of racist extremism, and secure a certain level of local political legitimacy by stressing the importance of ordinary ("mundane" and "banal") concerns shared with local populations about issues like immigration and "terrorism" (Rhodes 2009, see Eatwell 1998a). This effort to engage local people was accomplished by a relatively high level of activism in key wards. Hence at the local level a party that helped pensioners with their gardening, cleaned graffiti from streets and sponsored football teams created an impression at variance with national demonology, and this cognitive dissonance, created by BNP tactics, was exploited electorally. Certainly the conventional political establishment, especially New Labour, were caught off guard by the BNP's success (see Ford and Goodwin 2010). Wilks-Heeg makes the point that such a level of local representation not only took many people by surprise, it should have served as a warning signal about the parlous condition of local representative democracy in England – the success of the BNP was, in effect "'the canary in the coalmine'" (Wilks-Heeg 2009). Moreover, increased media interest meant that BNP councilors were able to articulate their views to a much broader audience and thereby exert greater influence on the national debate about policy and politics, particularly with regard to immigration. The debate about the poor provision of social housing, for example, would quickly degenerate into an emotive discussion about eligibility. The BNP, having deployed more traditional doorstep activism, sought to position itself as the legitimate champion of local white working class communities against the malignant consequences of policies pursued by central governments which prioritized multiculturalism.

Also in 2008 Nick Griffin shrugged off another leadership challenge from campaigners who sought greater internal
party democratization. This internal wrangle indicated that,
despite the significant electoral advances, some in the party
were not content with the authoritarian impact of structural
reform and, more specifically, Griffin's *modus operandi*. Yet
the revised party constitution of 2009 confirmed the leader's
executive authority to appoint and create party officers, to
determine internal structures, shape rules and procedures,
and make all major strategic, tactical and policy decisions.
Moreover, Griffin could only be removed by a postal ballot
of the membership and the challenger had to meet certain
restrictive criteria, such as being a member for five years with
two years of continuous service (see Goodwin 2011 p.78-79).
The formation of an "Advisory Council", which was designed
to provide the leader with guidance, could not obscure the
fact that the BNP was an irredeemably authoritarian and hierarchical structure. It was clear that in organizational terms
the leader would continue to be, not only the most important
political player, but the only acceptable source of legitimate
power and authority.

At the same time Griffin recommended internal reforms
to protect the party's inner ideological coherence from the
anticipated influx of newcomers. Members would be divided
into two categories: standard and voting members. Standard
members would be entitled to vote for a leader, or stand as a
candidate, but only voting members could propose policies
and vote at the national conference. Voting members had to
have two years of unbroken membership and demonstrate
ongoing commitment to the party. BNP membership was on
the rise and numbers which had stood at around 3,000 in
2002, were up to approximately 9,000 by 2005 (see Copsey
2008 p.196-8; Goodwin 2010 p.180), and by 2008 had risen
to around 12,000 (Goodwin 2010 p.180). The numerical level
of the membership was confirmed in 2009 when membership lists were made public by a discontented former activist
– 11,811 individuals drawn form all walks of life. Griffin

placed much more importance on the retention and training of rank-and-file members in an effort to sustain the BNP's activist base. Meanwhile the Education and Training Department, originally set up in 2007, was tasked with turning the party into a much more professional outfit, capable of dealing with mass communication and the rigours of early twenty-first century politics. The party also made an effort to foster a collective sense of purpose amongst members and activists by continuing to organize training events, summer schools, festivals and so on. A youth organization (interestingly re-named "BNP Crusaders"), a student group, a trade union ("Solidarity"), an association of ex-servicemen and even an associated (Great White) record label were the organizational elements of a strategy which was seen as part of a much broader cultural offensive (see Goodwin 2010 p.180-81; 2011 p.87). Certain social categories were identified for special attention, for example the BNP newspaper *British Countryman* focused on developing an agenda amenable to rural, agrarian elements, and had the telling tagline "for tradition, identity and freedom" whilst wealthier supporters were encouraged to join the Trafalgar Club. As Griffin himself explained "'the great failing of the BNP is that it focused almost exclusively on elections...the idea that we can merely be elected to power, and that the establishment will simply say 'here are the keys, good-bye we're off' is simply not going to happen'" (cited in Goodwin 2010 p.181).

The 2009 European elections once more demonstrated the electoral potential of the BNP, it polled 943,000 votes, easily the best electoral performance by a far right wing party in Britain. MEP candidates Nick Griffin and Andrew Brons were elected for the North West and Yorkshire and the Humber, but the party also did well in Wales and the East of England where it had been quite weak in the past. Although considered a less important election, and perhaps perceived as an opportunity for electors to register a "protest vote", the European contest undoubtedly constituted an important moment in the history of the BNP, and offered some indication that they were continuing on the road toward political respectability. Success in the 2009 European elections was followed by BNP membership of the Alliance of European National Movements (AENM) in Brussels, and this electoral performance also eased financial concerns for a party reliant primarily on its own membership for funds.

On 22 October 2009 Nick Griffin, amidst considerable controversy, was invited onto the topical current affairs debating programme *Question Time,* which attracted a record 8.2 million audience (Copsey and Macklin 2011a p.89, see Trilling 2012 p.167). Although Mark Thompson, BBC Director General, claimed that the BNP had met certain objective criteria to justify its invitation, the decision was "met with anguished outrage from the political establishment and the media" (Copsey and Macklin 2011a p.86). The BBC came in for strident criticism in certain quarters for facilitating a dialogue with fascism and protests took place outside various BBC venues. However the programme itself, in departing from its conventional format, simply degenerated into an attack on the policies of the BNP and Griffin's personal political integrity in particular. In such an atmosphere Griffin inevitably looked "shifty and evasive" (Copsey and Macklin 2011a p.88) and the BNP leader subsequently complained of a "lynch mob" mentality, although this was no doubt prompted partly by the inadequacy of his own performance which was widely regarded as feeble (see Eatwell 2010 p.222). The BNP claimed that there were record numbers of applications for party membership from the general public after the programme, a claim which was, of course, difficult to verify.

Also in 2009 the Equalities and Human Rights Commission (EHRC) found that the BNP's membership criteria, as set out in the party's constitution, contravened the Race Relations Act (1976). Restricting membership to "indigenous Caucasian", that is white Britons, was considered to be discriminatory, and the BNP, under considerable duress, was forced to amend its constitution to permit "non-white" members. There was of course little chance of such compliance making the BNP any more attractive to people from ethnic minority communities in Britain, although the party did claim to have recruited a few Sikh members. The constitutional changes were accepted by the BNP under the threat of legal action but it made little substantive difference to its "racist" orientation, which continued to prioritise an "all white" Britain. As Williams and Gable remarked at the time, although the alteration was made, "the BNP's ideological core and the minds of its members remain saturated with racism" (Williams and Gable 2009 p.8). The BNP remained deeply critical of the perceived folly of liberal multiculturalism, despite the fact that they began to borrow extensively (and shamelessly) from the rhetoric and vocabulary of multiculturalism in pressing their demands on behalf of the "oppressed" indigenous white population in Britain who were having their "identity" eroded (see Rhodes 2011). The BNP continued to position itself as the respectable and responsible, almost dispassionate, defenders of ordinary white folk. The "Activists' and Organisers' Handbook" (BNP nd 2011) talked of "simple sales techniques", the importance of "selling" the party and establishing "deep roots" in local communities by portraying themselves as "everyday citizens with justifiable concerns and with practical, positive answers" (BNP nd 2011 Part 1). There was definitely no room for the old "unshaven scruff or skinhead haircuts" and the handbook helpfully suggested the wearing of caps or hats and "smart casual" attire when out canvassing because "the impression the leafleter gives is every bit as important as the message in the leaflet" (BNP nd 2011 Part 1).

However, we now know that during this period the BNP also faced considerable financial difficulties (see Gable 2011 p.20-21). Although, since 2006, the party's annual turnover had increased six-fold, most of the contributions came from members rather than wealthy donors and it appears that the party seriously over-stretched itself (Goodwin 2011 p.91). Moreover, accusations of financial impropriety emerged and some members of the Advisory Council were expelled for drawing attention to and criticizing the absence of internal accounting transparency. Indeed the BNP's irregular and occasionally erroneous recording of donations prompted an investigation by the Electoral Commission in 2008, and European Union fraud investigators in 2009. The court case effectively ended in a stalemate with both sides claiming victory, although the drain on BNP resources was considerable (see Trilling 2012 p.173). Given the encouraging trajectory of the BNP's electoral development its internal constitutional reforms and the gathering financial crisis, the 2010 General Election in Britain was seen as both a test and an opportunity for the party.

In 2010 voters were offered the most detailed BNP manifesto ever produced (BNP 2010), which committed the party to the complete termination of immigration. Immigration was described as "an unparalleled crisis which only the BNP can solve" (BNP 2010 p.4). "Indigenous" British people, the BNP claimed, were set to become a minority within 50 years, and drastic steps were required to reverse this process. Using phraseology loaded with ambiguity the manifesto stated that "the BNP recognizes the right of legally settled and law-abiding minorities to remain in the UK and enjoy the full protection of the law, on the understanding that the indigenous population of Britain has the right to remain the majority population of our nation" (BNP 2010 p.4). Group identity, along with a sense of belonging and allegiance were, according to the document, part of human nature and the British people were "bound together by blood" which "ensures an overlap of culture, heritage and tradition" (BNP 2010 p.22 and p.44). Indeed, "British people may take pride from knowing that the blood of an immense column of nation-building, civilization-creating heroes and heroines runs through their veins. Being British is more than merely possessing a modern document known as a passport. It runs far deeper than that; it is to belong to a special chain of unique people who have the natural law right to remain a majority in their ancestral homeland" (BNP 2010 p.23). Moreover, the manifesto stated unequivocally that: "we desire the preservation of our culture, heritage and identity. Our national character and native institutions are a precious heritage which reflect our origins and are an expression of blood" (BNP 2010 p.44). Of course the unspoken signifier here - the elephant in the room - is unquestionably "race" and the desire to preserve and promote the white (British) race. As a result voluntary resettlement of ethnic minorities would be "encouraged" with the use of the foreign aid budget because, according to the BNP, no great civilization was created or sustained by multiculturalism (see BNP 2010 p.20 and p.22). Consequently, under a BNP administration the Race Relations Act would be repealed along with "all other far leftist social engineering projects" such as the Equalities and Human Rights Commission (BNP 2010 p.4). More menacingly the BNP claimed it would "confront" the Muslim "colonization" of Britain because the Islamic religion was fundamentally incompatible with the values of a modern western democracy (BNP 2010 p.5). Indeed, "a BNP government would outlaw all overt signs of Islamic colonization such as the burka, ritual slaughter, mosques and minarets (which are little more than symbols of territorial conquest)" (BNP 2010 p.34).

The BNP also advocated withdrawal from the EU as an institution designed to erode Britain's sovereignty and national identity. Repeal of the Human Rights Act (1998), and withdrawal from the European Convention on Human Rights were also deemed necessary to ensure that Britain was not exploited by "the world's scroungers" (BNP 2010 p.6). Interestingly, in seeking to defend British democracy, the manifesto also focused on the need for devolution of power to local communities and continued to articulate its populist preoccupation with citizen-initiative referenda. Without any hint of irony the BNP claimed to be opposed to the current "repressive" and "totalitarian" state which had been created as the result of the desire to manufacture a multicultural nation (BNP 2010 p.37-38). Rather ominously the BNP said it would forbid "interference" by "third parties" in the election process, and "hold media outlets criminally liable for knowingly publishing falsehoods" (BNP 2010 p.6). The BNP was also opposed to "the intrusion of non-British and alien cultural influences which undermine our traditional value systems" and would therefore "take steps to promote the traditional British concepts of civility and courteousness" (BNP 2010 p.7). The party also sought to attract support by emphasizing the need for a Bill of Rights and an English Parliament (BNP 2010). Detailed policies were outlined on crime, which included the re-introduction of capital punishment and new anti-treason legislation, the right to bear arms, ending "political correctness" in the police force, and even the establishment of a penal colony on South Georgia.

However, the BNP's 2010 manifesto was relatively weak, if not flimsy, on coverage of economics, apart from the ritualistic references to the need for profitability, protecting British manufacturing industry from international competition, and acting against foreign corporations (although the document included a bizarre idea to investigate the viability of local currencies). Much of what passed for "economic" policy took the form of simply reiterating the financial benefits of pursuing other objectives, such as ending immigration and withdrawal from the EU. Interestingly the document asserted unequivocally that "lower taxation must be the ultimate aim" and advocated raising the threshold for inheritance tax (BNP 2010 p.72). All economic policies were contingent upon a carefully considered assessment of the "national interest" – an examination to be conducted under the auspices of the BNP of course. However, the "Activists' and Organisers' Handbook" was rather more explicit in its economic orientation, claiming that the BNP "is pledged to the maintenance of a private enterprise economy within a broad framework of national economic policy" whilst "private property should be encouraged and spread to as many individual members of our nation as possible" (BNP nd 2011). Thus the BNP might have opposed liberal globalization, but it certainly did not question free market capitalism as a mode of economic production and wealth accumulation. Other policies covered the need for substantial investment in transport infrastructure, energy, technology, agriculture, housing, the environment (despite the fallacy of global warming), the necessity of discipline in schools, the long overdue restoration of "traditional" aesthetic standards, along with a strategy focusing on defence and foreign affairs (which included a plan for the introduction of National Service and withdrawal of troops from Afghanistan) - the document even contained an initiative to save the "British pub"! Hence the manifesto reflected a concerted effort to convince the electorate that the BNP had a well considered, carefully constructed, and broadly based policy portfolio.

The BNP therefore made a huge effort to position itself as a credible, democratic, accountable, populist right wing party. In this process it was aiming to shed its historical image as a single-issue, racist, Hitler-worshipping fan club consisting of delinquent dullards and political misfits. Yet the party proclaimed it would never compromise on its fundamental principles, which meant that the policy programme would ultimately precipitate a national and cultural renewal which was bound to be rooted in and reflect the ethnic identity of British "folk" (see BNP 2012 p.90). In short, as the manifesto concluded, the BNP aimed to put the "great" back into Britain (BNP 2010 p.90). During the election campaign itself, in an effort to solidify the image of protecting British identity (whilst simultaneously removing the stigma of Nazism) Griffin appeared in a TV broadcast replete with union jacks and Churchillian images. Attention was deliberately focused on Griffin's Parliamentary candidature in Barking where the BNP detected the possibility of a major political breakthrough. The 2010 General Election was to constitute the BNP's very own "great leap forward".

However, the 2010 election results all but destroyed the BNP's hopes and aspirations. In Barking Griffin finished third as the Labour Party increased its majority, and overall the BNP did particularly badly (Ashley 2010). The BNP stood 338 candidates in the General Election and 737 in local elections, a huge logistical effort – it failed to get even close to electing an MP, and it was effectively wiped out locally with its share of the vote falling dramatically in most places (see Lowles

2010). Griffin's disappointment, and that of his party, was palpable. When the BNP lost heavily in subsequent local elections, including the loss of all of its councillors in Barking and Dagenham, the party seemed to have passed its electoral peak and the BNP, in time-honoured fashion, turned inwards upon itself. The controversy surrounding Griffin's role in apparent financial corruption, along with his style of governance, precipitated a spate of resignations which were accompanied by the familiar routine of accusation, denial and mutual recrimination. Indeed the disappointing electoral return and ongoing financial difficulties (the audited accounts in 2009 indicated a debt of £400,000) led to a leadership challenge to Griffin by Andrew Brons in July 2011, which the latter lost by a very narrow margin, 1,157 to 1,148 (Trilling 2012 p.192-93). In a contest which focused on Griffin's financial propriety and honesty (rather than any ideological failures) the party became bitterly divided, which raised serious questions about the BNP's long-term viability (Williams 2011 p.18).

In this context the 2012 local elections were another huge disappointment – it lost all twelve of the council seats it was defending, with no far right candidate winning a seat (the first time this had happened since 2001). From a peak of 57 councillors the BNP was reduced to just four. Consequently, although the BNP may have become a feature on the political landscape, its electoral aspirations had to be dramatically scaled down. This electoral meltdown, along with the fact that the right wing Euro-sceptic UK Independence Party posed a significant electoral obstacle to democratic recovery, inevitably precipitated some serious questions about strategy, and it may even mean that in the longer term the BNP will retreat to the margins and revert to the tactic of street confrontation. Indeed, given the BNP's faltering electoral strategy Nick Griffin appears to be pinning his political hopes on capitalizing from the coming conflagration caused by continued immigration, diminishing oil revenues, social and economic crises, and the so-called "clash of civilizations" between the West and Islam. However, whether Griffin will actually be in control of the BNP when the anticipated upturn in fortunes materializes, remains in considerable doubt, not least because of his own fragile financial circumstances – he was declared bankrupt in January 2014.

Having noted the sense of disappointment pervading the party in recent years due to its declining electoral perfor- mance, and despite its internal wrangling, the BNP remains by some distance the most successful far right wing party Britain has ever had. Even if the party seemed at times as though it was on the verge of collapse, its electoral support has held up remarkably well. In fact the BNP's vote in General Elections has increased by a factor of 12 since 2001, and by a factor of 100 in local elections in the same period, while membership has increased seven-fold (Goodwin 2011 p.171). It also estab- lished itself for a time as a prominent political player on the local scene, exploiting apparent public anxiety about immi- gration and cultural diversity (Goodwin 2011 p.171). Indeed it is important to note that even though the 2010 election was a major disappointment, the BNP still polled more votes than the Greens (who got a candidate elected as MP) and they could boast many more votes than the NF or BUF ever achieved. Evidently the European elections, because of the traditionally low turn-outs, have provided the BNP with unprecedented opportunities to mobilize a protest vote whilst local electoral politics, without requiring a large outlay in terms of resources and manpower, has provided a productive arena for BNP. Because wards are often ethnically homogenous the BNP can exploit and mobilize the resentment voters feel toward conven- tional parties, particularly Labour (see Bottom and Copus 2011). Hence in political terms local constituency contact and a European electoral profile can, in certain circumstances, facilitate a diminution of the legitimacy deficit (see Goodwin 2010 p.173-74).

A breakthrough at the national Parliamentary level looks far less certain, although this may not necessarily be due to a lack of sympathy amongst voters for BNP type policies. As Goodwin notes "the failure of the BNP to more effectively mobilize its underlying electoral potential and achieve a wider breakthrough is not due to a lack of demand for policies and ideas associated with the extreme right but rather supply factors, such as the characteristics of the party itself (i.e. its ideology, strategy, organization and leadership) as well as the reaction of other political actors" (Goodwin 2010 p.170). In terms of the impact at General Elections the sustained effort to ameliorate the party's exoteric appeal by making it more "moderate", populist and voter-friendly has been of limited success, principally because of the First Past the Post voting system which makes it particularly difficult for smaller parties to make an electoral impact. However, taking the electoral performance of the party as a whole, by trying to attract a much wider audience via an emphasis on "freedom", "identity" and "democracy", rather than biological racism and anti-semitism, the BNP has achieved tangible successes, although nothing comparable to some of its more prominent counterparts in continental Europe.

Nevertheless, having made these observations with regard to electoral outcomes we are left with the troublesome issue of core ideology and how much of the BNP's policy re-calibration reflects a genuine deviation from classical fascist themes, and how much was/is simply a superficial political gambit, designed to court respectability and win elections. Has the BNP really embraced a post-fascist "ethnocratic liberalism" (Griffin 2000) or does the political reorientation conceal the persistence of perennial fascist objectives?

Something of the ambiguity inherent in the issue of BNP ideology has been reflected in the work of Nigel Copsey. Copsey has identified a more populist, moderate (yet illiberal) version of ethnocentric nationalism, which "occupies the political space between fascism and the mainstream right" (Copsey 2008 p.80). Although Copsey described the BNP as an anti-systemic party (Copsey 2008 p.80) he added that the "national-populists are not neo-fascist" because of their commitment to democracy (Copsey 2008 p.82). Copsey also maintained that the 2005 manifesto document was significant in that "it forces us to reconsider some old certainties regarding the ideological make-up of the British National Party" and he asked rhetorically whether Nick Griffin's party had "finally stepped out of traditional fascist, neo-fascist or even neo-Nazi territory into the realm of more respectable, *Front National*-style national populism? Could a case now be made for re-designating the BNP as a party of the 'national populist' right?" (Copsey 2008 p.161). Yet on the other hand Copsey also suggested that a more forensic examination of the party programme reveals "evidence of an instinctive susceptibility to illiberal thinking" (Copsey 2008 p.162) with an emphasis on enforced racial separation, and he confirmed that, "a culture of anti-semitism still pervades the party" (Copsey 2008 p.162). Therefore Copsey argued that recent changes were, above all else, an elaborate exercise in re-branding and public relations, because the core ideology remained essentially the same, and fascism was still the "ultimate objective" (Copsey 2008 p.102). As a consequence, according to Copsey, Nick Griffin's BNP has re-calibrated fascism "to suit contemporary sensibilities" in an effort to acquire electoral respectability and political legitimacy (Copsey 2008 p.82). Copsey argues that the BNP remains committed to an Anglo-centric socio-economic and cultural "revolutionary re-birth" which still perceives the nation in racial terms (Copsey 2008 p.163). For Copsey, despite the apparent emphasis on themes like freedom, security and identity, it is "the deep-seated discontent with the existing liberal system that gives rise to the totalitarian impulse within the party even if, at present, this impulse is being kept under restraint" (Copsey 2008 p.163). As a consequence, "despite cleverly disassociating itself from inter-war fascism, Nick Griffin's British National Party remains intuitively fascist" it therefore reflects "not so much a change of course as an opportune change of clothing" (Copsey 2008 p.164 and Copsey 2007 p.80).

Copsey's scepticism is well founded because the fact is that the BNP had not actually shed its ideological baggage, indeed it had not escaped the legacy of its history as a Nazi party because it was never part of its intention. As Eatwell has noted, "party literature since 2000 has at times contained 'coded' messages, which seem aimed at reassuring the 'traditionalists' that the party has not lost its extremist soul" (Eatwell 2004 p.63). Although the party has engaged in a concerted effort to re-write its own history in order to obfuscate its fascist ideological roots and locate the party in the populist political mainstream, this has not been motivated by a desire to re-cast the underlying principles, which still reflect a continuing commitment to the fascist credo - a doctrine that was most clearly reflected in the regimes of Fascist Italy and Nazi Germany. A distinction has to be made between the inner ideology, adhered to by party ideologues, and the surface appeal of the party which is designed to attract votes. Of course it may be the case that some members may indeed have decided to join as a consequence of the moderated party programme, and therefore genuinely adhere to a populist perspective – but the party vehicle is still given impetus by its core ideological dynamic, which remains fascist. As Trilling has pointed out, there is an important distinction to be made "between committed BNP members and those drawn to support the party" (Trilling 2012 p.4) and although political progress has been made by widening its right wing policy profile, the party remains, in essence, fascist [23]. "Despite the surface change, the inner doctrine was the same as ever: a belief in 'revolutionary' seizure of power at a moment of crisis; biological racism; a barely concealed conspiracy theory" therefore "throughout its existence the BNP has remained profoundly fascist" (Trilling 2012 p.86 and p.203).

We can illustrate this point and prove it beyond any reasonable doubt by focusing on the fact that the BNP still places a clear emphasis on the ethnic and cultural identity of the British people. The references to "'native peoples'" of "'almost identical stock, such as Saxons, Vikings and Normans'", "'the uniqueness of the people'", and those "'species and races'" which "'must be preserved'" (cited in Passmore 2002 p.119-120) indicate that there is unquestionably a genetic, sociobiological sub-text. As BNP leader Nick Griffin himself has put it: "'nationality and identity are based on ancient roots and belonging, not possession of a passport. And every new wave of new recruits must be taught this, or our struggle would be pointless'", moreover "'as long as our cadres understand the full implications of our struggle, then there is no need for us to do anything to give the public cause for concern…we must at all times present them with an image of moderate reasonableness…Of course we must teach the truth to the hardcore…But when it comes to influencing the public, forget about racial differences, genetics, Zionism, historical revisionism and so on" (cited in Goodwin 2011 p.7 and *Patriot* No.4 1999 in Richardson 2011 p.40). This ongoing emphasis on genetics is confirmed in other internal documents such as *Hostile media questions for BNP candidates and officials 2005* and *Language and concepts discipline manual 2005* (cited in Richardson 2011 p.48-49). Racial cleansing is unquestionably still the over-riding objective and as Richardson says, "in contrast to their frequent denials, the BNP is a racist party: it remains wedded to a belief in racial inequality and a racial explanation of social and historic progress; it also remains committed to a white Britain, with black communities 'repatriated' or otherwise removed from any public influence" (Richardson 2011 p.50). Moreover, coded anti-Semitic references to the Jewish conspiracy are made via a focus on Zionism, the role of the media, international finance, globalization and multiculturalism. This preoccupation is also clearly reflected in the recommended reading which still contains literature by the likes of A.K. Chesterton, Arnold Leese and Nesta Webster, as well as the usual dreary tomes dedicated to denying the validity of the Holocaust (see Richardson 2011).

However, the clearest indication of the BNP's real ideological intent is provided by the BNP's internal documents captured by Mike Sutton in 2007 from the "official" website before they were removed (Sutton 2013, see Sutton and Perry 2009). This trawl through the darkest depths of BNP ideology reveals a party still obsessed with racial purity, genetics and miscegenation, and absolutely intent on imposing authoritarian solutions – as Nick Griffin himself says "'mankind is divided into races'" and the BNP "'recognises such ineradicable facts of human nature and seeks to base its political programme on such realities, and not on the pernicious fantasy of 'human equality'...we believe, in a nutshell, in the human right to discriminate'" (cited in Sutton 2013). However, according to Griffin it was imperative that the electorate conclude that the BNP were "'just another party. That everything about us is 'normal'" and he concluded "'we do not seek power for its own sake, but so we can use it to do the things we must do to protect our people and secure a future for white children. That has always been our aim, and will always remain our aim'" (cited in Sutton 2013). The distinction between the surface appeal (exoteric/public) and the deeper ideological (esoteric/private) content – what Sutton and Perry refer to as "the stuff of nightmares" – is revealed as a fundamentally duplicitous tactical ploy (see Sutton and Perry 2009 p.94). Indeed "the ideological core of the BNP, as revealed in the political beliefs and commitments of party leaders and activists, still draws strength from Leese's anti-Semitic racial fascism and remains committed to the racial purification of the national space" (Richardson 2011 p.39). There is therefore absolutely no doubt that "the BNP should be viewed as a continuation of previous parties of the British fascist fringe" (Richardson 2011 p.58).

In this sense Roger Griffin is undoubtedly correct to conclude that "it is the constant slipping of the mask of Griffin and his activists to reveal unreconstructed racist and neo-Nazi attitudes beneath the photo-opportunistic smiles that has doomed to failure the BNP's bid to establish itself as a British democratic neo-populist party...The party's modernization is thus not authentic" (Griffin 2011 p.203). In actual fact, framing concerns in terms of patriotism, freedom, culture and identity is simply a cynically constructed populist code, and cannot conceal the fact that in reality the emphasis on biological racial preservation and xenophobic nationalism will inevitably mean prejudice, discrimination and, ultimately, forms of compulsion and violence. The surface ideology, which is protean and adaptable, and primarily designed to procure electoral advantage, should not obscure the inner core of the ideology, which will only ever really be fully revealed in practice. Despite dishonest protestations to the contrary by the BNP, fascism is being adapted, as a matter of political expediency, to suit the modern era and a more specific set of contemporary sociocultural and economic circumstances.

As a result of its tactical manouvring and apparent ideological flexibility the wider far right has adopted a rather ambivalent attitude toward the BNP. On the one hand recalcitrant racial nationalist ideologues have rebuked the BNP for abandoning the creed of national socialism, yet on the other there appears to be a grudging respect, indeed admiration, for its capacity to set the political agenda  (see Woodbridge 2011). Parties like the National Democrats, National Front, Freedom Party, British People's Party, Democratic Nationalists, Britain First Party, White Nationalist Party and Nationalist Alliance constitute a marginalized miasma of micro-sects who, despite their precarious existence, hope to either exploit the ideological space opened up by the BNP or, alternatively, feed off of the BNP's carcass in the event of its ultimate demise. There is little doubt that these are similarly fascist in inspiration, whether they adhere to a classic conception (as outlined via themes in the previous chapter) or a more populist variant. Take for example the British People's Party, launched in 2005, which advocates the creation of a "white workers' state", the repatriation of non-white immigrants, and the re-introduction of capital punishment. The aim of the BPP is "rebuilding our pride in our racial and national heritage" and the creation of "an energetic folk state" in order to "secure the existence of our people and a future for White children" (www.bpp.org.uk/policies2012). On the other hand the English People's Party, launched in 2010, represents a more populist perspective on the far right and describes itself as a "patriotic" party, whilst calling for a blanket ban on all forms of immigration (see www.englishpeoplesparty.org 2012). Both organizations are emblematic of the purist-populist axis on the contemporary fascist right in Britain.

Perhaps the organization most capable of threatening the political pre-eminence of the BNP as the standardbearer of the fascist right remains the National Front, which claims (rather disingenuously) an unbroken ideological heritage. The current Chairman of the NF is Ian Edward, who is hoping to re-activate electoral ambitions, and he states explicitly that "'we are a racial nationalist party'" (cited in Brown 2012). Indeed the NF, like much of the fascist right in Britain, retains a messianic commitment to the so-called "fourteen words": "we must secure the existence of our people and a future for white children" (a phrase derived from the racial supremacist group "The Order" in the USA). The National Front continues to hope that it can portray itself as the authentic voice of racial nationalism given the rising political temperature created by "Islamaphobia" and the BNP's recent difficulties, especially given Griffin's apparent capitulation over non-white membership. Indeed the NF have captured some prominent defectors from the BNP, such as Richard Edmonds, who has spent a lifetime inhabiting the fringes of fascist politics (see Collins 2011a). Interestingly Nick Griffin, obviously irritated by the capacity of the NF to damage his party, has derided them as "'neo-fascist'". This is, as Woodbridge points out, "an audacious use of terminology" (Woodbridge 2011 p.112) and reflects quite clearly Griffin's effort to expunge the memory of his own Nazi credentials, at least for the purposes of public consumption. Yet in an odd way it is possible that criticism from the fringes of the unreconstructed Nazi right is not entirely unwelcome for the BNP since,"there is some evidence that Griffin has courted such condemnation from the more extreme groups as part of his legitimation strategy" (Woodbridge 2011 p.119). High profile squabbles with neo-Nazi nutters might be construed as good for electoral business.

The fascist fringes of politics in Britain, populated by a plethora of mutually antagonistic ideological sects, are easily dismissed as an irrelevance, as Goodwin points out such groups are often ridiculed for having more initials than members, although "the potential for violence should not be ignored" (Goodwin 2011 p.6). Such parties "rely on miniscule memberships and few resources. Some are so weak they have been confined to specific areas, for example the DN in Bradford or the NNP in the Midlands. Although they aim to operate within legal frameworks, individual members have been linked with violence" (Goodwin 2011 p.5). This connection to the ultra-violent far right, which exists in the penumbra beyond conventional politics, is an important political fact and the key individuals on the fascist right who inhabit the shadowy world of extra-parliamentary, paramilitary neo-Nazism should be the subject of further detailed research and analysis. Groups like the Aryan Strike Force (ASF), Racial Volunteer Force (RVF), Britain First (BF) and the British Freedom Fighters (BFF) reject any kind of electoral activity as counter-productive and ultimately self-defeating. These subterranean subversives focus on an uncompromising ideological commitment to classical fascism and the use of violence as a matter of principle, whilst exploiting their contacts in the sub-cultural skinhead network of the "Blood and Honour" Nazi music scene in order to procure material resources. Roger Griffin has noted that some, largely autonomous, grouplets have formed an amorphous, leaderless, cellular network, its unpredictable, asymmetrical growth having been facilitated by the judicious use of the internet to attract and "educate" activists (see Griffin 2003). According to Griffin, this ill-defined, miniscule, "rhizomic", "groupuscular right", although largely invisible from the vantage point of conventional politics, nevertheless enables fascist ideas to be sustained and disseminated in onerous circumstances (Griffin 2003, see Griffin 2002b) [24]. Indeed "the minute bursts of spontaneous creativity that produce and maintain individual groupuscles constitute nodal points in a force-field or web of radical political energy that fuels the vitality and the viability of the organism as a whole" (Griffin 2003 p.46-47, see Griffin 2002b). Certainly, in extreme cases these anti-systemic, subcultural groups have the capacity to transform disaffected individuals into fanatical activists who are quite prepared to use the most extreme violence against their political opponents, society and the state.

However, in the context of the declining electoral viability of the BNP and the diffusion of the fascist fringe, the development of a non-party extra-Parliamentary movement of right-wing public protest in Britain is of particular interest. The English Defence League (EDL) has precipitated some extensive media attention which has focussed on the organization as leading a new and dangerous wave of violent, racist, street-based fascist-style politics (see Jackson 2011). The EDL was formed on 27 June 2009 as an organization which, initially at least, had strong links with various football gangs or "firms" and which was designed to organize demonstrations against militant Islamism. The EDL is, according to a recent report by Paul Jackson, a "new far right social movement" which has updated the old fascist strategy of "march and grow", and which aims to capitalize on an anti-Muslim prejudice which has an increasing resonance in British culture (see Jackson 2011 p.60-61). As a vehicle for radical right-wing political protest the EDL has made considerable headway as the electoral fortunes of the BNP have declined.

The EDL was initially led by ex-BNP member Stephen Yaxley-Lennon (alias "Tommy Robinson") and Kevin Carroll. The EDL claimed to be non-violent, ideologically distinct from the BNP, and non-racist – it has not as yet contested elections, and operates as a publicity-seeking pressure group concentrating purely on the issue of the Muslim religion. Apparently open to all, including members of minority ethnic communities, the single-issue orientation of the organisation has been to oppose the spread of Islamic fundamentalism. The EDL argued that it was simply protesting against the creeping "Islamification" of British society and the excesses of radical Muslims intent on establishing a state based on Sharia law (see englishdefenceleague.org2012). Describing itself as a "human rights" movement, EDL members were even filmed burning a Nazi flag on the BBC's *Newsnight* current affairs programme in an effort to distance themselves from accusations of fascism and white supremacism (see Jackson 2011 p.16). The EDL is co-ordinated principally through the internet and social media, and is organized into (approximately 130) loosely connected regional "divisions" (which also includes a "Jewish" Division). The EDL, which has boasted over 90,000 "supporters" on Facebook, has been particularly popular in places like Luton, Birmingham and the North West, where there are some relatively large Muslim communities. The EDL has also sought to develop an international presence with global connections, via the internet, to a variety of similar organizations in Europe, the USA and elsewhere (see Jackson 2011 p.27). Finance is derived principally from online merchandising and individual benefactors like wealthy IT entrepreneur Alan Lake. More recently the EDL has been looking toward cooperating with the British Freedom Party (which contains several disaffected BNP members) in an effort to explore electoral options and in April 2012 British Freedom announced that Yaxley-Lennon would be joining the party as its deputy leader (Trilling 2012 p.195). The EDL has certainly had little difficulty mobilizing 3,000-5,000 people for its "demonstrations", which often degenerate into opportunistic violence perpetrated against Mosques, the purveyors of halal meat or individual Muslims (see Treadwell and Garland 2011). The more recent emergence of the EDL faction calling themselves "the Infidels" is illustrative of not only a masculine, sub-cultural predisposition for violence, but also reflects the fractious nature of a social movement which affords ample opportunity for local, autonomous, grass roots initiatives.

However, the contention that the EDL is simply a civil rights organization was never really sustainable. Indeed such a view might be discarded as disengenuous given the prominence of BNP activists and known racists, and the significance of violent disorder as a tactic, which soon became associated with the organization. (Interestingly, although the BNP has apparently "proscribed" the EDL, evidence of substantive disciplinary action against those members involved with it has yet to emerge). Indeed, the culture of "hooliganism" within the organization has remained a "constant presence", and "as with many far right organizations in British history, its brand has become indelibly associated with violence and extremism" (Jackson 2011 p.18 and p.62). Despite the veneer of pluralism and diversity various EDL factions have engaged in extreme violence against ethnic minorities, they have attacked trade union offices, and they have also threatened to assault anti-capitalist protestors and public sector workers on strike (Woodson 2009, Townsend 2011, see Trilling 2012 p.189). Indeed, the websites, blogs and Facebook pages associated with the EDL features "'endless sickening, hate-filled comments about Muslims and other minorities of the type you would expect to find on a Neo-Nazi website. Calls for physical attacks on Muslims and the burning of mosques are commonplace'" (Bob Pitt cited in Jackson 2011 p.65). There was even a suggestion that some EDL members were in contact with Norwegian Anders Breivik in the period before he launched his murderous assault in July 2011 (Lowles and Creasy 2011, see Trilling 2012 p.189-90).

Thus in the EDL the emphasis on a visceral ethno-national ultra-patriotism and a British "way of life" slips easily into negative stereotyping which "creates a xenophobic discourse of exclusion" (Jackson 2011 p.9). Western culture, as a repository of rational enlightenment and liberal tolerance, is deemed to be under threat from a "backward", "barbaric", "inferior" and monolithic Muslim religion which is not only irredeemably violent and favourably disposed toward jihadi "terrorists", but wholly at odds with European values. Hence the reality is that the EDL is little more than a repository for a nationalistic Islamaphobia. Indeed this was a point taken up by Unite General Secretary Len McCluskey when he said that, "'trade unionists stand against everything the EDL stands for. Ultra-rightwing groups care about nothing other than stoking hatred, which is why they have no place in our communities'" (cited in Townsend 2011). Similarly Unite Against Fascism has argued that the EDL has well-documented links to the BNP and consists of "hardened fascists" at the centre of an organization which is "looking to build a new racist street movement" in order to "control the streets" (Bennett and Dhalu 2010, see Collins 2011 p.316). Indeed some anti-fascist activists have called for the EDL to be designated as an "extremist" organization, arguing that right wing violence is not being taken seriously as a threat and, moreover, that official initiatives like the government's "Prevent" programme have been organized and orientated in such a way as to focus only on Islamic fundamentalist extremism (see Rahman 2011, and Lowles 2011). Extraordinarily Adrian Tudway, the UK police's national co-ordinator for domestic extremism, even urged Muslim's to engage in dialogue with the group, arguing that they were not "extremist" in the conventional sense of being a threat to democracy (see Rahman 2011). As Gerry Gable noted, for some Muslims this was akin to asking the Jewish community to converse with Nazis (cited in Jackson 2011 p.68).

The conflict over the appropriate response highlights the confusion that the EDL has precipitated amongst activists, academics and journalistic commentators alike. There is little doubt that the EDL gives expression to unreconstructed racist voices and its marches are designed to be provocative, but it is a mistake to view the organization as simply a BNP for football "firms". Firstly, the organization can count on a broad swathe of support from those who not only reject Islamic fundamentalism, but are comfortable with the language of "British" culture and identity. Secondly, the lack of a clear programme, and the existence of anti-Islamic sentiment in mainstream discourse has meant that the group has been able to act as a convenient repository for youthful discontent. In the contemporary context, therefore, the EDL, despite its internal divisions, poses significant tactical and strategic problems for its opponents. However, it has far more of its own. If we take the rhetoric at face value, the fact that a single policy provides some kind of coherence for the EDL is both a source of strength and weakness. Any effort to move the EDL beyond anti-Islamism (in terms of nationalism, culture and identity) means it is easier to categorise it with the other more conventional racist and fascist organizations, in which case it will lose its strategic specificity, whilst on the other hand a static tactical focus on the issue of extremist religion risks confirming the organization as a one-trick political pony. It remains to be seen if the EDL can survive the high-profile defection of "Tommy Robinson" to the controversial "anti-extremist" think tank the Quilliam Foundation. In any event, the significance of the EDL lies not in the political pronouncements, which conceal a plethora of ideological motivations ranging from Christian fundamentalism to Nazism, but in the fact that the EDL remains a lightning-rod for disaffected white working class in Britain.

## The Nature of British Fascism: Oscillation between Optimism and Obscurity

It may be concluded, from this brief account of the far right in Britain, that its effect on British politics has been, at most, marginal. As far as British fascism is concerned it is indeed tempting to refer to Marx's correction of Hegel concerning the course of history, which repeats itself first as tragedy, then as farce. In the 1970s Rees stated that "only two fascist or fascistic movements have attained any real importance in British politics, the BUF and the NF; the rest, like so many sub-atomic particles, are notable for combining a very high energy with a very brief existence" (Rees 1979 p.7). Similarly in the 1980s Thurlow could argue that "British fascism was small beer. At no stage could it be considered a credible political threat" (Thurlow 1987 p.303). More recently Goodwin has argued that, "traditionally, the far right in Britain has been associated with failure", with Britain's far right regarded as the "'ugly duckling'" of the European genus (Goodwin 2007 p.241). Hence the unattractive triptych of BUF, NF and BNP has never quite been able to capture the attention of the onlooker for long enough to make a discernible impression.

Yet there is no doubt that when we are referring to the far right in Britain we are indeed actually dealing with variants of classical fascism. The internal wrangling, acrimonious splits and mutual recriminations which characterised the development of the fascist far right owed much more to personal rivalry and political tactics than significant theoretical or ideological disputes. Although there were qualitative differences in degree, for instance between the ethnocentric/cultural racism of Mosley, with his emphasis on moral idealism, aesthetic value and shared culture, and the genetic determinism of many of his followers and most other fascist groupings, it does not invalidate this basic hypothesis – the BUF, NF and the BNP were authentic political manifestations of the classical fascist phenomenon. The dynamic impetus and inspiration derived by such groups from continental fascism in the 1920s and 1930s, and the emphasis on themes (identified in the previous chapter) such as social Darwinism, instinctivism, violent activism, nationalism, authoritarianism, the corporatist "third way", anti-liberalism, anti-communism, anti-semitic conspiracy theories and racism, all betray their distinctly fascist heritage. Indeed those following in the tradition of Arnold Leese, such as Colin Jordan, John Tyndall, and Martin Webster, were clearly ideological Nazis. There is little scope for ambiguity or ambivalence here, the emphasis on biological conceptions of race, the evils of Jewry, international conspiracy and so on, betray an explicit adherence to specifically Nazi ideas as outlined by the likes of Rosenberg and Hitler (which were outlined in detail in chapter one).

However the picture alters somewhat with the arrival of the "new" BNP in the mid-1990s which, in attempting to move beyond electoral impotence, made a concerted bid for respectability and legitimacy. In the process "the BNP has unquestionably become the most successful far-right party in British history" (Goodwin 2007 p.241). The BNP, by emulating a continental paradigm provided principally by the French FN, made a clear effort to carve a national-populist niche for itself, and has been much more successful in electoral terms. Nick Griffin himself claims to have transformed the BNP from a "'bad political joke into a major factor in British politics'" (cited in Goodwin 2011 p.xiii). Of course the construction of legitimacy is crucial as a prerequisite for electoral break-through and the effort to secure and sustain such credibility has led the BNP, at a local and national level, to portray a more socially acceptable and moderate image to the public.

As we have seen, despite the BNP's lurch toward "respect-ability" and legitimacy, beneath the surface the party remains fascist in inspiration and there are still people within the BNP who adhere to a messianic version of British nationalism. The fact is that the "new" BNP has the same basic ideological dynamic driving it, despite the more sophisticated marketing strategy, and the party still undoubtedly attracts those on the far right who are committed to a more apocalyptic vision of politics. As a result the party has not been able to detach itself entirely from the image of violence, not just in terms of racial hatred and practical hostility to minority groups, but also with regard to individuals who have been investigated under the terms of domestic anti-terrorism legislation (see Goodwin 2010 p.182-83) [25]. This trend toward the accep-tance of more extreme methods is likely to continue given the fact that the electoral route appears to have been blocked since 2010. As Goodwin concludes, "the evidence suggests that 'traditional' right-wing extremist parties like the BNP will increasingly find their appeal restricted to dwindling pools of racially prejudiced angry white men. The fact that the party is not extending its appeal beyond smaller rumps of hostility suggests a bleak future" (Goodwin 2011 p.181).

The fact is, in a post-Auschwitz context, it would be absurd to expect parties which possess Fascist and Nazi sympathies to tell the truth, because to do so would simply court electoral oblivion. Therefore it would be naïve to assume that the BNP's overt orientation is anything more than calculated political opportunism, a superficial and cosmetic re-configuration designed to deceive. True to the history of fascist flexibility the surface rhetoric will take many different forms depending upon the contemporary context and immediate tactical advantage. Hence the likes of Nick Griffin and the new generation of fascists in the BNP might find it politically expedient to distance themselves from the memories of Hitler and Mussolini, and may find it convenient to march under the Union Jack rather than the swastika, but that the inner ideology has been, and contines to be, a variant of fascism is undeniable. In this sense the classical versions of Fascism and Nazism, identified and examined in the first part of this text, are not purely academic questions, nor is the ethnic cleansing and genocide of that period simply a subject of interest only to historians - the ideas which inspired those regimes remain active in Britain today (Trilling 2012). There is absolutely no reason at all to suppose, given the nature of those ideas, that British fascists would not, given the opportunity, emulate, albeit in a more politically and culturally specific way, the horrors of that particular period.

## NOTES

[1]   Thurlow refers to "Mosley's powerful mind" which "produced stimulating ideas" that were "usually expressed in a coherent and rational manner" (Thurlow 1998 p.118), and he describes Mosley as a "brilliant but erratic man" (Thurlow 1998 p.278). Indeed Thurlow says "of all the sawdust Ceasars and tinpot Fuhrers of the British fascist political tradition, only Mosley had the requisite political ability to look the part as a credible leader" (Thurlow 1998 p.281). Skideslky goes furthest in deference to Mosley's intellectual credentials, and concludes his work with a quote from Faust: "'whoever

strives can be redeemed'" (cited in Skidelsky 1981 p.520). In fact Skidelsky's biography offers an overly sympathetic account of its subject and the BUF, indeed in the Preface to the 1981 edition Skidelsky acknowledges that he under-emphasised the "dark side" of British fascism during that period. Certainly Mosley's son provided a more considered account when he argued that whilst his father dealt with high ideals on the one hand, on the other he "'let the rat out of the sewer'" (cited in Skidelsky 1981 p.512). Of course it is simply not possible to obscure Mosley's chilling distillation of fascist ideas in a plethora of footnotes – the important point is not so much that Mosely was a talented man or an intellectual, but that he was a fascist. Academic qualifications and scholarly credentials do not guarantee political wisdom, still less morality. For example it might be noted in this context that, of the fifteen Nazi participants attending the Wannsee Conference in 1941, eight held academic doctorates, whilst the *Einsatzgruppen A* mobile execution unit, under the command of Dr. Franz Walther Stahlecker, boasted eleven lawyers, nine with doctoral degrees - the gruesome human vivesector Josef Mengele held doctorates in anthropology and medicine. (See Herbert 2001 who confirms this observation with reference to the university educated leaders of the National Socialist police, and Weindling 1996 who focuses on the role of professional elites in extending the capacity of the Nazi state in pursuit of its racial utopia).

[2]   It is in this area that Skidelsky's biography is most troubling – he actually argues that the Jews need to shoulder some of the blame for the confrontation that took place, although he accepts that Mosley may have responded with "surplus hostility". Incredibly Skidelsky also maintains that legal responsibility for the violence that accompanied BUF meetings lay with the anti-fascist opposition (although he does acknowledge that ultimate responsibility is difficult to assign). Interestingly

Skidelsky also claimed that the Public Order Act was a value-judgement against the BUF, suggesting that "Fascists on the whole....acquitted themselves with aplomb in many difficult situations, and often with conspicuous courage" (Skidelsky 1981 p.361-62, p.381 and p.390). Also very odd is Thurlow's suggestion that "'the BUF, despite left wing propaganda to the contrary... displayed an unwillingness to use offensive violence against the state and anti-fascists'" (cited in Renton 2001 p.70, see also Thurlow 1998 p.xii). Meanwhile Cullen (1993), in using Home Office and MI5 archives (which he describes as "sufficiently impartial"), makes essentially the same observation, arguing that the BUF was "primarily the victim of offensive political violence, rather than its prime instigator" and "it is difficult to see what else the movement could have done" (Cullen 1993 p.247, p.264-5). (Cullen also claims that the "coercive core" of the BUF's ideology, to which the anti-fascists were self-evidently responding, is common to all "statist" politics, and he suggests that, in this context, only the anarchists are "innocent", although this rather glibly under-plays the massive qualitative difference between fascist and constitutional parties, see Cullen 1993 p.265). In fact it is quite clear that many in the BUF required little encouragement to embrace violence, and indeed Thurlow himself actually acknowledges elsewhere that the BUF used pro-active violence to attack rival fascist organizations (see Thurlow 1998 p.66, see Woodbridge 2012 p.57 note No.5). The BUF was an extremely aggressive political outfit whose aim was to control the streets in the manner of the continental fascist movements. In this context, given such a purpose and provocation, practical resistance was inevitable. (The political and moral obligation of physical resistance to fascism will be discussed in the conclusion to this text).

[3]     Some commentators have viewed the Regulation as a blot on Britain's liberal heritage. Thurlow argues that

the BUF were patriots rather than traitors, and Skidelsky maintains that, given the absence of treasonable intent, detention was unreasonable (Thurlow 1987 p.189-90 and p.302, see Skidelsky 1981). This is a controversial position to adopt given the BUF's evident affinity for the enemy. It is more remarkable that some of the most prominent aristocratic fascists evaded detention (Pugh 2005 p.306).

[4]   Baker (1984) argues that Chesterton was a cultural fascist given the nature and context of his anti-semitism – this is perhaps less plausible than Thurlow's case for Oswald Mosley in this regard (Thurlow 1987).

[5]   See *Patterns of Prejudice* vol 1 1967 p.23 which refers to a "British Fascist Programme"

[6]   Walker (1978) may have been correct to argue that to refer to NF supporters as "fascist" was "silly", but his observation missed the point. The ideology adhered to and professed by the party was what really mattered, and it was fascist.

[7]   Hence Thurlow's references to Tyndall's "post-Nazi synthesis" and the influence of Spengler and Francis Parker Yockey is somewhat misleading (see Thurlow 1981 p.29), although Thurlow retracted/clarified this somewhat (see 1987 p.258 and p.274) where he acknowledged a difference in degree rather than kind in Tyndall's work. See Hanna (1974 p.51), Taylor (1982 p.100) and Fielding (1984 p.56-72 and p.69).

[8]   The NF did reasonably well in the midlands as usual, however London, with its tradition of support for right wing groups, achieved the dubious distinction of leading the regional table of support. In London the NF averaged over 4% with Hackney South providing the best result of 9.4%. Taylor states of London, "the NF did well... against the national trend...largely because it was able to mobilize an existing potential among white electors for support related to the size of coloured populations, and additionally capitalize upon a political tradition of support for the extreme right in the East End of London

and in parts of the North and East of London where ex-East Enders have settled" (Taylor 1982 p.43). The clear implication was that NF support reflected white fears about the adjacent minority communities and a pre-existing extremist tradition. NF support, such as it was, was also facilitated by the break-up in 1974 of the Action Party, the successor to the UM, which hitherto had some influence in the East End.

[9]  According to some accounts the NF did best in those areas fearing the arrival of Malawi Asians e.g. Sandwell 27.5%. See Harrop and Zimmerman (1977 p.12), Taylor (1979 p.250-57, 1980 pp.268-70).

[10] Jordan actually stole a pair of red knickers from Tesco (a Jewish-owned company) – conduct hardly appropriate for a potential *Fuhrer*!

[11] Walker qualifies his statement shortly afterwards by stating that Steed's study (1978) "should serve to dampen some of the hysteria which greeted the NF's increasing electoral prominence in 1977" (Walker 1978 p.226, see below)

[12] *Guardian* 5 July 1977 cited in Steed (1978). Steed argues that the 1977 results, far from indicating a significant mobilization of white working class support in London, in fact reflected the winning of support that was actually or potentially available in 1974. In effect the variation in the NF's share of the vote 1974-77 was the product of differential turnout – while over three quarters of Londoners had voted in the October 1974 General Election, only around two fifths voted in the GLC election. Consequently in 1977 the NF's share of the vote was calculated as a percentage of a much smaller overall turn-out. In effect a methodological error in comparing elections precipitated erroneous conclusions. Taylor states of Steed's analysis "if this general interpretation is correct, it would seem that both the succour drawn by the NF from the 1977 GLC results, and the alarm that

these caused among other groups, was largely misplaced" (Taylor 1982 p.130). See Whiteley (1979 p.370-80).

[13] Many NF members' wives and relatives were encouraged to stand as candidates – Tyndall's father-in-law, mother-in-law and wife all stood. Interestingly Hill says that funding for the campaign actually came via South African diamonds (Hill 1988).

[14] According to Renton: "looking through the list of left wing campaigns in recent British history, one could find no better example of success than the Anti-Nazi League of the 1970s" (Renton 2001 p.195). This paean of praise for the ANL and Rock Against Racism is perhaps excusable, but certainly overstated.

[15] Distribution of material such as *Holocaust News* from the Institute for Historical Review/Historical Review Press and the *Journal of Historical Review* indicated clearly where NF sympathies lay (see Lipsdadt 1993 p.137). Other revisionist works distributed by the NF included *The Six Million Reconsidered* by William Grimstad, *Is Anne Frank's Diary Genuine?* by Robert Faurisson, and *The Man Who Invented Genocide* by James Martin. Indeed Verrall himself is widely believed to have penned the short revisionist tract *Did Six Million Really Die?* (1974) under the pseudonym Richard Harwood (see Lipstadt 1993 p.104). Holocaust denial has an interesting heritage. One of the earliest proponents of Holocaust denial was Maurice Bardeche who, along with Paul Rassinier claimed that victims exaggerated their experience and/or that genocide was a Zionist-inspired myth (see Neville 1999 Chapter 7 p.69; Cohn-Sherbok 1999 Chapter 25 p.254). George Lincoln Rockwell had also contended that the Holocaust was a profitable fraud, and anti-semite Harry Elmer Barnes blamed the Allies for the Second World War and for perpetuating the genocide myths (see Lipsdadt 1993 p.67). Meanwhile Austin App defended Nazi Germany and questioned the widely accepted figure of six million victims (see Lipsdadt 1993 p.85). Also

indicative of the genre in the late 1970s was *The Hoax of the Twentieth Century* written by Arthur R. Butz, which argued that international Zionism manufactured false-hoods in order to gain sympathy for Israel, and that the "death camps" were well equipped transit facilities used to keep Jews safe from the Red Army (see Lipsdadt 1993 p.123). We can leave Peter Neville to make the obvious point: "the techniques used by Holocaust deniers are regarded as an affront to professional historians because they distort documentary evidence or involve outright fabrication of evidence. More importantly, however, they are an affront to the survivors of the Holocaust" (Neville 1999 p.72). Holocaust denial is one of the most insidious features of modern fascist activity because victims, already defiled as *Untermenschen* during the single most horrific event in recent history, survived only to be dismissed as non-existent non-people by pseudo-historians and semi-educated crackpots. As Deborah Lipsdadt (1993) argues, despite the thin veneer of scholarship, Holocaust denial is not only cruel but, at its core, "poses a threat to all who believe that knowledge and memory are among the keystones of our civilization" (Lipsdadt 1993 p.19-20).

[16] For a full account see the internal report by the NF Directorate in August 1986, especially p.51 for full names and details of respective factions (NF Directorate 1986). Interestingly Ray Hill (1988 p.295-6) has argued that this particular fissure, like most others, owed more to personal animosities rather than fundamental ideolog-ical disagreement, since both factions claimed to base their political outlook on the Strasserite "Third Position". Goodwin in his recent survey of the BNP (2011) does not really examine the NF "political soldier" phenom-enon, which is disappointing because although the BNP is the focus of his attention, Griffin's earlier role in the NF's Strasserite adventurism highlights some interesting elements in the broader trajectory of his politics.

[17] Interestingly, the creation of this new nationalist cadre would require a high level of self-discipline and commitment which resulted in numerous exhortations to self-improvement by the leadership e.g. giving up excessive drinking and tobacco, and the need to study certain key texts and so on - evidently the new "National Warrior" was no longer to be found amongst the lumpen-proletariat or the beer-sodden skinheads on the terraces at football matches.

[18] Searchlight (1986) actually argued that events at this time within the far right conformed to a plan outlined by Colin Jordan (1986) in an article entitled *The Case for Politics Beyond Party* which appeared in the *League of St. George Review.* Jordan's plan, put briefly, was to have three groupings: one on the right fringe of the Conservative party; one to raise racial tension with Jews/minority ethnic communities; and one elite cadre. However, it is difficult to believe that such a series of events was so clearly and cleverly orchestrated. (At this point it is as well to note some very questionable research techniques deployed by *Searchlight* – the composite interview may yield some interesting material, but its academic utility as empirical evidence is extremely dubious).

[19] The denial of the Holocaust is evidently a controversial theme, and an issue where the BNP could be identified as having a distinctly pro-Nazi predisposition. The party not only distributed copies of *Holocaust News*, which declared the Holocaust a myth, it also publicized the revisionist work of controversial historian David Irving. The work of David Irving offered a more respectable revisionism – he argued that the number of Jewish deaths was exaggerated and that Hitler had no knowledge of the death camps. Irving therefore shifted responsibility to Hitler's over-zealous henchmen, Himmler and Heydrich, and he identified Jewish influence and the British Psychological Warfare Executive as the source of the myth of Hitler's culpability. The evidence against Hitler, Irving

infamously claimed, would not suffice in an English magistrates court to convict a vagabond of stealing a bicycle (see Griffin 1995 p.335-37). In this context see Irving's short-lived Focus Policy Group 1980-83, his book *Hitler's War* (1977) and his introduction to Fred Leuchter's Report (1988) which attempted to prove "scientifically" that mass killings did not take place (see Lipsdadt 1993 p.163. See also Wilkinson (1981 p.97), Hill (1988 p.245), and Gill Seidel (1986) *The Holocaust Denial*). The infamous *Protocols* were still "recommended reading" in the BNP, as was material on the "show trials" of Nuremberg and "misunderstood" Nazis such as Eichmann. It is also worth noting that some in the BNP also latched onto criticisms of the "Holocaust industry" made by the anti-Zionist Jewish academic Norman Finkelstein (2000). As a response to Daniel Goldhagen's (1996) *Hitler's Willing Executioners* Finkelstein's thesis, whilst making entirely legitimate criticisms of Israel's cynical manipulation of a historic tragedy, nevertheless inadvertently gave succour to some unreconstructed racists on the far right.

[20] The name C18 is derived from a numerical reference to the letters A and H in the alphabet – the initials of Adolf Hitler. The immediate catalyst for the formation of C18 was a meeting of the League of Saint George in Kensington Library in 1991 which was comprehensively routed by AFA. As Lowles says, "humiliatingly, the event's security team was taken out by a small group of anti-fascists posing as Nazis, who arrived early carrying forged entrance tickets...in a scene reminiscent of a warzone, the street outside the venue was littered with the bodies of unconscious skinheads" (Lowles 2001 p.10).

[21] Paul David "Charlie" Sargent once described C18 as "'thugs who follow an ideology'" (cited in Ryan 1998). This is more or less correct. In fact C18 became increasingly infatuated by race war, armed white supremacism and Ulster Loyalism, and its members gradually drifted away from the BNP (especially after the strategic shift in

1994) (see Lowles 2001). Eventually C18 was to implode as a consequence of internecine factional rivalries, state infiltration and, most importantly, the assiduous attention of Anti-Fascist Action/Red Action (see Lowles 2001, Birchall 2011). Eatwell, without providing any evidence, suggests that state infiltration of groups such as C18 and the National Socialist Alliance was designed to elicit information on criminal activity such as drug dealing "rather than to break extremism" (Eatwell 2000 p.185). This may be plausible, but it was not the primary cause of their demise (see note 22 below). In any event C18 failed in its primary political purpose (defence of the BNP) and, having detached itself from its progenitor, became thereafter a repository for an assortment of narcissistic Nazi lunatics. The leader-guard of the master race in Britain effectively degenerated into an infantile drinking club, articulating the impotent, incoherent rage of degenerate Hitlerite fantasists and racist thugs.

[22] This reference appears in a document which was accessed by the author via third party personal contacts, see also Griffin (1996b p.13) where he concludes "we have got better things to do than go looking for trouble". The phrase "drunken red Fenians" derives from the accurate observation that many leading members of the group Red Action were second or third generation Irish and committed, ideological Republicans. The reference to inebriation is, however, inaccurate – Red Action/AFA never permitted excessive drinking on mobilizations. There is little doubt that AFA/Red Action was responsible for the BNP's tactical re-orientation, although Nigel Copsey has claimed that by getting the BNP to alter its strategy and "modernize" it constituted, in effect, a tactical own goal by the anti-fascist activists. As Copsey says "if we accept that this modernization is at least partly responsible for the BNP's rise, it follows that militant anti-fascism, although perhaps successful in the short term, had a deleterious effect over the longer term"

(Copsey 2011 p.136-37, see p.130). Obviously any conclusion on this involves a certain degree of counter-factual conjecture. It is perfectly legitimate to speculate, however, on the possibility that the absence of physical opposition might have afforded the fascists much more room to manouvre and therefore made the BNP's project of street insurrection even more electorally profitable than the current alternative. Here notions of public "space" as a dynamic, contested phenomenon, become particularly pertinent (see Linehan 2012, also Rosenhaft 1983). Who is to say that the BNP would not have secured 50 MPs rather than 50 councillors if their preferred strategy had been left unopposed, without the aggressive attentions of AFA? The burden of proof is surely on the likes of Copsey – not those who shared the council estates with the fascists, who witnessed the nature of their tactics and were aware of the scope of their ambition, and who chose to resist. In a similar vein to Copsey (and others less worthy of mention), Roger Eatwell contends that the idea that street demonstration and violence have been effective in opposing the fascists is a "left-wing myth" (Eatwell 2000 p.179). Given the extremely serious situations which have often prevailed in certain localities when attempting deal with the real presence of fascist groups and their potential to do damage to communities, idle speculation by academic critics, delivered from the safety of their university libraries, lacks some credibility to say the least.

[23] Goodwin's work is worth noting in this regard since he stresses the importance of placing the membership of radical right wing parties at the centre of research because it facilitates a more detailed analysis and challenges certain stereotypes. Thus Goodwin argues that BNP members are not ignorant or poorly educated but "normal" with a desire to uphold democracy, nor are they anti-Semitic or Nazi, but simply concerned about their traditional way of life (see Goodwin 2008).

Goodwin appears to have dismissed the possibility that some individuals from his exceedingly small sample might have been tailoring their ideas to make a good impression. Even if it could be proven conclusively that some members or supporters held opinions at variance to classical fascist ideas it is hardly the point. The core ideology is the essence of the party and provides the ultimate political motivation.

[24] Roger Griffin argues that, although not all the groups are worthy of attention, ignoring this polycentric counter-cultural movements is "analogous to astronomers studying only celestial objects such as galaxies, supernovae and red dwarfs, and ignoring asteroid belts, sub-atomic particles and 'dark' matter" (Griffin 2003 p.29). One does not have to accept the overdrawn positivism of Griffin's methodology to concur with this point, although it has to be said that whilst it is part of an academic's remit to render complex and complicated social reality intelligible, the doyen of fascist studies quite often accomplishes the reverse. Griffin also posits that his "rhizomic groupuscularity" thesis might be applied to left wing groups "in keeping the tradition of revolutionary socialism alive in a democratic era in which the hegemony of capitalism seems unassailable. It certainly promises to produce fresh insights into the power of the al-Qaeda network" (Griffin 2003 not No.5 p.29). Whilst the former point now looks decidedly dated, given the financial collapse of 2008, the latter observation illustrates little more than Griffin's apparently obsessive concern to apply his own "heuristically useful" theoretical paradigms.

[25] In this context it is perhaps worth remembering, for example, that BNP candidate Robert Cottage was convicted of stockpiling explosives in his Lancashire home in 2007.

# 3. INTERPRETATIONS OF FASCISM

O bviously there are a very large number of interpretations and explanations of fascism, a bewildering variety of perspectives in fact (Pearse 2002 p.11). Indeed after many years of academic and scholarly debate about the value of various approaches "the scene resembles a desert battlefield littered with the burnt-out, rusting hulks of failed theories" (Knox 2000 p.56). Yet an appraisal of theory is absolutely crucial in order to facilitate a satisfactory understanding of the fascist phenomenon. Theoretical approaches provide an interpretive prism through which the significance of fascism can be studied and explained, and as we will discover they can be extremely insightful. However, theory is not simply about engaging fascism at a certain level of abstraction and offering analytical observations. The type of theory deployed in analyzing fascism can often contain or reflect much broader normative assumptions about how best to respond, and what specific values to prioritise and preserve in the struggle against fascism. Self-evidently, misreading fascism or producing theory which is opaque or insufficiently robust, can not only diminish our understanding, it can have profound consequences in terms of seriously attenuating the capacity to resist. Hence the interpretations of fascism carry a significance well beyond their actual utility in identifying and analyzing socio-political reality. Getting it right or wrong is not simply a matter of measuring academic competence or gauging competing conceptual paradigms – it is a question of the utmost practical importance.

The most useful approach to examining the competing theories of fascism, given the purpose of this text, is to divide a representative sample into broad categories in order to high-light competing approaches. Naturally these categories are not mutually exclusive or necessarily independent of each other, and such a technique may do an injustice to the complexity of some individual interpretations, but the tactic of taxonomic categorization is useful (indeed unavoidable) given the space available in relation to the quantity of material and the over-riding need to detail and decipher in a concise fashion the relative reliability of respective approaches.

## The "New Consensus": Palingenetic Ultra-Nationalism

The critical starting point for this perspective is the belief that it is necessary to see fascism as it saw itself and as its followers saw it – that is, the movement must be understood "on its own terms" (Mosse 1999 p.x). As George Mosse explained, "only then, when we have grasped fascism from the inside out, can we truly judge its appeal and its power" (Mosse 1999 p.x). Hence a cultural interpretation is crucial because it "opens up a means to penetrate fascist self-understanding, and such empathy is crucial in order to grasp how people saw the move-ment" (Mosse 1999 p.xi). This is a self-consciously cultural approach which focuses on fascism as a "revolutionary" system of beliefs with clearly identifiable objectives.

In many ways Roger Griffin's work on fascism serves as the emblematic epicentre of this particular perspective and Griffin supplies much of the academic literature to sustain its ongoing attraction. The crucial starting point for Griffin is his belief that fascism should be treated on a par with other utopian ideologies and that fascist ideas should be taken seri-ously. Fascism should therefore be accorded full ideological status, as Griffin says, "it should be stressed that fascism's anti-rationalism has not prevented it from producing a vast amount of highly articulate ideological writings, some of them displaying great erudition and theoretical verve" (Griffin 1995 p.6). Ideas are the key to understanding fascism, according to Griffin. Indeed it could even be argued that Griffin has become the (self-appointed) focal point of "fascist studies", the fashionable academic grouping which has provided the dynamic for what he has termed the "new consensus" on what actually constitutes the so-called "fascist minimum". As Griffin explains, "it is just possible that after seven decades in which the only island of agreement about the dynamics of fascism in an ocean of confusion, idiosyncrasy and contradiction was to be found in Marxist territorial waters, an archipelago of consensus may finally be surfacing among non-Marxists as well" (Griffin 1998 p.ix). Griffin argues that his own "attempt at offering a heuristically useful ideal type of fascism" actually "signalled something of a breakthrough in fascist studies" (Griffin 1998 p.13). Thus Griffin's suggestion is that his own work has facilitated the emergence of a new common sense which has evolved by stressing the centrality to fascist ideology of populist myths of national re-birth or regeneration – "palingenesis". Griffin argues that fascist ideology, the mythical core of which is populist, palingenetic ultra-nationalism, is designed to rescue the nation from decadence and decline, and may take a variety of forms according to the specific historical context. This ideology is, critically, anti-liberal, anti-bourgeois, anti-conservative and revolutionary in intent (Griffin 1998 p.3). This idealized explanatory abstraction, Griffin argues, is not an ossified and outmoded conceptual template but a useful scholarly instrument which might be utilized effectively to shed light on the fluid continuity of the fascist phenomenon.

Many of the most prominent scholarly commentators on fascism and the far right in Britain are quite happy to associate themselves explicitly with Griffin's theoretical perspective (see Copsey 2007 p.64, Macklin 2007). Indeed Griffin himself maintains that other theorists, such as Zeev Sternhell, Roger Eatwell, Stanley Payne, Walter Laqueur, Alexander de Grand and Mark Neocleous among others, have delivered definitions "broadly consistent" with his own (Griffin 1998 p.15, see note 45 p.19, and note 47 p.19; see Griffin 2000) although it might be noted that he appears somewhat perturbed by the fact that some theorists appear to distance themselves from his approach whilst apparently deploying the common denominator of its main tenet (see Bosworth 2009 Introduction, Passmore 2002). However, as Roberts et al (2002) have argued, there is a sense in which Roger Griffin has over-sold his perspective and has been far too anxious to portray any idealist or culturalist emphasis as confirmation of consensus (see Roberts et al 2002). At times Griffin has certainly been more equivocal and circumspect about the solidity of his "new consensus", portraying it as a premature attempt to "manufacture" agreement, a programmatic postulation, and a "conciliatory offer", rather than an empirical fact (see Griffin 2002a). Even if we do not accept the notion that Griffin's thesis concerning the "new consensus" actually set out to foster the process of convergence he then claimed to have discovered, and even if we remain ultimately unimpressed by its taxonomic coherence, there is certainly no doubt that Griffin's work has had a major (perhaps even profound) impact upon academic discussion surrounding fascism.

Certainly Griffin's work has distinct parallels with the perpective put forward by Roger Eatwell, another member of what might be termed the "fascism studies" academic establishment. Eatwell argues that fascism cannot be defined simply by reference to the two classic regimes, and that underpinning "stereotypical fascism, defined essentially by its style and negations, lay a coherent body of thought" although "the resulting ideology was elusive because it drew from both the right and left, seeking to create a radical 'Third Way' which was neither capitalist nor communist" (Eatwell 1996 p.xix, 1996b). Hence for Eatwell the "syncretic ideology" of fascism, which focused on the re-birth of the nation and imposing a corporatist socio-economic framework, is more complex and diverse than some accounts suggest and should be taken seriously as such (Eatwell 1996b p.312). Eatwell, however, criticises Griffin's approach because it over-emphasises the importance of myth and confuses propaganda with ideology.

In contrast, Eatwell (1992) advocates a "spectral-syncretic" model in analyzing fascism, which stresses ideology as well as practical policy output, because in practice Hitler and Mussolini distorted or deformed fascism by compromising with conservative elements. Although Eatwell emphasises the vague, inchoate nature of fascist theory, he nevertheless accepts the idea of fascism as a radical new synthesis, a "holistic-national radical Third Way" hostile to both communism and capitalism (Eatwell 1996 p.286, 1996b p.313). Eatwell evidently believes that quasi-Keynesian state intervention in the economy, accompanied by a degree of welfarism and product protectionism, constituted a qualitative departure from capitalism toward social egalitarianism, and he also argues that psychopathology may be as important as ideology in understanding the motivations of certain fascist activists (see Eatwell 1992, Eatwell and O'Sullivan 1989). Crucially Eatwell also questions the adequacy of "left" and "right" terminology when discussing fascism because, he argues, ideologies are multidimensional entities and there is inevitably a degree of synthesis and overlap – in short, fascism cannot be easily or precisely located on the conventional, spatial "left-right" ideological spectrum (Eatwell 1992, see Eatwell 2000 p.179, also see Eatwell and O'Sullivan 1989 where he refers, in this context, to "Marxism's central errors" and "the confusions of social science").

Despite a degree of congruence amongst some analysts regarding the importance of fascist theory and the idea of national palingenesis, the idea that this has produced a "consensus" is perhaps overstated, and it is probably appropriate to remain sceptical about any nascent agreement, even within the relatively restricted realm of "fascist studies" scholars (see Renton 1999 p.19, also Roberts et al 2002). Although there has been a certain synergy and over-lap in some perspectives, the palingenesis national re-birth position never really crystallized into a commonly held thesis. Moreover, Griffin's analysis is very much inferred from a study of what the fascist protagonists actually say themselves, as he explains, "one of my aims in developing my theory was precisely to generate a definition of fascism from the writings of fascists themselves, which they could recognize as valid" (Griffin 1998 note 46 p.19). In effect Griffin attempts to read fascism from the inside, in terms of its own self-understanding (Roberts et 2002 p.259). As a consequence fascist ideology is taken very much at face value while the actual political experience and social context of fascism is downgraded. However, the fact is that ideas and idealism on their own can generate nothing, they are not free floating in the ideological ether, they are related to structures and processes rooted in society. To ignore the reality of social context, and the power relations contained therein, can fatally distort and destroy the value of an overall interpretation. At its worst such a textual approach to the study of fascism can degenerate into a rather distasteful exercise in discourse analysis. As we have seen, to take the written or spoken word of fascists without examining explicitly the experience of fascist praxis and the social conditions which created it, risks being distracted by the ambitious architectural blueprints of a few ideologues which, in some cases, bore very little resemblance to the structure that was eventually constructed. Indeed, extrapolating from what exists of the ideological content in the early stages of a fascist movement, in order to try and identify its precise nature, risks major misinterpretation – it might seem logical to extrapolate from a tadpole and identify a whale, but a closer, more careful inspection of biological reality will actually reveal a frog.

It might also be added, with regard to the concept of palingenesis, it is not entirely clear that other important ideologies exclude the idea of populist ultra-nationalism. For example, various anti-colonial movements, which could not be described as fascist in any meaningful sense, adopted policies and programmes which might be identified as "palingenetic", and even moderate conservatives have been tempted by the rhetoric of renewal (Renton 1999 p.26). Hence Griffin's flimsy effort to impose his explanatory framework on the Provisional IRA (with its aim of Irish unity) may be quite logical from his theoretical perspective, but is entirely unconvincing (Griffin 1993 p.177). The desire for self-determination, independence and national liberation or "re-birth" are not necessarily fascist traits. Indeed, it is possible to argue that radical forms of fascism, like Nazism, were "internationalist" in intent (rather than purely "nationalist"), given their favourable predisposition toward all Aryan peoples as a racial category that transcended borders. On the other hand, even if we accept a degree of palingenetic purpose in fascism, it might be argued that the project failed abysmally. Lofty ideas about regeneration and renewal might be construed as part of an elaborate mythology, but rather than a national "re-birth", fascism was in fact mid-wife to an abortion (see De Grand in Roberts et al 2002 p.266). And then there is the critical issue of who benefitted from fascism – obviously of less concern to those infatuated by ideological rhetoric, but absolutely crucial for any real understanding of how and why fascism emerges, its ultimate political purpose and its social significance (see later).

It has also been persuasively argued that although the new consensus may not imply sympathy for fascist ideas, the perspective does lack an appropriately developed critical dimension (Renton 1999 p.28-29, Renton 1999a). As Renton has said, the danger of this academic approach to fascism "lies in the path it treads from an idealist definition of fascism to a positive description of fascism" (Renton 1999a p.25). This may be no part of their intention (as Griffin makes clear in his acrimonious rebuttal of Renton), but the actual effect of such a re-calibration of focus toward ideas and culture has the inevitable consequence of downplaying the dark side of fascism (see Griffin 1999a). The "new consensus" (such as it is) does not focus enough on the importance of socio-economic context (and the compromises it necessitates), it exaggerates theoretical coherence of fascist ideas, and it does not deal adequately with the actual effects of fascist practice. De-emphasizing practice and exaggerating revolutionary rhetoric (much of which was demagogic posturing) and culture, can lead to a distinctly partial, if not distorted, account. The danger is that by placing "palingenesis" front-centre as the core factor explaining fascism, and relegating structural socio-economics to contingency, not only reduces the study of fascism to an analysis of culture and ideas, it effectively puts the cart before the horse. There is also a sense in which the "over-heated introspection" of "fascist studies" gives disproportionate weight to peripheral fascist movements that were "marginal", "mimetic" and "downright insignificant" (Blinkhorn 2004 p.523 and p.524). We might also flag up at this stage that certain subsidiary assumptions by advocates of this culturalist perspective are also questionable – such as the notion that the "left-right" ideological spectrum should be abandoned (Eatwell), and the idea that fascism was "revolutionary" and fundamentally anti-conservative (Griffin) – both claims will be dealt with subsequently.

Therefore any meaningful insights derived from the "new consensus" perspective must be weighed against the obvious limitations of its conceptual frame of reference – in essence the "new consensus" raises as many questions as it answers, obscuring as much as it reveals. The "new consensus" is clearly not as coherent, or "heuristically useful" as Griffin and the others would like to think. As Martin Blinkhorn has suggested, the best approach here is to acknowledge that which is useful and interesting in the Griffin-inspired "fascist studies" ultra-nationalist, populist-palingenesis thesis, but realize the limitations of this particular "ideal type" explanation by accepting and emphasizing the importance of what lies beyond its scope (Blinkhorn 2004).

Of course it might be mentioned that many other contemporary analysts have made noble individual efforts to provide a definition of fascism which relate to some extent to the "new consensus", and some indeed are quite useful. For example, the work of Robert O. Paxton is worthy of note, and he has suggested that "fascism might be defined as a form of political behavior marked by obsessive preoccupation with community decline, humiliation or victimhood and by compensatory cults of unity, energy and purity, in which a mass based party of committed nationalist militants, working in uneasy but effective collaboration with traditional elites, abandons democratic liberties and pursues with redemptive violence, and without legal restraints, goals of internal cleansing and external expansion" (Paxton 2009 p.549 see Paxton 2005 Chapter 8 p.206). Self-evidently this formulation has some considerable merit, although very often the contemporary definitions given of fascism are distinctly descriptive and static – those in pursuit of a genuine "explanation" have to look further afield because describing what a political phenomenon actually "is" is not always the same as explaining "how" or, more importantly, "why".

## Psychology as the Critical Component

One of the more interesting "schools of thought" to grapple with the fascist phenomenon is what might be termed the "psychological" perspective, which has produced numerous insights into the fascist experience. Whether this constitutes a psychological analysis of the fascist leader, or a more general psychological evaluation of the society at large, or both, there are many analysts who see psychology as an indispensible instrument for a satisfactory explanation of fascism. As Kitchen correctly pointed out, "the sadistic behaviour of fascist gangs, the extraordinary mass hysteria generated by fascist rulers and the apparently pathological conduct of many fascist leaders seemed to be such striking characteristics of the fascist regimes that it was widely assumed that psychology was the only discipline capable of providing an adequate explanation of fascism" (Kitchen 1982 p.12).

Orthodox psychological interpretations have tended to concentrate on the fascist leaders (see Baker 1986 p.3-12), indeed numerous interpretive accounts of fascism argue that the personality traits, if not the pathological insanity, of the particular fascist leader is an indispensible explanatory factor. For example, such accounts may imply an innate genocidal consciousness on the part of Hitler, or might emphasise Mussolini's neurotic psyche and his will to power as satisfying some deep-seated psychological need. Many analysts seem comfortable using, at least in part, psychological categories and interpretations with regard to the fascist leaders. Ernst Nolte for instance emphasizes Hitler's psycho-pathological nature as an important variable in understanding fascism. According to Nolte Hitler's "infantilist", "mediumistic" and "monomaniacal" characteristics were a key to his, and National Socialism's, success, and "combined they raised him for a brief time to be lord and master of his troubled era" (Nolte 1969 p.372). Similarly, prominent German political scientist and historian Karl Dietrich Bracher also refers to "psychohistory" in the context of Hitler's sexual perversions and mother trauma (see Bracher in Laqueur 1982 p.206). Even some of the more complex, sophisticated and nuanced biographical accounts acknowledge the significance of a psychological dimension. For example, the most accomplished biography of Hitler, by Ian Kershaw, focuses some attention on the dictator's "extraordinary psychological make up" and the narcissism which precipitated a calamitous over-estimation of his own capacities (Kershaw 2009 p.512). As Kershaw explains, "not just external circumstances, but his own personal psyche, pushed him forwards, compelled the risk", and ultimately, of course, all of Germany shared in Hitler's "hubris", which was a prelude to experiencing the ultimate "nemesis" (Kershaw 2009 p.513).

Yet it is also possible to identify far more bizarre tributaries which feed into the burgeoning stream of the psychological perspective. For example Gonen (2000) in applying Freudian psychoanalytical postulates to Nazi ideas, maintains that the emphasis on German unity reflected a desire to retrieve the omnipotence of early infancy when "sheer willing by itself materialized results" (Gonen 2000 p.177). In this sense some aspects of Nazi ideology "can therefore be seen as contemporary political derivatives of infantile psychology" (Gonen 2000 p.177). The Germans, according to Gonen, embraced "psychogeographic solutions to identity conflicts", suffered from a paranoid "sickness phobia" and had, ultimately, lost touch with themselves (see Gonen 2000 p.176 and p.178-79). From Gonen's perspective, Nazism could be explained with reference to an an unusual "psychological blend" between anal and oral "national characteristics" and an ideology which articulated the emotional drives embedded deep within the human psyche – the Nazi's wanted to "eat territories and shit Jews" (Gonen 2000 p.203, see p.205-206).

Of course, much of the psychological attention has been focused, perhaps unsurprisingly, on Hitler himself. Tales of paranoia, manic depression, a craving for recognition, fractious relationships with paternal authority, fear of failure, and/ or a troubled family life have all featured in some accounts. Indeed many good trees have been sacrificed to produce a veritable torrent of tenuous psycho-analyses that have doubtless been extremely lucrative for publishers, given the apparently insatiable interest in the subject area. For example Raymond de Saussure emphasised the Fuhrer as a phallic force, with an authoritarian father ensuring homosexual inclinations and an Oedipus complex, whilst Hitler's general sexual inadequacy (the absence of a testicle) are seen as the motivating force behind his desire for dictatorship (see de Saussure 1943, also Mosse 1979a p.36). Robert Waite (1978) in his study, revealingly entitled *The Psychopathic God Adolf Hitler*, argues that Hitler was mentally deranged, and that his psychological disposition is the key factor in explaining National Socialism (see Thurlow 1980 p.7). Waite deconstructs Hitler's personality in detail and identifies an array of Oedipal conflicts and displacements, along with an insecurity about his own ancestry, which led him to "prove" his racial incorrubtibility by instigating genocide (Waite 1978, Marrus 1993 p.16).

To take another example, Rudolf Binion, in deploying his "psycho-historical" approach, argued that Hitler suffered from a "castration complex" which was symbolized by his temporary blindness during the war (Binion 1976 p.131). According to Binion Hitler was pampered at the breast, harboured a deep animus toward his father, and eroticized his mission to protect ("mother") the German people (see Binion 1976). More specifically Binion attempted to relate Hitler's hatred of the Jews to the fact that his mother was treated by a Jewish doctor shortly before she died. Thereafter a deep hatred toward the Jews was sublimated, only to be released subsequently in an explosion of anti-semitic rage (Binion 1976, see Rosenbaum 1998 p.240). Unable to assimilate his traumatic experience, Hitler's anti-Semitism "was a reaction against the guilt for his mother's agony of 1907...that reaction, long repressed, was released by a gas poisoning reminiscent of his mother's agony" (Binion 1976 p.35). Interestingly Cohn-Sherbok also develops the same theme, suggesting that "in 1907 Hitler's mother was diagnosed as dying of incurable cancer, and her doctor, Dr. Eduard Bloch, a Jewish physician, recommended an iodoform treatment. This was a costly and painful procedure...it may be that this early event in Hitler's life set in motion his deep-seated animosity to Jews" (Cohn-Sherbok 1999 p.34). Cohn-Sherbok claims that some observers have noted the similarity between the powerful and foul-smelling iodoform and the mustard gas which temporarily blinded Hitler in 1918 – hence he not only re-lived his mother's untimely demise but made the causal connection between Judaism and capitulation in the war. The conclusion that the poisoners should themselves be poisoned constitutes a convoluted but deeply inter-connected sequence of events, leading to the inescapable desire to exact revenge for both the death of his mother and the defeat of the Father-land (Cohn-Sherbok 1999 p.34).

Similar arguments can be made in relation to the contention that Hitler's apparent psychological derangement derived from the fact that four members of the committee that denied him entry into art school were Jewish (see Gluckstein 1999 p.23). Hence Hitler's political career is seen as an instru-mental effort to come to terms with any number of painful past experiences, such as the death of his mother, defeat in war, or indeed the inability to sustain a lasting relation-ship with a woman (see Marrus 1993 p.16, Hildebrand 1985 p.122). Much has even been made of Hitler's personal traits, such as: his fastidious obsession with cleanliness; his aversion to, or fondness for, certain foods (meat on the one hand, cake and chocolate on the other); hypochondria (including constipation and an ability to withstand pain – he declined anesthetic when undergoing dental treatment); his inability to forge lasting bonds of friendship; his long spells of disorganized, indisciplined indolence; and, of course, his spectacular tantrums (see Welch 1998 p.6-7, Stone p.85). Yet as Geary correctly points out – in none of this can be found any real evidence of clinical madness (see Geary 1994 p.8-9). Despite all the strenuous efforts to attach psychoses, and the mountain of minutiae dredged up by assiduous archivists, it appears that Hitler was, rather unhelpfully, not a lunatic. This has not prevented people from pursuing the more extraordinary pathways of personality disorder.

If we expand theme of psycho-dynamics even further and drill downward into personal motivations, we discover Kimberley Cornish in *The Jew of Linz* apparently attempting to "explain" Hitler's anti-semitism as a consequence of his envy of a wealthy and gifted Jewish pupil who attended the same school between 1904-05, namely Ludwig Wittgenstein (see Neville 1999 p.10). Thus the existence of the Third Reich and genocide is somehow conflated with the acting out of Hitler's innate impulses, which were triggered by a childhood jealousy. According to Neville, "some so-called 'psych-historians' have sought an explanation for Hitler's racism in his sexuality. His constant reference to Jews as 'seducers' of 'innocent German maidens' have suggested that Hitler may have contracted syphilis in his youth or undergone an unfortunate sexual experience. Alternatively, Hitler's difficult relationship with his father, or his key relationship with his mother, Klara, have been blamed for his latent, obsessive racism" (Neville 1999 p.12). It has even been argued that fascism can be explained in terms of the leader's lack of self-esteem, impotency, his disfigured genetalia, predisposition for necrophilia, syphilitic psychosis, excretory sexual perversion or the desire to satisfy anal erotic urges (see Rosenbaum 1998 and Stern 1975 p.17).

Interestingly, Norman Stone's biography contains several references to Hitler's lack of sexual experience, his unease about his own masculinity (including the unusually low level of the testis hormone in his blood) and indeed Hitler's "latent homosexuality" which was, according to Stone, reflected in Hitler's choice of "statuesquely handsome uniformed blond adjutants" (Stone 1992 p.21-22 and p.41). The precise relevance of these speculative observations is not adequately explained although Stone tells us, quite helpfully, that "no-one knows what went on inside Hitler's head" (Stone 1992 p.33). Some commentators have even sought answers to Hitler's psyche in his art work, although McDonough informs us that "art experts have suggested Hitler's style of painting does not reveal any deep psychological difficulty, certainly no psycho-pathic tendencies…his tendency to paint buildings is viewed as the product of an introverted personality, not deep mental difficulties" (McDonough 1999 p.5). It is perhaps fortunate for us all that Hitler's water-colours were unspectacular and conventional, if he had painted "the scream" (Edvard Munch), the consequences in terms of the output of puerile psycho-babble would have been incalculable.

Much of this material is, of course, constructed upon apochryphal "evidence" or the consequence of pure conjec-ture, amounting to little more than retrospective guesswork on a grandiose scale. Even if the facts could be incontrovert-ibly established, it is not clear how this emphasis on individual psychological idiosyncracies or personal peccadilloes could possibly *explain* fascism. If it was possible to prove beyond all possible doubt that Hitler had one testicle, or made Geli Raubal urinate on him for his own sexual gratification, would that particular variable make a critical difference to the overall explanation of fascism? It might stimulate Freudians into a frenzy of analysis, but it is unlikely to provide any clues beyond the illumination of basic sexual pathology and personal inter-relationships. Freakish abnormality in one person cannot explain fascism, or any phenomenon of a significant socio-political magnitude - focusing on Hitler's scrotal sack might be fascinating for some analysts, but it is fruitless as a means of finding deeper meaning. As Kershaw has correctly pointed out "of course personality counts in historical explanation. It would be foolish to suggest otherwise" (Kershaw 2009 p.xxvii) but personalities, no-matter how great, grotesque or charismatic, are not omnipotent – they make history, but not in the social circumstances of their own choosing.

Also psychology-based are the numerous accounts which stress the mental attitude and condition of the masses and their peculiar receptivity to the fascist message. There is a kind of logic to this approach, for as Albert Einstein noted in 1933, fascism seemed to constitute a "'psychic illness of the masses'" (cited in Friedlander 2009 p.3). Also in 1933 Harold Lasswell's thoughtful account spoke, more specifically, of how the Nazi's fulfilled a deep psychological need amongst the insecure and emotionally fragile lower middle classes, providing them with new targets for aggression and objects of devotion. Lasswell even speculated that focusing on an ancient religious scapegoat somehow expiated feelings of guilt for a general lack of personal piety, the Jew was therefore sacrificed in a cleansing gesture which reflected an aspiration for a feeling of moral worth (see Lasswell 1933 p.375 and p.378). Politics becomes in this context "a form of social therapy for potential suicides" (Laswell 1933 p.380). Emphasis here is often upon the conjunction of certain factors which conspired to produce a kind of collective neurosis amongst the masses, a psychotropic hysteria induced amongst the population by the use of certain techniques which facilitated communal seduction. Kornhauser for instance (*The Politics of Mass Society* 1959) saw fascism as a phenomenon symptomatic of a pervasive malaise in the structure of society itself (see King 1977 p.196). The significance of tribal instincts, group aggression and the desire to engage in hero-worship by the multitudes are emphasised in some cases - here fascism acts as a stimulant to satisfy collective psychological requirements.

Here there is a clear connection to the gloomy prophets of mass society who predicted the demise of civilization, drowned in the irrational and brutal impulses of the multitudes. The majority of the population, atomized and alienated in their newly industrialized urban sprawls, deprived of the primary ties of the old feudal order (community, church, family etc) embraced fascism in an attempt to overcome their isolation and insecurity. Indeed it might be argued that one of fascism's fundamental insights was to recognize that people want to "belong" and to be rescued from their "'desolate emptiness'" (see Fest 1973 p.428, Goebbels cited in Fest 1973 p.425). As Konrad Heiden admitted, "'even the devil is preferable to the emptiness of an existence that lacked larger significance'" (cited in Stern 1975 p.164). Fascism is thus seen as the result of the heightened psychological susceptibility of the masses to integrative appeals, and the desire to recreate a sense of belonging and community. Other psychology-based accounts, such as Wilhelm Reich's *The Mass Psychology of Fascism* (1933) (Reich 1997, see Griffin 1995 p.274) have also attempted to explain how and why people succumbed to the lure fascism (see Taylor 1985 p.205-6). Reich, in utilizing elements of Freudian psychoanalysis, insisted on the central role of sexual inhibition and repression in generating fanaticism and destruction (see Griffin 1995 p.274). Indeed Reich saw fascism as a response to the crises of sexuality and family, a way of resisting the new permissiveness and freedom in the sexual realm and fascism was thus considered to be a sado-masochistic response to the disruption of traditional modes of behaviour (see Renton 1999 p.80). According to Reich mankind was "biologically sick" and "politics is the irrational social expression of this sickness" indeed "the suppression of the natural sexuality of children and adolescents serves to mold the human structure in such a way that masses of people become willing upholders and reproducers of mechanistic authoritarian civilization" (Reich 1997 p.322). Mankind, in having lost "the sensation of his organs", has lost "the ability to react naturally" indeed has "replaced the natural self-regulatory intelligence of the body plasma by a goblin in the brain" (Reich 1997 p.343).

To take another specific example, Erick Erikson saw fascism as a kind of masculine adolescent rebellion caused by an infantile rejection of the father and a deep ambivalence toward the mother (Erikson 1942). Here Peter Nathan developed a similar theme in arguing that fascist "revolutionaries" in "over-valuing masculinity" and "fearing weakness", were often "the product of a particular kind of marriage: the marriage of a refined and 'good' mother, whom the child always idolizes, and of a tough boorish, unrefined and usually drunken, bullying father" (Nathan 1943 p.52-3 and p.43). Nathan also saw fascism as a means of overcoming a national inferiority complex and the terrifying fear of lonliness (see Nathan 1943 p.96), a feature which was explored in greater detail by Erich Fromm. In fact Fromm's *The Fear of Freedom* (1942), which unites psycho-analytical and Marxist approaches, is generally considered to be one of the more thoughtful expositions of such ideas (Griffin 1995 p.275). Fromm locates the basis of fascism in a pervasive fear of isolation, powerlessness, symbiotic sado-masochism and the identification between dictatorial leader and compliant subjects eager to "follow orders" (see Fromm 1942, Gregor 2000 p.42). Fascism, for Fromm, provided temporary emotional satisfaction and a feeling of superiority which compensated people for the fact that their lives had been culturally and economically impoverished (see Fromm 1942 p.190). In effect modern freedom was so frightening that fascism's followers sought comfort in submission, and in subordinating themselves to authoritarianism the masses were thereby relieved of the pain and powerlessness of being themselves (Fromm 1942, see Griffin 1993 p.191). In a similar vein T.W. Adorno and others in 1950 produced what they termed as the "F" scale in an attempt to expose the basic "authoritarian personality" and the authoritarian character of the masses, as the key to fascism. Those individuals inclined toward obedience obviously supported the Nazis, and were therefore seen as the cause of the Nazi triumph. Social determinants were not simply downgraded, they were discounted as Adorno's team divided the world into proto-Nazis and victims by virtue of personality (see Bauman 1991 p.152-53). Meanwhile, Klaus Theweleit, utilising the work of Reich and Fromm, identified a fascist disposition rooted more specifically in the authoritarian socialization of the middle classes - only the discipline of coercive institutions like the military could attempt to control the chaotic ego, and the manner of violent outbursts was, he argued, conditioned by this unstable psychological disposition  (see Peukert 1987 p.34).

It is interesting to note that even some prominent contemporary academics have incorporated psycho-analytical themes to explain the attraction of fascism. For example, Roger Griffin's approach delves into the socio-psychological in the sense that he spends some time examining the human impulse toward self-transcendence. Griffin's effort to apply a "syncretic amplification" of Koestler's theory, which emphasizes the significance of the "archicortex" and the "phylogenetically older animal brain" in the limbic system, along with his focus on paranoid and delusional pathology, the mobilisation of irrational drives and the structural defects in the neurology of the brain, provides Griffin's thesis with a discernible psychology-based dimension (Griffin 1993 p.186). The national myth of re-birth, in certain circumstances, apparently satisfies the need for self-transcendence. The lure of psychology is, it seems, difficult to resist.

However, "scholars should be careful when labelling individuals as psychologically or criminally motivated in their political choices. Unless an individual is demonstrably unstable or insane, personality is best treated as an important but not decisive factor in the development of social and political prejudices. Under most circumstances personality should be viewed as an historical and social process..." (Baker 1986 p.7). The interactions between psyche and external social reality, although often intrinsically interesting, are far too complex to succumb to over-simplified generalization, and conclusions can often degenerate into facile speculation. Of course if we accept that inherited traits have no unique explanatory importance we have to accept the painful fact that not all fascists and/or fascist sympathisers are psychopathic deviants, and may in fact be quite "normal" (see Billig 1978 p.31). The plain fact is that fascists are made rather than born. It is perhaps true that those interpretations of mass, rather than individual, psychology have more to offer in terms of explaining fascism, but they too tend to break down in comparative analysis. For example, if mass alienation and atomism are crucial variables it is difficult to see why no fascist movement of significance has emerged in the United States. While all these and other accounts are correct to utilize psychology in the examination of fascism (with regard to individual or group), when used in isolation such approaches cannot fully "explain" fascism, although they can and do provide telling insights (see Carr 1978). As Carr commented, "imperfect as the tools at our disposal are, there may be some merit in making tentative suggestions about the possible balance between personality and the totality of the historical situation" (Carr 1978 p.14). However, orthodox psycho-analytical approaches which use psychological techniques in isolation, without reference to other social forces, can only lead to a partial analysis and an incomplete picture: at worst the conclusions drawn can be absurd (see Kitchen 1982). In short, the psychosis-sanity axis can be easily over-drawn, and history is not made by the genitals alone.

## Theology and the Resonance of the Religious Signifier

Although perhaps not attracting widespread academic endorsement it is as well to acknowledge, at this point, what might be termed the "theological" interpretation of fascism, and there are a number of possible dimensions to this. As Stackelberg says of Nazism "early histories of the Third Reich tended to treat Nazism as a mysterious pathology, the incarnation of an evil force that ultimately could only be accounted for metaphysically, as if the devil had directly intervened in human affairs" (Stackelberg 1999 p.2). According to the likes of Jacques Maritain, history simply records a cosmic Manichean struggle between the forces of "good" and "evil" and fascism fits clearly and neatly into this template (see O'Sullivan 1983 p.24). As Yehuda Bauer has pointed out, Christian and Jewish theologians, such as Eliezer Berkovits, Irving Greenberg, Franklin H. Littell and Gregory Baum have, to varying degrees, seen fascism and the Holocaust as the direct consequence of human evil (see Cesarani 1996). Bauer himself has described Hitler as "'near ultimate evil'" (cited in Rosenbaum 1998 p.282) and there are obviously echoes of Hannah Arendt's work on the "banality of evil" in these interpretations. In fact Berel Lang has suggested that the Nazi's, despite the idealistic rhetoric of righteousness and sacred mission, and irrespective of the medical metaphors about eradicating a virus or infection, actually knew that their actions were fundamentally immoral because they made such a sustained effort to keep them secret (see Rosenbaum 1998 p.210-11). Hence Hitler, portrayed as saviour, saint or virologist was just a deception, a mask of rectitude to conceal the reality of absolute evil. The devil's most cunning trick, of course, was to convince people he did not exist. Indeed Lang argues further that the Nazis were not only conscious of their evil, they turned it into an art form – their purpose was to knowingly execute and relish in their nefarious misdeeds (see Rosenbaum 1998 p.214). The orchestra playing at the death camp becomes, in this scenario, an act of imaginative cruelty, part of a vile aesthetic of diabolical wickedness. Emil Fackenheim even suggests that Hitler's demonic depravity was so "radical", and of such a magnitude, that it actually defies human explanation – it is only fathomable by God (see Rosenbaum 1998 p.xiv, see Tismaneanu 2012). This is a perspective which emphasizes the identification of the "cloven hoof", the Fascist as "fallen", the Nazi as Iago.

Of course few humans fall into the category of actually knowing or believing they are evil, or resolve to press on regardless with what are self-evidently "evil" acts, fully conscious of their own willful malevolence. Moreover, all of this raises disturbing questions for theologians about Deity and the nature of omnipotence. If God knew and understood, why did he refuse to intervene? If he could have done so but chose not to, what does that say about the purpose of his divinity? Given the nature of fascism and, more specifically, the Holocaust, is it possible to conceive of God as all powerful *and* just? Yehuda Bauer has wrestled with these theological issues and his comments on the utility of religion (regarding the Holocaust specifically) are of broader significance – it is, in effect, a fascinating dead-end (Bauer 2001 p.212). Unfortunately theology thesis does not appear to be providing many answers, and if God knows he (she) isn't telling!

There are also those that argue, more prosaically, that the diminution in the influence of formal religion organized through the established churches somehow created a space which could be filled by particularly immoral political movements. "Among the original representatives of this view were Eric Voegelin and Gerhard Ritter, who both argued that Nazism had been primarily a moral disease originating in the Enlightenment, and who both prescribed a simple 'return' to Christian values as the best antidote" (Steigmann-Gall 2005 p.83). Indeed some accounts, which emphasize the centrality of "religion", actually perceive fascism as the logical consequence of a Godless society. Put simply, progressive secularization of society resulted in the diminution of the forces of light and created an imbalance in favour of the darker, more sinister elements. This led inexorably to the erosion of traditional Judeo-Christian moral standards and, ultimately, to the political success of the anti-Semitic, anti-Christian pagan empire(s). Of course the fly in the ointment for this theory resides in the fact that in practice many fascists remained committed Christians (including members of the SS) and the attitude of the churches was not uniformly hostile (to say the least). Certainly it is difficult to square fascist ideology with Christian ethics, but it is far from clear that the absence of Christianity and secularization somehow "explains" the rise of fascism. If this approach is designed to help us explain the success of fascism in some countries rather than others, it is necessary to prove that the ontological crisis was more acute in Germany and Italy than in, for example, the United States or France. This is deeply problematic and difficult to prove. Given the intractable nature of the difficulties involved here in trying to encapsulate fascism with reference to divinity and the simplistic dichotomies of "good" and "evil", or as a consequence of vaguely defined demonic conspiracies, the discussion of the validity of these particular perspectives is perhaps best postponed until the life hereafter.

However, there are those who refuse to relinquish the religious signifier when analyzing fascism and, perhaps more plausibly, see the movement as providing a kind of secular, ersatz religion. There is a debate amongst exponents as to whether political religion can be defined as a functional equivalent to religion or as a full religion in a phenomeno-logical sense. Phillipe Burrin, for his part, has argued that the adjective is more important than the noun (Burrin 1997 p.326). Burrin has therefore reiterated the enduring utility of the concept of political religion because, in the midst of the void left by religion, the emotions of exaltation and rever-ence, so typical of religion, were transposed upon secular political objects – thus a new "omni-politics" led inexorably toward the suppression of traditional religions as competitor faiths, despite the fact that the fascists shamelessly plagiarized certain components from Christianity (Burrin 1997 p.327-28).

Emilio Gentile has been a prominent contemporary expo-nent of this type of perspective, describing Italian Fascism as a "political religion" (Gentile 1990). Gentile has argued that Fascism, whilst not being "theological" in a conventional sense, facilitated the "sacrilisation of politics" (Gentile 1990 p.229). In fact "fascist religion placed itself alongside traditional reli-gion, and tried to syncretize it with its own sphere of values as an ally in the subjection of the masses to the state" (Gentile 1990 p.230). According to Gentile Italian Fascism developed the contribution made by the likes of Gabriele D'Annunzio, with his emphasis on martyrdom, sacrifice and purification.

Fascism deployed similar religious metaphors, myths, symbols and rituals in an effort to evoke a sense of identity and, ultimately, re-mould the soul of the Italian people (Gentile 1990 p.234-35). Mussolini did describe Fascism as "'a religious concept of life'" (cited in Gentile 1990 p.235) and Emilio Gentile maintains that "faith" was a key word for Fascists, indeed in the final analysis "culture and intelligence counted for less than commitment to the dogma of fascist religion" (Gentile 1990 p.238). The recent archival research of Christopher Duggan would tend to underscore this observation, indeed he stresses the importance of carefully choreographed religious and spiritual language and practice in securing the emotional attachment of many ordinary people to the regime (see Duggan 2013 p.51-52, p.104).

Similar observations have been made with regard to Nazism. In 1939 Carl Jung suggested that Hitler might be founding a new Islam, with Germany "'drunk with a wild god'" (cited in Burrin 1997 p.346 note No.32), and the religious motif in Nazism has sustained comparisons ever since. For example William Carr suggested that there was real value in the contention that Nazism was only really intelligible in terms of a pseudo-religious dimension (see Carr 1978 p.5). Interestingly, Michael Burleigh (2000, 2001) has also stressed the notion of Nazism as a substitute religion (see Passmore 2002 p.20). According to Burleigh fascism was the calamitous consequence of moral collapse and barbarism, it was an "assault on decency" perpetrated by ideological zealots intent on creating a sacralised political system based on "faith, hope, hatred and a sentimental self-regard for their own race and nation" (Burleigh 2001 p6 and p.1). Armed with their substitute, caricature religion, false messiah and pseudo-liturgies the Nazis, according to Burleigh, induced paroxysms of rapture and engineered a metaphysical, emotional engagement with the masses which prioritized fanatical faith, obedience, anger and self-pity, at the expense of the "customary politics of decency, pragmatism, property and reason" (Burleigh 2001 p.8). Indeed the Nazis, Burleigh argues, offered an eschatologically redemptive political religion which "sank a drillhead into a deep-seated reservoir of existential anxiety, offering salvation from an ontological crisis" (Burleigh 2001 p.255) [1].

Others have developed a similar theme suggesting that fascism satisfies the same psychological impulses which seek certainty, meaning and ritual in an unstable social environment. In this sense fascism might be seen as an ideology "with an extra ingredient" (see Gentile 2005 p.69). Fascism, by sacralizing the state and national community with supreme ethical, suprahuman significance produces "a symbology and liturgy certainly shaped by and articulated through the legacy of Christian discourse, but not descended from it 'genealogically'" (Griffin 2005a p.15-16). Along with others, Roger Griffin has evidently become more sympathetic to the heuristic value contained within the idea of a secular "political religion" separate from the traditional religious institutions rooted in society (see Griffin 2005, Linehan 2005 and Gentile 2005) [2]. Faith in fascism is seen as a matter of religious reverence as much as political predisposition. Of course, as we have noted (see earlier), the identification of fascism as having some kind of religious or spiritual dimension is something that the fascist movements themselves were anxious to convey and exploit.

However, although some have argued that the decline of religious values opens a space that can be occupied by pseudo-religions or political religions like Fascism and Nazism, "the principal weakness of this argument is that Germans and Italians had become more detached from traditional religious faith by 1920 than the French or British" (Paxton 2009 p.556). It could also be pointed out that pre-existing socio-cultural and political ties to established religion provided an obstacle to fascist success, and this is perhaps an easier point to sustain than the suggestion that the absence of transcendental monotheism or the structural manifestations of worship, somehow precipitates fascism. It might also be noted, as Mann does, that "fascism was too this-worldly and too instrumental really to be a religion" (Mann 2004 p.99). Fascism wanted to instill faith in its political project, and ransacked religious techniques in the process of attempting to secure this objective, but there was very little offered in the way of spirituality. Yet the idea of fascism as a political religion per se, as a route to individual or collective (rather than spiritual) transcendence, or as a repository of blind faith does, nevertheless, offer some clues as to the attraction of fascism in particular socio-economic contexts – but analysis of that said context is absolutely critical for a satisfactory explanation (as we shall see). It might also be added finally that the exponents of the "political religion" thesis, from Eric Voegelin and Pierre Sironneau onwards, have often been anxious to equate the fascist experience with Communism as a similarly "resentful", "apolcalyptic" and "utopian" ideology with religious pretentions (see Burleigh 2000 p.13, p.21 and p.23-24, see Burrin 1997). Which brings us neatly into the antechamber of the next "explanation" of the fascist experience to be considered - totalitarianism.

## Totalitarian Theory: The Decaying Corpse of Cold War Ideology

The phrase "totalitarian" was actually used by fascists quite frequently themselves to describe their own regimes, and it appears that Mussolini first used the term in a speech delivered on 5 January 1925 (see Eatwell 1996 p.57). Referring to the aspiration of a "total", unifying social and political transformation, this label has also been deployed subsequently by a significant range of scholars in order to examine and explain fascism's monopolistic control of political power (see Gentile 2002). However, the emergence of "totalitarian theory" in its most developed form was itself the product of a particular conjunction of factors after 1945, specifically the pervasive fear of Communism in the West and the Cold War.

The "totalitarian" theory became extremely popular in the immediate post-war period and, with various modifications, can still count on attracting some endorsement in academic circles. Many analysts, such as Sternhell, Bullock, Germino, Hildebrand, Talmon, Weber, Seton Watson, Krejci, Kedward,

Passmore, Pollard, Gentile and many others have adopted the language of totalitarianism to a greater or lesser degree [3]. The original pioneers of the "totalitarian" perspective tended to stress the notion of a monolithic state and a fanatical mass movement brainwashed by party ideology and this model, it was argued, could also be applied with equal accuracy to Communist systems of rule. In fact several observers had identified, at an early stage, an apparent similarity between Bolshevism and fascism, such as Luigi Sturzo, and Francesco Nitti who suggested in the 1920s that both ideological systems were based on similar principles (see Burleigh and Wipperman 1991 p.9). The essence of what became the "totalitarian" theory therefore developed from some of these rudimentary observations about the commonality between apparently contradictory ideologies.

In fact the "totalitarian" theory itself is perhaps most closely identified with work of Carl J. Friedrich whose six-point syndrome became the basis upon which the totalitarian explanation was constructed. Totalitarianism, he argued, was a system of rule qualitatively different from any in the historical experience of repressive, tyrannical and despotic governments. The six distinguishing features of totalitarian regimes were, he suggested (i) an elaborate, universal, official ideology (ii) a single mass party led by one man, superior to, or intertwined in, the government bureaucracy (iii) the use of terror by the party/regime (iv) monopolistic control of the mass media (v) the monopoly of weaponry (vi) central control of the economy (see Friedrich and Brzezinski 1965 p.21). These factors, it was argued, were equally applicable to both communist and fascist systems of rule, and it was the idea of this inner kinship between the two systems which was central to the totalitarian thesis [4]. As Freidrich and Brzezinski confirm, "...from all the facts available ... fascist and communist totalitarian dictatorships are basically alike ... that is to say in terms of structure, institutions and processes of rule" (Friedrich and Brzezinski 1965 p.15 and p.19). Both types of regime adapted autocracy to the conditions of the twentieth century, which made them absolutely inimical to human freedom, and both represented a distinct contrast to conventional western "constitutional" systems (Friedrich and Brzezinski 1965 p.20).

Others adapted and developed this theory, such as Schapiro (1972) who outlined the enduring value of the totalitarian argument, albeit in a marginally modified form, whilst many other academics subsequently embraced the concept more implicitly by accepting many of its core assumptions. Gregor, for instance, developed an interesting variation on the totalitarian theme by stressing the convergence of National Fascism and Leninist Bolshevism, maintaining that both utilised similar tactics to establish developmentalist, mass mobilising, modernising regimes. Gregor argued that "whatever differences distinguish Italian Fascism from its Bolshevik contemporary, these differences are not as interesting, or theoretically significant as their shared similarities" (Gregor 1979 p.302-3). Consequently, for Gregor there was essentially no difference between Fascist Italy and Communist Cuba, China or the Soviet Union - Lenin, Trotsky and Mussolini were all revolutionary nationalist modernisers (see Gregor 1979a p.244, 1969 p.346, and 1979 chapter 9 and Addenda). Hence Gregor concluded that, "for all the criticism levelled against the concept 'totalitarian', it remains vital" (Gregor 1979 p.319) [5].

Clearly "the central idea behind theory of totalitarianism is that there is a vital structural similarity between communist and fascist systems which in turn form an antithesis to the Western democratic system" (Kitchen 1982 p.25). In this way those of a liberal constitutionalist disposition were able to transform the concept of a straightforward linear ideological spectrum into a more satisfactory "horse-shoe" shape where "'extremists at both ends seemed close enough to touch'" (Felipe Fernandez-Armesto cited in Pearse 2002 p.118). This broad proposition was elaborated upon by other prominent scholars, such as Hannah Arendt, who reiterated that "practically speaking it will make little difference whether totalitarian movements adopt the pattern of Nazism or Bolshevism" (Arendt 1962 p.313). For Arendt any identifiable differences were negligible - the Soviet camps were "purgatory" on earth, the Nazi camps were "hell", and both types of regime possessed the capacity to destroy the realm of civil freedom and enforce hitherto un-experienced levels of repression (see Arendt 1962).

Ernst Nolte's perspective may also be pertinent here, with his assertion that fascism can be understood as a response to the threat of "Asiatic" Bolshevism – hence the death camp and Gestapo are seen as a clumsy reaction to the gulag and the Cheka. Evidently Nolte has one foot firmly implanted in the totalitarian camp (see Kitchen 1982 Chapter 4). Such was the importance and impact of Nolte's work that it stimulated a sustained debate in West Germany, especially given the fact that he argued that Stalin's crimes preceded Hitler's, were of the same order (or worse) and in many ways precipitated Nazi genocide, so in short there was a causal relationship between "class murder" and "race murder". "For Nolte Nazi crimes were nothing more than a response to the extermination carried out by the Bolsheviks, which was the ultimate, decisive matrix for all the twentieth century's horrors. Hitler was thus guilty of a deplorable excess in his historically justified effort to defend Germany and the West from the Communist threat" (Traverso 1999 p.76-77). Indeed Stackelberg even suggests that Nolte's avowed revisionist purpose was to re-cast the Nazi regime in a more positive light and to blame communism: "for Nolte, National Socialism was a justified, if excessively radical, response to the greater menace of Soviet communism...unconvincing though his interpretation may have been, its obvious aims were to at least partially rehabilitate Nazism while at the same time incriminating and discrediting the left" (Stackelberg 1999 p.10, and p.259). In this sense, when Nolte and others examine fascism, Communism is actually identified as the real culprit, the "original sin" (see Zizek 2005).

Of course many accounts have emphasized not only the existence of an ideological and practical identity between fascist and Communist systems, but have made a particular point of stressing the similarity of outcomes in terms of destruction and death. Engel, for example, argues that the Holocaust "was not the only instance of mass murder in human history. In fact it was neither the largest nor proportionately the most extensive case. Estimates of the number of Soviet civilians who died as a result of their government's deliberate actions against them between 1929 and 1950 vary widely, but all vastly exceed the number of Jews killed by the Third Reich" (Engel 2000 p.1). Meanwhile Eatwell concurs and compares the Holocaust to the "deliberately induced" Ukrainian famine under Stalin, in which more people perished than in the Nazi death camps (Eatwell 1996 p.277). For his part Rees contends that Stalin "committed crimes that, in part at least, are reminiscent of aspects of the Nazis' 'Final Solution'…in May 1945 most of Europe swapped one cruel dictator for another" (Rees 2005a p.345-46, see p.366). Many others have developed similar observations, for instance Noel O'Sullivan (1983) stresses the affinity between fascism and communism in terms of inherent ideas and unpalatable consequences, suggesting that Stalin's drive to eliminate the Kulaks was not at all dissimilar to Hitler's Final Solution to the "Jewish Problem". Meanwhile Passmore (2002) notes that "the collapse of Communism in 1989 brought to light new evidence of the horrors of Stalinism, and gave totalitarianism a new lease of life" (Passmore 2002 p.19). Tismaneanu is one of the more recent exponents of this perspective, stating that Communism and fascism, in sharing a number of "phobias, obsessions and resentments" merged into "a baroque synthesis" which represented "the incarnation of diabolically nihilistic principles of human subjugation" (Tisnaneanu 2012 p.x and p.xi). According to Tismaneanu the two totalitarian ideologies were radically evil, "rooted in ideological frenzy and utopian hubris", and contained an "eschatological fervor" which produced a record sheet of "absolute failure" (Tismaneanu 2012 p.15, p.19 and p.27). Hence totalitarianism offers "important and still valid interpretive keys for understanding the unique blending of ideology, organization and terror in unprecedented attempts to create perfectly homogenized communities through genocidal methods" (Tismaneanu 2012 p.224). Tismaneanu, his text teeming with self-righteous indignation, is in absolutely no doubt about the identity between fascism and Communism.

However, it is interesting to note that even "radical" antifascist commentators are prone to occasional slippage toward totalitarian rhetoric, for example, when Sewell claims that "the rise of fascist barbarism in Germany was mirrored in the USSR by the consolidation of Stalinist totalitarianism" (Sewell 1988 p.82), or when Renton refers (almost in passing) to the supposed similarities with the Soviet Union: "the origins of the Russian tyranny were different – *yet Stalinism was as murderous as fascism*" (Renton 2001 p.11 italics added). The pervasiveness of this approach in practical terms was highlighted more recently in 2009 when a Polish Minister Elzbieta Radziszewska sought to extend the restrictions on dangerous "totalitarian" propaganda by banning the sale of Che and Lenin t-shirts. Some members of the European Parliament have even argued for the banning of communist insignia like the hammer and sickle and the red star (see Zizek 2005). Indeed one Professor Wojciech Roszkowski asserted in the daily paper *Rzeczpospolita* that "'communism was a terrible, murderous system... It's very similar to National Socialism. There's no reason to treat the systems – and their symbols – any differently'" (cited in Zizek 2009 p.57-58). Karl Deitrich Bracher confirmed the continuing utility of theory by maintaining that "'all justifications for getting rid of the concept of totalitarianism are inadequate, so long as we do not come up with a better word for this phenomenon...the rejection of the concept comes primarily from those to whom it may very well apply'" (cited in Gregor 2000 p.136-37). According to Bracher, who doubtless speaks for many others, if you are apt to reject the coherence and value of totalitarianism as an explanatory theory, you are probably a totalitarian.

Yet totalitarianism is an inherently weak, if not fundamentally flawed "explanation" of fascism. Of course as Markwick explains "at first sight there seems much to commend in the view not only that Soviet communism and Italian Fascism were close 'totalitarian' cousins, if not twins like Stalinism and Nazism, but also that the threat of communism begat fascism in its Italian, German and other European guises" (Markwick 2009 p.339). However the emphasis on the apparent ideological affinity between fascist and communist regimes is entirely spurious, and totalitarianism as a theory of fascism is exceedingly flimsy not least because the totalitarian approach completely ignores the respective social bases of communist and fascist regimes – that is, the fundamental divergence in the mode and relations of production (Friedrich and Brzezinski refer to public ownership as a "variation" from private ownership! See Friedrich and Brzezinski 1965 p.23). The economic systems of fascism and communism did not just diverge at certain points, they were fundamentally different. Thesis also overstates the monolithic structure of many communist regimes, which makes it extremely difficult to apply to certain historical examples, for instance Hungarian Communism, Vietnamese Communism, Cuban Communism or even Soviet Communism prior to 1929 [6].

Totalitarian theory is also unsatisfactory on a conceptual level because of its exclusive emphasis on the techniques and methods of particular regimes. As a result it ignores the pre-power movement-phase of the phenomenon, omitting any mention of the enormous differences in the ideological content and social aspirations of fascism and communism - the former being regressive, socially reactionary and racist, the latter being essentially laudable and humane. If the regimes were indeed essentially similar one would assume a degree of ideological convergence, and this is obviously not the case. Friedrich and Brzezinski do acknowledge that purposes and intentions were "not wholly alike" yet they dismiss this fact as relatively unimportant (see Friedrich and Brzezinski 1965 p.19). This is rather like insisting upon analysing the mode of transport whilst completely ignoring the intended destination. Moreover, Paxton makes the pertinent point that "a camp is a camp. But as soon as one examines the historical routes to power and the ways the two regimes related to the societies they ruled, profound differences appear...Nazism had the ultimate aim of establishing the hegemony of a master race; Stalinism's ultimate aim was to establish a totally egalitarian society worldwide under Russian hegemony" (Paxton 2009 p.562). The fact that, from the victims' perspective, death was the ultimate consequence for some groups of people cannot alter the reality that the social dynamics and intended purposes of the respective regimes differed profoundly. Indeed, as Traverso says "Kolyma was a form of destruction that was not theorized by Stalin's regime, and in fact was in contradiction with the principles proclaimed by the USSR" (Traverso 1999 p.65 see p.69). Therefore there is a sense in which the Stalinist system was repugnant because it betrayed its own ideology - the Nazi regime was repulsive because its ideology was meticulously adhered to. This particular point was actually underscored by Primo Levi who succinctly observed that "it is possible, even easy, to picture a Socialism without prison camps. A Nazism without concentration camps is, instead, unimaginable" (Levi 2008 p.393). A coercive authoritarianism which aims at social equality may be extremely unpleasant and unpalatable, but it is qualitatively different from a coercive authoritarianism which seeks to impose the dominance of a master race via the extermination of entire ethnic groups.

There is another, substantive (if more controversial) objection to totalitarian theory which, in the context of the Cold War, was very easy to overlook. Totalitarian theory seriously undervalues the respective achievements of each regime, especially certain Communist systems which, given their respective historical starting points and the contextual socio-economic difficulties encountered, made some remarkable social advances. Health care in Cuba, full employment in the Soviet Union or cheap social housing in East Germany should not be so glibly dismissed. Conveniently, the various faults in "free" western liberal democratic "constitutional" regimes, against which "totalitarian" systems are invariably counter-posed and compared, are not seriously addressed at all. Of course it is perfectly legitimate to examine the methods and techniques of rule, and brutality and repression must be condemned, but even here, on the totalitarian theorists own chosen (relatively narrow) ground, their case for an identity between communist and fascist systems is very weak. Much as it might offend assiduously cultivated liberal sensibilities, it is entirely legitimate and indeed desirable to distinguish between a forced or necessary repression and a voluntary or inherent coersion. Objectives and circumstances must be taken into account when analysing methods, and one need only take a cursory look at relatively recent historical examples, such as Communist Cuba and Apartheid South Africa, to confirm this point. Repression, like war and violence is a dynamic phenomenon in which we can perceive various levels and types, and indeed just like war and violence, repression is in some cases justified.

In any case, if we *are* to concentrate on methods and techniques, surely it is inappropriate to suggest a qualitative similarity between the Soviet gulags and psychiatric "hospitals" (reprehensible though they were) and the systematic genocide and torture perpetrated in the Nazi extermination factories. Even with regard to the Stalinist period in the Soviet Union a distinction is clearly discernible between the bureaucratic, dispassionate, systematic industrialised genocide in what was undertaken by Hitler's regime, which had as its objective the extermination of an entire human group, and the mixture of civil war excesses, purge, slave labour and starvation which characterised Stalin's brutal Empire (see Paxton 2009 p.562). To put it bluntly the Soviet gulag at Ozerlag was hideously brutal, but it was a labour camp which measured its success in terms of the miles of railway track constructed by inmates, and some died in the process – the productivity of Auschwitz was calculated by counting the dead as a consequence of pre-planned, systematic murder (see Sonia Combe cited in Traverso 1999 p.69-70). Indeed it is also interesting to note the selective historical memory of some academics, anxious to note the excesses of Stalinism, who insist on including figures of fatalities resulting from starvation and official neglect, but who nevertheless tend to ignore or overlook the massive loss of life associated with, for instance, industrialization in Britain, famine in Ireland and India, or as a consequence of civil war, colonialism and the trans-Atlantic slave trade (see Harman 1996 p.10). As Alain Badiou has persuasively argued, if the only criteria for judgement is the "black farce" of counting the number of deaths caused, then the advocates of bourgeois democracy, who scribble so vociferously about the sanctity human rights, are also standing upon a heap of corpses (see Badiou 2010 p.3).

Clearly the brutal repression of Stalin's gulags, which were a barbaric legacy of autocracy and the desire for rapid industrialisation, cannot be precisely equated with the horrendous finality of mechanized mass extermination perpetrated by the Nazis. Death was often a by-product of malevolent mistreatment in the former, while it was the inevitable consequence of the latter's inexorable, ideologically motivated desire to eliminate whole categories of people in the name of Aryan supremacy. As Primo Levi quite correctly concluded – the Nazi camps constituted something quite unique in human history (Levi 2008 p.391) therefore any forced and superficial comparisons with other, albeit deeply unpalatable regimes, do a grave injustice to historical reality and merely trivialize the horrors of the Holocaust.

The fact is that totalitarian theory was the political product of a Cold War mentality which regarded it as tactically advantageous to emphasise theoretical and practical identity between communism and fascism, even though they are in fact antonyms (see Markwick 2009). Indeed Kershaw, whilst arguing that totalitarianism is a "concept" rather than a "theory", points out that "the concept is unusual in political science typologization in attempting to lump together systems which, in their self-image, were wholly antagonistic towards each other" (Kershaw 1989 p.50). The fact that liberalism prioritizes a particular version of libertarian individualism antithetical to both ideologies does not make fascism and communism the same, or even similar. So the idea of such a convenient ideological symmetry was an assiduously cultivated, politically manufactured illusion, and fascism was in actual fact a mass populist, demagogic, pseudo-revolutionary parody of its mortal enemy and antithesis, Bolshevik-Communism (as we will see). It is also important to stress that, given the true status of communism as the ideological nemesis of fascism, many of its most ardent adherents were at the forefront of struggle against it, and became the first victims of fascist regimes. Those contemporary analysts, many of whom are comfortably ensconsed in academia, who are so anxious to deploy trite categories in order to manufacture a simplistic symbiosis between fundamentally divergent political paradigms, would do well to reflect more seriously upon those brave communists who were intimidated, imprisoned and murdered in the fight *against* fascism.

Evidently the actual value of "totalitarianism" as an analytical tool to explain fascism is therefore strictly limited: "only when the insistence on the essential identity of fascism and communism is denied, is theory capable of producing valid insights into the nature of fascism, but when this occurs totalitarianism is given a different meaning and the original premises of theory are abandoned" (Kitchen 1982 p.35). As a consequence one is forced to conclude that "totalitarianism", given its methodological weakness and theoretical inadequacy as an instrument of analysis, was/is little more than a "boo" label - an epithet essentially applied to regimes and movements which are considered politically and ideologically distasteful. Totalitarian theory is therefore of minimal value to a proper understanding of fascism.

Given this conclusion it is perhaps surprising to note that such notions are making something of a comeback in the academic community. By re-calibrating the totalitarian analysis, and integrating it within a conceptual framework which stresses the significance of "political religion" (see earlier), the likes of Emilio Gentile and Roger Griffin are attempting to rescue theory. Both political religion and totalitarianism, which is re-cast and described as a "process", a "purpose", an "experiment in political domination" and a "vision of life" rather than a completed project, are thus both seen as complementary, constitutive elements of fascism (see Gentile 2005 p.57-58, Linehan 2005 p.103). The founding of the journal *Totalitarian Movements and Political Religions* in 2000 may be indicative of a growing scholarly preoccupation, although achieving a consensus on the precise utility of this particular "conceptual cluster" may be harder to achieve, despite Griffin's best efforts (see Griffin 2005a). Injecting the apparently lifeless body of totalitarian theory with the serum of "political religion" may have some academic mileage in it, certainly in terms of facilitating esoteric conference papers and edited collections, and it may even yield the occasional insight, but it is unlikely to resurrect the original, decaying corpse of totalitarianism as articulated by the cold war warriors in the west – that particular cadavar should be buried and forgotten.

## Historiographical and Sociological Insight: Engaging with Context

Other approaches to fascism emerge out of what might be termed conventional historiography and the sociological method of analysis. This category obviously encompasses a very wide range of diverse interpretations, many of which make a substantive contribution to the study of fascism - indeed some of them are absolutely critical to a proper understanding of the nature of fascism.

In some senses, of course, many of those who adopt an historicist approach tackle the fascist phenonemon as limited in time – that is, the product of a specific set of contingent historical circumstances. The study of the fascist regimes, for instance, has definite dates which provide neat, discernible junctures that can frame scholarly analysis. This much is axiomatic. Stanley Payne's "retrodictive theory" for example sees fascism as the revolutionary product of a particular conjunction of specific conditions at a historical moment, the collusion of a variety of factors such as a cultural *fin de siècle*, heightened nationalism, secularization, political fragmentation, economic crisis, social conflict, fear of communism, international status deprivation and so on, which created the specific conditions for fascist success (see Payne 1997). However the focus upon a specific historical period has led some to suggest that the context which produced and sustained the phenomenon of fascism was so unique that the experience is extremely unlikely to be repeated. For example, D.C. Watt in the Introduction to *Mein Kampf* (1974 p. xxii) suggests that "the plague has run its course" and therefore may be examined more clearly, whilst Pugh argues that "there is a strong case for saying the Second World War effectively put an end to fascism properly understood" (Pugh 2009 p.504). Hugh Trevor-Roper epitomizes this historicist attitude toward the specificity of fascist experience when he says, "the public appearance of fascism as a dominant force in Europe is the phenomenon of a few years only. It can be precisely dated. It began in 1922-3 ... it ended in 1945 with the defeat and death of the dictators" (Trevor-Roper 1981 p.19). From this viewpoint fascism is seen as the expression of an age or specific epoch, a brief and distinctive period of European history representing a parenthesis in the normal progressive liberal democratic development of free nations.

Similarly many of the historical approaches either view fascism as the work of pre-eminent individuals, or else the culmination of particular national histories. The idea that fascism may be reduced to an analysis of the life and ideas of the respective leaders is a common one, especially with regard Hitler and Nazism (see Rees 2005). This explanatory emphasis, which focuses on the personality and power of the fascist leader, has been reflected in the enormous number of biographical publications. As Paxton says, "most studies of fascism focus on the leader with the fascination of a bird watching a snake" (Paxton 2009 p.559). For example, the likes of Bullock, Bracher, Stone and others, to varying degrees, reduce the study of National Socialism to a straightforward scrutiny of prominent personalities, inter-personal contacts, situations and circumstances. Hence as Bracher has asserted with regard to the German experience, "Nazism may be called Hitlerism" (Bracher 1982, see also Kershaw 1985 p.69 and Fest 1973). Here fascism is often seen as, essentially, the implementation of a blueprint worked out by the evil genius, as Trevor-Roper implies in his introduction to the Hitler-Bormann documents when he says that Hitler "devised, made and carried out a great revolution from start to finish, from nothing to world empire" (Hitler 1961a p.2). Meanwhile Fest, to take another example, essentially concurs with this perspective by suggesting that "...to a virtually unprecedented degree he created everything out of himself at once: his own teacher, organiser of a party, and author of its ideology, tactician and demagogic saviour, leader, statesman, and for a decade the 'axis' of the world" (Fest 1973 p.3). Thus, according to this approach Hitler was, remarkably, the Marx, Lenin, Trotsky and Stalin of his revolution, its Rousseau, Mirabeau, Robespierre and Napoleon.

Great stress, in such accounts, is often placed on the unique qualities of the fascist leader and therefore his ultimate culpability. For instance many historical accounts of Germany under Nazism stress Hitler's will to power, indeed according to Fest the crime of mass extermination was "planned and committed by Hitler" (Fest 1973 p.5). Although Fest acknowledges the importance of social circumstances (via his periodic "interpolations"), he does nevertheless claim that "in him (Hitler) an individual once again demonstrated the stupendous power of a solitary person over the historical process" (Fest 1973 p.7). Here the fascist phenomenon is essentially personalised by stressing the leader's special "gifts", identifying their evil enchantment and emphasizing the power of political leaders to shape the societies they governed. Here the facts are deployed to demonstrate the power of one exceptional individual to change the course of human history. One of the more recent examples of this approach is the work by Laurence Rees (2012) who utilises a Weberian approach to analyzing Adolf Hitler's mystical "dark charisma", and the study has the revealing sub-title "leading millions into the abyss". Here Hitler is seen as the "archetypal" prophet-dictator with extraordinary oratorical skills capable of offering the masses a seductive combination of messianic certainty and redemptive hope. Even Ian Kershaw's broad ranging biography, by far the best of its type, not only places Adolph Hitler centre-stage in the story of Nazism (which is entirely plausible), but also claims that ultimately the German dictator was the "main author" of war and the "chief inspiration" of genocide: "never in history has such ruination – physical and moral – been associated with the name of one man…Hitler's name justifiably stands for all time as that of the chief instigator of the most profound collapse of civilization in modern times" (Kershaw 2009 p.968-69). Similarly Ernst Nolte also argued that, not only was fascism very much a product of its era (see Nolte 1969 p.18), but he also emphasized the crucial indispensability of key individuals, and he stressed the reliance of German, Italian and French fascism on the powerful personalities of Hitler, Mussolini and Maurras (Nolte 1969).

In this way fascism is "explained" by the extraordinary, almost superhuman qualities of key individuals, especially the leaders, who are portrayed in terms usually reserved for characters in fiction – the Pied Piper of Hamelin or Svengali. However it is interesting to note that whilst guilt is easily located as a consequence of an apparently logical account of the key protagonist(s) - many other individuals and groups are conveniently spared the burden of scrutiny and blame, despite their co-operation, complicity and collusion. Hence the difficulty in such a biographical approach can be that by locating blame so clearly with a single individual, the other critical contextual aspects are either downplayed or ignored. For example, the culpability of the fascist dictator is assumed to an extraordinary degree by Nolte when he suggests that "after the Fuhrer's death the core of the leadership of the National Socialist state snapped back like a steel spring wound up too long, to its original position and became a body of well-meaning and cultured central Europeans...these men were better people than most of the world has assumed" (Nolte 1969 p.504). Indeed Maser articulates explicitly what most of these accounts imply when he says "Hitler's ability not only to win over the majority of the German people, but to lead them so completely astray, has no precedent in history" (Maser 1973 p.258) [7]. Nor is this fascination with the leader a product of our own distance from actual events, since Hermann Rauschning, writing at the time, also "explained" Nazism in terms of the qualities possessed by the great dictator. Rauschning contended that Hitler was a kind of mystical "medicine-man" with special powers capable of hypnotizing an entire nation (Rauschning 1939 p.254). Of course, what has been said of Hitler's role can also be said (although perhaps to a lesser degree) of Mussolini. For instance, Wiskemann's account of Italian Fascism maintains that the relationship between Mussolini and National Fascism was one of dependency by the latter on the former, their fortunes thereby inextricably linked (Wiskemann 1969). Similarly Gregor emphasises the importance of Mussolini in synthesizing various ideological elements and bonding it to a political strategy designed by him to win power, which he exercised more or less alone (see Wiskeman 1969 and Gregor 1979a).

Although no-one could possibly deny the crucial value of biographical study as a method of presenting and understanding history, and whilst the actual role and contribution of the respective dictators should not in any way be underestimated, the obsessive concentration on the role of the leader is not necessarily very helpful in explaining fascism as an ideology and social force. There is absolutely no doubt that the historical/biographical approach can yield interesting information and essential descriptive data, but it is simply erroneous to claim that one person, nomatter how great or grotesque, can manifest or manipulate the entire historical process. Individuals make history, but not as they please or in conditions of their own choosing. Fascism was not simply the projection of the dictator's will, and to suggest this not only produces a partial picture, it provides a convenient alibi for those individuals, groups and institutions who facilitated fascism in various ways. In adopting such a focused approach not only are certain rather uncomfortable facts often ignored or underplayed (for example who financed, supported and benefited from fascism) but, interestingly, it is an approach which tends to confirm the fascist leaders' own view of themselves. This is, it might be argued, "the last triumph of fascist propagandists" (Paxton 2005 p.9). Identifying and analyzing the primary exponent of a political creed is not quite the same as identifying causes and providing explanations.

Similarly, the idea that fascism, if not the product of an exceptional individual, was the result of a peculiar national history, forms the basis of some appraisals. Fascism is thus seen in some ways as the consequence of a "special path", or a kind of national sickness afflicting a particular country at a certain time, perhaps even the result of inherent national characteristics. For instance William Montgomery McGovern, G.L. Mosse and William L. Shirer broadly take the view that Nazism was to a large extent the (inevitable) outcome of a peculiarly German history (see Hildebrand 1985 p.157, Szaz 1963, McGovern 1946, Mosse 1979, and Shirer 1985 especially Chapter 4). Emphasis here is placed, generally, on the legacy of specifically German ideas and traditions, although sometimes the structural disjuncture between economic modernization and liberal political democratization ("misdevelopment") is identified as a key factor in facilitating a "reactionary protest potential" (see Eley 1983). Here it is customary to mention the malignant influence of Prussian militarism and prioritize the pre-figurative impact of *Kaiserreich* authoritarianism. As Hans-Ulrich Wehler, an exponent of this perspective, explains: "'in the widespread susceptibility towards authoritarian policies, in the hostility towards democracy in education and political life, in the continuing influence of pre-industrial ruling elites, there begins a long inventory of historical problems'" (Wehler cited in Gregor 2000 p.65). Nazism is therefore seen as the logical teleological outcome of specifically Germanic thought and experience. F.D. O'Butler's work *Origins of National Socialism* (1941) is probably the most explicit and articulate exposition of such an approach. O'Butler traces the genesis and growth of Nazi ideas, beginning with the German "romantics", and the likes of Herder, Fichte, Jahn, Hegel, Nietzsche, Schopenhauer, Wagner and Spengler are each seen as embodying a particular aspect of Nazism - the racial myth, authoritarianism, nationalism, militarism and so on. In this way an evil thread is traced through German history, culminating in the deadly and derivative ideas of Rosenberg, Goebbels and Hitler. As O'Butler explains, "the rise and triumph of National Socialism is not fully explicable unless it is realised how very much its outlook was an extension of the traditional outlook of Germany...German thought and German politics goose-stepped together down the years" (O'Butler 1941 p.278 and p.284). National Socialism is here seen as a product of the inherent susceptibility of Germanity to such ideas and the cunning triumph of the dark-side of the German soul.

In some ways Daniel Goldhagen's controversial thesis fits well here, with his notion that the hatred of the Jews ("eliminationist anti-semitism") and Nazi genocide, were an integral and unique manifestation of German thought and culture. Goldhagen concludes that the German people as a whole were culpable for what transpired, and cannot be exonerated by claims about fear or ignorance (Goldhagen 1996; see Neville p.2). According to Goldhagen over 100,000 (and perhaps even as many as 500,000) German people were involved in the extermination programme, which represented an extremely wide network of participation and knowledge, which in turn implies a singular, straightforward national responsibility on the part of what were in effect Hitler's willing accomplices in genocide. As Goldhagen concludes: "the inescapable truth is that, regarding Jews, German political culture had evolved to the point where an enormous number of ordinary, representative Germans became – and most of the rest of their fellow Germans were fit to be – Hitler's willing executioners" (Goldhagen 1996 p.454).

The vast majority of Germans are thus seen as having harboured a homicidal animus toward the Jews which had a long historical trajectory, and they became, under Hitler, a nation driven "crazy" with pathological anti-Semitism. In Goldhagen's schema, Germany was pregnant with murder long before the arrival of the Nazis, and Hitler simply acted as "midwife" (see Rosenbaum 1998 p.340). However, although no-one could seriously doubt the importance and impact of specifically German anti-Semitism, this view, which stresses generalized public intent and culpability, is extremely odd because if the sadistic Germans were so keen on murderous genocide, why were Hitler and the SS so determined to keep the precise details of such a potentially popular policy shrouded in secrecy? Why use euphemisms such as "*Sonderbehandlung*" ("special handling") to describe a policy that, according to Goldhagen, most Germans happily subscribed to? The Goldhagen hypothesis is simply not supported by the empirical evidence. It is interesting to note that in the German translation of Goldhagen's book many of the assertions were softened and in the title itself *Scharfrichters* ("Executioners") became the less inflammatory *Vollstreckers* ("Executors") in recognition, possibly, of the offence it might cause. Despite the intial praise heaped on Goldhagen for his work, his perspective is, at best, a distortion of historical reality. Indeed Norman Finkelstein's forensic critique claims, in a withering attack on what he termed "Goldhagen's conceptual meat grinder", that Goldhagen "mangles the scholarly record", "manages to get nearly everything about the Nazi Holocaust wrong" and concluded that thesis is "worthless as scholarship" (Finkelstein 1997 p.50, p.84, p.66 and p.40). Of course any narrow, monocausal formula, which explains Nazism and the Holocaust purely in terms of specifically German antecedents and national character, is not only reductive and simplistic in ignoring several important European comparators, it does a considerable injustice to those Germans (including millions who voted for left wing parties) who rejected anti-Semitism and resisted, many of whom paid with their lives.

It is not difficult to construct an Italian counterpart to this, as Thurlow, Gregor and Lyttleton do, albeit implicitly and with much more subtelty (see Thurlow 1980b p.19, Gregor 1969 and Lyttleton 1973). In this way Mussolini's Fascists can be seen as the logical consequence of Sorel's preference for cathartic violence, the elite theories of Mosca and Pareto, the nationalism of Rocco and Corradini, Papini's condemnation of the respect for human life, the action-oriented revolutionary impulses of d'Annunzio with his belief in purification through sacrifice, aligned to Marinetti's futurist fascination with war and violence. Indeed in some cases the search for historical/ ideological antecedents may lead far beyond the nation and epoch under scrutiny, although it might still be implied that the nation concerned has a peculiar susceptibility to particularly unsavoury concepts and practices. William Montgomery McGovern's account is a classic of this genre, as the fascist rejection of liberalism is identified as a clear consequence of an infatuation with a wide variety of political ideas, all of which assiduously undermined individual liberty and democracy (McGovern 1946). In the pantheon of precursors McGovern cites not only the usual suspects, such as Luther, Rousseau, Fichte, Nietzsche, Hegel, Sorel and Pareto but, incredibly, the likes of Walter Bagehot, Thomas Carlyle, T.H. Green and Immanuel Kant. Together, according to McGovern, these theorists contributed to the construction of an authoritarian, etatist ethos which was exploited by fascism and became the basis of its ideological edifice. As McGovern explained, "political doctrines, like children's diseases, are remarkably contagious" (McGovern 1946 p.8). Others have made similar observations, for example, Hayes goes to extraordinary lengths to illustrate the lineage of distasteful ideas which led to fascism, and as a consequence the likes of Plato, Hobbes and Machiavelli are portrayed as almost proto-fascist (see Hayes 1973 p.40). In this way a conspiratorial cabal of contemptible theorists is assembled together and pronounced guilty of facilitating a crime they could not possibly have imagined. Obviously this kind of interpretation has been influenced by Allied perceptions of war-guilt although they no doubt contain a degree of historical validity in the sense that certain pre-figurative ideas fed into the fascist ideological framework. However, focusing upon such ideological precursors, whether they be authoritarian ideas, anti-democratic preconceptions or a favourable predisposition toward the tactical use of violence, is of dubious utility when it comes to explaining fascism because such ideas and notions are not fascist per se. Moreover, fascism simply cannot be explained solely in terms of a particular nation's historical development, by its inherent capacity to perpetrate evil, or by a heightened susceptibility to unpalatable ideas.

The attitudes and assertions of what might be termed the "historicists" often overlap or are loosely tied to the various sociological or socio-structural interpretations of fascism which seek, more plausibly, to explain the phenomenon in terms of the configuration of social forces existing at the time. Although this approach has been challenged in the recent era it is clearly capable of producing pertinent insights into the nature of fascism (see Baldwin 1990). Indeed emphasizing the autonomy of fascism from any social base can leave behind a vacuum in which regime and society exist independently of each other – this is clearly quite unsatisfactory (Baldwin 1990 p.27). In this sense Ian Kershaw's impressive work acts as a more sophisticated biographical bridgehead between those who would emphasise individual personality and "will to power", and the critical context of socio-structural dimensions (Kershaw 1995). Here agency and contingency are synthesized and afforded scope to facilitate a more nuanced interpretation – unidimensional historicism evolves into a more sophisticated "interactionism" by accommodating the various insights of social history and sociology (see Renton 2001 p.55-59) [8].

There are some useful and interesting sociologically informed accounts which stress the explanatory power of class (Pearce 2002 p.96). As early as 1923 Luigi Salvatorelli identified fascism as an essentially middle class phenomenon, and examined the relationship between social classes and political formations (see Kitchen op cit 1982 p.60). Fascism was seen as an independent movement of the disgruntled and dispossessed middle and lower middle classes, who followed the fascist leaders as the personal embodiment of the aspirations of the petit bourgeoisie. Similarly American sociologist Seymour Martin Lipset analysed the social bases of political movements and described fascism as an "extremism of the centre", which reflected the middle class nature of fascist support (Lipset 1960, see Griffin 1995 p.285). Lipset also stressed the anxiety of the increasingly resentful and proletarianised middle class as a significant factor, threatened by predatory capital from above and organised labour from below, and seeking compensation for a discernible decline in prestige and status (Lipset 1960, Kitchen 1982 p.63, see Taylor 1985 p.204, Germani 1968 p.65). Fascism, from this perspective, is viewed as a kind of extremist populism of the middle classes. However, the fact is that fascist movements did gain a measure of working class support, and the social class composition of the respective fascist parties was not radically dissimilar to the societies they sought to dominate (Pearse 2002 p.97). The fascist parties managed to appeal to all classes, albeit for very contradictory reasons, so the utility of focusing on the role of the petit bourgeoisie seems somewhat limited, and large-scale capitalists enterprises benefitted much more from fascist practice than the middle class trader or small-scale independent entrepreneur (Pearse 2002 p.118). As Paxton says of Lipset, "his eyes glued on the early stages" he "overlooked the establishment's role in the fascist acquisition and exercise of power'" (Paxton 2005 p.210). Other commentators, such as Talcott Parsons, highlighted the imperfect integration of social classes and the existence of structural dysfunctions in capitalist formations, whilst identifying the concomitant creation of diffuse needs amongst the disaffected sections of society as a key reason for the ultimate success of fascism (Parsons 1954, see Griffin 1995 p.277). In short, this kind of perspective sees endemic social conflict and weak democratic traditions resulting in acute domestic difficulties which threatened to destroy the solvent which bound communities together. By claiming to integrate people from all walks of life the fascists, therefore, offered the prospect of a social truce (if not harmony) and a system of values that, apparently, transcended sectional class interests. There is evidently some value in this approach given fascism's capacity to offer existential validation to a variety of social classes.

Much of the sociological literature surrounding fascism has also focused on the somewhat nebulous notion of "social development", an idea that has been enthusiastically embraced by some analysts. Indeed there are a few explicitly "developmentalist" theories which emphasise the apparently similar historical development of Italy and Germany - both achieved nationhood late, and both (especially Italy) had to overcome a stubborn agricultural economic base and the persistence of feudal traditions. As a consequence, it is argued, both nations not only retained pre-capitalist, authoritarian and feudal forms, but both were unable to fully functionalize bourgeois-democratic structures and thereby institutionalize political conflict (see Corner 1986; Renton 2001 p.19). This developmentalist angle focuses on the "modernist" qualities of the fascist regimes as a means of catching up with other industrially developed Western nations, so in this sense it was felt that fascism offered a sort of "special path" to the modern world. In the 1960s Barrington Moore put forward such a theory, and suggested that fascism capitalised on structural socio-economic difficulties which previous regimes were unable to resolve and in focusing on the glorification of the peasant, fascism represented an attempt to make conservative reaction popular and plebian (Moore 1966). In this way traditional conceptions of hierarchy, discipline and obedience were endorsed via more romantic conceptions of social solidarity (Moore 1966 p.447; see Griffin 1995 p.293). A.J. Gregor has also argued that the Fascist phenomenon in Italy represented, essentially, a modernising movement. Fascism was, according to this view, "a developmental dictatorship appropriate to partially developed or underdeveloped, and consequently status deprived, national communities in a period of intense national competition for place and status" (Gregor 1969 p. xiii, see 1979a p.243 and 1979) [9]. Fest, in the conclusion to his study, makes similar claims for Nazism when he says that the regime should be viewed as, "the terroristic or Jacobin phase of a widespread social revolution that propelled Germany into the twentieth-century" (Fest 1973 p.760) and both Ralf Daherndorf and David Schoenbaum have spoken of the push toward economic and social modernity via fascism (see Schoenbaum 1967, McDonough 1999 p.127, Neocleous 1997).

In fact the idea of particular national development or national exceptionalism can be over-stated, as illustrated in the case of the German *Sonderweg* (special development) thesis (see Gregor 2000 p.63). This perspective argues that Germany, and more particularly its bourgeois class, failed to shrug off feudal, absolutist monarchical-aristocratic forms and embrace liberal democracy, as the rest of western Europe had done, and that this somehow created favourable conditions for the success of Nazism (see Stackelberg 1999 p.24). Thus an unstable mix of modern industrialization and pre-industrial cultures and institutions created the conditions in which Nazism could develop and flourish. However criticism of the "special path" notion has been widespread, not least because it could be argued that the *Kaiserreich* was not particularly feudal or archaic, but was actually one of the most modern (pro)capitalist structures in Europe (Renton 2001 p.26, see Kocka 1988). So in this sense the counter-argument suggests that German socio-economic experience was not vastly different to either Britain or France. Even in Italy, although the south was hardly industrialized at all, the north contained some of the most developed industrial regions in Europe, such as those areas situated around Turin and Milan. So the picture in both cases is more mixed than the proponents of the specificity of national developmentalism tend to suggest. Moreover, even if the "special" path thesis provides some explanation as to why the particular configuration of circumstances precipitated fascism in a particular national context, it is much weaker on analyzing what took place after power had been achieved.

In addition there is also the difficult question of trying to determine exactly which aspects of "modernization" were specifically the product of fascism and which would have occurred anyway, the specific examples of industrialization, urbanization and secularization each offering a case in point. Disentangling political motive and social consequence here is highly problematic and, of course, there is little genuine unanimity on what actually constitutes "modernization" (Pearce 2002 p.99). It is certainly worth bearing in mind the fact that "modernization", as such, does not constitute a one-way fast-track to freedom and democracy. Modernity may not be inherently "progressive" in terms of improving lives or facilitating human liberty, and a synthesis between modernism and pathological barbarism is entirely feasible. Irrational doctrines can also be pursued methodically and in accordance with a "rational" plan divorced from ethically valid norms (see Woodley 2010 p22 and p.24). Indeed it might be plausibly argued that modernity itself contains a (potential) "dark side", for example, in the early twentieth century racism was perceived as a distinctly modern perspective, based on "expert", "scientific" assumptions about health, medicine and the universal beneficence of social engineering (see Bauman 1991 p.61). The fascist regimes themselves certainly patronized the exponents of modernity, like city planners, architects and engineers, whilst modern media techniques were deployed to secure popular acquiescence, and of course war was waged with the most sophisticated technology available. In fact the V1 and V2 rockets built at Peenemunde were the practical manifestation of a fascist obsession with modernity, so were the *autobahn* and the draining of the Pontine marshes, even perhaps the scepticism about the utility of organized Christianity. It should also be noted that the apparently anti-modern agrarian romanticism of the Nazis anticipated the application of new mechanization and agricultural techniques (regarding husbandry, breeding, plowing, planting, fertilization and so on) to improve efficiency. Moreover, it must also be remembered that the death camps were models of modern technical design and organization. Nazism and Fascism were indeed modernizing movements although they articulated a particular dystopian vision of the future.

Clearly history does not always move in a linear fashion from pre-modern barbarism via progressive "development" toward "modernization", and to claim otherwise suggests an implausibly crude conception of the historical process, which rests ultimately upon the essentially arbitrary choice of indicators whose relationship to each other is ambiguous and the measurement of which is inherently problematic. At worst the vague concept of modernization confuses chronology with morality and becomes a normative, teleological theory of history unreflectively derived from Western European assumptions about the value of such a process (see Knox 2000 p.55). In any case it would seem that any effort to *explain* fascism primarily in terms of a route to "modern" technological, industrial and economic development per se is incomplete and unsatisfactory because such "progress" preceded fascism and did not depend upon it, although it is true that in both countries such a process may have continued, or been enhanced to some degree. However, if we are to see fascism simply in terms of its capacity to facilitate national modernisation, without more substantial contextual elaboration, then we would have to explain what was specifically "fascist" about Oliver Cromwell or Peter the Great since each, after all, was a prophet and practitioner of modernisation.

It is also the case, of course, that in some ways fascism (and Nazism in particular) represented a reaction *against* the spirit and techniques of modernism. This has led commentators such as H.A.Turner, J.Herf, Hans Rogger and George Mosse to identify the contradictions within Nazism with regard to "modernism" and "anti-modernism" (Turner 1971-72, Herf 1981 especially p.808, Organski 1968 p.19). Herf, for instance, refers to the "reactionary modernism" and "technological romanticism" of Nazism, with its paradoxical combination of irrationalism and technics (Herf 1981 p.822, see Herf 1984). Hitler may have utilised the most sophisticated technological equipment to convey his message, and envisaged, among other things, a completely modern integrated transport system and brand new cities, but he also looked "forward" to a rural/ agrarian utopia which was in fact based on classical colonial values inspired by the British Raj. It might also be pointed out that the old feudal aristocracy were not derided or dismissed, let alone liquidated as an unwanted pre-modern social anachronism, and many of them were welcomed straight into the upper echelons of the SS. Consequently the Nazi regime's practical infatuation with the engineer should not obscure some of the more arcane and contradictory elements of fascist ideology. Hitler was fascinated by technology, he enjoyed his Mercedes-Benz, and he identified himself with the technological expertise of his confidant Ferdinand Porsche (who became an honorary member of the SS), but the Fuhrer also professed fealty to Teutonic notions of nobility, medieval conceptions of the *volk*, and promoted the idea of the soldier-peasant. Il Duce, like the Futurists, glorified the cutting-edge dynamism of the new technology (especially aviation), and he was photographed on a motorbike, driving fast cars and flying aeroplanes. However Mussolini not only fetishised ancient Rome he made a point of being pictured bare-chested, tilling the fields like an agricultural labourer, and such bucolic symbolism was not entirely perfunctory because Fascism emphasized the innate value of agrarian work and rural life. Here Neocleous's account of the conflict over the realization of the opposed potentialities of modernity in mass society, and the notion of "radical reaction", clearly reflects some of the complexity inherent in this aspect of fascism and he quite correctly concludes that fascism, in effect, faces both ways at once (Neocleous 1997 p.59).

In general we might conclude that certain historical approaches which stress fascism's specificity are dangerously complacent in their attempt to confine fascism to a particular epoch, for in some accounts it appears to preclude the possibility that fascism might re-emerge, albeit perhaps in a significantly modified form. The identification of fascism with the machinations of evil men is only partially rewarding and tends to obscure other more important contributory factors. Similarly the "rogues-gallery" approach of seeking out national antecedents and/or intellectual precursors, oversimplifies a complex social phenomenon and always involves a degree of selective speculation and arbitrary choice, since ideas are easily taken out of context, misinterpreted and distorted. Whilst care must also be taken when utilising middle-class and/or developmentalist theories, those more sociologically-informed approaches to the explanation of fascism do, at least, possess the inestimable merit of relating fascism to the social reality out of which it emerged.

## Marxist Analyses: Towards an Explanation?

Most of theories and interpretations that have sought to explain fascism are, more or less, what Kitchen (1982) refers to as "autonomic" approaches. That is they view fascism as a phenomenon independent of capitalism and its development. However, Marxism offers a different and a potentially more rewarding perspective. Although a bewildering number of interpretations may be located within this category, and there has certainly been no definitive Marxist explanation of fascism, in general they have the primary virtue of analysing fascism in terms of economics and class relations. In Marxism the emphasis is upon a materialist conception of history which was described succinctly by Friedrich Engels as: "'that view of the course of history which seeks the ultimate cause and the great moving power of all historic events in the economic development of society, in the changes in the modes of production and exchange, in the consequent division of society into distinct classes, and in the struggles of these classes against one another'" (Engels cited in Novack 1980 p.29). This starting point would seem to be indispensible for a comprehensive and satisfactory explanation of fascism and its functional significance, given that societies are constructed upon the contextual reality of how the economy is organised and, more specifically, who owns and controls economic power and wealth. As Ernst Gottschling explained, "'capitalist society is the soil on which the fascist state was able to come into being'" (cited in Gregor 2000 p.143). Any significant socio-political phenomenon therefore must be seen in terms of its relationship to the economic structure (in this case capitalism), as a critically important factor in its emergence and development.

However, the relationship between the economic sub-structure or base, and the political super-structure is a complex one, and the Marxist approach has been justifiably criticized for reducing  intricate social reality to a crude, simplistic, determinist formula (see Schuddekopf 1973 p.96). Some Marxists, in short, have vulgarized Marx's theory of the reciprocal, dialectical relationship which exists between economics and politics. Fascism has been seen by certain Marxist theorists and practitioners as merely an instrument of the agents of capitalism. In this scenario the capitalist class, specifically the most reactionary and chauvinistic elements of finance capital, were seen as creating and manipulating a fascist movement in order to save their economic system and forestall the ("inevitable") communist revolution. This overly mechanistic and retarded "agent" theory (what Kitchen refers to as a "heteronomic" approach) was expounded by the Comintern in the 1920s and 30s, and led to the adoption of the "social fascist" thesis, which proved to be a major misinterpretation of the nature of fascism (see Kitchen 1982).

Although Zinoviev actually coined the phrase "social fascism", as early as 1924 Stalin had declared that Social Democracy was "'objectively the moderate wing of fascism.... these two are not contradictory, they complement one another. They are not antipodes but twins'" (cited in Kitchen 1982 p.3; see Griffin 1995 p.260). "The 'social fascist' logic was for Stalinists obvious: if the political and economic situation was 'objectively' revolutionary, then the subjective factor of reformism, i.e. social democracy, became the major impediment, and had to be undermined" (Townshend 1996 p.111). Stalin and the Communists were effectively arguing that all those Social Democrats who refused to embrace the Communist credo were in fact the "enemy" and therefore the accomplices of fascism. Indeed the SPD leaders were described as a faction of German fascism behind a socialist mask, and in 1928 the Sixth World Congress of the Comintern confidently predicted the final death agony of the capitalist system. The consequences of this misguided strategy, which called for the destruction of social democracy, were tragic indeed. Coop-eration, for example, between the KPD and SPD against the Nazis was never seriously considered, and individual Social Democratic workers were simply urged to join the Communist movement. Joint action was therefore deliberately disregarded as a defensive strategy and, as Poulantzas pointed out, "the blindness of both the PCI and KPD leaders...(was) staggering" (Poulantzas 1974 p.47) [10].

Official Communist orthodoxy at the time clearly identi-fied a revolutionary potential in the masses and envisaged capitalism collapsing through its own internal contradictions. Indeed on occasions it was stated that fascism might even be a "necessary stage" on the road to the pre-determined prole-tarian revolution (see Mandel's Introduction to Trotsky 1971 p.24). The massive growth in the Nazi vote was thus seen as an indicator of revolutionary potential in the context of capi-talist crisis, rather than a looming catastrophe for the working classes. This concept of historical inevitability ("after Hitler it will be our turn") meant that many Communists were not only myopically optimistic, but were unable or unwilling to counter fascism, conceptually or otherwise. Indeed, "by failing to distinguish between bourgeois democracy and fascism, the Comintern was blindly prepared to sacrifice the organizations of the working class in the interests of a formalistic theory" (Kitchen 1974 p.116). Events themselves were to prove the bank-ruptcy of Comintern policy and the magnitude of the defeat for the organised working class (Beetham 1983 p.21; see Renton 1999 p.60). At the Seventh Congress, in the summer of 1935, Dimitrov belatedly outlined a new "Popular Front" policy which acknowledged the qualitative difference between fascism and social democracy and attempted to facilitate class cooperation against the common enemy by identifying fascism as the product of a smaller section of imperialistic finance capital. However, the belated revision of their strategy did little to allay the fears of socialists and democrats about Communist motives (and of course 1939-41 was to represent yet another supreme example of ideological contortionism by an international Communist movement entirely subservient to the national interest of the Soviet Union, as interpreted by Stalin).

Communist policy remained centred on the belief that fascism was created and controlled by capital and, interestingly, this belief still formed the basis of interpretations of fascism in Eastern Europe in the post-war period. As Paterna, Fischer, Gossweiler, Markus and Patzold put it "'in 1933 and in the following years, the financial powers in the German Reich...*controlled the economic policy decisions of the Hitler government*'" (cited in Gregor 2000 p.141 italics added). The work of Jurgen Kuczynski and Kurt Gossweiler has also stressed the importance of capital and/or divisions therein, in explaining Nazi policy, and the underlying tenor of such approaches is exemplified by one standard GDR text which claimed that Hitler was "'the political spokesman of the real dictators of Germany - the men of coal, iron, steel, the chemical and electrical industries, as well as the big banks ... he was the tool, the creature of the German monopoly bourgeoisie'" (cited in Taylor 1985 p.203; see Barkai 1990 p.10-15). Marxist *cui bono* determinism therefore survived long after fascism had been defeated, although few western scholars took it seriously as possessing any real explanatory value. As Baldwin has commented, "only rare students of the subject, equipped with a heroic capacity for reductionism, are willing to explain Barbarossa or the Holocaust in terms of the economic interests they served" and the idea that the key actors in the historical drama of the fascist period were Krupp and the Perone brothers is simply implausible (Baldwin 1990 p.17).

However there is a tradition of dissent within the Marxist school which refused to be contained within the straight-jacket of the Comintern's conceptual orthodoxy, and this dissent provides the basis for a more adequate understanding of fascism (see Beetham 1983). For example, Communist leader Palmiro Togliatti offered "disquisitions of considerable subtlety and acuity" (Bosworth 1998 p.50) while Angelo Tasca propounded a much more sophisticated analysis of fascism (and was expelled from the PCI as a result). These approaches stressed the fact that fascism was more populist and eclectic than conventional Communist orthodoxy acknowledged, consisting of diverse and possibly divergent social and political factions. Antonio Gramsci's reference to "Ceasarism" and the re-configuration of hegemony offered insights which transcended the primitive class reductionism of the Stalinist International, whilst Thalheimer's skillful use of Marx's analysis of Bonapartism facilitated a more thoughtful account, which emphasized the contradictory nature of fascism and the relative autonomy of the political sphere (see Renton 1999 p.65). There were also, in 1930s, Social Democrats who, having rejected "Kautskyism" in the light of Hitler's success, became more radical and produced similarly useful insights. The work of Otto Bauer, who stressed the ruling class motive of breaking the equilibrium in the conjuncture of class forces, is a particularly good example of a Marxism attempting to come to terms with the exceptional specificity of fascist movements (see Kershaw 1989 p.51) [11]. Certainly both Zetkin and Trotsky were among the first to recognize the inadequacy of the "social fascist" thesis by stressing the unique danger of fascism and the necessity of a more considered strategic and tactical response (see Trotsky 1971 and 1969; Renton 1999 p.54). Zetkin actually realized that the initial Communist reaction to the fascists, which saw them as a bizaare collection of mad adventurers or "fools" (as Zinoviev had called them) obscured the fact that they were beginning to represent many people who were suffering economically and unable to express themselves politically (see Wistrich 1976 p.158). Trotsky's analysis, delivered in exile, was also insightful.

Trotsky's prognosis was more accurate because he recognized that fascism, as a mass movement, was constructed around the interests of fanatical petit bourgeois elements, and he also realized the magnitude of the threat, arguing that the fate of humanity rested on the outcome of the struggle against fascism (see Wistrich 1976). Trotsky also predicted that the plebian "socialist" demagogy of the fascist movements would be quickly discarded once power had been achieved, and this would serve as a prelude to a period of unmitigated barbarism as the full implications fascist ideology - the discarded refuse of European political thought - were fully revealed. Fascism, Trotsky insisted, would be no ordinary military-police dictatorship and he warned, "'should fascism come to power, it will ride over your skulls and spines like a terrific tank'" (cited in Townshend 1996 p.112). According to Trotsky the KPD's theoretical inadequacy in prioritizing the counter-revolutionary sins of the Social Democrats, was compounded by the tactical error of effectively dividing and bewildering the working class. For Trotsky effective opposition had to emphasise a united front led by the working class, including those associated politically with the Social Democrats – they might march separately but should strike as one against the common enemy. The Comintern, having conducted a stunning strategic volte face in 1935 by accepting the tactical class collaborationism of the Popular Front, which entailed cooperation with bourgeois parties and anti-fascist elements, caused Trotsky to criticize the new formulation as being far too heterogeneous and subordinating the working class to bourgeois leadership. This was a tactical and strategic dispute that was to be worked out with still more tragic consequences during the civil conflict in Spain between 1936-39, to the ultimate benefit of Franco and his Falange. Nevertheless fascism was, according to Trotsky, a direct consequence of the bankruptsy of bourgeois capitalist society, the rotten reformism of social democracy and an opportunistic, politically inept Communist leadership.

Of course it might be argued that Trotsky's pristine version of Marxism was over-optimistic about the potential of the international working class in the context of its struggle against a supposedly moribund capitalism, and there is a certain lack of precision in his analytical categories – his relatively undifferentiated (and confusing) use of "Bonapartism" ("pre", "preventive", "senile" as well as "fascist") being a case in point (see Kitchen 1974). Trotsky's theory of fascism could not only be confusing, it was saturated with a bitterness directed at the errors of his erstwhile comrades. However, this "did not prevent him from subjecting the official communist interpretation of fascism to a penetrating critique for its abstract formalism and inability to differentiate between particular stages and varieties of the fascist phenomenon" and Trotsky undoubtedly "showed a sharp eye for the practical consequences of a false political theory" (Wistrich 1976 p.157 and p.163). As Kershaw has noted, "the unorthodox (or deviant) Marxist analyses of Leon Trotsky, Otto Bauer and, especially, August Thalheimer, each drawing differently shaded analogies between fascism and Bonapartism, as developed in Marx's *Eighteenth Brumaire*, are impressive – not least given the sterility and mistakes of orthodox Communism at the time – in their intellectual attempts to grasp the nature of the new type of political danger which they faced" (Kershaw 1989 p.50). In their effort to draw out the distinction between social and political power these theorists did much to rescue Marxism from a theoretically redundant economic reductionism.

Given the description of fascism already outlined earlier in the first chapter of this text, the tendency by some Marxists to re-assess the relationship between economics and politics, capitalism and fascism, and hence to revise Comintern orthodoxy, seems entirely sensible. Orthodox Marxist interpretations were vitiated by a fatal premise because theory, which construed fascism as an inevitable or typical stage in capitalist development, emerged from "an over-evaluation of objective and infrastructural forces and a corresponding devaluation of subjective and superstructural factors" (Hoare 1963 p.99). Indeed it could be argued that early Marxism's inability to identify and explain the epochal significance of Auschwitz and genocide raised serious doubts about its capacity to answer the broader questions about the nature of society and capitalism (see Traverso 1999). Although, as we have seen, there was an extremely close relationship between fascism and capitalism, and businesses did benefit considerably from fascist policies, the relationship was obviously not straightforward: "the monopolies did not simply pay the piper and call the tune" (Kitchen 1982 p.70). The ruling class does not, in reality, simply dictate terms to political representatives in a simplistic manner because political superstructure and economic base interact reciprocally and possess their own internal dynamics. The reductive, instrumentalist view that fascists were just the agents of capital was clearly inadequate because, as Poulantzas put it, "the superstructure itself is not just a wrapping inside which the productive forces develop; it intervenes decisively in the production process" (Poulantzas 1974 p.41). In short, politics matters.

Tim Mason probably went furthest amongst Marxists in asserting the "primacy of politics", arguing explicitly that ideology and political will (in Nazi Germany) triumphed over economic calculation (Mason 1993, Mason 1968 p.165, see Mandel's Introduction to Trotsky 1971 p.30-31 and note no.46; also Hildebrand 1985 p.114 and p.133). According to Mason, domestic and foreign policy (especially after 1936 and the second Four Year Plan) became more independent of the will of the dominant economic class "and even in some essential aspects ran contrary to their interests" (Mason 1968 p.167). Henceforth, Mason argues, the economic elite displayed no common political priorities and thereafter fragmented into its constituent parts [12]. In essence Mason acknowledged that his earlier analyses, which placed class conflict in the foreground, were only partial and could not do justice to the full story and central legacy of fascism. As Mason explained, "it was apparently the case that both the domestic and foreign policy of the National Socialist government became, from 1936 onwards, increasingly independent of the influence of the economic ruling classes" (Mason 1996 p.54). Of course Mason had a point, for there are a number of instances where fascist rule clearly did not square with the priorities of capitalist development, or where events could not be explained by a reductionist account of class conflicts - the most obvious example being, of course, the Holocaust. "In Auschwitz we see a genocide in which racial hatred was virtually the one and only motive, carried out in disregard of any economic, political or military consideration" (Traverso 1999 p.3).

Given its critical significance, this point is worth developing. Although (as we have noted) the camps were models of "modern", "rational", capitalist contractual relations and businesses made extraordinary profits out of their construction and the slave labour provided therein; and although the use of the "Jewish threat" and the general persecution of minorities can be viewed as helping to bind social classes together and stabilise a divided nation by isolating an unfortunate "out group" - the genocidal operation clearly did not conform completely to capitalist requirements. For example, at a time when transport facilities were scarce, rolling stock and other valuable resources were devoted to the transportation of victims across Europe, and in a period when German industry desperately required manpower, skilled workers were murdered. The actual physical annihilation of the Jews therefore served no really useful purpose for capitalism, ideological or otherwise (see Carr 1987). Indeed the way the political sphere had "emancipated itself" from the needs of economics is most clearly marked by the racial policies implemented by the SS "where the translation of ideology into practice was in flat contradiction to the interests of the war economy and yet was allowed to continue" (Mason 1996 p.74). The racial utopianism of Nazi ideology transcended the practical "hard headed" economic requirements of businesses and this is most clearly illustrated by the language of the Nazi Ministry of Occupied Territories which phrased its priority as follows: "'economic questions should not be considered in the solution to the Jewish question'" (cited in Hilberg 1985 Volume Three p.1007). As Sparks concludes, "there is no possible explanation of this mass murder in terms of the drive to accumulate capital or win an imperialist war, to secure the rule of capital or even the state over the subject population. The only possible reason can be that it was the autonomous logic of the fascist state" (Sparks 1980 p.41, see Hildebrand 1985 p.141).

Such a prominent and pertinent example illustrates, therefore, significant scope for independent action by the fascists, and this reflects the fact that it is entirely appropriate to view politics as relatively autonomous from the economic base. The reality is that the relationship between fascism and capitalism was not always harmonious and the likes of Mussolini and Hitler always contained a certain threat to capital given fascism's capacity for independent, ideologically driven initiative. As Trotsky said as early as 1932 "while it makes use of fascism, the bourgeoisie nevertheless fears it" (Trotsky 1969 p.15) indeed "'the big bourgeoisie like fascism as little as any man with aching molars likes to have his teeth pulled'" (cited in Renton 1999 p.71). The most productive approach therefore, is to see the relationship between fascism and the capitalist classes as a "genuine bargain" between two social forces, with both sides having to make real compromises and tangible concessions (see Sparks 1980 p.33). Although fascism was not a movement that existed independent of capitalism or capitalist influence (it was not designed to be so) it was not an instrument of those classes or that economic system either - this is what Kitchen refers to as a "syncretic" approach, that is, neither "autonomic" nor "heteronomic" (Kitchen 1982). Fascism must therefore be seen as one of the options for capital in its effort to maintain its position of social superiority during a period of severe systemic crisis. In essence the capitalists, faced with an economic collapse and the disintegration of the politically dominant class, turned to fascism as an alternative political force in the hope that it could provide a radical populist means of securing economic regeneration and maintaining overall capitalist hegemony. However, there was no mono-causal dynamic connecting capital and fascism, no simplistic purchase of power or pulling of strings, but a compromise based upon an association (rather than an identity) of interests. Indeed, political submission to the fascist dictatorship was the necessary condition, the price that had to be paid, for the continued economic supremacy of capital over labour. As Marx explained in the *Eighteenth Brumaire of Louis Napoleon*, in order to save its purse the capitalist class must sometimes forfeit the crown - and the sword that safeguards the bourgeoisie must at the same time be hung over its own head as the sword of Damocles (Marx 1978 p64, Beetham 1983 p.27) [13].

Although the orthodox economic determinism of Communist theory, as represented by the Communist International, proved unsatisfactory and indeed led to grievous practical political errors, two important points nevertheless need to be remembered: firstly, it did represent the first serious attempt to analyse a new and complex political phenomenon in its social context (we have the benefit of hindsight of course, which in nearly all cases bestows a greater clarity of vision); and secondly, despite its manifest inadequacy it did provide a useful starting point for the development of an altogether more appropriate thesis. We might also add, of course, the not inconsiderable observation that many Communists actually died playing their part in the struggle against fascism, for as Evans correctly points out with regard to Germany, "of all the groups who held out against Nazism in the early years of the Third Reich, the Communists were the most persistent and the most undaunted. They paid the greatest price as a consequence" (Evans 2006 p.65 see p.70-71). Self-satisfied liberal intellectuals who are so often desperate to criticize Marxist analyses might do well to bear this in mind.

It can be concluded from our overview of interpretations that, standing above the superficiality of isolated psychological explanations; beyond the futile moralizing of theological rumination; in opposition to the facile comparisons of totali-tarian theory; eschewing the simplistic idea that fascism was inevitable given national history/characteristics or the instrumental consequence of charismatic leaders; tran-scending the unelaborated findings of sociological analysis; and superseding the vulgar mechanistic determinism of early communist orthodoxy, there stands a theoretical perspective which is capable of a more differentiated understanding of fascism, and which does full justice to the complex patterns of historical reality. Marxism, if used thoughtfully as a tool of analysis, whilst paying due regard to the relative autonomy of the political sphere and acknowledging the reciprocal symbi-otic relationship that exists between the economy and other facets of social life, is capable of producing the most cred-ible *explanation* of fascism (given the description outlined earlier in this book). The Marxist analysis certainly retains considerable heuristic value. Using an un-dogmatic and crit-ical application of Marxist principles it is possible to arrive at a theory which is rooted in the analysis of social forces, acknowledges the reality of economic power, and evaluates the nature of the historical process in the material world - yet which is flexible enough to accommodate all that is of value from other interpretations. This approach does not demand a belief in historical inevitability or require a treatise on the ultimate victory of communism - ideas about predestination are best relinquished and left to theologians. However, a Marxist approach, which acknowledges the importance of capital accumulation and class conflict as central to the anal-ysis of social phenomena, is much more plausible than most academic alternatives. At least Marxism is capable of asking the most important questions – how does fascism emerge, and who benefits? Marxism, of course, cannot guarantee a convincing explanation, but an analysis of history, economics and social class are prerequisites to any proper understanding, and by stressing the importance of social context this theory can elucidate the central fact that fascism emerges as a direct consequence of the crises inherent in capitalism itself.

This deeper, more analytical approach is also important for another crucial reason – if, in certain circumstances, moral responsiblity requires us to hate – it is important to hate precisely – a point which will re-surface in the conclusion to this text (see Mason 1996 p.230).

## Examining Fascism: Re-Asserting the Central Significance of Social Function

Quintin Hoare noted many years ago that although fascism "is one of the most familiar terms in our political vocabulary, it is hardly ever used in a way that suggests both an analytical grasp of its essential nature, and a real awareness of its autonomy as a category" (Hoare 1963 p.99). In terms of fascism's "essential nature" we may conclude from our analysis that fascism is composed of a number of constituent elements or themes, which we have isolated and assessed, and which *taken together* constitute the essence of the phenomenon. These themes were discernible in the experience of classical fascism. Fascism was underpinned and validated by reference to a pre-rational "instinctivism" and a distorted version of "social Darwinism". It embodied a virulent xenophobic nationalism which embraced militarism, encouraged war and justified imperialism. Fascism advocated and constructed an authoritarian state which it counter-posed to plutocratic, pluralistic liberal parliamentary democracy, and presided over a severely disciplined and hierarchically ordered society. The fascist mass party, which contained a preponderance of young, middle class elements, was essentially populist and led by a charismatic, dictatorial leader. Fascism also, whilst claiming to be socialist in some sense, aspired to a corporatist "third way" between capitalism and communism. As it turned out, despite being collectivist (in stressing the primacy of "national interest" and society over the individual), fascism was vehemently opposed to social egalitarianism. Critically, fascism accommodated capitalism in practice, and utilised references to "socialism" (and anti-capitalism) as rhetorical, demogogic devices, designed to attract mass support. Fascism was also racist in asserting the cultural and/or biological superiority of its nation/race. However, although the congruence of these factors make it legitimate to talk in terms of "fascism" as a generic concept, which could be applied to both the Italian and German experience, differentiation between the two is essential - there was a distinct qualitative difference between the Italian and German versions of fascism. The Nazi pre-occupation with race definitely sets their ideas apart and the emphasis on sociobiology, genetic determinism and anti-semitism precipitated a version of racism which gave it a distinctive character. In short, the visceral racism of Nazism infected practically everything the Nazis attempted or accomplished.

Although interpretations of fascism are varied, with many producing extremely valuable insights, it is nevertheless also evident that any satisfactory assessment must be rooted in an analysis of social formation and social function. The purely intellectual, ideological and diachronic dimension of fascism makes little sense unless there is an emphasis upon empirical and epochal reality. Concept should never take precedence over context, and abstraction should always take accurate account of socio-economic environment (and indeed proven historiography). Ideological production can only really be adequately explained in relation to the existing social and material interests which determine consciousness and lived experience. Any account which abstracts political and ideological purpose from the reality of the social structure that creates it, is unlikely to be adequate (see Rossi/Tasca 1938 p.338). Therefore, an examination of social context is essential if fascism is to be genuinely explained and understood, rather than simply identified and described. As Paxton has pointed out, if fascism is analysed closely, it looks much more like a "network of relationships than a fixed essence" (Paxton 2005 p.207).

As we have seen, fascism emerged and crystallized during a period of acute social, economic and political crisis, and ultimately secured capitalism as an economic and social system. Despite a vague and eclectic ideological synthesis the fascists "either shared power with powerful conservative groups, or acquired a predominant position in the state under their tutelage" (Kallis 2004 p.23). The existing power blocs made a "satisfactory" (rather than "ideal") strategic choice in favour of fascism as the "least worst" option (see Woodley 2010 p.132). This fact, despite the odd anomalous exception, reflected the underlying political predisposition of fascism as a social force. Fascism offered a populist solution to the problem of generating mass support for a fundamentally inequitable social system. As Ralph Miliband quite rightly pointed out, "had they done nothing else the fascist dictators, by the subjugation of all manifestations of working class power and influence would have richly earned the gratitude of employers and of the economically dominant classes generally" (Miliband 1980 p.82). Hence, when Eatwell says that fascism "involves a rejection of existing society and the power of Establishment groups" he is evidently wide of the mark (Eatwell 1996b p.314). The idea that fascists were instruments of capital might be simplistic and vulgarly reductive - capitalists were partners rather than puppetmasters - but there can be no serious doubt that the bourgeoisie (in general terms) managed to sustain their economic system and continued to flourish. Even under fascist dictatorship, which sought to interfere into all areas of social life, politics continued to be largely constrained and cast in a mould shaped by the inherent requirements (and contradictions) of capitalist economics. In general (to paraphrase Mason) the notion that the economy gets the system of government it needs is a better point of analytical departure than the idea that people get the government it wants or deserves (see Mason 1996 p.53).

It is important to be clear here. The capitalist classes certainly did not create fascism – the fascist Behemoth was far too popular and plebian to have originated in the boardroom - but the bourgeoisie was willing use the movement because there was no credible political alternative, and the dominant class was absolutely determined to benefit from its consequences. Fascism, despite its ideologically driven and dynamic propensity for independent initiative, nevertheless served a useful function for traditional social elites. The requirements of an exploitative capitalist class were thereby fused with the ideological demands of a demonic dictatorship in a functional, if uneasy, symbiosis. This relationship needs to be acknowledged and Max Horkheimer's oft quoted maxim: "anyone who wont talk about capitalism should keep quiet about fascism" remains perfectly valid. Capitalists may not have been the key actors in the grotesque drama that unfolded in Germany and Italy, but they retained the deeds to theatre and they made absolutely certain that they were rewarded handsomely for accommodating the brash and brutal new inhabitants of the political stage.

Of course the analysis of fascism also raises some extremely important subsidiary issues. For example, the whole question of fascist ideology calls into question the idea of "revolution". Many academics, analysts and commentators have taken at face value the fascist slogan "'everything must change'" (cited in Stone 1992 p.57) and therefore have stressed fascism's radical "revolutionary" credentials. For example, Knox argues that the widespread assumption that only "the left" could make revolutions contains a hidden, indefensible teleology which claims to "know where history was going", and that this fact was fatally exposed by the "putrescence of Communism" (see Knox 2000 note 6 p.4). Indeed Knox claims that Fascism and Nazism, far from aiming to avert revolution, were destined to make it (Knox 2000 p.227). Meanwhile Mosse has argued that a "revolution" from the right is entirely conceivable if revolution, as a neutral analytical concept, is defined as a rapid, forceful and fundamental re-ordering of society in conformity with a projected utopia (Mosse 1999 p.xi-xii, see Knox 2000, Schoembaum 1967). Many analysts would therefore concur with Copsey, who argues that the "'revolutionary' right occupies the most extreme point on the right-wing scale", which is the realm of "generic fascism, which takes ultra-nationalism to the revolutionary extreme" (Copsey 2008 p.79, see Copsey 1994) [14]. Similarly, Thurlow's work contains the assumption that British fascism was somehow "revolutionary" in intent (see Thurlow 1998 p.119, also Thurlow 1980a p.19) whilst Griffin states explicitly that fascism "is revolutionary, not counter-revolutionary" (Griffin 1993a p.16, see Griffin 2000a). Yet Seton Watson encapsulates a critical confusion by suggesting that, on the one hand, to deny the epithet "revolutionary" to fascism is doctrinaire and perverse, although he acknowledges that the aim was *not* social revolution (Seton-Watson 1979 p.365). This ambiguity is even apparent in Griffin's work, specifically the subtle elision in his definition of "revolution" from "fundamental (structural) change" to "revolutionary spirit" (see Griffin 2000a p.187-88). Indeed, to note yet another illustrative example, Schoenbaum suggested that the fascist "revolution" was ultimately a "state of mind" (see Schoembaum 1967 p.54). In fact Hitler himself actually illustrated and pre-figured the terminological ambiguity by describing himself as "'the most conservative revolutionary in the world'" (cited in Bobbio 1996 p.19). At a conceptual level this is all rather confusing. Does a "revolution" require a *social* transformation, and what precisely does this mean?

The only satisfactory way to delineate the precise nature of fascist "radicalism" is to analyse more closely the idea of "revolution", which is more accurately divided in to its political, cultural and socio-economic dimensions. It might be persuasively argued that fascists precipitated a dramatic, even "revolutionary" political transformation from democracy to dictatorship. Moreover, they did (and will, given the opportunity) make drastic alterations to society in terms of implementing racist policies, imposing order, restricting civil freedom and so on. It is also possible to concur that fascism's "semiotic territorialisation" represented some kind of qualitative cultural transformation (see Griffin 1999). However, it is worth bearing in mind that fascist efforts at social engineering were for the most part either cosmetic, transient or illusory (see Stephenson 2008 p.102). Moreover, under Fascism and Nazism the underlying economic structure remained substantially in tact, and the commitment to capitalism, free enterprise, private property and material inequality was fundamentally unaltered. So in this sense Fascists, and even Nazis, were ultra-conservative rather than revolutionary. For all the anti-system rhetoric, in this key sense fascism was fundamentally inert and intent upon the preservation of the prevailing social structures (see Kallis 2004 p.19). In fact fascism, in many ways, simply created the illusion and the spectacle of comprehensive, total, "revolutionary" transformation, whilst essentially sustaining the prevailing social structure. Florid fascist rhetoric about the creation of a "new man" or precipitating a "revolution of the soul", and retrospective academic analysis which highlights "revolutionary spirit", cultural aesthetics and the radical re-coding of social symbology, cannot obscure fascism's fundamentally conservative essence.

If we focus on social and economic function in the two classic examples it is absolutely clear that fascism was a deeply reactionary, indeed counter-revolutionary, political paradigm. Despite the fact that Mussolini was influenced by "revolutionary" syndicalism, and irrespective of Hitler's contempt for bourgeois self-interest, fascism functioned, in the final analysis, to sustain hierarchical and exploitative social relations. However, although fascism maintained and protected a social hierarchy which was based on private property and capital accumulation, it nevertheless liquidated the bourgeois political system which appeared incapable of preserving that order. Therefore fascism can be described as "revolutionary" only in a very narrow and limited sense, and it certainly did not aim to transform class relations or the underlying structure of society - fascism aspired to the replacement of the traditional political elites *within* the pre-existing socio-economic framework. Fascism was therefore a political "revolution" which protected prevailing inequalities and preserved social stability - although it may have appeared radical and dynamic it was fundamentally inert. As Neocleous says, "the fascist political revolution is the *alternative* to social revolution" (Neocleous 1997 p.56). Despite its extravagant claims and pretentious posturing fascism could not conceal its ultimately defensive, counter-revolutionary purpose as a "revolt on behalf of order" (Fest 1973 p.105). Indeed, the fascists "like to call themselves revolutionaries, but one discovers best by their actions what they really want to change. Their revolution consists of hardening the character and purifying and energizing the community rather than making the social structure or the economic system more just or more free" (Paxton 1998 p.7). Although fascism was, self-evidently, more than a muscular Conservatism it was not "revolutionary" in the sense in which the term has been understood from 1789 onward, as a fundamental transformation in the social order and a re-distribution of power (see Paxton 2005 p.11). Therefore Hobsbawm was quite correct to consider fascists, in effect, "the revolutionaries of counter-revolution" (Hobsbawm 1994 p.117).

Fascism cannot be detached from the socio-economic variables that facilitated its emergence, growth and success – as such, it represented a particularly nasty and obnoxious form of capitalism which was, nevertheless, qualitatively different from other versions of capitalism (e.g. the liberal democratic or conservative authoritarian forms). Fascism was, therefore, an "exceptional state", the product of the particular character of the capitalist crisis and the fact that traditional social elites, which were fractured themselves as a consequence of economic dislocation, were incapable of sustaining political control in their own interests. Able to forestall socialist alternatives and prevent parliamentary progress, but unable to secure popular support to sustain their own authoritarian preferences, they therefore provided the political space for fascism to develop. In emphasizing its patriotic vision fascism could mobilize the population via mass party and periodic plebiscitory affirmation, thus providing an opportunity for capitalism to regenerate itself by effectively destroying the left and liberating the productive process from the fetters imposed upon it by organized labour. There is absolutely no doubt that key elements in the traditional ruling class attempted, quite cynically, to use fascism in this way. Fascism thereafter became a regime characterized by the mutual dependency between a mass political movement pursuing a nationalist, racist and authoritarian ideology, and capitalist interests which were anxious to ensure social stability, restore economic profitability and protect private property.

However, it must also be remembered that because of its mass base and the awesome authority of its leader - in effect its "relative autonomy" - fascism posed very a serious threat to dominant social elites themselves. The idea of a vulnerable ruling class - agrarian, industrial, military and bureaucratic - is not simply the retrospective rhetorical rationalization of the assorted moneybags who had chosen to accommodate an evil ideology. In the power-cartel of fascism, the dictator and mass party developed the capacity not only to dominate the other components in the army, big business and elsewhere, they actually possessed the potential to destroy them. However, in terms of the dangers posed by classical fascism to its erstwhile collaborators, the destructive dynamic only really became clearly evident in the final phases of the war when the power alliance between dictator and social elites began to collapse. By then their complicity in a barbarous war and genocidal murder was a well-established fact. As the power of fascist dictators expanded exponentially, and as the more esoteric, irrational aspects of fascist ideology were shifted toward centre stage, the capacity of fascism to work against the objective interests of capitalism and the bourgeoisie also increased. One fact, nevertheless, is absolutely incontrovertible - for the vast majority of ordinary people, and especially for the organised working class, fascism was a disaster. As Leon Trotsky said, "the historic function of fascism is to smash the working class, destroy its organisations, and stifle political liberties when the capitalists find themselves unable to govern and dominate with the help of democratic machinery...fascism, as a mass movement, is the party of *counter-revolutionary* despair" (Trotsky 1969 p.8 and p.10 italics added).

In addition to the question of fascism's "revolutionary" integrity there is also the thorny issue of whether fascism is actually a "right wing" ideology, and whether fascism can be clearly and unambiguously located upon the conventional, spatial "left-right" spectrum. Some analysts have questioned the utility of the generally accepted left-right continuum in the analysis of ideology, arguing that the political spectrum is circular rather than linear, with the extremes of left and right occupying simultaneously opposite and adjacent positions, whilst others argue that a more sophisticated graph or matrix should be used to reflect highly differentiated ideological positions. On the other hand some have suggested that fascism is a "centrist" ideology incorporating elements of both "left" and "right", radicalism and reaction (Lewis 1987) whilst others have maintained that not only should a distinct differentiation be made with forms of Conservatism, but that fascism is somehow "left wing". As Eatwell says "it is important not to view fascist ideology solely within a right-wing framework. Some fascists were former socialists, often disillusioned with the revolutionary potential of the working class, and attracted by the motivating power of myths" (Eatwell 1998b p.1188). Many commentators clearly agree with the substance of this approach, for instance Whisker suggests that fascism shared a common Marxist heritage with Bolshevism (Whisker 1983), whilst Griffiths, to take another example, argues that left wing characteristics are to be found in most varieties of fascism and that left and right are sometimes difficult to distinguish from each other (Griffiths 2005 p.1, p.5, see p.11 and p.126). In similar mode, the idea of "left-fascists", deployed by the likes of Roger Griffin (and, incidentally replicated in much journalistic material) highlights an analagous position (see Griffin 2003), while the likes of Rogger and Weber, Brittan, Thurlow, Green, Gregor (and indeed John Tyndall) have all argued that the existence of fascism and/or economic liberalism on the "right" makes it difficult to think conceptually in conventional "right-left" terms (see Rogger and Webber 1965 p.2). Thus Thurlow's observation regarding fascism that there is "no common agreement as to whether its roots lie in the political right or left" (Thulow 1999 p.1) may be a statement of fact, but simply highlights the depth of theoretical confusion. Interestingly, the idea that there is little substantive difference between "left" and "right" on the political spectrum is an assessment which broadly conforms to the assumptions made by fascists themselves, to the effect that their dynamic new movement(s) had rendered obsolete the conventional ideological distinctions (see Paxton 2005 p.12).

In fact, abandoning or amending the primary ideological metaphor of "left" and "right" can only add to the confusion surrounding fascism. Indeed this type of ideological obfuscation (deliberate or otherwise) is, in some ways, simply an updated and adapted version of "totalitarian theory". The apparently sophisticated idea of ideological reconfiguration is little more than totalitarian theory in a tuxedo, and the general acceptance by so many commentators of the need to equate "extremists" reflects not only the intellectual rehabilitation of thinkers like Arendt and Schapiro but also denotes, as Slavoj Zizek has pointed out, the capitulation of a liberal left which has tacitly accepted the unchallengeable primacy of (so-called) "moderate" forms of neo-liberal democracy (Zizek 2002 p.3). The reference to the similarity between "extremist" ideologies and the "totalitarian" threat, according to Zizek, sustains a kind of *Denkverbot* or prohibition against critical thinking which, by shamefully exploiting the horrors of the gulag and the Holocaust, effectively blackmails people into renouncing radical political engagement (Zizek 2002 p.4). The underlying assumption is that all sensible, rational people will opt for the "moderate" liberalism that prevails in the west. Of course an even better option from a neo-liberal capitalist perspective is to dismiss the "ideological" language of left and right altogether as an irrelevance in the new global order.

When analysing ideologies it is important to assess content, purpose and function as well as, form and method, and in so doing it becomes clear that fascism is ideologically adjacent to conservatism and opposite to socialism/communism (hence the notion of "left-fascism" is a confusing oxymoron). Although sub-division and the appraisal of subtle variation is crucial for more precise differentiation (e.g. types of "left" and "right": democratic/authoritarian, individualist/collectivist, radical/pragmatic) the "left-right" spectrum remains an indispensable analytical framework. Fascism and communism are mutually exclusive because the ideas, values and objectives differ dramatically, and more specifically this dichotomy reflects deeply divergent attitudes toward the "pole star" ideal of equality (Bobbio 1996). As a conceptual tool therefore, the idea of an ideological continuum from "left" to "right" retains its taxonomic value as a means of classification because "left" and "right" are emphatically *not* identical, or similar, or even two sides of the same coin, and the fact that there are various intermediary positions between and within "left" and "right" does not invalidate the model, any more than grey invalidates the contrast between black and white or dusk denudes the distinction between day and night (see Bobbio 1996 p.5).

We can conclude therefore that fascism was/is, despite all the confusion and ambiguity (contrived and otherwise) a right wing, counter-revolutionary ideology.

## NOTES

1]   It is important to consider Burleigh's work because his perspective has generated considerable debate. For example Gregor suggests there is "much of potential interest in this model" because it focuses on the link between the rational and emotional in politics, the communication and interpretation of dogma, cult forms and submission to authority  (Gregor 2005 p.9). In fact, despite the impressive historiographical detail, Burleigh's thesis and the notion of fascism as a political religion, constitutes a contradictory effort to downgrade the importance of the idea that ideology serves material interests, whilst blaming (in characteristically condescending fashion) narcissistic, ill-educated, sadistic, barbarian mobs for perpetrating violence. In effect Burleigh engages in an ultimately unsuccessful effort to re-calibrate the old totalitarian perspective about the similarities between fascism and communism.

Gregor rightly points out that a weakness in Burleigh's book is the extraordinary array of apparently unrelated targets, such as radical politics, hippies, left-wing intellectuals, Maoism, and political correctness (see Gregor 2005 p.10) – he might have added others, such as Bolshevism, Lenin, Trotsky, Stalin, the Soviet Union, George Bernard Shaw, Cuba and film director Ken Loach! (These attacks mark a stark contrast to Burleigh's evident admiration for Claus Schenk von Stauffenberg, who was a "tall, physically impressive Catholic" a "big man in every sense of the word", and an "accomplished cellist and horseman" who provided "elan" to the resistance against Hitler – a resistance which was, essentially, decent and honourable. Burleigh appears not to mind the fact that many of the military conspirators had been enthusiastic supporters of Hitler in the first place, and remained so right up until the point when it was clear they were going to lose the war) (see Burleigh 2001 p.713-716). Gregor is therefore correct to suggest that imprecise ideological digression and lack of analytical rigour seriously undermines the integrity of the Burleigh analysis. To take an illustrative example, Burleigh says that most Soviet citizens fought the Nazis for the elementary reason that their homeland was under dire threat from a murderous enemy rather than because they supported the political system (Burleigh 2001 p.500). This may indeed be the case, but probably underestimates the number who consciously fought for a better world by actively ridding it of the abomination of Nazism – and in any case, how many British soldiers fought Nazism in order to preserve free enterprise, still less pointless political anachronisms like the House of Lords or the Royal family?

In the final analysis the rich historical detail and insightful erudition contained in Burleigh's work cannot compensate for a fairly flimsy attempt to engage in political theory or indeed the frequent lapses into right-wing anglo-centric political prejudice. Burleigh is, in essence, strong on "when" and "where", but relatively weak on "why", and provides little in the way of explanation.

The emphasis on point-scoring, so apparent in Burleigh, is also evident in Emilio Gentile's work (see Gentile 2005). His shrill rebuttal of Richard Bosworth's critique brings to mind Woody Allen's observation that academics are like the Mafia – they only ever kill their own!

2] It is also interesting to note, as an addendum, that Ernst Nolte also delved into the metaphysical in his analysis. Although it would be erroneous to suggest that Nolte adhered in any way to a theocratic explanation, his foray into the extra dimension is perhaps best noted here. Nolte maintained that fascism, apart from everything else, was what he termed as a "metapolitical" phenomenon, which embodied resistance to transcendence at both a theoretical and practical level. By this he meant opposition to man's theoretical (e.g. philosophical or theological) capacity to conceive of and act upon an idea or goal that stands above his defective and humdrum existence. This novel adjunct to Nolte's thesis considers fascism as some kind of obstacle to the abstraction of life and thought. Quite why Hitler's utopia of a racially pure soldier-peasant society (with all its attendant features) should be considered in this way is obscure. Hitler's utopia may have been hideous, but it does appear to have possessed more transcendental qualities (in Nolte's terms) than, for instance, pragmatic Conservatism. In truth Nolte's contention is both mystifying and unsatisfactory. For a devastating critique of Nolte's work see Kitchen (1982 chapter 4). (See also Stern (1975) p.97). However, Nolte's work is actually credited with having revived scholarly interest in fascism (see Griffin 1995 p.297).

3]   Of course observations about "totalitarian" systems can make the same point in coming from the opposite direction – hence criticism of various left wing ideas as, implicitly or explicitly, *Linksfaschismus*. See bibliography, for example both Linz and Sternhell (1982 p.30 and p.379), Kedward (1971 p.240), Bullock (1962 p.402), Passmore (2002 p.32) and Talmon (1952) *The Origin of Totalitarian Democracy*. See also Roger and Weber (1965), Krejci (1987), Seton Watson (1979 p.357). An echo of this perspective is found in other more recent interpretations. For example Noel O'Sullivan (1983), in his unusual account, explains fascism in terms of the development of an "activist" style of politics. This "activism", he contends, resulted from mass democracy and an increased participation in politics which, together with the emergence of an excessive "optimism" about what politics could actually achieve, resulted in fascism. Thus the seeds of fascism are seen to exist and grow within the development of liberal democracy itself: "from the outset the modern liberal democratic tradition was vulnerable to extremist interpretations and the advent of fascism, in consequence, cannot be said to have marked its 'disintegration'. It marked, rather, the final disclosure of ambiguities which had been present from the beginning" (O'Sullivan 1983 p.64). O'Sullivan seems to suggests that the democratic process is not antithetical to fascism but, on the contrary, is part of the problem, constituting merely a prerequisite for "extremism", fascist or otherwise. Much of this, of course, is ploughing the same field as Hayek (1944), who saw any state intervention (nomatter how popular or democratically accountable) as the road to totalitarian serfdom, and Karl Popper (1945) who warned against the enemies of the "open society" (see F.A. Hayek *The Road to Serfdom* and Karl Popper *The Open Society and Its Enemies*).

4]    This idea was also posited (perhaps surprisingly) by Otto
      Strasser (1940a) and by historian Friedrick Meinecke as
      early as 1930, see Hildebrand (1985 p.108).

5]    Gregor leaves National Socialism out of the account, save
      certain tortuous references to "post-industrial totalitari-
      anism" in Germany (1979 p.326). It is indeed difficult to
      see how Nazism could fit into Gregor's "modernization"
      theory given the degree of industrial development in
      Germany in 1933 (see later).

6]    Arendt (1962) added a tortured appendix to her book
      shortly after the Hungarian rising of 1956, which
      destroyed many of the assumptions upon which her
      work, and the totalitarian theory, were based. See
      Mosse (1979) for a more guarded critique of the
      totalitarian theory.

7]    In Maser's case this preoccupation with the leader has led
      him to study Hitler in prodigious detail - interviews are
      conducted with school-fellows and army colleagues, he
      even assesses Hitler's medical records, daily routine and
      menu in an attempt to shed light upon the evil dictator
      (see Maser 1973, 1973a and 1970). Even an accomplished
      historian like William Carr, who was not prone to dwell on
      irrelevant detail, was nevertheless drawn into an account
      of Hitler's gastric flatulence (see Carr 1978 Chapter 5 "A
      sick man?"). For their part, Petrova and Watson (1995)
      pore over the precise details surrounding Hitler's death
      (research based on, we are told, not only newly acquired
      forensic details, unpublished photographs and unseen
      watercolours by the Fuhrer, but an actual examination
      of Hitler's skull). The precise value of such obsessive
      fascination remains unclear. Lest anyone assume that
      the historiographical obsession with scarcely relevant
      minutiae is confined to Hitler, it is worth mentioning
      Dorril's work on the BUF, where he tells us that Mosley's
      signature and handwriting "displayed a wish to impress...
      (and) portrayed intelligence, will-power and the desire
      to achieve great things" (Dorril 2006 p.13).

8]   Although Renton notes a "methodological retreat" in the first volume of Kershaw's work, which "slips toward a more customary biography of Hitler" (Renton 2001 p.62)

9]   As we saw earlier, Gregor saw Communist regimes in the same way, and so embraces both the totalitarian and developmentalist theses. Gregor also says that he would like to think that his work is the best brief outline of Fascism as an ideological and political system available in English (Gregor 1979a p.ix). It isn't. For a start, quite apart from theoretical inadequacies, Gregor revealed a distinct sympathy for fascist ideology as "'coherent'" and "'persuasive'" (cited in Bosworth 1998 p.79). Indeed, whilst writing in the journal *The European*, Gregor even pondered the merits of Mosley's Union Movement (see Rees 1979 p.24-5 note No.104; Renton 1999 p.27). Hence Gregor's odd claim to "objectivity" is somewhat suspect.

10]  See Poulantzas (1974 p.209) where his rather recondite analysis refers to the PCI position as "infantile leftism" and the KPD stance as "sham ultra leftism". Poulantzas attributes the deficiency in Marxist analyses to the inability to grasp the nature of the imperialist chain, and Italy/Germany's weak position therin.

11]  Beetham (1983) contains several very interesting pieces by Bauer. See Mandel's Introduction to Trotsky (1971) who analyses various communist theories and regards Trotsky's as the most proficient and useful.

12]  More controversially Mason also suggests that the working class, by exploiting labour shortages, was able (to some degree) to defend its own collective interest against the regime in a continuing cycle of repression and concession, without actually possessing the power to challenge the regime itself (see Mason 1993 and 1996).

13]  Hence Passmore's observation that "those Marxists who did abandon the primacy of capitalist defence produced accounts not clearly differentiated from non-Marxist ones" is over-stated (Passmore 2002 p.15).

14]   See also Copsey's confusing comments about the BNP's economic policy under Tyndall. On the one hand Copsey quite correctly points out, "had Tyndall's BNP ever come to power, such a system would have been used to discipline the labour force and, where adjudications took place, they would have invariably favoured capital since the BNP remained committed to the maintenance of a private enterprise economy albeit within the parameters of national economic policy" (Copsey 2008 p.97). Yet he continues, "there can be no doubt that in its formula for ultra-nationalist rebirth, what the British National Party had aspired to was economic revolution...what all this foresaw was not some 'tinkering' with the prevailing system but a 'total' transformation of British economic life – the onset of a new, post-liberal economic order" (Copsey 2008 p.97). Copsey therefore asserts, "for sure this was a revolutionary right intent on overthrowing pluralist, representative democracy and replacing it with an illiberal system of totalitarian control" (Copsey 2008 p.98).

# CONCLUSION

## FASCISM, THE FAR RIGHT IN BRITAIN
## AND THE RESPONSE OF THE LEFT

*"...what happened could happen again...A new Fascism, with its trail of intolerance, of abuse and of servitude, can be born outside our country and be imported into it, walking on tiptoe and calling itself by other names, or it can loose itself from within with such violence that it routs all defenses. At that point, wise counsel no longer serves, and one must find strength to resist"* (Primo Levi 2008 p.396)

---

The far right in Britain (as we have noted) can only really be explained with reference to the historical experience of classical fascism, and organizations like the BUF, NF and BNP have not only been fascist, but at times explicitly Nazi, in their ideological orientation. However, apart from very short periods in the 1930s, 1970s and in the current era, the far right has been politically ineffective in Britain. Indeed, for the most part the fascist fringe has only really attracted a "hotch-potch of wierdos, paedophiles, social misfits and egomaniacs" (Bullstreet 2001 p.5). However, the importance of the groups and individuals which together constitute the British far right lies in their contribution to the continuity of an unbroken heritage which keeps alive a tradition of fascist ideas in onerous circumstances (Billig 1978 p.350). The fact that the BNP, as the most significant right wing fascist organization, has had to adapt itself to try and meet the challenges of the twenty-first century, underscores this observation. As a consequence, of course, it is necessary and appropriate to identify qualitative differences between classical and contemporary forms (see Prowe 1994): for instance, the focus on anti-communism has receded as the political threat from the left has diminished, and anti-semitism has been obscured (but not eliminated) by opposition to immigration, multiculturalism and Islam, whilst military expansionism and rural romanticism also appear rather less relevant today. Nevertheless, some of these differences are a reflection of a purely tactical re-orientation – it would certainly be naïve to assume that the BNP has assimilated democratic values and practices. Fascists today may be intent on fighting their political battles on a new terrain, utilizing a variety of different tactics, but the underlying ideological dynamic is still heading in very much the same direction as before and they occupy, broadly speaking, the same position on the ideological spectrum. Hence the contention that the BNP is "part of the extreme right" but is "not fascist" (Passmore 2002 p.24) is both misleading and potentially dangerous [1].

Given the relative failure of British fascism, many academics, journalists and commentators have sought an explanation for this in the inherent moderation of British political culture which, they argue, not only rejects fascism but eschews extremism of all varieties. As Macklin says "the 'classic' Liberal histories of British fascism stress that the political bestiality of British fascism was repelled by the essential gentleness of English 'civic culture'" (Macklin 2007 p.2). British (English) people are seen as far too sensible and circumspect to embrace such an apparently radical creed. Consequently, as Kushner has noted, "the decency factor continues to dominate when explanations are sought for the failure of British fascism" (Kushner 1994 p.28). In fact Roger Griffin, the chief architecht of the so-called "new consensus" in "fascist studies", is one of the most high profile exponents of such a view. Griffin maintains that the core of British culture contains within it an innate distrust of demagogy and a pervasive aversion to fanaticism. Indeed Griffin argues that fascism was "an abortive political movement in the overwhelming

majority of cases, and British fascism only confirms the rule...
it will only develop into a significant popular movement
when an unusual conjuncture of structural forces are present
in that society; and that it will only be in a position to seize
state power in a set of conditions so rare as to be considered
'freak'" (Griffin 1996  p.141 and p.142). So Griffin suggests
that it is only in a very narrow set of  extremely abnormal
circumstances that people might be seduced by fascism's anti-
systemic, palingenetic ultra-nationalistic political liturgy.

Since Griffin is so pre-eminent in the academic field, and
his perspective on the reasons for the abject failure of British
fascism are emblematic of the dominant orthodoxy, his views
are worthy of more detailed examination. Roger Griffin
explains that fascism is a "revolutionary political creed, and
hence a force which except in the most exceptional historical
conditions will only appeal 'naturally' to a small minority of
temperaments – most people being by nature reactionary/
conservative or reformist/gradualistic in their politics, if not
apolitical. This radically narrows the potential support base
for fascism's intensely revolutionary and utopian form of politics" (Griffin 1996 p.146). Moreover, in terms of the British
experience Griffin maintains that fascism was a "latecomer"
into a society which has developed an abundance of non-
fascist or anti-fascist political and cultural themes denying it
ideological space, and fascist ideas have been further marginalised by the "irreducible pluralism of modern society",
therefore whilst it was poisonous and potentially lethal in
local areas, British fascism was a "storm in a tea-cup" (Griffin
1996 p.162 and p.163). This is why, according to Griffin, fascist
seeds may continue to germinate but they will inevitably
shrivel up long before they flower because the conditions for
growth have "disappeared for good" (Griffin 1993 p.112). As
Griffin succinctly puts it: "to imagine a conjuncture of events
in which an overtly anti-liberal, hyper-nationalist, and revolutionary political force such as fascism might come to govern
the country is to indulge not so much in counter-factual speculation as political science fiction" (Griffin 1996 p.162), and

as a consequence contemporary fascism possesses little more than "nuisance value in the macro-political scheme of things" (Griffin 2002 p.19). Fascist organisations, Griffin says, have therefore had to de-materialize into hard-core leaderless, "rhizomic" cellular networks (e.g. via the internet), or have mutated into right-wing populist parties in order to survive as their post-war habitat contracted (Griffin 2002 p.20). The ascendancy of liberal capitalism has effectively ensured the defeat of fascism. This is a very clear position, articulated by one of the most prominent academic experts on fascism, and it would also be fair to say that conventional wisdom on the subject broadly concurs with Griffin's viewpoint - in essence, the consistent political failure of fascism somehow reflects Britain's immunity to extremism, and the prospects for fascism in Britain are exceedingly bleak.

However, there are reasons to be sceptical about some of the assumptions underpinning this consensus and the notion of British "exceptionalism" which underpins it (see Eatwell 2000, 1992b), indeed there may even be a critical sense in which Roger Griffin's perspective is manifestly myopic. Certainly the speculative idea that a fascist or fascist-type regime could *not* occur in Britain seems dangerously complacent. In fact it is entirely sensible to be far less sanguine about fascist ideology and the condition of the far right in Britain, and the capacity of fascist ideas to do harm in the future should not be underestimated.

The ballot box, party membership figures or Parliamentary representation are not the only criteria by which success or impact should be judged. The metaphor of the sturdy liberal tide-barriers erected against any potential fascist flood is an interesting one, and there may be some mileage in it (Griffin 1996), however the real danger is not necessarily that the damns will be dramatically destroyed by a tidal wave of fascist votes, but that democratic values, institutions and processes are effectively eroded from within. The slide into a qualitatively different type of regime may be much more gradual and incremental, as Paul Wilkinson once pointed out in a moment of clarity, "perhaps the greatest danger of all to our democratic societies does not stem so much from the more obvious external threats, but from a kind of creeping fascism from within, the gradual encroachment of our democratic liberties, values and institutions by authoritarianism, unbridled militarism, and a paranoid retreat into narrow and aggressive nationalism..." (Wilkinson 1981 Preface).

In fact it is interesting to note just how far things have moved in this direction. The tone for the early twenty-first century was undoubtedly set by the authoritarian populism of Thatcherism in the 1980s, with its emphasis on a strong state, hierarchical social order and strident nationalism (it is always worth remembering that Thatcher supported the Apartheid regime in South Africa and befriended the vile dictator Pinochet) (see Hayes 1994). The course set by Thatcher has been followed with little deviation by subsequent administrations, indeed New Labour has guided the British state into some very deep waters. As Mark Neocleous has pointed out, the scope afforded to fascist-type ideas within liberal democracy by the "anti-terrorist/security" agenda is significant and growing exponentially (Neocleous 2009). The most cursory glance at the so-called "war on terror" (and the nationalistic military interventionism that has accompanied it) reveals that the nature of the British state has itself been radically transformed. As prominent human rights lawyer Gareth Peirce has explained, well established legal principles, which have been in place since the seventeenth century, have been distorted or destroyed in the name of "national security" – habeas corpus has been abandoned, secret courts preside to hear secret evidence where guilt is inferred by association, whilst torture has been used and justified (Peirce 2010) [2]. Reference here might also be made to the official treatment of asylum seekers and the more pervasive prejudicial attitudes towards the Muslim community generated by state-led "counter-terrorism". Indeed, in many ways the counter-terrorist strategy has been constructed upon implicit notions about the nature of Islam and the minority Muslim community which conform to an agenda that has been set by, and suits, the unreconstructed racists on the extreme right of the political spectrum.

So in this sense, on some issues, not only does the BNP's Nick Griffin stand in close ideological proximity to certain contemporary policy makers in Britain, he is very much looking over their shoulder and setting the agenda – and the sclerosis of a secretive, unaccountable, coercive authoritarianism continues to spread throughout the British state. In this sense a rigid distinction between liberal-conservative authoritarian state practice and aspects of fascist ideology is problematic because of clear similarities and continuities in terms of policy priority, practice and political purpose (see Kallis 2000a p.96). Conservative authoritarianism may not be the same as fascism, but there are certain, identifiable family resemblances and although the difference between fringe and fabric may be qualitative and disnernible, they are both cut from the same cloth (Hayes 1994, 1995). In any event, as Kershaw has correctly remarked, "even if a collapse into new forms of fascism is inherently unlikely in any western democracy, the massive extension of the power of the modern State over its citizens is in itself more than sufficient cause to develop the highest level possible of educated cynicism and critical awareness" (Kershaw 1995 p.213). Clearly, Roger Griffin's focus on the miniscule and diminishing "revolutionary" threat of fascist ideology (from outside, as it were) means that he is, to some extent, looking in the wrong direction - really significant changes are already taking place behind his back.

Moreover, it might be argued that the fashionable emphasis on the "unBritishness" of fascism and the inherent tolerance of the British people reflects an uncritical acceptance of what is, in effect, a convenient cultural myth or "noble lie". As Ken Lunn put it "the somewhat smug notion that Britain, or British society, was somehow immune to the tendency to support or sympathise with fascist regimes needs to be shaken...British society cannot be simply assumed to be devoid of elements of sympathy for the ideological dimensions of fascist activity" (Lunn 1996 p.173). If we look at public attitudes in Britain we can identify a "latent support for the extreme right in British politics" (see John and Margetts 2009). As Robert Ford (2010) has pointed out, drawing on a range of survey data, there is a clear constituency for ideologies that stress authoritarianism, ethnic nationalism and xenophobia (Ford 2010 p.147). Hostile sentiments about immigration and asylum seekers, and support for the far right agenda is particularly pronounced among white working class respondents, but is certainly not confined to this category (Ford 2010 p.154, see p.158). Indeed, from 2000 onwards the "issue agenda shifts steadily in favour of the extreme right" with anxiety focusing on immigration, crime and terrorism (Ford 2010 p.156). Ford concluded that, "the polling evidence suggests that the extreme right in Britain is currently realizing only a fraction of its electoral potential" (Ford 2010 p.158). As the folk-memory of a war against fascists fades into the historical distance  the discontent with a self-serving and corrupt political class in Britain has been growing. At the same time an electoral system produces major parties which share an ideology dominated by a commitment to neo-liberal economics and state authoritarianism, thereby attenuating any sense of meaningful  ideological choice. Given the gradual authoritarian transformation of the state and the rightward drift in public attitudes it is indeed interesting to note just how far ordinary Britons have assimilated or accommodated proto-fascist assumptions, structures and processes as constituent components of  ordinary everyday political "normality".

There is, in short, no impenetrable damn of liberal tolerance separating conventional politics from fascism, despite the comforting assurances of some academics. As Cronin has pointed out, the claim that British fascism has "failed" is "naively simple" (Cronin 1996 p.1) and the idea of "failure" tends to obscure the uncomfortable fact that fascism has made significant political progress, has set the political agenda on certain specific issues, and retains the capacity to do severe damage to the social fabric. In fact Kushner has made the interesting observation that the emphasis on the neo-Nazi "other" provides a comforting illusion about the nature of British society and culture, which remains imbued with racist notions, indeed Kushner believes that in Britain there is a "desire to play with fascist toys at arms' length" (Kushner 1994 p.44). Put simply, the focus on the abject "failure" of the caricature villains of the "fascist other" actually enables British society to ignore its own particular imperfections, some of which owe a debt to certain political and social preconceptions held in common with elements on the far right. Therefore, Britain's relationship with the ideology of fascism is more ambivalent and ambiguous than one might expect, given the abject electoral failure of explicitly fascist political parties.

The question of the re-emergence (or resurrection) of fascism in some form is therefore far from redundant, indeed there is "no more insistent or haunting question posed to a world that still aches from wounds that fascism inflicted on it" (Paxton 2005 p.172). In fact, when assessing the actual prospects for fascism in Britain it is important to view such a possibility in terms of three critical, inter-related variables, two of which will be dealt with in the next sub-section, while the third will form the basis of a conclusion.

## The Ruling Class and Neo-Liberal Economics as Critical Contingent Variables

Of course, when evaluating the possible future trajectory of fascism in Britain there are a number of obvious focul points – for instance the quality of fascist leadership, the mechanics of the electoral system and, more generally, the extent to which conventional Parliamentary politics can absorb social discontent in the era of austerity. However, by far the most important factors are: the political disposition of prevailing social elites (most of which have embraced the dominant ideology of neo-liberalism as reflective of their best interests), and the projected performance of the British economy. "Since the fascist route to power has always passed through cooperation with conservative elites, at least in the cases so far known, the strength of a fascist movement in itself is only one of the determining variables in the achievement (or not) of power", indeed "the only route to power available to fascists passes through cooperation with conservative elites. The most important variables, therefore, are the conservative elites' willingness to work with the fascists (along with a reciprocal flexibility on the part of the fascist leaders) and the depth of the crisis that induces them to cooperate" (Paxton 2005 p.98 and 1998 p.16).

In fact there is really very little evidence to suggest that the ruling class in Britain would be averse to a more abrasive authoritarian regime if it was felt that the circumstances required it. Naturally, as Terry Eagleton pointed out some time ago, "bourgeois society has expended an enormous amount of historical energy in the evolution of its liberal democratic ideologies, and won't willingly dispense with this elaborate ideological stabilization of the class struggle in order to hand over political power to a shabby bunch of paranoid petit-bourgeois thugs whom it would not tolerate in its drawing rooms" (Eagleton 1976 p.100). However, it has always been the conservative and nationalist ruling classes that facilitated fascism's success by incorporating them into government, albeit in an attempt to use them for their own purposes (Noakes 1990 p.74). We have noted how such elites compromised with classical fascism in Italy and Germany – it was the arch conservative Von Papen who, having persuaded Hindenburg to appoint Hitler as Chancellor, declared "'we've hired Hitler'" (cited in Neville 1999 p.19, see Noakes 1990); and it was the liberal Giolitti who confidently exclaimed that the Fascists would be like "'fireworks: they'll make a great deal of noise but only leave smoke behind'" (cited in Bosworth p.156). The fascists did not storm the structures of state power, the front door was unlocked from the inside by Conservatives. "Everywhere the 'fascist solution' was endorsed by such powerful individuals, groups and institutions in order to strengthen the popular appeal of the existing state...without any exception, fascist movements/parties climbed to power through the complicity of indigenous elite sectors in the framework of a conscious political experiment with more popular forms of authoritarianism" (Kallis 2000a p.79 and p.96).

This particular point is worth developing, since a kind of anti-fascist national myth has evolved in Britain as a consequence of the conflict with Nazi Germany (and Fascist Italy) between 1939-45. The uncomfortable fact is that participation in the war against Hitler (and Mussolini) reflected a desire to protect certain long-held strategic, geo-political and economic interests, rather than a battle over ideological principle or morality. In short, the ruling class in Britain was drawn into an anti-fascist position by the foreign policy of Hitler because the Nazi design for continental supremacy posed a threat to Britain's traditional interests, it certainly did not reflect any deep antipathy toward fascist ideology – in fact many members of the British ruling class (and beyond) were really rather impressed by fascist ideas and the "achievements" of fascist regimes (see Griffiths 1980). As Pugh points out, "for the British Government fascism in Italy was an experiment deserving of success", "many leading politicians sympathized with Hitler" and "the support shown for the main elements in the fascist critique by public figures, including those who never described themselves as fascists, suggests that there was little really alien in their ideas" whilst "aristocratic Conservatives were especially susceptible to the appeal of fascism" (Pugh 2005 p.38, p.130, p.73 and p.78).

One might also cite, in this regard, the utterances of the Conservative Party's very own "anti-fascist" war-lord Winston Churchill who could not bring himself to support the Spanish Republic against the forces of General Franco (see Hobsbawm 1994 p.113). On a visit to Fascist Italy as Chancellor of the Exchequer, Churchill remarked that: "if I were an Italian I am sure I would have been with you from the beginning to the end in your victorious struggle against the beastial appetites and passions of Leninism...But in England ... we have our own way of doing things", "'your movement has rendered a service to the whole world..She has provided the necessary antidote to the Russian poison'" (Churchill cited in Mussolini 1939 p.283-5, and cited in Behan 2003 p.113). Churchill proceeded to explain Italian Fascism's significance as a triumph of western civilization and applauded its capacity to mobilise the masses against the "cancerous" common enemy of communism (see Ali 2013). Churchill did not disguise his admiration for Hitler either: "'I have always said that if Great Britain was defeated in war, I hoped we should find a Hitler to lead us back to our rightful position among the nations'" (Churchill cited in Ali 2013). Winston Churchill's opposition to fascism was neither ideological nor ethical in motivation.

It is also always worth remembering that in the inter-war period the influence of the fascist phenomenon extended widely throughout the political "right" and there was a "flourishing traffic" in ideas and personnel between fascism and the Conservatives in Britain (Pugh 2005 p.5). Certain sections of the ruling class in Britain not only flirted shamelessly with fascism between the wars, but many Conservatives saw fascism as simply a more virile and robust expression of their own ideas, a kind of Ultramontane version of Conservatism. As Griffiths says, certain sections of the "British Right" fell for fascist overtures "hook, line and sinker" (Griffiths 1980 p.377). In effect therefore the conflagration after 1939 represented a war of interests rather than ideas - it was a war conducted against fascists rather than the ideology of fascism. This dimension has, of course, been distorted somewhat by the post-war reaction to the reality of the Holocaust, which not only revealed the evil essence of Nazi practice, it precipitated a retrospective rationalization by those same Conservative elements. As Griffiths says, "the present's view of the past has been coloured by the events that have taken place in between" (Griffiths 1980 p.375). This revision may have been an understandable reflex in response to Genocide, but it should not be allowed to obscure the nature of the relationship between Conservatism and fascism before the war. Unquestionably, if the war had gone badly, Britain would have supplied its very own own Petain or Quisling, and those most eager to collaborate (such as the dim-witted Nazi sympathizer Edward VIII) would have come from the Establishment and the Conservative right (Hayes 1995). In fact Skidelsky mentions revealingly, with regard to the BUF, that the Conservative Establishment mistrusted Mosley and felt that if there was going to be fascism in England it "would be introduced under the auspices of the National Government, not by a grass-roots fascist movement" (Skidelsky 1981 p.420) [3]. The fact that the anti-fascist consensus survived the war, and that an anti-Nazi folk memory continues to exist, does not invalidate the contention that it is the Conservative right and conservative elements in the ruling class who are most likely be seduced by, and succumb to, the fatal allure of fascist theory and practice. Fascism prevails when people of power and privilege accede to it, and that class of people in Britain, given "appropriate" circumstances, is no less susceptible than any other comparable European country.

As a consequence it is not difficult to envisage a similarly misguided accommodation between the ruling elites in the UK and a suitably British version of fascist-authoritarian nationalism which, denuded of its more obvious fascist signifiers, might nevertheless provide a bridgehead to a far more sinister future. It is also worth noting that even after 1945 some Tory elements tried to tempt Mosely back into the Conservative fold (Dorril 2006 p.549) and many "liberal-minded" post-war Conservatives were not averse to a more authoritarian paradigm if the alternatives were considered still more unsatisfactory. An instructive example in this context was Tory grandee Sir Ian Gilmour, one of the Conservative Party's leading "anti-Thatcher" moderates in the 1980s and author of *Inside Right* (1978), who talked about theoretical case for ending democracy if the results of the electoral process were undesirable. Hence the idea that there is some kind of inpenetrable ideological firewall separating fascists from the more mundane varieties of the traditional Conservative right is conceptually misguided and historically inaccurate (see Levy

1999 p.116). The major difference between the fascist and the non-fascist Right is the fact that fascism exists by mobilizing the masses from below (see Hobsbawm 1994 p.117). As Ralph Miliband once noted, "...it is not very difficult to conceive of a British form of Conservative authoritarianism, which would maintain some of the features of traditional constitutionalism, proclaim its dedication to ultimately democratic objectives, assure one and all that the state of emergency would not last a day longer than necessary, and insist that the measures taken under that state of emergency, though no doubt drastic, were clearly essential for national recovery and renewal" (Miliband 1984 p.154). In this sense "fascism is never far beneath the surface of bourgeois democracy" (Eagleton 1976 p.106). It is always worth remembering that in Germany the Nazi vote was only 2.6% in 1928 and declining just before they achieved power, whilst in Italy, after Italian Fascists performed abysmally in the elections of 1919 the socialists actually carried a coffin to Mussolini's house in a mock funeral procession, but by 1922 Mussolini was in control of the state (and six weeks after that, incidentally, dining with King George V at Buckingham Palace). Circumstances can change in the blink of an eye.

Although there is little value in being drawn into facile counter-factual conjecture, it is nevetheless obvious that any fascist or proto-fascist type of regime in Britain would differ significantly from that which occurred on the continent in the 1920s and 30s, simply because of the qualitative variation in the contextual circumstances and national history – in effect, those aiming to construct such a regime in this country would have to make use of the materials at hand, so in this sense fascism of the classical kind is indeed historically specific. As Tom Nairn observed as long ago as 1970, no reactionary regime "could possibly overlook those priceless symbols of nationhood, Westminster, the Crown and the Constitution" (Nairn 1970 p.28). In any case, a British variant of fascism would inevitably attempt to avoid being tainted as somehow subservient to a foreign creed, and be duly deferential to British traditions, institutions, history and culture. Therefore, "it is possible for fascism itself to recur, but of course it would not necessarily arise or come to power in the same form as in the past. History never repeats itself exactly. A given form of exceptional regime and a given type of political crisis have different features according to the historical period in which they appear" (Poulantzas 1974 p.358). The work of Aristotle Kallis on "fascistization", and the idea of experimentation with selective elements of fascism, is clearly pertinent in this context (see Kallis 2003).

Contemporary fascists are unlikely to wave swastikas, wear paramilitary uniforms or swear ostentatious allegiance to the army - they are far more likely to wear pin-striped suits and profess adherence to the basic business virtues of profitability and efficiency which pervade our culture – the dominant ideology is always bound to be absorbed and modified to produce a particular political synthesis, the precise character-istics of which will undoubtedly reflect the prevailing ethos of the era. Fascism thus seeks out in each national culture those themes through which it is best able to mobilize the masses against democracy and the left, thereby convincing Conserva-tives of the rectitude of their cause and the utility of their movement  (see Paxton 2005 p.40, see Kallis 2003). Therefore British fascism is unlikely to be a straightforward replica of classical fascism, and even the current crop imbecilic fascists realize that simply copying the rhetoric and aesthetics of old style-fascism is the equivalent of purchasing a one-way ticket to political oblivion. Fascism will never, unfortunately, do us the service of returning without a disguise. However, "if we under-stand the revival of an updated fascism as the appearance of some functional equivalent and not as an exact repetition, recurrance is possible" (Paxton 2005 p.175).

Such a hypothetical scenario cannot possibly carry the burden of being described as a prediction, and even such a speculative prognosis might be dismissed as overly pessimistic or even a sign of pronounced paranoia. However, this would be missing the point. The significance of making observations about prospective political arrangements is to identify from which direction the threat will emerge. Much depends on the political attitude and ideological flexibility of those Conservative elites who wield power, and how much ground they are prepared to concede in order to preserve their wealth and privilege. In normal circumstances of course the ruling class, although mendacious and meticulously self-serving, is able to sustain its hegemony without recourse to such severe alternatives. However it is important to acknowledge that there is no logical compatibility between capitalism and democracy or liberalism, and that political forms are not generated spontaneously - there is, in other words, great scope in the type of political regime which capitalism can accommodate. Fascism will evolve, if at all, as a consequence of an accommodation with the most Conservative and reactionary elements of the ruling social and political elites, many of whom  might very well have distinct reservations about specific aspects of fascist policy. However, in the context of economic turmoil and heightened class conflict, the rejection of particular ideological facets might weigh far less heavily than the notion that a fascist-type regime might be the only reliable political force capable of winning popular support and pulling the cart out of the mud (see Taylor 1985 p.154). Fascism becomes attractive when the ruling class are in despair, and are willing to throw in their lot with ideological fanatics and, in the final analysis, "there are no limits to which monopoly capitalism will not go to ensure its continuing hegemony; anyone who regards that statement as a piece of leftist paranoia has only to think of Buchenwald" (Eagleton 1976 p.101). Vita-Finzi once said, citing an old Persian proverb, that in certain situations the ruling class is quite capable of concluding that "'dirty water will do for putting fires out'" (Vita-Finzi 1968 p.231-2).

This brings us onto the second significant element in this particular equation – much depends on how Britain's economic position develops, because the rhetoric of state authority, strident nationalism, racism and social discipline is far more likely to resonate in an atmosphere of political and social dislocation created by seemingly intractable economic crisis. Obviously the financial collapse of 2008 is of considerable relevance here.

The recent spectacular crisis in the financial markets, as credit expansion, asset price inflation and speculation reached its inevitable crisis point, has not only left the global economy "in tatters" but raised some very serious questions about the long-term viability of western free market capitalism (Chang 2010 p.xiii). Such questions are particularly pertinent for Britain which, as a consequence of de-industrialisation under Thatcher, developed an economy distorted in favour of the provision of financial services. As the apostles of laissez-faire capitalism dissolved into the ether and books on Keynesian economics were hastily dusted off, the British government engaged in the most extraordinary bale-out of the banking sector. Ordinary citizens, who had little or no knowledge of sub-prime speculative excess or unsustainable leverage ratios, were expected to pay the price in terms of cuts in jobs and services, as politicians organised one of the most colossal state interventions in economic history (Chang 2010 p.8). Of course political elites in Britain are now, under the guise of the Coalition's "austerity programme", busy attempting to stabilize the very same neo-liberal economic model that produced catastrophe in the first place, and although perhaps the era of free market triumphalism has been brought to an abrupt end, the capitalist economic system still remains intact (Milne 2011, Callinicos 2010 p.2). Although the financial and economic crisis once again clearly exposed the chaotically irrational contradictions within capitalism, the extraordinary state sanctioned subsistence of the self-serving financial alchemists was never likely to be accompanied by any acknowledgement that capitalism itself, constructed upon inequality and exploitation, is systemically dysfunctional. Indeed the great success of the political elites has been to convince the population that there was really no alternative to the course of action taken by the governments after 2008. However, as Seumas Milne has commented, the consequences of the crash are only just beginning to manifest themselves: "the evidence is piling up that the full impact of the crisis is only starting to make itself felt – and that both the economy and politics will be transformed before it has run its course" (Milne 2011).

In effect, what recent economic events have starkly revealed is that the "freak" configuration which Roger Griffin identified as the only context within which fascism might flourish, is not actually unusual but an integral part of the dynamic of capitalist development. Each successive economic crisis, of course, opens up space for discursive ideological alternatives, and in the context of economic disarray and disintegration the urge to submit to a more authoritarian and nationalistic capitalist formula may become overwhelming. In such a situation the generally accepted notions of democracy and liberty then "mirrors the logic of a gesture meant to be refused" (Zizek 2009 p.135) [4]. In a society which is apparently in the process of imploding, the attraction of fascistic ideologies may become far more compelling as disaffected voters become attracted by the superficial radicalism of far right wing parties with their anti-system rhetoric. In such a situation fascist ideology, with its emphasis on collectivism, is quite simply more dangerous because it is more convincing than the sterile individualism that lies at the core of neo-liberalism. One of the fundamental insights of the fascist right is the emphasis on the social dimension and its acknowledgment that people need to feel a sense of social belonging, that is, the need to believe that there is more to existence than being an autonomous and atomised agent cast adrift  in the free market wilderness. The ideological vision of fascism is, in the context of socio-economic crisis, eminently more attractive, intellectually and emotionally, than the austere individualism offered by neo-liberals. The key point here is that in order to fulfill their need for social identity and political participation in a community which is evidently fragmenting as a result of persistent and progressively more critical economic crises, it is possible that people may embrace an extremely unpalatable ideology - even an ideology as barbarous and grotesque as a suitably modified version of fascism. In difficult times desperate people will seize upon anything to provide an "explanation" for their predicament and some prospect of respite, and they will gravitate toward any idea or movement which will provide hope and give their lives a larger existential significance.

The point of such conjecture is simply to acknowledge that the social, economic, cultural and psychological conditions that made fascism possible have not actually been eradicated. As Enzo Traverso explains, with regard to fascism's paradigmatic political criminality, "modern society is not immune to the danger of a repetition, perhaps in other forms and with other targets, of a horror comparable to the death camps" (Traverso 1999 p.54). It may even be the case, as Zigmunt Bauman has so eloquently explained, that the emphasis on technological rationality and efficiency in "modern" social formations actually makes it far easier for such ideas to manifest themselves into material reality (Bauman 1991). After all it was the rational, routine, technical, bureaucratic, impersonal and ethically blind organization of society that made the Holocaust possible. As Bauman says, "the Holocaust was not an irrational outflow of the not-yet-fully-eradicated residues of pre-modern barbarity. It was a legitimate resident in the house of modernity" (Bauman 1991 p.17). From Bauman's perspective the complex chain of causal and functional dependencies characteristic of state organization in the modern world is capable of obscuring the moral calculus and consequences of individual actions until "humanity" is rendered, in effect, invisible. In such a scenario, not only do Stanley Milgram and Phillip Zimbardo still make some sense, civilization itself remains incapable of guaranteeing the moral use of the extraordinary powers it has unleashed. As Bauman says, "if there was something in our social order which made the Holocaust possible in 1941, we cannot be sure that it has been eliminated since then" indeed "there seems to be less hope than before that the civilized guarantees against inhumanity can be relied upon to control the application of human instrumental-rational potential, once the calculation of efficiency has been awarded supreme authority in deciding political purposes" (Bauman 1991 p.86 and p.116). In short, the way modern society is organized may make immoral conduct more, rather than less, likely (Bauman 1991 p.198). In this sense fascism is an inevitable, immanent feature of capitalist society, even if its success is not predetermined and perhaps even unlikely (see Dandeker 1985).

The essential requirement is to recognize that such a danger still exists and, moreover, to be precise about where the danger actually comes from. As Mandel stated in the late 1960s "the actual breeding ground of fascism is not to be sought among the non-conformist minorities, but among the philistines muttering 'respectability, honour, loyalty'" (Mandel Introduction to Trotsky 1971 p.37), and "'when you look at the long and gloomy history of man you will find more hideous crimes have been committed in the name of obedience than have ever been committed in the name of rebellion'" (C.P. Snow cited in Landau 1998 p.7). Fascism or a fascist-type regime will emerge, if at all, out of an accommodation with Conservatism and ruling elites, and as a consequence of capitalist economic collapse, because essentially fascism is a right wing socially conservative political force and, as such, would offer predominant socio-economic and political elites a better chance of securing their overriding objectives in a period of profound uncertainty. In this sense, self-evidently, *Pecunia non olet* (Bauman 1991 p.103).

## Anti-Fascism: Reformism or Radical Resistance?

Clearly, as we have seen, the subtle dialectics of social change are not always positive or progressive – negations, interpenetrations and the laws of transformation are perfectly capable of casting dark shadows as well as light - there is no unilinear impetus toward greater "social progress". Beliefs are there to be acted upon, no matter how gruesome or grotesque, and the possibility of a version of fascist ideology being lived-out in

Britain is no more ridiculous or fanciful than mankind living-out any of the other pathological nightmares it has chosen to live-out from time to time. History is not a heritage park and it has the unsettling habit of repeating itself, even if it does so in ways which make it difficult to discern.

This brings us to the third contingent variable, in terms of evaluating the prospects for fascism, which is the quality and integrity of the explicitly "anti-fascist" forces in society. The response of the so-called "left" to the current crisis in capitalism, the concomitant drift toward authoritarianism and the growth of right wing extremism, is absolutely crucial. Indeed, the reaction of the "left" to the radical right has often been critically important in determining the success of fascist movements, and the consequences of adopting ineffectual tactic or erroneous strategy can be devastating (Fryth 1985, Kirk and McElligott 1999). There is, therefore, a heavy responsibility on leftist political groups, parties and movements to resist not just fascist groups and fascist ideology, but also the socio-economic conditions which tend to produce it – exploitation, unemployment, poverty and inequality.

Unfortunately New Labour's contribution in this regard has been little short of abysmal. Tony Blair's legacy is not just a "liberal" imperialist participation in immoral and illegal war, but political corruption, privatization, de-regulation, deteriorating public services, demoralized trade unions and, crucially, growing inequality. New Labour has been, from its inception, infatuated with the idea of convincing big business and the rhodium-plated super-rich that the party is economically "prudent" and "responsible", and in doing so it has capitulated completely to the impersonal forces of neo-liberalism. In effect New Labour has bought into the new consensus which was constructed around Thatcherite assumptions about the appropriate role of the state and the enduring utility of free markets. As a consequence New Labour, despite the odd dissenting voice, has supported free enterprise economics and been complicitous in the drift toward a more authoritarian state. It is this reality which makes the warnings of people

like David Miliband, a chief architect and exponent of New
Labour, so completely vacuous – quoting the findings of the
Searchlight Educational Trust he argued that insecurity in
society is, "fuel for the far right's hate" which lures people
"towards more aggressive forms of identity politics", conveniently ignoring the fact that whilst in power his party did
so much to perpetuate that insecurity (Miliband 2011). New
Labour's position on fascism and the drift toward authoritarian politics is therefore analogous to that of a voodoo
witch-doctor who can see quite clearly the visible symptoms of
severe infection, but who is quite unable to identify causes or
administer a cure, and indeed is perfectly capable of making
the condition significantly worse. In short, supporting New
Labour means endorsing the economic (and political) system
that not only produces vast inequality but which, crucially,
is capable of spawning fascism. Resistance against fascism is
always "a manifestation of the struggle between rich and poor"
and New Labour has effectively lost any lingering interest in
fighting that particular battle (Martell 1996 p.14).

Perhaps even more significantly, at a more general conceptual level, the liberal-left in Britain has effectively abandoned
anti-fascism as an irrelevance. For them the war has already been
won, a victory which was secured as the beneficent by-product of
social diversity and political pluralism. In essence, the liberal-
left intelligentsia has become obsessed with identity politics,
which has not only replaced the traditional radical emphasis
on class conflict, it has prioritised a social schema based on a
particular conception of certain cultural attributes. The new
"post-modern" left is fascinated by ethnicity, sexuality and
gender, along with the new social movements which purport
to represent those specific interests, whilst the "white working
class" is simply reconfigured as another marginalized cultural
category. As Milner argues, the new notions that emerged
to identify, articulate and defend cultural and sub-cultural
difference, and which produced "quasi-socialistic" political
movements, were actually sustained by the monetary demand
for a "commodifiable" counter-cultural text – gay lifestyle, black

consciousness or sisterhood became the new zeitgeist, and they positioned themselves in the market along with everything else (Milner 1999). Of course the outcome has been hardly equitable since the "solutions" to discrimination were mostly individualist and consumerist, rather than contained within an egalitarian-collectivist strategy which required meaningful, structural social change. As Milner says, "for all their apparent success, the new social movements have not challenged the fundamentally class-divided nature of late-capitalist society. It is difficult to avoid the suspicion that this has been so because, insofar as they derive their primary identities from an intelligentsia which is itself a socially privileged class, they remain reluctant to threaten class-based inequalities" (see Milner 1999 p.166). The consequences of this have been significant.

Unfortunately the "new left" has not only reinforced the sectarian separatism of "special interests" and undermined the idea of class struggle, it has tended to "Balkanise" the working class, thereby effectively fragmenting the forces of resistance to the far right. In essence the liberal-left have helped to prevent the various tributaries of doubt, anxiety and anger from coalescing into a political force capable of defeating the drift toward authoritarianism and the ideology fascism. Fashionable post-modern cynicism about collective action and the utility of meta-narratives has meant that, in the resulting cacophony of competing claims, "no melody can be sung in unison" (Bauman 2011 p.49). Despite the odd tactical success, the ultimate consequence has been socially and politically conservative because not only is working class unity undermined and division institutionalised, capitalism has been (is) perfectly capable of accommodating (and commercializing) the social categories prioritized by the new "radicals". Yet the doxa of "identity", "diversity" and "multi-culturalism", deployed as a political method (rather than a desirable end-product of more equitable social order) has assumed the status of a sacred cow on the liberal left.

There is, however, a much more dangerous dimension to this perspective because there is a sense in which the liberal-left have prioritised and deployed descriptive social categories which actually underscore the political preconceptions of the far right. In some ways, for example, the pre-occupation with ethnic identity and cultural pluralism merely reinforces the racial categories emphasised by unreconstructed fascists. Moreover, if tolerance is thin on the ground, then multiculturalism can easily degenerate into lawfully sanctioned mutual suspicion, hostility and hatred. It is not at all surprising therefore that the BNP, in its more modern manifestation, has been perfectly prepared to play the "cultural identity" card – the contours of the ideological territory mapped out by the trendy left are familiar to the far right and easy to navigate. In short, the "politically correct" intelligentsia, so infatuated with notions of "post-modernity", are playing into the hands of the very forces they claim to have transcended. Indeed it might even be argued that "multiculturalism" is effectively the ideology of the "end of ideology", the utopian dream of those liberal individualists on the left who were always so obviously uncomfortable with the language of class and confrontation (see Bauman 2011). It is also worth pointing out that actually standing up to the tyranny of the socio-economic status quo and resisting the forces of fascism requires a certain level of moral courage and political fortitude – evidence of which is meagre amongst the narcissistic liberal left [5].

Meanwhile, on the so-called "revolutionary" left in Britain "anti-fascist" strategy has often (although not always) been utilised as part of a broader effort to re-oxygenate the tired politics of Trotskyism. Of course, simply using anti-fascism to re-activate sectarian schemes or realise hopelessly ambitious political aspirations is both cynical and dangerous. However, the more disturbing aspect to their (hyper) active "revolutionary praxis" has been the fact that in most cases the tactics deployed have been conspicuously unsullied by any kind of contact with the working class – the one social group that is not only destined to lose most by an agenda set by the far right, but which is the only social force capable of securing the social transformation required to defeat fascism permanently.

Hence the objective for any "real" left must be to develop an anti-fascist strategy that has at least the possibility of engaging and mobilizing ordinary working class people. This means, of course, challenging the insidious, patronizing liberal perception of members of the "white working class" as either fascist-fodder or passive victims.

In the context of neo-liberal hegemony, declining trade union membership and the untimely demise of the Labour Party this may itself seem like a Sisyphean task of extraordinary proportions. Yet something like this was achieved, albeit on a micro-scale, by organizations like Anti-Fascist Action, which not only harnessed the creativity of ordinary people, it engaged in much more robust resistance to fascist organizations in the 1980s and 1990s (see Birchall 2010). In response to a fascist movement intent on "controlling the streets" it was AFA, rooted in local communities, which did a great deal of effective work in challenging the BNP and its pseudo-paramilitary affiliates. While liberal Parliamentarians postured for the media and middle class "revolutionaries" talked amongst themselves, militant anti-fascists "did most of the heavy lifting" (Birchall 2010 p.18). Many on the left were uncomfortable with such a ruthless approach, but as Gramsci once pointed out, "'what is the point in continuing to call yourself a Socialist and a revolutionary if all it means is that you get beaten up and shot'" (cited in Behan 2003 p.43). Here the lesson of the *Arditi del Popolo (ADP)*, the first effective anti-fascist organization (consisting of communists, socialists, republicans and anarchists) is important to learn (Behan 2003 p.4) [6]. The left in Britain has been far too preoccupied with the notion of free speech and the idea that fascism should be exposed to the penetrating light of democratic debate in the hope that sensible, rational people will see through the lies and half-truths of fascist discourse. Prioritizing freedom of speech above political reality is to commit a categorical error because fascists only ever use democracy in order to destroy it, although fascists are perfectly prepared to milk the Parliamentary cow before it is butchered. In any event, freedom of speech, like most other civil rights, is a contingent liberty, it cannot be an absolute right in all circumstances because everything depends on political circumstances and social consequences. Opposition to fascism cannot be gauged by the criteria of conventional political activity because the stakes are just far too high. Fascism is, in effect, the political equivalent of plutonium, so there is no genuinely "safe" way to engage with it at any level – active resistance is the only principled position to adopt. It is certainly no use relying on police forces or parliaments to eradicate fascism – in this sense Alexander "Sasha" Pechersky, a former Red Army soldier who led the rebellion in Sorbibor, will always be a more relevant and inspiring role model for genuine community-based anti-fascists than the pathetic political careerists and cynical opportunists who have come to dominate liberal "leftist" politics in the contemporary era.

Yet it is also important to note that there is really no escape from ideological confrontation (in the sense of taking up theoretical challenge posed by the radical right) because ideas are powerful. Certainly, the revisionist tendency toward the retrospective rationalization or "normalization" of fascism as an ideology should be assiduously resisted. Understanding fascism does not require acceptance, foregivess or justification, and any narrative of fascism should remain unremittingly hostile. Yet expecting ordinary people to support the anti-fascist position as a consequence of some reductive class formula which stresses "inevitable" social contradiction would be a fundamental mistake. It makes sense, in order to oppose the pollution of social and intellectual life by right wing fascist-type ideas, to offer a clear and unambiguous conceptual alternative which stresses that ultimately, the struggle against the  poisonous creed of fascism is, necessarily, a fight against the socio-economic framework which incubates it. Capitalism, its violence encoded in the system of acquisition and exploitation, has destroyed the lives of far more people than fascism ever has. Today 15% of the world's population consumes almost 80% of its wealth and the gap between rich and poor in Britain is greater than when Charles Dickens chronicled the squalor of Victorian England (see Callinicos 2000). Despite their best efforts, the likes of Fuku-yama and the apostles of neo-liberalism have been unable to exorcise the ghost of Marx, and the great socio-economic questions remain unresolved because the toxic elixir of unfet-tered capitalism has been exposed as "calamitous nonsense" (Milne 2012 p.xiii).

There is certainly a heavy political price to be paid if the political agenda is contructed around issues prioritized by the enemies of the working class. As Mandel noted many years ago, "if the movement lets itself be led around by the nose without offering significant resistance, and allows its power to be taken from it step by step, at the first really sharp change in the economic situation some clever adventurer might really be inspired to smash it" (Mandel Introduction to Trotsky 1971 p.36). Nevertheless, "there seems to be something in humanity which will not bow meekly to the insolence of power. It is true that power only really succeeds by winning the collusion of its underlings. The evidence, however, is that this collusion is usually partial, ambiguous and provisional" (Eagleton 2011 p.100). Militant anti-fascists need to build upon this resis-tance in the belief that "liberty, equality and fraternity" is a more inspiring slogan than Mussolini's exhortation to *Credere, Obbedire, Combattere* (Believe, Obey and Fight), and sure in the knowledge that egalitarianism and internationalism remain the only certain anti-dote to fascism. As Angelo Tasca (Rossi) said: "humanity must find salvation in its deeper self, and the deepest and most enduring feelings are those pertaining to enlightened moral consciousness ... the sun will shine on those who have managed to preserve the foundations of humanity that fascism is trying so hard to destroy forever" (Rossi/Tasca 1938 p.336).

*If we could learn to look instead of gawking,*
*We'd see the horror in the heart of farce,*
*If only we could act instead of talking,*

*We wouldn't always end up on our arse.*
*This was the thing that nearly had us mastered;*
*Don't yet rejoice in his defeat, you men!*
*Although the world stood up and stopped the bastard,*
*The bitch that bore him is in heat again.*

Bertolt Brecht *The Resistible Rise of Arturo Ui*

## NOTES

[1]   Passmore claims that highlighting the similarities between historic fascism and the current far right means omitting important features of the definition, such as hostility to electoral democracy and paramilitarism (Passmore 2002 p.88-90). To accept the BNP's 'national-populist' commitment to democracy and/or rejection of sub-state violence as anything other than a cynical tactical manouvre is to miss the real point. Although Passmore does accept that national-populism might be equally as dangerous, the ideological confusion unquestionably suits those fascists seeking to re-calibrate their image (see Passmore 2002 p.108).

[2]   A cursory consideration of the contemporary "debate" about the "legitimate" use of torture illustrates the point very well – who could have envisaged, prior to the "war on terror", such a deliberation taking place in a "liberal-democratic" society? The ground has shifted, and what was conventionally regarded as obscene and unjustifiable, has now become "necessary in the circumstances". This regression in discourse is not purely academic, it rarely is, because such public discussion often defines the limits of what is "acceptable".

[3]   Of course it also ought to be remembered that historically Conservatives have not been averse to threatening armed rebellion if the cause was right, as they did before the First World War when a united Ireland threatened the political and social pre-eminence of Ulster Unionists. The

highly questionable activities of the Security Services in the 1970s in reaction to Wilson's Labour administration, and their role in Northern Ireland during the period of the "troubles" might also be noted in this regard.

[4]    Zizek argues that "we are the ones we have been waiting for" (Zizek 2009 p.148) urging "preventive action" and Jacobin-Leninist forms to avoid capitalist catastrophe. Where his perspective is less plausible is in relation to the more specific tactics of anti-fascism. He argues that "interpretive demystification" is easier when dealing with a liberal democrat because of the tension between ideological content and form – the former belies the latter, and the disjuncture between aspirational ideas (freedom, democracy) and reality is clear. Yet he argues it is much more difficult to accomplish the same task and "enlighten" "our own" exploited worker who blames the Jews for his misery, and is seduced into directing their rage to the wrong target. This raises serious questions about, for instance, tactical orientation toward the EDL, which is overwhelmingly working class. In fact it would seem no less of a challenge to convert an unemployed supporter of the EDL than a  liberal Coalition-voting lecturer. Zizek acknowledges that "many" communists deserted the cause and joined the Nazis in the 1920s and 1930s, and some communists in France have turned to Le Pen – why the reversal of that process is so extraordinarily difficult to achieve is not adequately explained (Zizek 2009 p.68). Indeed if the experience of AFA in Britain is anything to go by, where more members flirted with right wing "extremism" than with the Liberal Democrats, then Zizek is simply wrong. The key point is surely that more members of the EDL are receptive to radical ideas about changing society and, moreover, possess the willingness to actually do something about it. The liberal, as Zizek is well aware, always has the capacity to resort to cynical disavowal ("yes I know very well, but...."). This

is an important issue for the left in Britain, and there is very little evidence that it is being taken seriously at all.

[5]    This may sound like a particularly harsh assessment. However, those people believing that this point is over-drawn should consult the record of the British "left" with regard to Ireland during the so-called "troubles". Check, for example, the number of articles devoted to the subject in the *New Left Review*. Any analysis of the Labour Party in relation to the same subject will reveal bi-partisan complicity in state sanctioned murder and torture.

[6]    Behan's claim that the ADP has similarities with the "united front" of the Anti-Nazi League in the UK is risible. Behan says "the ANL, like the ADP in the early 1920s, does not shy away from physically confronting Nazis" (Behan 2003 p.119). At the very least Behan is being economical with the truth because in many instances "shy away" is precisely what they did (Waterloo train station in 1992 is only the most obvious example). However, this certainly does not mean that Eatwell is correct in suggesting that the success of street resistance is essentially a "myth" (see Eatwell 1998b p.1188, 1992b p.184, and 2004 p.75-76).

# BiBLiOGRAPHY

Adam, C. (1978) "How to Spot an NF Child" *New Statesman* 27 January

Allardyce, G. (1979) "What Fascism is Not: Thoughts on the Deflation of a Concept" *American Historical Review* vol 84 No.2 pp.367-88

Ali, T. (2013) "When Tabloids Attack: L'Affair Miliband" *Counterpunch* October 11-13

Allen, M. (2002) *The Business of Genocide* Chapel Hill, University of North Carolina Press

Andreski, S. (1968) "Some sociological considerations on fascism and class" in Woolf, S. (ed) *The Nature of Fascism* London, Weidenfeld and Nicolson Chapter 6 pp.97-103

Anti-Fascist Action (nd) *Heroes or Villains?* London, AFA

Andrew, C (1989) "100 Years On: Lessons of Hitler's Evil Enchantment" *Daily Telegraph* 20 April

Arendt, H. (1962) *The Origins of Totalitarianism* London, Allen and Unwin

Ashley, J. (2010) "To see how fascism can be throttled, look at Barking" *Guardian* 29 November

Auschwitz-Birkenau State Museum (1995) *KL Auschwitz: Seen by the SS* Oswiecim, ABSM

Aycoberry, P. (1999) *The Social History of the Third Reich 1933-1945* New York, The New Press

Badiou, A. (2010) *The Communist Hypothesis* London, Verso

Baker, D. (1985) "A.K. Chesterton, the Strasser Brothers, and the Politics of the National Front" *Patterns of Prejudice* vol 19 No.3 pp.23-33

Baker, D. (1986) "The Appeal of Fascism: Pathological Fantasy or Intellectual Coherence?" *Patterns of Prejudice* vol 20 No.3 pp.3-12

Baker, D. (1996) "The Extreme Right in the 1920s: Fascism in a Cold Climate or 'Conservatism with Knobs on?'" in Cronin, M. (ed) *The Failure of British Fascism: The Far Right and the Fight for Political Recognition* Basingstoke, Palgrave Macmillan Chapter 2 pp.12-28

Baldwin, P. (1990) "Social Interpretations of Nazism: Renewing a Tradition" *Journal of Contemporary History* vol 25 No.1 January pp.5-37

Bambery, C. (1992) *Killing the Nazi Menace: How to Stop the Fascists* London, Bookmarks

Bankier, D. (1988) "Hitler and the Policy-Making Process on the Jewish Question" *Holocaust and Genocide Studies* vol 3 No.1 pp.1-20

Barkai, A. (1990) *Nazi Economics* Oxford, Berg

Barkai, A. (1996) "Volksgemeinschaft, 'Aryanisation' and the Holocaust" in Cesarani, D. (ed) *The Final Solution: Origins and Implementation* London, Routledge Chapter 1 pp.33-50

Barkai, A. (1996a) "The German *Volksgemeinschaft* From the Persecution of the Jews to the 'Final Solution'" in Burleigh, M. (ed) *Confronting the Nazi Past: New Debates on Modern German History* London, Collins and Brown Chapter V pp.84-97

Barker, M. (1982) *The New Racism* London, Junction Books

Barrington Moore Jnr (1966) *Social Origins of Dictatorship and Democracy* London, Penguin

Bartov, O. (1996) "Operation Barbarossa and the Origins of the Final Solution" in Cesarani, D. (ed) *The Final Solution: Origins and Implementation* London, Routledge Chapter 7 pp.119-136

Bartov, O. (1996a) "Savage War" in Burleigh, M. (ed) *Confronting the Nazi Past: New Debates on Modern German History* London, Collins and Brown Chapter VIII pp.125-139

Bauer, Y. (2001) *Re-Thinking the Holocaust* Newhaven, Yale University Press

Bauman, Z. (1991) *Modernity and the Holocaust* Cambridge, Polity

Bauman, Z. (2011) *Culture in a Liquid Modern World* Cambridge, Polity

Baynes, N.H. (ed) (1969) *The Speeches of Adolf Hitler Volumes I and II* New York, H. Fertig

Bean, J. (1999) *Many Shades of Black: Inside Britain's Far Right* London, New Millenium

Beckman, M. (1993) *The 43 Group* London, Centreprise

Beetham, D. (ed) (1983) *Marxists in Face of Fascism* Manchester, Manchester University Press

Behan, T. (2003) *The Resistible Rise of Benito Mussolini* London, Bookmarks

Bendersky, J.W. (1983) *Carl Schmitt: Theorist for the Reich* Princeton, Princeton University Press

Benewick, R. (1972) *The Fascist Movement in Britain* London, Allen Lane

Bennett, W and Dhalu, S. (2010) "Time to stand up to the bigots" *Morning Star* Thursday 4 November

Bergen, D. (2008) "Occupation, imperialism and genocide, 1939-1945" in Caplan, J. (ed) *Nazi Germany* Oxford, Oxford University Press Chapter 9 pp.219-245

Bessel, R. (ed) (1987) *Life in the Third Reich* Oxford, Oxford University Press

Bessel, R. (1987a) "Political Violence and the Nazi Seizure of Power" in Bessel, R. (ed) *Life in the Third Reich* Oxford, Oxford University Press Chapter 1 pp.1-15

Bessel, R. (ed) (1998) *Fascist Italy and Nazi Germany: Comparisons and Contrasts* Cambridge, Cambridge University Press

Betz, H-G. and Immerfall, S. (eds) (1998) *The New Politics of the Right: Neo-Populist Parties and Movements in Established Democracies* Basingstoke, Macmillan

Billig, M. (1978) *Fascists: A Social Psychological View of the National Front* London, Harcourt, Bryce and Jovanovich

Billig, M. (1989) "The Extreme Right: Continuities in Anti-Semitic Conspiracy Theory in Post-War Europe" in Eatwell, R. and O'Sullivan, N. (eds) *The Nature of the Right* London, Pinter Chapter 9 pp.146-166

Billig, M. and Cochrane, R. (1981) "The National Front and Youth" *Patterns of Prejudice* vol 15 No.4 pp.3-15

Binion, R. (1976) *Hitler among the Germans* New York, Elsevier

Birchall, S. (2010) *Beating the Fascists: The Untold Story of Anti-Fascist Action* London, Freedom Press

Blinkhorn, M. (1990) *Fascists and Conservatives* London, Unwin Hyman

Blinkhorn, M. (1994) *Mussolini and Fascist Italy* London, Routledge

Blinkhorn, M. (2004) "Afterthoughts Route Maps and Landscapes: Historians, 'Fascist Studies' and the Study of Fascism" *Totalitarian Movements and Political Religions* vol 5 No. 3 pp.507-26

Bobbio, N. (1996) *Left and Right: The Significance of Political Distinction* Cambridge, Polity Press

Bosworth, R. (1998) *The Italian Dictatorship: Problems and Perspectives in the Interpretation of Mussolini and Fascism* London, Arnold

Bosworth, R. (2002) *Mussolini* London, Arnold

Bosworth, R. (2005) *Mussolini's Italy: Life Under the Dictatorship* London, Allen Lane

Bosworth, R. (ed) (2009) *The Oxford Handbook of Fascism* Oxford, Oxford University Press

Bosworth, R. (2009a) "Dictators Strong or Weak? The Model of Benito Mussolini" in Bosworth, R. (ed) *The Oxford Handbook of Fascism* Oxford, Oxford University Press Chapter 14 pp.259-275

Bosworth, R. and Dogliani, P. (eds) (2002) *Italian Fascism: History, Memory, Representation* London, Macmillan

Bottom, K. and Copus, C. (2011) "The BNP in Local Government" in Copsey, N. and Macklin, G. (eds) (2011) *British National Party: Contemporary Perspectives* London, Routledge Chapter 7 pp.142-62

Bracher, K. (1982) "The Role of Hitler: Perspectives of Interpretation" in Laqueur, W. (ed) *Fascism* London, Pelican Chapter 5 pp.193-212

Bracher, K. (1988) *The German Dictatorship: The Origins, Structure and Consequences of National Socialism* London, Penguin

Brecht, B. (1972) *The Resistible Rise of Arturo Ui: A Gangster Spectacle* New York, Samuel French

British National Party (1982) *A New Way Forward: Political Objectives of the British National Party*

British National Party (1982a) *A Modern Political Movement* BNP

British National Party (1982b) *Constitution of the British National Party* BNP

British National Party (1992) *Fight Back! The Election Manifesto of the British National Party* BNP

British National Party (1993) *What We Stand For* BNP

British National Party (2005) *Rebuilding British Democracy: General Elections Manifesto 2005* Welshpool, BNP

British National Party (2010) *Democracy, Freedom, Culture and Identity: British National Party General Elections Manifesto 2010* Welshpool, BNP

British National Party (no date, received 2011) *Activists' and Organisers' Handbook* BNP Education and Training

Broszat, M. (1981) *The Hitler State: The Foundation and Development of the Internal Structure of the Third Reich* London, Longman

Brown, J. (2012) "The National Front's long march back to politics" *Independent* 23 April

Browning, C. (1992) *The Path to Genocide: Essays on Launching the Final Solution* Cambridge, Cambridge University Press

Browning, C. (1993) "Beyond 'Intentionalism' and 'Functionalism': A Reassessment of Nazi Jewish Policy from 1939 to 1941" in Childers, T. and Caplan, J. (eds) *Reevaluating the Third Reich* New York, Holmes and Meier Chapter 10 pp.211-233

Browning, C. (1996) "Hitler and the Euphoria of Victory: The Path to the Final Solution" in Cesarani, D. (ed) *The Final Solution: Origins and Implementation* London, Routledge Chapter 8 pp.137-147

Buchheim, C. (2001) "The Nazi Boom: An Economic Cul-de-Sac" in Mommsen, H. (ed) *The Third Reich Between Vision and Reality: New Perspectives on German History 1918-1945* Oxford, Berg pp.79-94

Bullock, A. (1962) *Hitler: A Study in Tyranny* Harmondsworth, Penguin

Bullstreet, K. (2001) *Bash the Fash: Anti-Fascist Recollections 1984-93* London, Kate Sharpley Library

Burleigh, M. (ed) (1996) *Confronting the Nazi Past: New Debates on Modern German History* London, Collins and Brown

Burleigh, M. (2000) "National Socialism as a Political Religion" *Totalitarian Movements and Political Religions* vol 1 Issue 2 pp.1-26

Burleigh, M. (2001) *The Third Reich: A New History* London, Pan Books

Burleigh, M. and Wippermann (1991) *The Racial State: Germany 1933-45* Cambridge, Cambridge University Press

Burrin, P. (1997) "Political Religion: The Relevance of a Concept" *History and Memory* vol 9 Issue 1-2 pp.321-49

Bytwerk, R. (ed) (2008) *Landmark Speeches of National Socialism* Texas, A&M University Press

Callinicos, A. (2000) *Equality* Cambridge, Polity

Callinicos, A. (2010) *Bonfire of Illusions: The Twin Crises of the Liberal World* Cambridge, Polity

Caplan, J. (1993) "National Socialism and theory of the State" in Childers, T. and Caplan, J. (eds) *Reevaluating the Third Reich* New York, Holmes and Meier Chapter 5 pp.98-113

Caplan, J. (ed) (2008) *Nazi Germany* Oxford, Oxford University Press

Carocci, G. (1975) *Italian Fascism* Harmondsworth, Pelican

Carr, W. (1978) *Hitler: A Study in Personality and Politics* London, Edward Arnold

Carr, W. (1987) "Nazi Policy Against the Jews" in Bessel, R. (ed) *Life in the Third Reich* Oxford, Oxford University Press Chapter 6 pp.69-82

Carsten, F. (1964) *The Rise of Fascism* London, Batsford

Cecil, R. (1972) *The Myth of the Master-Race: Alfred Rosenberg and Nazi Ideology* London, Batsford

Cesarani, D (ed) (1996) *The Final Solution: Origins and Implementation* London, Routledge

Chabod, F. (1974) *A History of Italian Fascism* Bath, C. Chivers

Chang, Ha-Joon (2010) *23 Things They Don't Tell You About Capitalism* London, Allen Lane

Childers, T. (1976) "The Social Basis of the National Front Vote" *Journal of Contemporary History* 11 pp.17-42

Childers, T. (1979) "The Social Bases of the National Socialist Vote" in Mosse, G. (ed) *International Fascism* Chapter 7 pp.161-188

Childers, T. and Caplan, J. (1993) (eds) *Reevaluating the Third Reich* New York, Holmes and Meier

Cohn-Sherbok, D. (1999) *Understanding the Holocaust* London, Cassell

Collins, M. (2006) "When is a terrorist not a terrorist? When he is a Nazi" *Searchlight* September No.375 pp.8-9

Collins, M. (2011) *Hate: My Life in the British Far Right* London, Biteback Publishing

Collins, M. (2011a) "Edmonds heads out the front door" *Hope not hate* 6 October

Copsey, N. (1994) "Fascism: The Ideology of the British National Party" *Politics* vol 14 no.3 pp.101-8

Copsey, N. (1996) "Contemporary Fascism in the Local Arena: The British National Party and 'Rights for Whites'" in Cronin, M. (ed) *The Failure of British Fascism: The Far Right and the Fight for Political Recognition* Basingstoke, Palgrave Macmillan Chapter 7 pp.118-140

Copsey, N. (2000) *Anti-Fascism in Britain* Basingstoke, Macmillan

Copsey, N. (2007) "Changing Course or Changing Clothes? Reflections on the Ideological Evolution of the British National Party, 1999-2006" *Patterns of Prejudice* vol 41 No.1 pp.61-82

Copsey, N. (2008) *Contemporary British Fascism: The British National Party and the Quest for Legitimacy* Basingstoke, Palgrave Macmillan

Copsey, N. (2011) "From Direct Action to Community Action: The changing dynamics of anti-fascist opposition" in Copsey, N. and Macklin, G. (eds) *British National Party: Contemporary Perspectives* London, Routledge Chapter 6 pp.123-141

Copsey, N. and Macklin, G. (eds) (2011) *British National Party: Contemporary Perspectives* London, Routledge

Copsey, N. and Macklin, G. (2011a) "'The Media = Lies, Lies, Lies!': The BNP and the Media in Contemporary Britain" in Copsey, N. and Macklin, G. (eds) *British National Party: Contemporary Perspectives* London, Routledge Chapter 4 pp.81-102

Corner, P. (1986) "Liberalism, Pre-Fascism, Fascism" in Forgacs, D. (ed) *Re-Thinking Italian Fascism* London, Lawrence and Wishart Chapter 2 pp.11-20

Corner, P. (2002) "State and Society 1901-1922" in Lyttleton, A. (ed) *Liberal and Fascist Italy* Oxford, Oxford University Press pp.17-43

Corner, P. (2002a) "Italian Fascism: Whatever Happened to Dictatorship?" *The Journal of Modern History* vol 74 No.2 pp.325-351

Corni, G. (2009) "State and Society: Italy and Germany Compared" in Bosworth, R. (ed) *The Oxford Handbook of Fascism* Oxford, Oxford University Press Chapter 15 pp.279-295

Coupland, P. (1998) "The Blackshirted Utopians" *Journal of Contemporary History* vol 33 No.2 April pp.255-272

Cressy, S. (2010) "The Extremist Defence League" *Searchlight* October No.424 pp.12-13

Crew, D. (ed) (1995) *Nazism and German Society 1933-45* London, Routledge

Cronin, M. (ed) (1996) *The Failure of British Fascism: The Far Right and the Fight for Political Recognition* Basingstoke, Palgrave Macmillan

Cronin, M. (1996a) "Introduction: 'Tomorrow We Live' – The Failure of British Fascism?" in Cronin, M. (ed) *The Failure of British Fascism: The Far Right and the Fight for Political Recognition* Basingstoke, Palgrave Macmillan Chapter 1 pp.1-12

Cronshaw, C. (1997) "The Two Sides of the Democratic Coin" *Spearhead* October No.344 pp.16-17

Cross, C. (1961) *The Fascists in Britain* London, Barrie and Rockliff

Cullen, S. (1993) "Political Violence: The Case of the BUF" *Journal of Contemporary History* vol 28 No.2 April pp.245-67

Dandeker, D. (1985) "Fascism and Ideology: Continuities and Discontinuities in Capitalist Development" *Ethnic and Racial Studies* vol 8 No.3 pp.349-67

Davidowicz, L. (1975) *The War Against the Jews* New York, Holt, Rinehart and Winston

De Grand, A. (1995) *Fascist Italy and Nazi Germany: The 'Fascist' Style of Rule* London, Routledge

De Grand, A. (2000) *Italian Fascism: Its Origin and Development* Lincoln, University of Nebraska Press

De Saussure, R. (1943) "Collective Neurosis of Germany" *Free World* February pp.121-26

Del Boca, A. and Giovana, M. (1970) *Fascism Today* London, Heinemann

Dorril, S. (2006) *Blackshirt: Sir Oswald Mosley and British Fascism* London, Viking

Duggan, C. (2013) *Fascist Voices: An Intimate History of Mussolini's Italy* London, Vintage Books

Durham, M. (1998) *Women and Fascism* London, Routledge

Eagleton, T. (1976) "What is Fascism?" *New Blackfriars* 57/670

Eagleton, T. (2011) *Why Marx was Right* New Haven & London, Yale University Press

Eatwell, R. and O'Sullivan, N. (eds) (1989) *The Nature of the Right* London, Pinter

Eatwell, R. (1992) "Towards a New Model of Generic Fascism" *Journal of Theoretical Politics* 4/2 pp.161-94

Eatwell, R. (1992a) "Why Has the Extreme Right Failed in Britain?" in Hainsworth, P. (ed) *The Extreme Right in Europe and the USA* London, Pinter Chapter 7 pp.175-192

Eatwell, R. (1996) *Fascism: A History* London, Vintage

Eatwell, R. (1996a) "The Esoteric Ideology of the National Front in the 1980s" in Cronin, M. (ed) *The Failure of British Fascism: The Far Right and the Fight for Political Recognition* Basingstoke, Palgrave Macmillan Chapter 6 pp.99-117

Eatwell, R. (1996b) "On Defining the 'Fascist Minimum': The Centrality of Ideology", *Journal of Political Ideologies* vol.1 No.3 pp.303-19

Eatwell, R. (1998) "Britain: The BNP and the Problem of Legitimacy" in Betz, H-G and Immerfall, S. (eds) *The New Politics of the Right: Neo-Populist Parties and Movements in Established Democracies* Basingstoke, Macmillan Chapter 9 pp.143-55

Eatwell, R. (1998a) "The Dynamics of Right-Wing Electoral Breakthrough" *Patterns of Prejudice* vol 32 No.3 pp.3-31

Eatwell, R. (1998b) "Continuity and metamorphosis: British fascism 1945-1989" in Larsen, S. and Hagtvet, B. (eds) *Modern Europe After Fascism 1943-1980s* New York, Colombia University Press Chapter 43 pp.1184-1218

Eatwell, R. (2000) "The extreme right and British exceptionalism: the primacy of politics" in Hainsworth, P. (ed) *The Politics of the Extreme Right: From the Margins to the Mainstream* London, Pinter Chapter 8 pp.172-192

Eatwell, R. (2004) "The extreme right in Britain: The long road to 'modernisation'" in Eatwell, R. and Mudde, C. (eds) *Western Democracies and the New Extreme Right Challenge* London, Routledge Chapter 3 pp.62-79

Eatwell, R. (2010) "Responses to the extreme right in Britain" in R. Eatwell and M. Goodwin (eds) *The New Extremism in 21st Century Britain* Abingdon, Routledge Chapter 10 pp.211-230

Eatwell, R, and Goodwin, M. (eds) (2010) *The New Extremism in 21st Century Britain* Abingdon, Routledge

Eley, G. (1983) "What Produces Fascism: Pre-Industrial Traditions or a Crisis of a Capitalist State?" *Politics and Society* March vol 12 No.1 pp.53-82

Engel, D. (2000) *The Holocaust: The Third Reich and the Jews* Harlow, Longman

Erikson, E. (1942) "Hitler's Imagery and German Youth" *Psychiatry: Journal for the Study of Interpersonal Processes* vol 5 pp.475-93

Erdmann, K. (1981) "National Socialism, Fascism, Totalitarianism" *Australian Journal of Politics and History* No.27 pp.354-63

Evans, D. (1975) "News from the Nazi Front" *International Socialism* No.80 July/Aug pp.5

Evans, R. (2006) *The Third Reich in Power: How the Nazis Won Over the Hearts and Minds of a Nation* London, Penguin

Evans, R. (2008) "The Emergence of Nazi Ideology" in Caplan, J. (ed) *Nazi Germany* Oxford, Oxford University Press Chapter 1 pp.26-47

Fest, J.C. (1973) *Hitler* London, Weidenfeld and Nicolson

Fielding, N. (1984) "Ideology, Democracy and the National Front" *Ethnic and Racial Studies* vol 14 pp.56-72

Finkelstein, N. (1997) "Daniel Jonah Goldhagen's 'Crazy' Thesis: A Critique of *Hitler's Willing Executioners*" *New Left Review* I/224 July-August pp.39-87

Finkelstein, N. (2000) *The Holocaust Industry: Reflections on the Exploitation of Jewish Suffering* London, Verso

Fischer, C. (1995) *The Rise of the Nazis* Manchester, Manchester University Press

Forgacs, D. (ed) (1986) *Rethinking Italian Fascism: Capitalism, Populism and Culture* London, Lawrence and Wishart

Ford, R. (2010) "Who might vote for the BNP? Survey evidence on the electoral potential of the extreme right in Britain" in Eatwell, R. and Goodwin, M. (eds) *The New Extremism in 21st Century Britain* Abingdon, Routledge Chapter 7 pp.145-168

Ford, R. and Goodwin, M. (2010) "Angry White Men: Individual and Contextual Predictors of Support for the British National Party" *Political Studies* 58 (1), pp.1-25

Foster, J. (1996) "The Relation Between Operation Barbarossa as an Ideological War of Extermination and the Final Solution" in Cesarani, D. (ed) *The Final Solution: Origins and Implementation* London, Routledge Chapter 5 pp.85-102

Fraenkel, H. (1940) *The German People Versus Hitler* London, George Allen & Unwin

Frei, N. (2001) "People's Community and War: Hitler's Popular Support" in Mommsen, H. (ed) *The Third Reich Between Vision and Reality: New Perspectives on German History 1918-1945* Oxford, Berg pp.59-77

Frei, N. (2005) "Auschwitz and the Germans: History, Knowledge and Memory" in Gregor, N. (ed) *Nazism, War and Genocide: New Perspectives on the History of the Third Reich* Exeter, University of Exeter Press Chapter 9 pp.147-165

Friedlander, S. (2009) *Nazi Germany and the Jews 1933-45* London, Phoenix

Friedrich, C.J. and Brzezinski, Z.K. (1965) *Totalitarianism, Dictatorship and Autocracy* Cambridge Mass, Harvard University Press

Fritzsche, P. (2008) "The NSDAP 1919-1934: from fringe politics to the seizure of power" in Caplan, J. (ed) *Nazi Germany* Oxford, Oxford University Press Chapter 2 pp.48-72

Fromm, E. (1942) *Fear of Freedom* London, Kegan Paul

Frye, C. (1966) "Carl Schmitt's Concept of the Political" *Journal of Politics* 28 pp.818-830

Fyrth, J. (ed) (1985) *Britain, Fascism and the Popular Front* London, Lawrence and Wishart

Gable, S. (2011) "Myths and lies on the BNP debt mountain" *Searchlight* August No.434 pp.20-21

Geary, D. (1994) *Hitler and Nazism* London, Routledge

Gellately, R. (1993) "Enforcing Racial Policy in Nazi Germany" in Childers, T. and Caplan, J. (eds) *Reevaluating the Third Reich* New York, Holmes and Meier Chapter 2 pp.42-65

Gentile, E. (1990) "Fascism as Political Religion" *Journal of Contemporary History* vol 25 No.2-3 May-June pp.229-251

Gentile, E. (2002) "Fascism in power: the totalitarian experiment" in Lyttleton, A. (ed) *Liberal and Fascist Italy* Oxford, Oxford University Press pp.139-174

Gentile, E. (2005) "Fascism, Totalitarianism and Political Religion: Definitions and Critical Reflections on Criticism of an Interpretation" in Griffin, R. (ed) *Fascism, Totalitarianism and Political Religion* London, Routledge Chapter 1 pp.32-81

Gentile, G. (1960) *Genesis and Structure of Society* Urbana, University of Illinois Press

Germani, G. (1968) "Fascism and class" in Woolf, S. (ed) *The Nature of Fascism* London, Weidenfeld and Nicolson Chapter 5 pp.65-96

Germino, D. (1959) *The Italian Fascist Party in Power: A Study in Totalitarian Rule* Minneapolis, University of Minnesota Press

Geyer, M. (1987) "The Nazi State Reconsidered" in Bessel, R. (ed) *Life in the Third Reich* Oxford, Oxford University Press Chapter 5 pp.57-67

Gilbert, M. (1987) *The Holocaust: The Jewish Tragedy* London, Fontana

Gillete, A. (2002) *Racial Theories in Fascist Italy* London, Routledge

Gilmour, I. (1978) *Inside Right* London, Quartet Books

Gluckstein, D. (1999) *The Nazis, Capitalism and the Working Class* London, Bookmarks

Goldhagen, D. (1996) *Hitler's Willing Executioners: Ordinary Germans and the Holocaust* New York, Knopf

Gonen, J. (2000) *The Roots of Nazi Psychology: Hitler's Utopian Barbarism* Lexington, University Press of Kentucky

Goodrick-Clark, N. (1992) *The Occult Roots of Nazism: Secret Aryan Cults and Their Influence on Nazi Ideology* New York, New York University Press

Goodwin, M. (2007) "The Extreme Right in Britain: Still an 'Ugly Duckling' but for How Long?" *Political Quarterly* vol 78 No.2 pp.241-50

Goodwin, M. (2008) "Research, revisionists and the radical right" *Politics* 28 (1) pp. 33-40

Goodwin, M. (2010) "In search of the winning formula: Nick Griffin and the 'modernisation' of the British National Party" in R. Eatwell and M. Goodwin (eds) *The New Extremism in 21st Century Britain* Abingdon, Routledge Chapter 8 pp.169-190

Goodwin, M. (2011) *New British Fascism: Rise of the British National Party* London, Routledge

Gordon, P. and Klug, F. (1986) *New Right New Racism* London, Searchlight Publications

Gordon, R. (2009) "Race" in Bosworth, R. (ed) *The Oxford Handbook of Fascism* Oxford, Oxford University Press Chapter 16 pp.296-316

Gregor, A.J. (1969) *The Ideology of Fascism* Basingstoke, Macmillan

Gregor, A.J. (1977/78) "Fascism and the Countermodernisation of Consciousness" *Comparative Political Studies* 10 pp.239-58

Gregor, A.J. (1979) *Italian Fascism and Developmental Dictatorship* Princeton NJ, Princeton University Press

Gregor, A.J. (1979a) *Young Mussolini and the Intellectual Origins of Fascism* Berkeley, University of California Press

Gregor, N. (ed) (2000) *Nazism* Oxford, Oxford University Press

Gregor, N. (ed) (2005) *Nazism, War and Genocide: New Perspectives on the History of the Third Reich* Exeter, University of Exeter Press

Gregor, N. (2005) "Nazism – A Political Religion? Rethinking the Voluntarist Turn" in Gregor, N. (ed) (2005) *Nazism, War and Genocide: New Perspectives on the History of the Third Reich* Exeter, University of Exeter Press Chapter 1 pp.1-21

Greil, A. (1977/78) "The Modernisation of Consciousness and the Appeal of Fascism" *Comparative Political Studies* 10 pp.213-38

Greil, A. (1977/78a) "What does it mean when I call you a Fascist?" *Comparative Political Studies* 10 pp.269-278

Griffin, N. (1996) "Woe to the Vanquished!" *Spearhead* No.329 July pp.12-14

Griffin, N. (1996a) "Will no-one rid us of these turbulent reds" *Spearhead* No.330 August pp.12-13

Griffin, N. (1996b) "The Unholy Alliance" *Spearhead* No.333 November pp.12-13

Griffin, N. (1996c) "Still 'no electoral road'?" *Spearhead* No.334 December pp.12-13

Griffin, N. (1997) "Democracy and British Freedom" *Spearhead* No.340 June pp.14-16

Griffin, N. (1997a) "Mr. Plod Gets Wet" (transcript of police interview with Nick Griffin) *Spearhead* September No.343 pp.14-17

Griffin, N. (1997b) "Hard Times, Soft Soap" *Spearhead* October No.344 pp.14-15

Griffin, R. (1992) "The Fascist Phoenix" *Politics Review* vol 2 No.2 November pp.2-5

Griffin, R. (1993) *The Nature of Fascism* London, Routledge

Griffin, R. (1993a) "Was Nazism Fascist?" *Modern Historical Review* September 5/1 pp.15-17

Griffin, R. (ed) (1995) *Fascism* Oxford, Oxford University Press

Griffin, R. (1996) "British Fascism: The Ugly Duckling" in Cronin, M. (ed) (1996) *The Failure of British Fascism: The Far Right and the Fight for Political Recognition* Basingstoke, Palgrave Macmillan Chapter 8 pp.141-165

Griffin, R. (ed) (1998) *International Fascism: Theories, Causes and the New Consensus* London, Arnold

Griffin, R. (1999) "Notes Toward the Definition of Fascist Culture: The Prospects for Synergy between Marxist and Liberal Heuristics" *Renaissance and Modern Studies* vol 42 Autumn pp.95-115

Griffin, R. (1999a) "Fascism is more than reaction" *Searchlight* September pp.24-26

Griffin, R. (2000) "Interregnum or Endgame? Radical Right Thought in the 'Post-Fascist' Era" *Journal of Political Ideologies* July vol 5 No.2 pp.163-78

Griffin, R. (2000a) "Revolution from the Right: Fascism" in Parker, D. (ed) *Revolutions and the Revolutionary Tradition in the West 1560-1991* London, Routledge pp.185-201

Griffin, R. (2002) "Paper tiger or Cheshire cat? A spotter's guide to fascism in the post-fascist era" *Searchlight* November No.329 pp.18-21

Griffin, R. (2002a) "The Primacy of Culture: The Current Growth (or Manufacture) of Consensus within Fascism Studies" *Journal of Contemporary History* vol 37 No.1 pp.21-43

Griffin, R. (2002b) "The Incredible Shrinking Ism: The Survival of Fascism in the Post-Fascist Era" *Patterns of Prejudice* 36 3 pp.3-8

Griffin, R. (2003) "From Slime Mould to Rhizome: An introduction to the groupuscular right" *Patterns of Prejudice* vol 37 No.1 pp.27-50

Griffin, R. (ed) (2005) *Fascism, Totalitarianism and Political Religion* London, Routledge

Griffin, R. (2005a) "God's Counterfeiters? Investigating the Triad of Fascism, Totalitarianism and (Political) Religion" in Griffin, R. (ed) *Fascism, Totalitarianism and Political Religion* London, Routledge Introduction pp.1-31

Griffin, R. (2011) "Alien Influence? The international context of the BNP's 'modernization'" in Copsey, N. and Macklin, G. (eds) *British National Party: Contemporary Perspectives* London, Routledge Chapter 9 pp.190-206

Griffiths, R. (1980) *Fellow Travellers of the Right: British Enthusiasts for Nazi Germany 1933-39* London, Constable

Griffiths, R. (2005) *Fascism* London, Continuum

Guerin, D. (1973) *Fascism and Big Business* New York, Monad Press

Halperin, S. (1964) *Mussolini and Italian Fascism* Princeton, Van Nostrand

Hamann, B. (2001) "Hitler and Vienna: The Truth about his Formative Years" in Mommsen, H. (ed) *The Third Reich Between Vision and Reality: New Perspectives on German History 1918-1945* Oxford, Berg pp.23-37

Hamilton, A. (1971) *The Appeal of Fascism: A Study of Intellectuals and Fascism 1919-45* London, Blond

Hanna, M. (1974) "The National Front and other Right Wing Organisations" *New Community* III pp.49-55

Harman, C. (1996) "A barbarian apart" *Socialist Review* June pp.10

Harris, H.S. (1966) *The Social Philosophy of Giovanni Gentile* Urbana, University of Illinois Press

Harris, S. (1973) "Spearhead of British Racialism" *Patterns of Prejudice* vol 7 No.4 pp.15-19 and p.33

Harris, G. (1991) *The Dark Side of Europe: The Extreme Right Today* Edinburgh, Edinburgh University Press

Harrop, M. and Zimmerman, G. (1977) "The Anatomy of the National Front" *Patterns of Prejudice* vol II July-August pp.12-13 and p.18

Harrop, M., England, J. and Husbands, C. (1980) "The Bases of National Front Support" *Political Studies* 28 pp.271-283

Hayes, M. (1994) *The New Right in Britain: Introduction to Theory and Practice* London, Pluto

Hayes, M. (1995) "A Family Affair" *Fighting Talk* May Issue 11 pp.13-14

Hayes, M. and Aylward, P. (2000) "Anti-Fascist Action: Radical Resistance or Rent-a-Mob?" *Soundings* Issue 14 Spring pp.53-62

Hayes, P. (1973) *Fascism* London, Allen and Unwin

Hayes, P. (1987) *Industry and Ideology: I.G.Farben in the Nazi Era* Cambridge, Cambridge University Press

Hayes, P. (1993) "Polycracy and Policy in the Third Reich" in Childers, T. and Caplan, J. (eds) *Reevaluating the Third Reich* New York, Holmes and Meier Chapter 9 pp.190-210

Heiden, K. (1934) *A History of National Socialism* London, Methuen

Hepple, T./Searchlight (1989) *From Ballots to Bombs: The Inside Story of the National Front's Political Soldiers* London, Searchlight Publishing

Herbert, U. (1995) "Labor as Spoils of Conquest, 1933-45" in Crew, D. (ed) *Nazism and German Society 1933-45* London, Routledge Chapter 7 pp.219-273

Herbert, U. (1996) "'The Real Mystery in Germany'. The German Working Class During the Nazi Dictatorship" in Burleigh, M. (ed) *Confronting the Nazi Past: New Debates on Modern German History* London, Collins and Brown Chapter I pp.23-36

Herbert, U. (2001) "Ideological Legitimization and Political Practice of the Leadership of the National Socialist Secret Police" in Mommsen, H. (ed) *The Third Reich Between Vision and Reality: New Perspectives on German History 1918-1945* Oxford, Berg pp.95-108

Herf, J. (1981) "Reactionary Modernism: Some Ideological Origins of the Primacy of Politics in the Third Reich" *Theory and Society* 10 pp.805-833

Herf, J. (1984) *Reactionary Modernism: Technology, Culture and Politics in Weimar and the Third Reich* Cambridge, Cambridge University Press

Hilberg, R. (1985) *The Destruction of the European Jews (Volumes One, Two and Three)* London, Holmes and Meier

Hilberg, R. (1993) *Perpetrators, Victims, Bystanders: The Jewish Catastrophe 1933-1945* New York, HarperPerennial

Hildebrand, K. (1985) *The Third Reich* London, Allen and Unwin

Hill, R. and Bell, A. (1988) *The Other Face of Terror: Inside Europe's Neo-Nazi Network* London, Grafton

Hillman, N. (2002) "'Misfits, dullards and outcasts': Fascist support after World War Two" *Searchlight* November No.329 pp.22-23

Hitler, A. (1961) *Hitler's Secret Book* New York, Grove Press

Hitler, A. (1961a) *The Testament of Adolf Hitler: The Hitler-Bormann Documents* London, Cassell

Hitler, A. (1973) *Table Talk 1941-1944* London, Weidenfeld and Nicolson

Hitler, A. (1974) *Mein Kampf* London, Hutchinson

Hoare, Q. (1963) "What is Fascism?" *New Left Review* I/20 pp.99-111

Hobsbawm, E. (1994) *Age of Extremes: The Short Twentieth Century 1914-1991* London, Abacus

Holland, D. (1984) *The Political Soldier* NF Nat Ed Group

Holmes, I. (1997) "The Line in the Sand: The white race is earth's most endangered species" *Spearhead* September No.343 pp.20-21

Husbands, C. (1975) "The National Front: A Response to Crisis?" *New Society* No.32 May pp.403-405

Husbands, C. (1984) "When the Bubble Burst: Transient and Persistent NF Supporters 1974-79" *British Journal of Political Studies* 14 pp.249-260

Husbands, C. (1988) "Extreme Right-Wing Politics in Great Britain: The Recent Marginalisation of the National Front" *West European Politics* vol 11 No.2 pp.65-79

Jackson, P. (2011) *The EDL: Britain's 'New Far Right' Social Movement* Northampton, RNM Publications

James, H. (1993) "Innovation and Conservatism in Economic Recovery: The Alleged 'Nazi Recovery' of the 1930s" in Childers, T. and Caplan, J. (eds) *Reevaluating the Third Reich* New York, Holmes and Meier Chapter 6 pp.114-38

Joes, A. (1977/78) "On the Modernity of Fascism" *Comparative Political Studies* 10 pp.259-268

John, P. and Margetts, H. (2009) "The latent support for the extreme right in British politics" *West European Politics* vol 32 No.3 May pp.496-513

Kallis, A. (2000) *Fascist Ideology: Territory and Expansionism in Italy and Germany 1922-1945* London, Routledge

Kallis, A. (2000a) "The 'Regime Model' of Fascism: A Typology" *European History Quarterly* vol 30 No.1 pp.77-104

Kallis, A. (ed) (2002) *Fascism Reader* London, Routledge

Kallis, A. (2003) "Fascism, 'Para-Fascism' and 'Fascistization': On the Similarities of Three Conceptual Categories" *European History Quarterly* 33 2 pp.219-50

Kallis, A. (2004) "Studying Inter-war Fascism in Epochal and Diachronic Terms: Ideological Production, Political Experience and the Quest for Consensus" *European History Quarterly* 34 1 pp.9-42

Kallis, A. (2009) *Genocide and Fascism: The Eliminationist Drive in Fascist Europe* London, Routledge

Kedward, H. (1971) *Fascism in Western Europe 1900-1945* New York, New York University Press

Kershaw, I. (1985) *The Nazi Dictatorship: Problems and Perspectives of Interpretation* London, Arnold

Kershaw, I. (1987) "Hitler and the Germans" in Bessel, R. (ed) *Life in the Third Reich* Oxford, Oxford University Press Chapter 4 pp.41-55

Kershaw, I. (1989) "The Nazi State: An Exceptional State?" *New Left Review* I/176 July-August pp.47-67

Kershaw, I. (1991) *Hitler* London, Longman

Kershaw, I. (1993) "Working Towards the Fuhrer: Reflections on the Nature of the Hitler Dictatorship" *Contemporary European History* vol 2 Issue 2 pp.103-18

Kershaw, I. (1995) "The 'Hitler Myth': Image and reality in the Third Reich" in Crew, D. (ed) *Nazism and German Society 1933-1945* London, Routledge Chapter 6 pp.197-215

Kershaw, I. (2009) *Hitler* London, Penguin

King, R. (1977) "Support for fascism and the Radical right: some explanations" in Nugent, N. and King, R. (eds) *The British Right* London, Saxon House Chapter 8 pp.192-221

King, R. and Nugent, N. (eds) (1979) *Respectable Rebels* London, Hodder and Stroughton

King, S. (1999) "Griffin heads for victory" *Searchlight* October No.292 pp.4-7

Kirk, T. and McElligott, A. (eds) (1999) *Opposing Fascism: Community, Authority and Resistance in Europe* Cambridge, Cambridge University Press

Kitchen, M. (1974) "Trotsky and Fascism" *Social Praxis* vol 2 Issue 1-2 pp.113-133

Kitchen, M. (1982) *Fascism* Basingstoke, Macmillan

Kitchen, M. (1995) *Nazi Germany at War* London, Longman

Knox, M. (2000) *Common Destiny: Dictatorship, Foreign Policy, and War in Fascist Italy and Nazi Germany* Cambridge, Cambridge University Press

Knox, M. (2002) "Fascism: ideology, foreign policy and war" in Lyttleton, A. (ed) *Liberal and Fascist Italy* Oxford, Oxford University Press pp.105-138

Kocka, J. (1988) "German History before Hitler: The Debate about the German *Sonderweg*" *Journal of Contemporary History* January vol 23 No.1 pp.3-16

Kogan, N. (1968) "Fascism as a political system" in Woolf, S. (ed) *The Nature of Fascism* London, Weidenfeld and Nicolson Chapter 1 p.11-18

Koonz, C. (1987) *Mothers in the Fatherland: Women, the Family and Nazi Politics* London, Jonathan Cape

Kushner, T. (1994) "The fascist as 'other'? Racism and Neo-Nazism in contemporary Britain" *Patterns of Prejudice* vol 28 No.1 pp.27-45

Landau, R. (1998) *Studying the Holocaust: Issues, Readings and Documents* London, Routledge

Laqueur, W. (ed) (1982) *Fascism: A Reader's Guide* London, Pelican

Laqueur, W. (1996) *Fascism* Oxford, Oxford University Press

Lasswell, H. (1933) "The Psychology of Hitlerism" *Political Quarterly* vol 4 Issue 3 pp.373-384

Lecomber, T. (1997) "Success and failure – the new politics and the old" *Patriot* Issue No.1 Spring pp.16-19

Levi, F. (2005) "Anti-Jewish Persecution and Italian Society" in Zimmerman, J. (ed) *Jews in Italy under Fascist and Nazi Rule 1922-1945* Cambridge, Cambridge University Press Chapter 10 pp.199-206

Levi, P. (2008) *If This Is A Man : The Truce* London, Abacus

Levy, C. (1999) "Fascism, National Socialism and Conservatism in Europe 1914-1945: Issues for Comparativists" *Contemporary European History* 8/1 pp.97-126

Lewis, D. (1987) *Illusions of Grandeur: Mosley, Fascism and British Society, 1931-81* Manchester, Manchester University Press

Linehan, T. (2000) *British Fascism 1918-1939: Parties, Ideology and Culture* Manchester, Manchester University Press

Linehan, T. (2005) "The British Union of Fascists as a Totalitarian Movement and Political Religion" in Griffin, R. (ed) *Fascism, Totalitarianism and Political Religion* London, Routledge Chapter 3 pp.103-124

Linehan, T. (2012) "Space Matters: Spatialising British Fascism" *Socialist History* 41 pp.1-21

Linz, J (1982) "Some Notes Toward a Comparative Study of Fascism in Sociological Historical Perspective" in Laqueur, W. (ed) *Fascism* London, Pelican Chapter 1 pp.13-78

Lipset, S.M (1960) *Political Man: The Social Bases of Politics* New York, Doubleday

Lipstadt, D. (1993) *Denying the Holocaust* London, Penguin

Lombardini, S. (1968) "Italian fascism and the economy" in Woolf, S. (ed) *The Nature of Fascism* London, Weidenfeld and Nicolson Chapter 9 pp.152-164

Longerich, P. (1999/2000) *The Wannsee Conference in the Development of the Final Solution* Holocaust Education Trust Research Paper vol 1 No.2

Lowles, N. (2001) *White Riot: The Violent History of Combat 18* Bury, Milo Books

Lowles, N. (2006) "2006 local elections analysis" *Searchlight* June No.372 pp.4-7

Lowles, N. (2010) "Defeated: BNP leader weakened after poll disaster" *Searchlight* June No.420 pp.8-12

Lowles, N. (2011) "It's time to act against the EDL" *Searchlight* August No.434 p.14

Lowles, N. and Creasy, S. (2011) "Comrades in Arms" *Searchlight* August No.434 pp.6-7

Ludtke, A. (1995) "The 'Honor of Labor': Industrial workers and the power of symbols under National Socialism" in Crew, D. (ed) *Nazism and German Society 1933-1945* London, Routledge Chapter 2 pp.67-109

Lunn, K. and Thurlow, R. (eds) (1980) *British Fascism* London, Croom-Helm

Lyttleton, A. (ed) (1973) *Italian Fascisms from Pareto to Gentile* London, J. Cape

Lyttleton, A. (1979) "Fascism in Italy: The Second Wave" in Mosse, G. (ed) *International Fascism* London, Sage Chapter 2 pp.45-71

Lyttleton, A. (1998) "The 'Crisis of Bourgeois Society' and the Origins of Fascism" in Bessel, R. (ed) *Fascist Italy and Nazi Germany: Comparisons and Contrasts* Cambridge, Cambridge University Press Chapter 1 p.12-22

Lyttleton, A. (ed) (2002) *Liberal and Fascist Italy* Oxford, Oxford University Press

Macklin, G. (2007) *Very Deeply Dyed in Black: Sir Oswald Mosley and the Resurrection of British Fascism After 1945* London, IB Tauris

Macklin, G. (2011) "Modernizing the Past for the Future" in Copsey, N. and Macklin, G. (eds) *The British National Party: Contemporary Perspectives* London, Routledge Chapter 1 pp.19-37

Mack Smith, D. (1985) *Mussolini* London, Paladin

Mallman, K-M, and Paul, G. "Omniscient, Omnipotent, Omnipresent? Gestapo, Society and Resistance" in Crew, D. (ed) *Nazism and German Society 1933-1945* London, Routledge Chapter 5 pp.166-196

Mann, M. (2004) *Fascists* Cambridge, Cambridge University Press

Markwick, R. (2009) "Communism: Fascism's 'Other'?" in Bosworth, R. (ed) *The Oxford Handbook of Fascism* Oxford, Oxford University Press Chapter 18 pp.339-361

Marrus, M. (1993) *The Holocaust in History* London, Penguin

Martell, S. (1996) "The Nature of the Beast" *Fighting Talk* July Issue 14 pp.12-14

Marx, K. (1978) *The Eighteenth Brumaire of Louis Bonaparte* Peking, Foreign Language Press

Maser, W. (1970) *Hitler's Mein Kampf: An Analysis* London, Faber

Maser, W. (1973) *Hitler* London, Harper and Row

Maser, W. (1973a) *Hitler's Letters and Notes* London, Heinemann

Mason, T. (1968) "The Primacy of Politics – Politics and Economics in National Socialist Germany" in Woolf, S. (ed) *The Nature of Fascism* London, Weidenfeld and Nicolson Chapter 10 pp.165-202

Mason, T. (1993) *Social Policy in the Third Reich: The Working Class and the 'National Community'* Oxford, Berg

Mason, T. (1996) *Nazism, Fascism and the Working Class* Cambridge, Cambridge University Press

Mazower, M. (2009) *Hitler's Empire: Nazi Rule in Occupied Europe* London, Penguin

McDonough, F. (1999) *Hitler and Nazi Germany* Cambridge, Cambridge University Press

McGovern, M. (1946) *From Luther to Hitler: The History of Fascist-Nazi Political Philosophy* London, Harrap

McKibben, R. (1969) "The Myth of the Unemployed: Who Did Vote for the Nazis?" *Australian Journal of Politics and History* 15 pp.25-40

Melograni, P. (1979) "The Cult of the Duce in Mussolini's Italy" in Mosse, G. (ed) *International Fascism* London, Sage Chapter 3 pp.73-90

Michaelis, M. (1978) *Mussolini and the Jews: German-Italian Relations and the Jewish Question in Italy 1922-1945* Oxford, Clarendon Press

Miliband, D. (2011) "Insecurity is fuel for the far right's hate" *Guardian* 28 February

Miliband, R. (1980) *The State in Capitalist Society* London, Quartet

Miliband, R. (1984) *Capitalist Democracy in Britain* Oxford, Oxford University Press

Milne, S. (2011) "The fallout from the crash of 2008 has only just begun" *Guardian* 10 March

Milne, S. (2012) *The Revenge of History: The Battle for the 21st Century* London, Verso

Milner, D. (1999) *Class* London, Sage

Mommsen, H. (1982) "National Socialism: Continuity and Change" in Laqueur, W. (ed) *Fascism* London, Pelican Chapter 4 pp.151-192

Mommsen, H. (ed) (2001) *The Third Reich Between Vision and Reality: New Perspectives on German History 1918-1945* Oxford, Berg

Moore B. Jnr. (1966) *Social Origins of Dictatorship and Democracy* Harmondsworth, Penguin

Morgan, P. (1995) *Italian Fascism 1919-1945* Basingstoke, Macmillan

Morgan, P. (2009) "Corporatism and the Economic Order" in Bosworth, R. (ed) *The Oxford Handbook of Fascism* Oxford, Oxford University Press Chapter 8 pp.150-165

Mosley, O. (1934) *The Greater Britain* London, BUF/Jeffcoats

Mosley, O. (1938) *Tomorrow We Live* London, Black House Publishing

Mosley, O. (1946) *My Answer* Ramsbury, Mosley Publications

Mosley, O. (1947) *The Alternative* Ramsbury, Mosley Publications

Moss, S. and Crase, J. (2009) "Is fascism on the march again?" *Guardian* 9 June

Mosse, G. (1968) "Fascism and the intellectuals" in Woolf, S. (ed) *The Nature of Fascism* London, Weidenfeld and Nicolson Chapter 12 pp.205-225

Mosse, G. (ed) (1979) *International Fascism: New Thoughts and New Approaches* London, Sage

Mosse, G. (1979a) "Towards a General Theory of Fascism" in Mosse, G. (ed) *International Fascism: New Thoughts and New Approaches* London, Sage Introduction pp.1-41

Mosse, G. (1999) *The Fascist Revolution: Towards a Generic Theory of Fascism* New York, Howard Fertig

Mudde, C. (1996) "The war of words: Defining the extreme right party family" *West European Politics* 19 (2) pp.225-248

Mudde, C. (2000) *The Ideology of the Extreme Right* Manchester, Manchester University Press

Muhlberger, D. (2003) *The Social Bases of Nazism* Cambridge, Cambridge University Press

Mussolini, B. (1939) *My Autobiography* London, Hutchinson

Mussolini, B. (1968) *Fascism: Doctrine and Institutions* New York, H. Fertig

Mussolini, B. (1975) *The Corporate State* New York, H. Fertig

Mussolini, B. (1976) *The Political and Social Doctrine of Fascism* New York, Gordon Press

Nathan, P. (1943) *The Psychology of Fascism* London, Faber and Faber

National Front (1983) *Let Britain Live* NF

National Front (1986) *Powderkeg Britain* NF

National Front (no date, received 1986) *Statement of Policy* NF

National Front (no date, received 1990) *Constitution of the National Front* NF

N.F. Directorate (1986) *Attempted Murder: A State-Reactionary Plot to Destroy the National Front* N.T Press

Neocleous, M. (1997) *Fascism* Buckinghamshire, Open University Press

Neocleous, M. (2005) "Long live death! Fascism, resurrection, immortality" *Journal of Political Ideologies* vol 10 Issue 1 pp.31-50

Neocleous, M. (2009) "The Fascist Moment: Security, Exclusion, Extermination" *Studies in Social Justice* vol 3 Issue No.1 pp.23-37

Neumann, F. (1944) *Behemoth: The Structure and Function of National Socialism 1933-1944* Oxford, Oxford University Press

Neville, P. (1999) *The Holocaust* Cambridge, Cambridge University Press

Nichols, A. (1981) "Germany" in Woolf, S. (ed) *Fascism in Europe* London, Methuen Chapter 4 pp.65-91

Nidam-Orvieto, I. (2005) "The Impact of Anti-Jewish Legislation on Everyday Life and the Response of Italian Jews" in Zimmerman, J. (ed) *Jews in Italy under Fascist and Nazi Rule, 1922-1945* Cambridge, Cambridge University Press Chapter 8 pp.158-181

Noakes. J, and Pridham. G (eds) (1974) *Documents on Nazism 1919-1945* London, Cape

Noakes, J. (1990) "German Conservatives and the Third Reich: an ambiguous relationship" in Blinkhorn, M. (ed) *Fascists and Conservatives* London, Unwin Hyman Chapter 5 pp.71-97

Noakes, J. (1996) "Nazism and High Society" in Burleigh, M. (ed) *Confronting the Nazi Past: New Debates on Modern German History* London, Collins and Brown Chapter III pp.51-65

Noakes, J. (2008) "Hitler and the Nazi State: leadership, hierarchy and power" in Caplan, J. (ed) *Nazi Germany* Oxford, Oxford University Press Chapter 3 pp.73-98

Nolte, E. (1969) *Three Faces of Fascism* New York, Mentor

Novack, G. (1980) *Understanding History: Marxist Essays* New York, Pathfinder Press

Nugent, N. (1977) "The Ideas of the British Union of Fascists" in Nugent, N. and King, R. (eds) *The British Right* London, Saxon House Chapter 6 pp.133-64

Nugent, N. (1977a) "The political parties of the extreme right" in Nugent, N. and King, R. (eds) *The British Right* London, Saxon House Chapter 7 pp.165-191

Nugent, N. and King, R. (eds) (1977) *The British Right* London, Saxon House

O'Butler, R.D. (1941) *The Roots of National Socialism* London, Faber and Faber

Organski, A. (1968) "Fascism and modernization" in Woolf, S. (ed) *The Nature of Fascism* London, Weidenfeld and Nicolson Chapter 2 pp.19-41

O'Sullivan. N (1983) *Fascism* London, Dent

Overy, R. (1994) *War and Economy in the Third Reich* Oxford, Clarendon Press

Parsons, T. (1954) *Essays in Sociological Theory* Glencoe, Free Press

Passmore, K. (2002) *Fascism: A Very Short Introduction* Oxford, Oxford University Press

Passmore, K. (2009) "The Ideological Origins of Fascism Before 1914" in Bosworth, R. (ed) *The Oxford Handbook of Fascism* Oxford, Oxford University Press Chapter 1 pp.11-31

Paxton, R. (1998) "The Five Stages of Fascism" *The Journal of Modern History* vol 70 No. 1 March pp.1-23

Paxton, R. (2005) *The Anatomy of Fascism* London, Penguin

Paxton, R. (2009) "Comparisons and Definitions" in Bosworth, R. (ed) *The Oxford Handbook of Fascism* Oxford, Oxford University Press Chapter 29 pp.547-65

Payne, S. (1997) *A History of Fascism 1914-45* London, UCL Press

Pearce, R. (2002) *Fascism and Nazism* London, Hodder & Stoughton

Peirce, G. (2010) *Dispatches from the Dark Side: On Torture and the Death of Justice* London, Verso

Petrova, A. and Watson, P. (1995) *The Death of Hitler: The Final Words from Russia's Secret Archives* London, Richard Cohen Books

Peukert, D. (1987) "Youth in the Third Reich" in Bessel, R. (ed) *Life in the Third Reich* Oxford, Oxford University Press Chapter 3 pp.25-40

Peukert, D. (1993) *Inside Nazi Germany: Conformity, Opposition and Racism in Everyday Life* London, Penguin

Peukert, D. (1993a) "The Genesis of the 'Final Solution' from the Spirit of Science" in Childers, T. and Caplan, J. (eds) *Reevaluating the Third Reich* New York, Holmes and Meier Chapter 11 pp.234-52

Picciotto, L. (2005) "The Shoah in Italy: Its History and Characteristics" in Zimmerman, J. (ed) *Jews in Italy under Fascist and Nazi Rule 1922-1945* Cambridge, Cambridge University Press Chapter 11 pp.209-223

Pois. R (ed) (1970) *Alfred Rosenberg: Selected Writings* London, Cape

Pollard, J. (1998) *The Fascist Experience in Italy* London, Routledge

Poole, A. (1996) "Oswald Mosley and the Union Movement: Success or Failure?" in Cronin, M. (ed) *The Failure of British Fascism: The Far Right and the Fight for Political Recognition* Abingdon, Routledge Chapter 4 pp.53-80

Poulantzas, N. (1974) *Fascism and Dictatorship* London, NLB

*Protocols of the Wise Men of Zion* (1920) New York, Beckwith

Prowe, D. (1994) "'Classical Fascism' and the New Radical Right in Western Europe: Comparisons and Contrasts" *Contemporary European History* 3 (3) pp.289-313

Pugh, M. (2005) *'Hurrah for the Blackshirts!': Fascists and Fascism in Britain Between the Wars* London, Jonathan Cape

Pugh, M. (2009) "Britain and its Empire" in Bosworth, R. (ed) *The Oxford Handbook of Fascism* Oxford, Oxford University Press Chapter 26 pp.489-506

Rabinbach, A. (1979) "The Aesthetics of Production in the Third Reich" in Mosse, G. (ed) *International Fascism* London, Sage Chapter 8 pp.189-222

Rahman, L. (2011) "Still battling blackshirts" *Guardian* Monday 3 October

Rauschning, H. (1939) *Hitler Speaks* London, Thornton and Butterworth

Rees, L. (2005) *The Nazis: A Warning From History* London, BBC Books

Rees, L. (2005a) *Auschwitz: The Nazis and the Final Solution* London, BBC Books

Rees, L. (2012) *The Dark Charisma of Adolf Hitler: Leading Millions into the Abyss* St. Ives, Ebury Press

Rees, P. (1979) *Fascism in Britain: An Annotated Bibliography* Sussex, Harvester

Rees, P. (1984) *Fascism and Pre-Fascism in Europe: A Bibliography of the Extreme Right* Sussex, Harvester

Reich, W. (1997) *The Mass Psychology of Fascism* London, Souvenir Press

Renton, D. (1999) *Fascism: Theory and Practice* London, Pluto Press

Renton, D. (1999a) "Fascism is more than an ideology" *Searchlight* August pp.24-25

Renton, D. (2001) *This Rough Game: Fascism and Anti-Fascism* Gloucester, Sutton Publishing

Renton, D. (2005) "'A day to make history?' The 2004 elections and the British National Party" *Patterns of Prejudice* vol 39 Issue 1 pp.25-45

Reznikoff, C. (2010) *Holocaust* Nottingham, Five Leaves Press

Rhodes, J. (2009) "The Banal National Party: The Routine Nature of Legitimacy" *Patterns of Prejudice* vol 43 Issue 2 pp.142-60

Rhodes, J. (2011) "Multiculturalism and the Subcultural Politics of the British National Party" in Copsey, N. and Macklin, G. (eds) *The British National Party: Contemporary Perspectives* London, Routledge Chapter 3 pp.62-78

Richardson, J. (2011) "Race and Racial Difference: The Surface and Depth of BNP Ideology" in Copsey, N. and Macklin, G. (eds) *The British National Party: Contemporary Perspectives* London, Routledge Chapter 2 pp.38-61

Roberts, D., De Grand, A., Antliff, M. and Linehan, T. (2002) "Comments on Roger Griffin, 'The Primacy of Culture: The Current Growth (or Manufacture) of Consensus within Fascist Studies'" *Journal of Contemporary History* vol 37 No.2 pp.259-74

Robertson, E. (1988) "Race as a Factor in Mussolini's Policy in Africa and Europe" *Journal of Contemporary History* January vol 23 No.1 pp.37-58

Rodogno, D. (2009) "Fascism and War" in Bosworth, R. (ed) *The Oxford Handbook of Fascism* Oxford, Oxford University Press Chapter 13 pp.239-257

Rogger, H. and Webber, E. (eds) (1965) *The European Right: A Historical Profile* London, Weidenfeld and Nicolson

Rosehaft, E. (1983) *Beating the Fascists: The German Communists and Political Violence 1929-33* Cambridge, Cambridge University Press

Roseman, M. (2005) "Shoot First and Ask Questions Afterwards? Wannsee and the Unfolding of the Final Solution" in Gregor, N. (ed) (2005) *Nazism, War and Genocide: New Perspectives on the History of the Third Reich* Exeter, University of Exeter Press Chapter 8 pp.131-146

Rosenbaum, R. (1998) *Explaining Hitler: The Search for the Origins of His Evil* London, Macmillan

Rossi, A. (Tasca, A) (1938) *The Rise of Italian Fascism* London, Methuen

Ryan, N. (1998) "Combat 18: Memoirs of a street-fighting man" *Independent* 1 February

Saldern, von A. (1995) "Victims or Perpetrators? Controversies about the role of women in the Nazi state" in Crew, D. (ed) *Nazism and German Society 1933-1945* London, Routledge Chapter 4 pp.141-165

Sarfatti, M. (2005) "Characteristics and Objectives of the Anti-Racial Laws in Fascist Italy 1938-1943" in Zimmerman, J. (ed) *Jews in Italy under Fascist and Nazi Rule 1922-1945* Cambridge, Cambridge University Press Chapter 4 pp.71-80

Saroop, N. (1989) "British culture must prevail in the ethnic melting pot" *Daily Telegraph* 8 March

Sarti, R. (1971) *Fascism and the Industrial Leadership in Italy 1919-1940* Berkeley, University of California Press

Sarti, R. (1990) "Italian fascism: radical politics and conservative goals" in Blinkhorn, M. (ed) *Fascists and Conservatives* London, Unwin Hyman Chapter 2 pp.14-30

Saussure de, R. (1943) "After Ten Years of Hitler: Collective Neurosis of Germany" *Free World* February pp.121-26

Schapiro, L. (1972) *Totalitarianism* London, Pall Mall Press

Schieder, W. (2001) "Fatal Attraction: The German Right and Italian Fascism" in Mommsen, H. (ed) *The Third Reich Between Vision and Reality: New Perspectives on German History 1918-1945* Oxford, Berg pp.39-57

Schleunes, K. (1970) *The Twisted Road to Auschwitz: Nazi Policy Toward German Jews 1933-1939* Urbana, University of Illinois Press

Schmidt, C. (1973) *The Corporate State in Action: Italy Under Fascism* New York, Russell and Russell

Schmitt, C. (1976) *The Concept of the Political* New Brunswick, Rutgers University Press

Schnapp, J. (ed) (2000) *A Primer of Italian Fascism* Lincoln, University of Nebraska Press

Schoenbaum, D. (1967) *Hitler's Social Revolution: Class and Status in Nazi Germany 1933-39* London, Weidenfeld and Nicolson

Schuddekkopf, O. (1973) *Fascism* London, Weidenfeld and Nicolson

Seidel, G. (1986) *The Holocaust Denial: Anti-Semitism, Racism and the New Right* Leeds, Beyond the Pale

Seton-Watson, H. (1979) "The Age of Fascism and its Legacy" in Mosse, G. (ed) *International Fascism* London, Sage Chapter 15 pp.357-376

Settenbrini, D. (1979) "Mussolini and the Legacy of Revolutionary Socialism" in Mosse, G. (ed) *International Fascism* London, Sage Chapter 4 pp.91-123

Sewell, R. (1988) *Germany: From Revolution to Counter-Revolution* London, Fortress Books

Shirer, W. L. (1985) *The Rise and Fall of the Third Reich* London, Secker and Warburg

Siegfried, K-J. (1996) "Racial Discrimination at Work: Forced Labour in the Volkswagen Factory, 1939-45" in Burleigh, M. (ed) *Confronting the Nazi Past: New Debates on Modern German History* London, Collins and Brown Chapter II pp.37-50

Skidelsky, R. (1981) *Oswald Mosley* London, Macmillan

Skidelsky, R. (1981a) "Great Britain" in Woolf, S. (ed) *Fascism in Europe* London, Methuen Chapter 12 pp.257-282

Smith, A. (1979) *Nationalism in the 20th Century* London, Robertson

Smith, S. (1997) "How we won Millwall" *Patriot* Issue No.1 Spring pp.6-9

Sole-Tura, J. (1968) "The political 'instrumentality' of fascism" in Woolf, S. (ed) *The Nature of Fascism* London, Weidenfeld and Nicolson Chapter 3 pp.42-50

Sparks, C. (1974) "Fascism in Britain" *International Socialism* No.71 Sept pp.13-29

Sparks, C. (1977) "Fighting the Beast: Fascism – The Lessons of Cable Street" *International Socialism* No.94 Jan pp.11-14

Sparks, C. (1980) *Never Again! The Hows and Whys of Stopping Fascism* London, Bookmarks

Spiller, J. (1999) "A Future for British Fascism?" *Politics Review* Nov pp.10-12

Stackelberg, R. (1999) *Hitler's Germany: Origins, Interpretations, Legacies* London, Routledge

Steed, M. (1978) "The National Front Vote" *Parliamentary Affairs* vol 31 pp.282-293

Steigman-Gall, R. (2005) "Nazism and the Revival of Political Religion Theory" in Griffin, R. (ed) *Fascism, Totalitarianism and Political Religion* London, Routledge Chapter 2 pp.82-102

Steinbacher, S. (2005) *Auschwitz: A History* London, Penguin

Stephenson, J. (2008) "Inclusion: building the national community in propaganda and practice" in Caplan, J. (ed) *Nazi Germany* Oxford, Oxford University Press pp.99-121

Stern, J.P. (1975) *Hitler: The Fuhrer and the People* Hassocks, Harvester Press

Sternhell, Z. (1982) "Fascist Ideology" in Laqueur, W. (ed) *Fascism* Chapter 9 pp.325-406

Sternhell, Z. (1994) *The Birth of Fascist Ideology: From Cultural Rebellion to Political Religion* Princeton, Princeton University Press

Stone, N. (1992) *Hitler* London, Coronet

Strachan, E. (1996) "Nature's Eternal Morality" *Spearhead* No.330 August pp.11

Strasser, O. (1940) *Hitler and I* London, Cape

Strasser, O. (1940a) *Germany Tomorrow* London, Cape

Stevenson, J. (1990) "Conservatism and the failure of fascism in interwar Britain" in Blinkhorn, M. (ed) *Fascists and Conservatives* London, Unwin Hyman Chapter 14 pp.264-82

Streit, C. (1996) "Whermacht, Einsatzgruppen, Soviet POWs and Anti-Bolshevism in the Emergence of the Final Solution" in Cesarani, D. (ed) *The Final Solution: Origins and Implementation* London, Routledge Chapter 6 pp.103-118

Stephenson, J. (1996) "Women, Motherhood and the Family in the Third Reich" in Burleigh, M. (ed) *Confronting the Nazi Past: New Debates on Modern German History* London, Collins and Brown Chapter XI pp.167-183

Stumke, H-G. (1996) "From the 'People's Consciousness of Right and Wrong' to 'the Healthy Instincts of the Nation': The Persecution of Homosexuals in Nazi Germany" in Burleigh, M. (ed) *Confronting the Nazi Past: New Debates on Modern German History* London, Collins and Brown Chapter X pp.154-166

Sutton, M. and Perry, B. (2009) "Politicking the personal: examining academic literature and British National Party beliefs and wishes about intimate interracial relationships and mixed heritage" *Information and Communication Technology Law* vol 18 No.2 June pp.83-98

Sutton, M. (2013) Internal BNP documents (personal correspondence)

Szaz, Z. (1963) "The Ideological Precursors of National Socialism" *Western Political Quarterly* 16 pp.924-945

Talmon, J. (1952) *The Origins of Totalitarian Democracy* London, Secker and Warburg

Tannenbaum, E. (1972) *The Fascist Experience: Italian Society and Culture 1922-45* New York, Basic Books

Taylor, S. (1977) "The National Front: Backlash or Bootboys?" *New Society* 41 Aug pp.283-285

Taylor, S. (1982) *The National Front in English Politics* London, Macmillan

Taylor, S. (1985) *Prelude to Genocide* London, Duckworth

Thurlow, R. (1976) "Authoritarians and Populists on the British Far Right" *Patterns of Prejudice* vol 10 No.2 March/April pp.13-20

Thurlow, R. (1976a) "Racial Populism in England" *Patterns of Prejudice* vol 10 No.4 July/Aug pp.27-33

Thurlow, R. (1977) "Political Witchcraft: Roots of Fascism" *Patterns of Prejudice* vol 11 No.3 May/June pp.17-22

Thurlow, R. (1978) "National Front Ideology: The Witches' Brew" *Patterns of Prejudice* vol 12 No.3 May/June pp.1-9

Thurlow, R. (1980) "Fascism and Nazism – No Siamese Twins" (I) *Patterns of Prejudice* vol 14 No.1 pp.5-15

Thurlow, R. (1980a) "Fascism and Nazism – No Siamese Twins" (II) *Patterns of Prejudice* vol 14 No.2 pp.15-23

Thurlow, R. (1981) "Destiny and Doom: Spengler, Hitler and British Fascism" *Patterns of Prejudice* vol 15 No.4 pp.17-33

Thurlow, R. (1987) *Fascism in Britain: A History 1918-85* Oxford, Basil Blackwell

Thurlow, R. (1998) *Fascism in Britain: From Oswald Mosley's Blackshirts to the National Front* London, IB Tauris

Thurlow, R. (1998a) "The Guardian of the 'Sacred Flame': The Failed Political Resurrection of Sir Oswald Mosley After 1945" *Journal of Contemporary History* vol 33 No.2 pp.241-254

Thurlow, R. (1999) *Fascism* Cambridge, Cambridge University Press

Tismaneanu, V. (2012) *The Devil in History: Communism, Fascism and Some Lessons of the Twentieth Century* Berkeley, University of California Press

Tooze, A. (2007) *The Wages of Destruction: The Making and Breaking of the Nazi Economy* London, Penguin

Tooze, A. (2008) "The economic history of the Nazi regime" in Caplan, J. (ed) *Nazi Germany* Oxford, Oxford University Press Chapter 7 pp.168-195

Tower Hamlets Trades Council/Hackney Legal Action Group (1978) *Brick Lane 1978: The Case for the Defence* London, THTC

Townsend, M. (2011) "Far right will target strikers, unions warn" *Guardian* 20 Nov 2011

Townshend, J. (1996) *The Politics of Marxism: The Critical Debates* London, Leicester University Press

Traverso, E. (1999) *Understanding the Nazi Genocide: Marxism after Auschwitz* London, Pluto

Treadwell, J. and Garland, J. (2011) "Masculinity, Marginalisation and Violence: A Case Study of the English Defence League" *British Journal of Criminology* 51 4 pp.621-634

Trevor-Roper, H. (1981) "The Phenomenon of Fascism" in Woolf, S. (ed) *Fascism in Europe* London, Methuen Chapter 2 pp.19-38

Trilling, D. (2012) *Bloody Nasty People: The Rise of Britain's Far Right* London, Verso

Trotsky, L. (1969) *Fascism: What it is and How to Fight It* New York, Pathfinder Press

Trotsky, L. (1971) *The Struggle Against Fascism in Germany* New York, Pathfinder Press

Turner, H. (1971-72) "Fascism and Modernisation" *World Politics* 24 pp. 547-564

Turner, H. (1985) *German Big Business and the Rise of Hitler* Oxford, Oxford University Press

Tyndall, J. (1966) *Six Principles of British Nationalism* London, Albion Press

Tyndall, J. (1988) *The Eleventh Hour: A Call for British Rebirth* Welling Albion Press

Tyndall, J. (1996) "World over-population: nature will cope and nature, as always, will be right" *Spearhead* No.329 July pp.6-8

Tyndall, J. (1996) "When authority collapses" *Spearhead* No.331 September pp.6-9

Tyndall, J. (1997) "The Evils that Bask in Freedom's Glow" *Spearhead* August No.342 pp.6-8

Tyndall, J. (1998) "Unity – Now!" *Spearhead* March No.349 pp.6-9

Vita-Finzi, P. (1968) "Italian fascism and the intellectuals" in Woolf, S. (ed) *The Nature of Fascism* London, Weidenfeld and Nicolson Chapter 13 pp.226-244

Wachsmann, N. (2008) "The policy of exclusion: repression in the Nazi state 1933-1939" in Caplan, J. (ed) *Nazi Germany* Oxford, Oxford University Press Chapter 5 pp.122-145

Waite, R. (1993) *The Psychopathic God: Adolf Hitler* New York, De Capo Press

Walker, M. (1978) *The National Front* Glasgow, Fontana/Collins

Wanrooij, B. (2002) "Italian Society under Fascism" in Lyttleton, A. (ed) *Liberal and Fascist Italy* Oxford, Oxford University Press pp.175-195

Webber, G. (1984) "Patterns of Membership and Support for the British Union of Fascists" *Journal of Contemporary History* October 19 pp.475-606

Weber, E. (1964) *Varieties of Fascism* Princeton, Van Nostrand

Weightman, G and Weir, S. (1978) "The National Front and the Young" *New Society* April 27 p.186-193

Weindling, P. (1996) "Understanding Nazi Racism: Precursors and Perpetrators" in Burleigh, M. (ed) *Confronting the Nazi Past: New Debates on Modern German History* London, Collins and Brown Chapter IV pp.66-83

Welch, D. (1998) *Hitler* London, UCL Press

Whisker, J. (1983) "Italian Fascism: An Interpretation" *The Journal of Historical Review* vol 4 No.1 Spring pp.5-27

Whiteley, P. (1979) "The National Front vote in the 1977 GLC Elections: An aggregative data analysis" *British Journal of Political Science* 9 pp.370-380

Whittam, J. (1995) *Fascist Italy* Manchester, Manchester University Press

Wilford, R. (1986) "Fascism" in Eccleshall, R., Geoghegan, V., Jay, R. and Wilford, R. (eds) *Political Ideologies* London, Hutchinson Chapter 7 pp.217-250

Wilkinson, P. (1981) *The New Fascists* London, Grant McIntyre

Wilks-Hegg, S. (2008) "The canary in the coalmine? Explaining the emergence of the British National Party in English local politics" *Parliamentary Affairs* 62 (3) pp.377-98

Williams, D. (2011) "BNP bear fight" *Searchlight* August No.434 pp.18-19

Williams, D. and Gable, S. (2010) "The BNP is still a racist party" March No.417 pp.8

Williamson, D. (1998) *The Third Reich* London, Longman

Winkler, H. (1979) "German Society, Hitler and the Illusion of Restoration 1930-33" in Mosse, G. (ed) *International Fascism* London, Sage Chapter 6 pp.143-159

Wiskemann, E. (1969) *Fascism in Italy: Its Development and Influence* London, Macmillan

Wistrich, R. (1976) "Leon Trotsky's Theory of Fascism" *Journal of Contemporary History* vol 11 No.4 October pp.157-184

Woodbridge, S. (2011) "Ambivalent Admiration? The response of other extreme-right groups to the rise of the BNP" in Copsey, N. and Macklin, G. (eds) (2011) *British National Party: Contemporary Perspectives* London, Routledge Chapter 5 pp.103-122

Woodbridge, S. (2012) "Local and Vocal: Arnold Leese and British Fascism in Small-Town Politics" *Socialist History* 41 pp.43-59

Woodley, D. (2010) *Fascism and Political Theory: Critical Perspectives on Fascist Ideology* London, Routledge

Woodson, T. (2009) "Well connected: English Defence League remix – a familiar story" *Searchlight* September No.411 pp.4-5

Woolf, S. (ed) (1968) *The Nature of Fascism* London, Weidenfeld and Nicolson

Woolf, S. (1968a) "Did a fascist economic system exist?" in S. Woolf (ed) *The Nature of Fascism* London, Weidenfeld and Nicolson Chapter 8 pp.119-151

Woolf, S. (ed) (1981) *Fascism in Europe* London, Methuen

Woolf, S. (1981a) "Italy" in S.Woolf (ed) *Fascism in Europe* London, Methuen Chapter 3 pp.39-63

Worley, M. (2011) "Why Fascism? Sir Oswald Mosley and the Conception of the British Union of Fascists" History 96 (321) January pp.68-83

Zimmerman, J. (ed) (2005) *Jews in Italy under Fascist and Nazi Rule 1922-1945* Cambridge, Cambridge University Press

Zizek, S. (2002) *Did Somebody Say Totalitarianism? Five Interventions in the (Mis)Use of a Notion* London, Verso

Zizek, S. (2005) "The Two Totalitarianisms" *London Review of Books* vol 27 No.6 17 March

Zizek, S. (2008) *In Defense of Lost Causes* London, Verso

Zizek, S. (2009) *First as Tragedy, Then as Farce* London, Verso

Zuccotti, S. (1987) *The Italians and the Holocaust: Persecution, Rescue and Survival* New York, Basic Books

www.bpp.org.uk/policies (accessed 12 November 2012)

www.englishpeoplesparty.org (accessed 20 November 2012)

www.englishdefenceleague.org (accessed 10 May 2011)

MJH.

www.ingramcontent.com/pod-product-compliance
Lightning Source LLC
Chambersburg PA
CBHW020450270326
41926CB00008B/551